LIFE OF A

KLANSMAN

LIFE OF A
KLANSMAN

A FAMILY HISTORY IN WHITE SUPREMACY

Edward Ball

FARRAR, STRAUS AND GIROUX

New York

Farrar, Straus and Giroux
120 Broadway, New York 10271

Copyright © 2020 by Edward Ball
All rights reserved
Printed in the United States of America
First edition, 2020

Owing to limitations of space, illustration credits can be found on pages 393–95.

Library of Congress Cataloging-in-Publication Data
Names: Ball, Edward, 1959– author.
Title: Life of a Klansman : a family history in white supremacy / Edward Ball.
Other titles: Family history in white supremacy
Description: First edition. | New York : Farrar, Straus and Giroux, 2020. |
    Includes bibliographical references and index.
Identifiers: LCCN 2020003403 | ISBN 9780374186326 (hardcover)
Subjects: LCSH: Lecorgne, Constant, 1832–1886. | Lecorgne family. | New Orleans (La.)—
    Race relations—19th century. | Reconstruction (U.S. history, 1865–1877)—Louisiana—
    New Orleans. | Racism—Louisiana—New Orleans—History—19th century. | White
    supremacy movements—Louisiana—New Orleans—History—19th century. | White
    League (La.)—Biography. | Ku Klux Klan—Biography. | Creoles—Louisiana—
    History—19th century. | New Orleans (La.)—Biography.
Classification: LCC F379.N553 L433 2020 | DDC 305.8009763/35—dc23
LC record available at https://lccn.loc.gov/2020003403

Our books may be purchased in bulk for promotional, educational, or business use.
Please contact your local bookseller or the Macmillan Corporate and Premium Sales
Department at 1-800-221-7945, extension 5442, or by e-mail at
MacmillanSpecialMarkets@macmillan.com.

www.fsgbooks.com
www.twitter.com/fsgbooks • www.facebook.com/fsgbooks

1 3 5 7 9 10 8 6 4 2

for my children,

Abigail

and

Theodore Ball

The more images I gathered from the past . . . the more unlikely it seemed to me that the past time actually happened in this or that way, for nothing about it could be called normal: most of it was absurd, and if not absurd, then appalling.

—W. G. SEBALD, *Vertigo*

CONTENTS

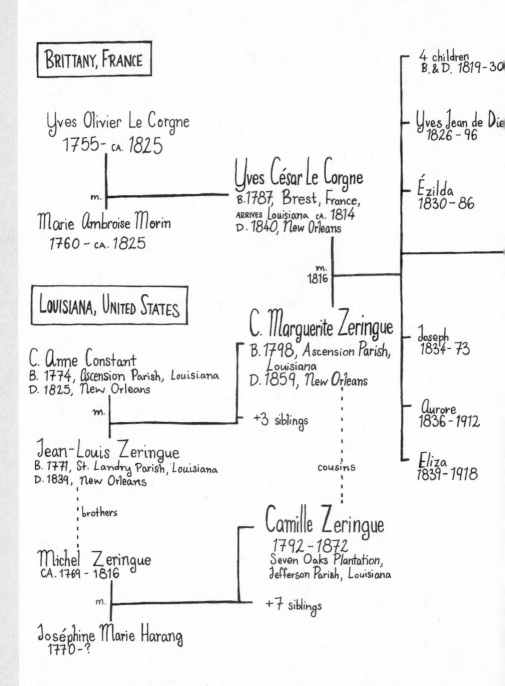

BRITTANY, FRANCE

Yves Olivier Le Corgne
1755 - CA. 1825

m.

Marie Ambroise Morin
1760 - CA. 1825

Yves César Le Corgne
B. 1787, Brest, France,
ARRIVES Louisiana CA. 1814
D. 1840, New Orleans

m.
1816

LOUISIANA, UNITED STATES

C. Anne Constant
B. 1774, Ascension Parish, Louisiana
D. 1825, New Orleans

m.

Jean-Louis Zeringue
B. 1771, St. Landry Parish, Louisiana
D. 1839, New Orleans

brothers

Michel Zeringue
CA. 1769 - 1816

m.

Joséphine Marie Harang
1770 - ?

C. Marguerite Zeringue
B. 1798, Ascension Parish,
Louisiana
D. 1859, New Orleans

+3 siblings

cousins

Camille Zeringue
1792 - 1872
Seven Oaks Plantation,
Jefferson Parish, Louisiana

+7 siblings

4 children
B. & D. 1819 - 30

Yves Jean de Die
1826 - 96

Ézilda
1830 - 86

Joseph
1834 - 73

Aurore
1836 - 1912

Eliza
1839 - 1918

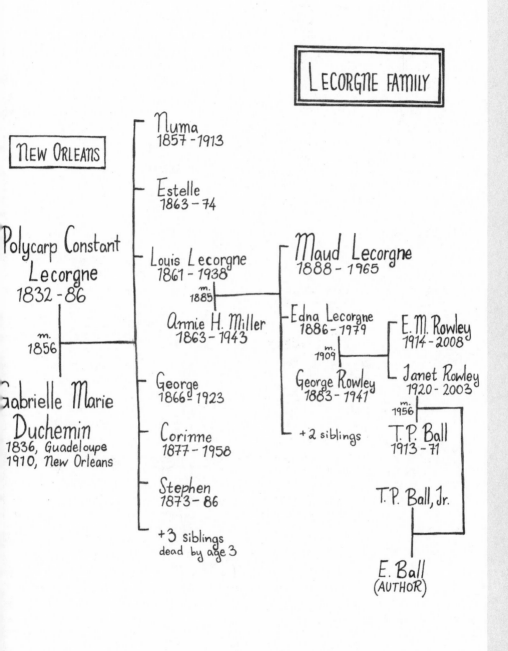

LECORGNE FAMILY

NEW ORLEANS

Numa
1857 - 1913

Estelle
1863 - 74

Louis Lecorgne
1861 - 1938
m. 1885

Annie H. Miller
1863 - 1943

Polycarp Constant
Lecorgne
1832 - 86
m. 1856

Gabrielle Marie
Duchemin
1836, Guadeloupe
1910, New Orleans

George
1866 - 1923

Corinne
1877 - 1958

Stephen
1873 - 86

+3 siblings
dead by age 3

Maud Lecorgne
1888 - 1965

Edna Lecorgne
1886 - 1979
m. 1909

George Rowley
1883 - 1941

+2 siblings

E. M. Rowley
1914 - 2008

Janet Rowley
1920 - 2003

T. P. Ball
1913 - 71
m. 1956

T. P. Ball, Jr.

E. Ball
(AUTHOR)

LIFE OF A
KLANSMAN

My mother had a soft view of the person who became our Klansman.

—He was the one with the pretty name, she said. *Constant Lecorgne.*

—Who can pronounce that? I said. He was French, and no one in New Orleans is French anymore.

This talk took place in the kitchen. I was a teenager.

—His name was unusual, my mother said. *Polycarp* Constant Lecorgne.

She pronounced the last part *Le-corn.* She said the middle name with a French effort, *Cohn-stah.*

—What kind of a name is that?

—Polycarp Constant. It's pretty.

My mother's name was Janet. She thought it plain. Whereas this family member, the one called Polycarp, had a fancy name. And he was French, meaning "Latin," meaning more cultured, or more virile, or something.

—*Polycarp Constant Lecorgne,* she said. It's like a melody.

—It is strange, I said.

—Look it up.

I went away to page through an encyclopedia, came back to report.

—Polycarp was a saint, about A.D. 100, in the city of Smyrna, on the Mediterranean. He was a bishop, killed by the Romans.

—Our Polycarp was Catholic, my mother said. He did not like his first name, so he used his second, *Constant.* He was not a saint.

—What do you mean?

—I mean it is too bad what he got up to with that White League. I mean it is sweet and bitter. The beautiful name. The business with the Ku-klux.

This is a story that begins with a woman making notes and talking about family and ends with a lot of people dead in a ditch. This is a family story. Yet it is not a family story wrapped in sugar, the way some people like to serve them.

When my mother died, in 2003, my brother and I went to New Orleans to bury her. We had her placed in the family tomb. We paid the cemetery to chisel her name—Janet Rowley Ball—on the stone door of the vault. Above her name was the name of her own mother, Edna Lecorgne.

Edna Lecorgne was a granddaughter of Polycarp Constant Lecorgne, our Klansman.

My brother and I emptied the contents of the house. (Our father was long dead, and we two the only children.) There was little in the way of books, but there were files. Our mother, Janet, was a filer. She had a big oak desk with two file drawers. Out of one I pulled a batch of folders marked "Lecorgne."

There was some furniture in the house explained by these Lecorgne files. A dining room set—Victorian, with a marble-topped breakfront. And a rolltop desk—tall, with pigeonhole letter slots and a barrel-like door over the desk. The furniture came from the Lecorgnes, and it was born during the years of the one with the pretty name.

When we were growing up, my brother and I and family sat at that Victorian dinner table, where, in a manner of speaking, we ate with our Klansman one thousand times. The Lecorgne family, and it seems Constant himself, owned the dinner furniture. The table, a couple hundred pounds of cherrywood, had a scalloped pedestal, curling knees for legs, and feet like claws. It came with a massive breakfront, seven feet high, with a red marble counter at the waist, little shelves and a beveled mirror above. The dining room was the grandest in a plain house.

As I was growing up, we ate every night at the same table. The story came out when necessary. If a visitor admired the furniture, my mother had this to say.

—Carpenter Lecorgne had a customer who could not pay his bill. Or maybe it was someone who did not want to pay, and who wanted to barter. So a deal was made, and the client paid with the dining room furniture. When? Oh, that was sometime in the late 1800s.

Lecorgne is not my family name. The Lecorgnes were my mother's people, and her mother's. Yet in the chain of being, and by inheritance, the Lecorgnes are, of course, my people. Our Klansman was my grandmother's grandfather.

Aunts and uncles had the name Lecorgne. Albert Lecorgne, "Uncle Albert," sometimes came to eat. When you shook his hand, you could feel calluses where his fingers met his palm. That was because Uncle Albert belonged to a line of Lecorgne carpenters. Polycarp Constant Lecorgne had been a carpenter.

Bertha Lecorgne, "Aunt Bert," also came around, although to me she is a dim memory of an unsteady walk. Then there was Maud Lecorgne, "Aunt Maud." She really was the caretaker of the Klan story.

The Klansman? I've known about him since childhood. I have been afraid of his story.

From the oak desk of my mother I took the manila folders back to my home in Connecticut. I put them in a file cabinet. They stayed there for ten years. In 2013, I took out the files. I studied the family trees and read notes about the Lecorgnes. Their lives unrolled in somebody's cursive. The longhand was unfamiliar, it looked antique. I knew my mother's handwriting; she wrote in a style from the time she went to school. This cursive was older. I turned over a page and saw the name "Maud Lecorgne." It was Aunt Maud's hand.

Aunt Maud's grandfather, Constant Lecorgne, was a family hero of sorts. That is, he was a hero before standards changed, and his memory became too hot. Then he was forgotten, deliberately. Maud's grandfather was a hero because he fought for whiteness, for our tribe. And if you measure the results, he won.

There is a Creole saying—*On lave son linge sale en famille*, "Wash your dirty laundry inside the family." Meaning, keep quiet about the bad stories, show no conflict, say nothing that dirties reputation. The adage is a reminder always to disguise.

I want to tell the story of this ordinary man with the unusual name. Because he helped to lay out and to tend the garden of whiteness in which we dwell.

Aunt Maud lived in New Orleans with her sister, Edna Lecorgne, my mother's mother. (Maud was a *great*-aunt to me, but she went by the simpler *Aunt*.) When I was a child, our family many times visited New Orleans, my mother's hometown. Eventually we moved there, and the city is one of the places I grew up. Edna and Maud Lecorgne, the two sisters with antique names, were in their seventies when I was a boy of nine or ten. They lived in a bungalow on Nelson Street, near Tulane University. The bungalow was brick and painted yellow, set up high against floods, eight feet above grade, ten steps up to the porch, deep eaves, built in the 1920s. Tulane University a half mile in one direction, the Mississippi River a half mile in the other. On the porch, a heavy door with glass on the top half. The door opened into the living room.

To a boy of ten, older women like Edna and Maud carried a thick smell. A musty aroma filled the six rooms of that bungalow. The smell was interrupted in places by the scent of a syrupy cologne, which appeared at the threshold of each woman's bedroom. At those doors, the sweet eau de toilette that Edna and Maud used, from the Maison Blanche department store, shocked the nose.

Aunt Maud wore black, horn-rimmed eyeglasses with a silver underwire. She had a flat, oval face and long white hair held tight in a bun at the back. Small, like most of the Lecorgnes. She owned a closetful of gingham dresses, indistinguishable one from the other. The thick seams of her heavy stockings ran like highway lines down the backs of her legs. Her shoes were black, laced, and thick-soled, with a two-inch heel.

Her sister, my grandmother Edna, was not talkative about family history. Instead, it was Maud who had the lore in hand. Aunt Maud knew the names and dates. She had her journals and documents, she had family trees.

Aunt Maud was a schoolteacher during her working life. For forty years she taught in the white public schools in New Orleans. English was her subject, mainly, and in retirement, genealogy became her vocation. She was quiet and inward. Maud never married, she had no children. Our ancestors were her offspring.

I remember now some of the story of our Klansman, as Maud Lecorgne possessed it. Pulling out Aunt Maud's ledgers and family notes, reading her Victorian longhand, it came back. The scene that follows dates from the 1960s, when I was a boy. Though these words are reconstructed, they do derive from facts. If there had been a recorder, it might have heard certain lines that Aunt Maud said.

—Come here, young man. I can tell you about our people.

—Aunt Maud, can I have a Coke cola?

She made up a Coke with ice.

—The Lecorgnes have lived no place but here in New Orleans since the time of Napoleon. The first of us was a man named Yves. You say *Eve*, like Adam's wife. Yves Lecorgne was French, of course, and he came from Brittany, in the west of France. He was an officer in Napoleon's navy, a man who landed up in New Orleans and who stayed. He found a bride named Marguerite Zeringue. She was a Creole, and they had five children, and one of them was my grandfather.

The air conditioner rattled in the window.

—My grandfather, Constant Lecorgne, was a carpenter. He built houses for plain people, and worked on boats, and he hammered many other things. Later, he was a fighter in the White League. The only difference between the White League and the Ku-klux was the League was not secret. And for his efforts, my grandfather had his head split open at the Battle of Liberty Place, on Canal Street. The White League won back the rule of white people. For a long time, nobody said that was a bad thing. Except perhaps the Negroes.

"The Negroes" was the phrase always on the lips of white people like us, being polite. Everything is in order when you place a definite article in front of a proper name. The Negroes, the Jews, the Indians.

—My grandfather went with the Ku-klux. I am talking about the time before the civil rights. Long time before. We would not have had them, the civil rights, had my grandfather lived. He would not have allowed the civil rights to happen.

The memories of Aunt Maud reached back many years. She was born in 1888, in New Orleans. New Orleans is the place where everybody among my mother's people got themselves born, and it has remained that place.

She used that more familiar, more intimate phrase, "the Ku-klux." It is what Aunt Maud and most people in her generation called the white militias.

Aunt Maud kept a photograph of a plantation house hanging in the hall outside her bedroom. It was placed so that you had to look at it on the way to the bathroom. The plantation was called Seven Oaks, a monster of a house in a Greek Revival style, built about 1840. Seven Oaks plantation, for Aunt Maud, was the memory of what the Lecorgnes wanted to be.

—The Lecorgnes married right into Seven Oaks when Yves Lecorgne, the first immigrant in the family, found his bride, Marguerite Zeringue. Seven Oaks was a place run by the Zeringue family, and the Zeringues and Lecorgnes became like two braids in a rope. At least for a time.

These days did not last. The Lecorgnes, perched halfway up the pyramid of Southern society, with its layers of caste, began a long slide to the white lowlands. Maud knew the name for this decline.

—The Lecorgnes were some of the *petits blancs*. The little whites. They have been working men, some of them working women. The women kept house, and they made a lot of children. There is more to that than they get credit for, the women. But the Lecorgnes were not always common people. They came from much better. Then, for generations, *petits blancs* we became. The one to remember is Constant Lecorgne, my grandfather, because he was a Redeemer.

—A Redeemer? Isn't that when souls go up to heaven?

—No, that is the Assumption. My grandfather was a Redeemer because he helped to end Reconstruction. He put the state of Louisiana back into white hands. If he had not fought, if he did not have his head split open in the Redemption, we would not be here now, sitting in this nice little bungalow off Carrollton Avenue. To make the Redemption happen, my grandfather fought for the White League, and he might have done other things. There are some things that should remain secret.

Seven Oaks plantation—built 1840, demolished 1976

Life had wrapped Aunt Maud in a curtain of sadness. Even as a boy I could see it. Her speech was spare, her manner reserved, and she never raised her voice. In the judgment of her time, she was somewhat a diminished woman. People called her a "spinster," a word then in common use, though not spoken in her presence. I imagine that in Maud's youth she grew sexual roots, like everyone, but no plant came above ground. I suspect these facts enlarged her idea of the family life that had preceded her. The Lecorgnes and Zeringues, in her telling, must have had big personalities, tall highs and bad lows.

Aunt Maud died at seventy-seven and took her stories. After that, few in my mother's family said much about our people named Lecorgne. But things circle around, and eventually the Klansman returned. At her death, Maud's family history files went to her sister, my grandmother Edna; and when Edna died they came to her daughter, my mother. When my mother died, they came to me.

My aunt Maud's notes and story of the Ku-klux offer a glimpse down the damp hall of American history, where the Ku Klux Klan is a perennial mold in the national house. It spread first during Reconstruction, the twelve years that followed the Civil War. This was the start of the Ku-klux, the movement in which my predecessor Constant Lecorgne played his part. By 1880, the fungus vanished, cleared by its own success in winning back white supremacy, after years when whiteness looked weak.

Forty years later, during the 1910s and '20s, the Ku-klux came out of its dry winter, and the second Klan spread wider than the first. This time it grew into a national movement with giant membership, menacing rites, and festive parades through cities. It was this second Klan that produced the familiar uniform of white sheets and white hoods. The first Ku-klux, the one of our Klansman, had varied disguises, anything to hide identity: robes decorated with stars, cornmeal sacks for hoods, painted masks. The revived Ku-klux lived about fifteen years. But a sex and money scandal took down its leaders, and the Klan shrank again with the Depression. After the rise in Germany of National Socialism, Nazi promises of "Aryan" purity made the cause of whiteness look like a call for tribal violence and democracy's end.

A third variety of the Ku-klux mold appeared during the civil rights movement of the 1950s and '60s. Although local and disorganized this time, Klan partisans in the hundreds staged bombings, marked civil rights leaders for death, and harassed their white allies. The third Ku-klux withered during the 1970s, as an open campaign for domination lost its appeal to most whites. The upper hand in the culture wars—are we to have white power alone, or some effort at pluralism?—went to a more humane side.

In the next decades, the spores of white supremacy spread again: white power movements in the 1980s, survivalist camps in the 1990s, nationalist militias in the 2000s. The ideas and the blood spirit of the Ku-klux fall and rise. Once more, they are in the air, public, and popular.

Our Klansman, my aunt Maud's grandfather, was not a leader but a follower, a foot soldier. His story is not rare. Violent white supremacy is a populist phenomenon, with many in the rank and file, and few leaders. Anyone who thinks that to have a Klansman among one's relatives is a strange or deviant thing may be surprised by the reality. In 1925, the Ku Klux Klan could claim five million members, white and Christian. It is likely that leaders of the movement exaggerated their numbers for publicity reasons. Let us assume that actual Klan membership stood at four million. Take four million Klansmen, people on the march in 1925, and estimate the number of their descendants. Count forward one hundred years to their grandchildren and great-grandchildren. By a good formula in demography, the four million Klansmen of 1925 have as their direct descendants in 2025 about one hundred thirty-seven million living white Americans. One hundred thirty-seven million people comprise one-half of the white population of the United States. Fifty percent of whites can claim a family link to the Ku-klux. Perhaps the gentle reader of these words is one. If not, someone near you.

One-half of whites in the United States could, if they wished, write a Klan family memoir. Of course, one has to know the names of a few ancestors and want to find out about their lives. What is strange, maybe, is that no such memoirs are to be found. The rarity is not in having a Klansman around. The unusual thing is to bring him out of the closet to interrogate under light.

A story of this kind might come from the hand of a president. The forty-fifth president of the United States is the son of a man, Fred C. Trump, who was arrested in New York one Memorial Day during the 1920s at a rally staged by the Ku Klux Klan. On May 31, 1927, in Queens, New York, about one thousand Klan marchers made their way through the borough's dense streets. They wore robes and hoods. The parade turned into a riot when the Klansmen attacked a smaller Memorial Day march of Italian Americans. Whites beat up other whites because the second Klan, led by Protestants, was anti-Catholic as well as anti-color. Fred C. Trump, age twenty-five, resident of the Jamaica section of Queens, was among seven arrested. The forty-fifth president, in his retirement, if he possessed the means of reading and writing, might himself produce a family history entitled "Life of a Klansman." The public awaits.

CAYUNE, NEW ORLEANS, L

MISS MAUD LECORGNE

MISS LE CORGNE FUNERAL HELD

Retired Teacher Dies

White supremacy is not a marginal ideology. It is the early build of the country. It is a foundation on which the social edifice rises, bedrock of institutions. White supremacy also lies on the floor of our minds. Whiteness is not a deformation of thought, but a kind of thought itself.

Our Klansman's story is not just a family story, it belongs to many. It is particular, but it carries with it a genealogy of race identity, of whiteness. It is a story of whiteness that is born into one life and grows, branching out into a tree that shelters others.

I have no first-person testimony for this tale—no letters or diaries, speeches or interviews. There are court records, however. There is thick circumstantial evidence. There are newspaper accounts, victim testimony, wills, property records, sacramental records, interviews with black families struck by Klan violence, supremacist manifestos, and traces of white oral tradition. I use evidence to draw out the life of the man with the pretty name. It is not necessary to invent anything to tell the story of our Klansman. Invention is where fantasy wrinkles the real, where what we would like to have occurred deflects what actually happened. However, invention is not the same as conjecture, which is a light that gives roundness to sketches of facts. To suppose an event occurs or a feeling moves people is permitted as a narrative device, as long as you keep the lamp of inference visible in the hand. Sometimes it is a help to speculate, if you make clear when you do so.

This is a piece of microhistory. The idea of microhistory is that the life of an ordinary person contains the kernel of a million; an individual carries the culture in microcosm. And I have to say this. The story that follows is not that a writer discovers a shameful family secret and turns to the public to confess it. The story here is that whiteness and its tribal nature are normal, everywhere, and seem as permanent as the sunrise.

PART I

THE KU-KLUX ACT

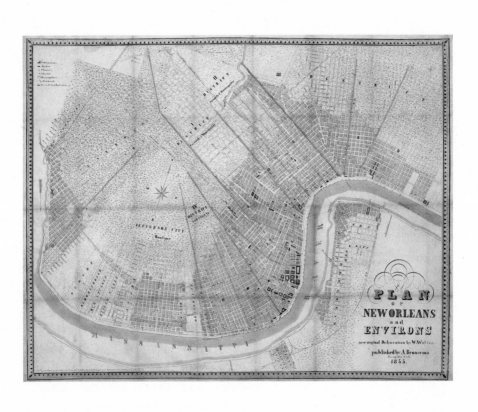

PLAN OF NEW ORLEANS and ENVIRONS

new original Delineation by W. Walter

published by A. Bronorma

1855

1

The middle of the week is good for an attack, for the surprise. It is March 4, 1873, in the city of New Orleans, a Tuesday night. About 9:00 p.m., a man called Polycarp Constant Lecorgne emerges from his house by the levee of the Mississippi River. He is a forty-one-year-old carpenter. Constant Lecorgne and his wife, Gabrielle Duchemin, live in a neighborhood called Bouligny. They have six children, and Gabrielle is pregnant with another. Gabrielle and the children remain in the house when Constant leaves for the night. He carries a gun, probably a revolver. The U.S. Army confiscated most of the long guns years ago.

The newspapers tell much of the story. The *Catholic Messenger.* The *New Orleans Republican.* The *Times,* the *Picayune.* Newspapers tell a crisp story, and court records say more.

At home, the family of Constant Lecorgne speaks French, their first language. French is a tongue of preference, as it is for about one-quarter of the city, black as well as white. French is the language of Creoles, English the language of most business and politics. The family's house by the levee of the river is a rental. Constant and Gabrielle once lived in a house they owned, but ten years ago they lost it, along with all their money. They can no longer afford to buy. Constant is a ship carpenter who works on the barges and steamers, the passenger boats and freighters that ply the Mississippi. The house is close to his work, a stone's throw from the water.

Constant has brothers and sisters, five of them. All have families, all live nearby. People named Lecorgne are scattered through Bouligny. The neighborhood of Bouligny lies three miles upstream on the Mississippi from the old center of New Orleans. It is a square mile of clapboard houses and workshops on the shoulder of the river, a place the Lecorgnes regard as theirs. Before they start to move away from Bouligny, which eventually occurs during the 1940s, the family lives in this part of New Orleans for one hundred years.

The Lecorgne who carries a gun leaves the rented house on Valmont Street and makes his way east some blocks through Bouligny. Constant meets others. A cousin by marriage named Ernest Livaudais, who is a musician, good on trumpet. He was the bugler in his company during the Civil War, which ended some years ago. Tonight, Livaudais does not carry a horn, but a gun. Constant and Ernest Livaudais continue downriver and join another man, Joseph Guillotte. The carpenter and the bugler defer to Guillotte. He is the leader of tonight's action, a raid on Precinct 7, stationhouse of the Metropolitan Police.

Guillotte, Livaudais, and Lecorgne: these three are the French fingers of the gang. They speak French to one another, and to other Creoles. They speak English to the people they call *les Américains*, "the Americans." Creoles are French-speaking natives of Louisiana, white or black. The English-speaking are *les Américains*, people who came to the city after the United States bought Louisiana, in the early 1800s. The Americans have grown to three-quarters of the population since then, and they dominate the Creoles. Constant and the others dislike being dominated, but it is their portion.

They rendezvous with more men, about thirty. Half of them Americans, half of them Creoles, all of them white.

The gang moves in the direction of Lawrence Square, an acre of green at the middle of Bouligny. At its edge is police precinct 7, a two-story garrison. Court papers say the men have "guns, muskets, pistols, swords, bayonets, and other warlike instruments." Their muskets are single-load rifles they managed to hide when the U.S. Army, the goddamn Yankees, ordered every house in New Orleans to surrender its weapons, after the war. Lawrence Square looks handsome. A big church called St. Stephen overlooks the square, as do a town hall and food markets. The main street, Napoleon Avenue, runs past St. Stephen, and streetcars on railroad tracks rumble past every half hour.

Constant Lecorgne and his comrades come to Berlin Street, on the southeast corner of the square, and there they find their target.

Tonight, probably, the gang does not wear hoods. Chances are that no one wears a Ku-klux robe. Costumes like hoods and robes are good for the parishes, the rural parts outside New Orleans. The parishes are what people in Louisiana call their counties. It is there, in the black villages, that a man must take steps to disguise himself. To bring rough justice to the doors of *les nègres*, "the blacks," a man needs camouflage. But tonight is not a night ride with clubs and ropes and whips. Tonight, a hood would get in the way. This is the first strike of an insurrection, and the costume of the Ku-klux, and the usual tools, do not fit the job.

Almost everybody in the gang is a soldier. A few years back, everyone fought in the other insurrection, the one to make up the Confederate States of America. The Confederate States was the slave nation that died on the birthing table during the Civil War. The white South calls the fight the "war between the states," or the "lost cause." It ended in 1865, eight years ago. The black South and the Northern states call it "the rebellion." Eventually everyone will agree to call it the Civil War.

The men are veterans, they know tactics. Constant Lecorgne was a second lieutenant in the Eighteenth Louisiana Infantry during the war. Joseph Guillotte, leader of tonight's assault, went with the Twenty-Second Infantry. Ernest Livaudais fought with the Thirtieth Louisiana Regiment, along with another man in the raid, Kendrick Chandler.

The newspapers call them "Ku-kluxers." The men think of themselves as guerrillas or vigilantes—they are vigilant in bringing order to a disrupted world. Last year the same men went with the so-called Louisiana Legion. And before that, the gang belonged to a group called the Knights of the White Camellia. The guerrillas put on and take off names like their costumes.

In this raid, the gang calls itself the "McEnery Militia." They are in the fight for a man named John McEnery, a politician. John McEnery ran for governor last fall, and whites say he should have won, had the other side not stolen the election. The McEnery Militia says it is taking back power from the coloreds and the carpetbaggers. They are taking it back from the U.S. Army. The army is the occupier, the carpetbaggers are the thieves, and *les nègres* are the lackeys of both. The

McEnery Militia wants change. They want to return things to the way they were. If they take the target, the garrison, the rest will come.

Joseph Guillotte gives the sign, and the men surround the police station. It is a wooden building, two stories, four rooms down, four up. Five patrolmen in the Metropolitan Police are on duty downstairs. Also downstairs is a Western Union telegraph office, with an operator on shift. Upstairs is closed and dark.

The cops inside are the "Metropolitans." They are few, but they are armed, and the stakes are life and death. If Constant is shot, he leaves his wife, Gabrielle, and six children, or seven, if the baby lives. A mile from the precinct are Gabrielle and the kids—Numa, Louis, Estelle, Georges, St. Mark, and Corinne. The oldest is fifteen, the youngest nearly two. They want their father to live. On the other hand, if Constant is shot, it would be seen by most whites as a hero's death.

Guillotte shouts and they are on it. Constant runs with others around the building. The men shoot up the doors and windows. This is the right fight, and they are in it for everyone. Constant is like the blade on a knife. He is in the door, a gun pointing at heads. I imagine the shouting in French, the cursing in English. *Bâtards coquins!* "Get the hell out!" The police are not ready for them, the Metropolitans surrender. Two of the cops are Creoles of color, French-speaking and black. They get extra attention, some roughing up, the butt of a gun on the head. But no one, yet, is shot. The police are chased into the street and made to run, leaving Precinct 7 in the hands of the Ku-klux. The gang keeps hostage the telegraph operator, a man named Patrick Sheeley, so they can use him to communicate with their friends and enemies.

Now it is ours. We are taking the city back. The Ku-klux are patriots. We are soldiers for the white tribe. That is what my ancestor seems to have believed.

Men are posted at doors and windows. They talk and wait. Everyone knows there will be a counterattack from the army. It is only a matter of time.

Precinct 7 stands in a line of shops and cafés, butchers and grocers, on Magazine Street. Tracks of a trolley run past the door. It is late, 11:00 p.m., and few stragglers walk by. There is nothing open but a barrelhouse, pouring beer. But there has been talk of a raid for weeks, and the street knows what is happening. Some shouts of encouragement to the raiders from whites, some curses and muttering from blacks. Some blacks disappear when they see an armed white gang. Some get out of sight but look back. Here are those bastards, again.

Down the street on Lawrence Square stands St. Stephen Church, all but finished, in a construction site. The big, new sanctuary has been going up for years, a replacement of the old building. It is nearly done, opening in a month. St. Stephen is the mother church for Constant Lecorgne and his family. Everybody goes on Sundays—the Lecorgne brothers and sisters, all of their children, and all of the cousins and in-laws. They all baptize their babies at the church font and bless their dead at the altar.

From the window of the precinct, gun in hand, Constant can see the rear of the new church. It is twice as big as the previous one, with a high, two-hundred-foot spire. He can see the new stained glass. He and Gabrielle have christened their children at St. Stephen, and buried the ones who did not survive. No one strays far from the church, no matter what comes. The raid happens in sight of the place. It means God must be witness.

Around midnight, a visitor arrives with an entourage. He is a man named Frederick Ogden—Colonel Ogden, to his men. Ogden is a leader of the white insurgency. *Les Américains* have Fred Ogden as their leader. The Creoles have their own, French leader. He is out of sight, out of town, for the time being. But tonight, Constant is a soldier in Fred Ogden's militia.

Ogden reminds the men that the taking of the precinct is just the first of two strikes. If the station holds, the rest of New Orleans falls, tomorrow. The city will surrender after the second raid, the one downtown. A raid that Ogden will lead on the main armory, in the garrison known as the Cabildo. Fred Ogden won local fame during the Civil War, when he rose to colonel and led a regiment of eight hundred rebels.

Everyone shakes Fred Ogden's hand, everyone gets his hand on a shoulder. Fred Ogden is a businessman by day, a militiaman by night. During the day, he sells equipment for the cotton business. He has good manners, he is well spoken. Constant is a woodworker. His speech is rough, his voice sometimes raised. The businessman with the fine habits, the craftsman with the rougher manners—they are partners in the same cause. They speak in English, Constant's second language, Ogden's first. Constant and other white Creoles flicker between French and English.

Fred Ogden repeats the plan. Tomorrow, we have three hundred, and the Cabildo is ours.

The Cabildo has the armory for the Metropolitan Police. It is old and beautiful. When the city was capital of the colony of Louisiana, it went up as the courthouse. The Cabildo lies three miles away, a trolley ride downtown, in the section the Americans call the French Quarter. The French know it as the *Vieux Carré*—the Old Quarter. Since the end of the War Between the States, the Cabildo has been a symbol of the occupation. Not the colonial occupation, or a foreign invasion. The domestic occupation, the invasion of the U.S. Army, the Yankee army.

Ogden talks to the men, Constant listens. The colonel does not want them to die. These are the necessary blows in the fight for the rights of whites. When the counterattack comes, it is time for glory, not death. This is the kind of talk Ogden shares to raise the morale of his men. You are the leading fist in the coup. You are the knife that tests the flesh. If the precinct holds, tomorrow comes the fight that releases us all from the nigger tyranny.

The raiders make the Western Union man send word to the newspapers. Telegraph lines carry the story to the North: the Ku-klux has taken a stand. A few hours later, *The New York Times* runs an item—"A Riot in New Orleans." It looks like a rebellion, the paper says, but do not be alarmed. "No hysterics are necessary about another civil war," says the paper.

Fred Ogden leaves. His visit exhilarates. The men are drunk with responsibility. Now comes a wait—twenty-four hours, maybe. If the governor of Louisiana tells the Metropolitans to take back the precinct, or if the army comes from its barracks, then they have a fight. A guard is posted, and rotations are worked out. Guns are cocked at the windows. A few more fighters come in during the night, reinforcements who join the raid. It is 2:00 a.m . . . 3:00 . . . 4:00. But no attack comes. No Metropolitans, no army.

I have some papers of the Lecorgnes, and among them I find what appears to be his photograph. Constant Lecorgne was a workingman, and he took instructions when he posed for a camera. The description of the Lecorgne men from these days, in military records, is that they have a "florid complexion." They are pale white, flushed with blossoms of red. Dark hair, whitening early, and blue eyes.

Polycarp Constant Lecorgne lives in New Orleans
all his life, 1832–86.

Constant Lecorgne stands about five feet, eight inches, a man with delicate, birdlike hands. He has perfect fingernails. Narrow shoulders, and slight, maybe 150 pounds. He has a sturdy mustache, and long wavy hair, which he wears in a romantic flip. An oval face and thin lips, his features like lines, as though painted in strokes. The face is interrupted by a clenched jaw and a sharp chin.

The Lecorgnes have an underbite. I also have an underbite, it comes from them.

The mouth is turned down, the brow furrowed. Constant scowls. His scowl leaves lines like slashes on his forehead.

On March 5, at 9:00 p.m., the night after the attack on the precinct, Colonel Fred Ogden and his three hundred men mass downtown, on the street called Chartres. With clubs and guns and knives, the mob swarms toward the Cabildo, the arms depot. In the air is the rebel yell, the yodeling whoop the attackers used as soldiers in the Civil War.

This time, the Metropolitans are prepared. The chief of police, Sidney Badger, has sent word to the federal commander in New Orleans, James Longstreet, whose army troops fire over the heads of the mob. Longstreet has two small cannons that he fills with powder but not shot. As Ogden and the mob advance, Longstreet opens fire with his blank artillery. The Ku-klux scatters. They return with rifle and pistol fire, hiding in doorways. The cannons blast again, to the sound of crashing windows. One man falls dead. Ogden gives orders to pull back, and the big gang drains into the side streets. The raid on the Cabildo fails.

There is a Creole expression, which I feel sure Constant knows— *Crachez dans l'air, il vous en tombera sur le nez,* "When you spit in the air, it falls back on your nose."

Three miles uptown, at the precinct in Bouligny, Constant and his gang wait. They are the thin line of the white uprising, the one that still holds. At 2:00 a.m. on March 6, the counterattack comes. The Metropolitan Police surround the building, shoot into windows. Constant, according to his testimony at court, retreats to the shelter of a staircase. He has a house full of children sleeping at home, and he does not care to die.

The Metropolitans come in through the doors. Constant is caught next to the telegraph office. He sees his cousin, Ernest Livaudais. He has known Ernest for years, heard him play music, gone to church with him. One of the Metropolitans shoots Livaudais in the arm. A comrade named Kendrick Chandler has a rifle. Chandler puts the shoulder stock on the floor, barrel aimed at the ceiling, preparing to surrender. Someone in the police squad shoots, a bullet ricochets off the muzzle of Chandler's gun, goes into his chest—or so says the inquest. Chandler falls. Constant stands six feet from the man. Chandler dies the next day.

Half of the gang flees the building and disappears. Thirteen make a last stand and are caught. They are dragged and pushed with gun barrels out to the street, then arrested. A Black Maria rounds them up. Polycarp Constant Lecorgne, the one with the pretty name, is herded into the wagon, thrown in the city jail. The Ku-klux spasm comes to an end.

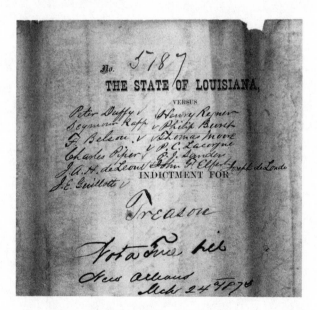

"P.C. Lacorgne" and comrades, indicted for treason against the U.S. government and breach of the Ku Klux Klan Act, in 1873

The New Orleans district attorney, James Beckwith, writes the indictment, *United States v. Peter Duffy, et al.* The lead defendant,

Duffy, is one of the thirteen. Constant is arraigned. He and his gang face two charges. The first is treason. Theirs was a violent attempt to overthrow the government. "P.C. Lacorgne," says the indictment, which misspells his name, "traitorously did attempt" to subvert the state "in contempt of the allegiance due by him to the commonwealth." The second charge is violating the 1871 Enforcement Act, the so-called Ku Klux Klan Act. With that law, Congress is trying to stop white militiamen who put on robes and hoods, who torment and kill black people, and who attack the government.

Constant stands accused. He is charged with treason. If he hangs for it, I will not have the pleasure of telling his story. He is a fighter for whiteness. Which he knows, and we also know, is not treason at all.

PART II

GRANDS BLANCS / BIG WHITES

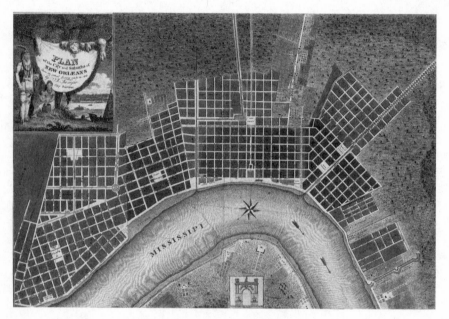

Map of New Orleans, 1817

2

Anyone who has passed through New Orleans knows the church, St. Louis Cathedral. It stands in the middle of the old city, in the *Vieux Carré*, the French Quarter, facing the river. The story of our Klansman starts here, with a wedding.

The levee of the Mississippi River rises above the streets, a dam between the city and the water. Stand on top of it with your back to the water and look down into Jackson Square. Three acres of green, wrapped by an iron fence. Pebbled paths ribbon between oaks and palmettos. An equestrian statue, a fountain, and at the edge of the square, the creamy stucco face of the cathedral. Each year the church is photographed at least ten million times, counting one picture for every tourist who glances at it.

When I was growing up, I spent a thousand nights along these streets in the heart of New Orleans. I mean, these streets of the hard-drinking, bad-behaving, overeating, many-sexed city that makes its living by selling itself to visitors. I miss it. The city cannot not be missed when you leave.

Travel back two hundred years and step into the church, and let us look at what lies behind the door.

It is October 8, 1816, and a wedding is under way. Here is the bride, eighteen-year-old Marguerite Zeringue—pronounced *Zeh-rang*—plus her people. Marguerite's family is large. She has eleven aunts and uncles, siblings of her father, and each of them has children, her cousins. Marguerite's parents own a rice farm on the Mississippi. Some of the Zeringues are here, some from her mother's family, and at least one enslaved worker. Here is the groom, Yves Le Corgne, age twenty-nine. He is *Eve Le-corn-ye*—the syllables smooth when spoken. Yves is alone, save maybe a few friends; he has no family of his own in New Orleans. He is a sailor with the French navy, or he used to be a sailor, until one day, when he came ashore from a vessel flying the French flag. That was a few years ago. That was when Yves gave up on France and quit the navy. He is what Creoles call *les Français étrangers*, "foreign French." Meaning, he is a new immigrant, an unknown who got off a boat.

The church has a vaulted ceiling, an altar of colored marble and gilded wood, on top of which stand three women. A mural is painted on the rear wall showing Louis IX, the sainted king of France, proclaiming the Crusades. The Louis whose name became Louisiana.

Louisiana started as a French colony in 1718, then became a possession of Spain in 1763. The church went up during the Spanish phase. The colony returned to France briefly after 1800, and then the United States bought Louisiana, in 1803. It is a meandering story, more so when you name the Native people, the Chickasaw and Choctaw, who are driven aside when the whites come.

But to the ceremony. When Yves Le Corgne and Marguerite Zeringue stand at the altar, France is their mother country, as it is for half the whites in New Orleans, at least in fantasy.

I have no portraits of the bride and groom. They do not hire a portrait painter, and it is many years before the advent of photography. But I can see them to a degree, by inference. I see them by thinking about their great-grandchildren, the people named Maud, and Edna, and Albert Lecorgne, whom I knew as a boy in New Orleans.

Yves Le Corgne as I picture him is slight, with thin features and a sharp chin. His brown hair is straight, cut to an inch or two in length, and combed forward in the Empire style. Many men, certainly white men with French roots, wear their hair in a style imported from Paris. It is copied from the emperor, Napoleon Bonaparte, and spread by imitation to the fingertips of the French-speaking world.

Marguerite Zeringue is reed-thin and petite, probably, with dark hair. White Creole women in Louisiana also keep up Empire fashion, which encourages Marguerite to wear her hair shoulder length but pinned up, with corkscrew curls falling from her ears. The style means Marguerite's wedding dress might be high-waisted, gathered in below her breasts, a light fabric falling, no corsets or stays, ending in a billow at the ankle.

Witnesses have written their names in the register. Marguerite's parents are here, Jean-Louis and Ann Zeringue. So is a witness named Jean DeBlanc. The Zeringue family are close to Jean DeBlanc. He has known them for decades, from a time when he and they both lived on a slow stream called Bayou Lafourche, one hundred miles from New Orleans. Now they are friends in the city. Jean DeBlanc is a man with a future. In fifty years, DeBlanc's son, a flamboyant lawyer with a florid name—Alcibiade—will lead a white supremacist movement. And in fifty years, a son of the pair getting married, a carpenter with a florid name—Polycarp Constant Lecorgne—will join the flamboyant lawyer called DeBlanc in a campaign of violent rage. It is an arrangement of symmetries, but these things do not yet matter. There is a wedding to finish, and no one here knows what is coming.

Also on hand, maybe, is a young woman named Polly. She is twenty-one, black, and an enslaved servant. Polly has been working for years in the home of Marguerite's parents. Today, she is a breathing gift. Marguerite's parents are presenting Polly to their daughter as a wedding present, handing her over like a living dowry.

Yves Le Corgne, the solitary groom, sees his bride ascend the aisle. Yves's people, his family, live five thousand miles away, in France. Some say that Yves, a petty officer in Napoleon's military, absconded from the French navy. The truth is fugitive, like the man, because there is no record of his arrival in New Orleans. There is only the wayfaring stranger who gets married.

Marguerite's family, the Zeringues, have two kinds of capital that Yves does not: slaves and social position. The Zeringues are Creole: they are French in language and life, and they have lived in Louisiana for nearly one hundred years. The Zeringues are enviable—to whites, that is. They have a rice farm on the Mississippi, five miles upriver from New Orleans. At 175 acres, it is a small plantation, with eleven enslaved workers, the latter fact thought prestigious.

Yves Le Corgne possesses little. Yves is marrying up, lifting himself to a higher class. Marguerite is marrying down, and her parents, I imagine, do not care for it.

The wedding is in French, first language of the bride and groom. English is spoken by a minority population, *les Américains*. The Americans have been streaming in, a few hundred one season, a thousand the next, since President Thomas Jefferson bought Louisiana from France, thirteen years ago. But the Americans and their language are second-class goods. Only one or two speakers of English can be seen at this Creole event.

The priest looks up.

—*Yves César Le Corgne, voulez-vous prendre cette femme, Marguerite Constance Zeringue, pour votre épouse?* Do you wish to take Marguerite as your wife?

The office done, the priest blesses the couple with holy water. A rustling of clothes, recessional music, and the church empties. At night, the French sailor takes his wife to their bed. My aunt Maud Lecorgne had a saying about petite women, and Marguerite apparently was small. As Maud put it, Yves's bride is so thin he has to shake the sheets to find her.

What lies behind the eyes of Yves Le Corgne, the new immigrant with a highborn wife? His youth says something.

Yves César Le Corgne is born in January 1787 in *Bretagne*, Brittany to the English, in the northwest of France. His parents, Yves Le Corgne and Marie Morin, are peasants who farm and fish. Their home is a tiny island called Molène. A half-mile square, population three hundred, Molène lies seven nautical miles out from the regional harbor on the mainland, the city of Brest. Looking out their cottage door, the Le Corgnes see nothing but ocean.

The region of Brittany juts out from France into the Atlantic in the shape of a spear, and Brest, population twenty-five thousand, lies at the tip of the spike. Brest is a port for the French navy and home of the *Académie de marine*, the naval academy. Shipyards proliferate.

The ocean turns the economy, and to send men to sea is the main task. Men are dispatched to war from Brest and sent north to fish *la Manche*, the English Channel. Young Yves Le Corgne shuttles back and forth from Brest to his island home two hours distant, Molène. He takes to the water, like everyone.

The French Revolution erupts in 1789. Yves is a toddler when riot sweeps away the monarchy in Paris. The Terror and guillotine replace Louis XVI and Marie Antoinette, but the violence is four hundred miles and worlds from Brittany. What a boy might see, dimly, is decay in the power of elites. The church and priests tremble, landlords and the rich look weak and fearful as they hold tight to lordship and money.

Napoleon Bonaparte seizes power in 1799, and soon the wars of empire recruit a generation. In the harbor at Brest, Yves sees warships coming together and sailing off. In December 1801, a giant mobilization takes place, as upwards of forty thousand sailors and soldiers leave from Brest on an expedition to the Caribbean. They are going to the old French colony, Saint-Domingue. Yves, at age thirteen, would have seen the massing of men and watched the flotilla from his front door. The mission of the fleet, everyone knows, is to put down the revolt of the enslaved who have thrown off French rule in the Caribbean. Napoleon is sending an army to take back Saint-Domingue and to impose slavery once again in the country called Haiti. It is for the magnificence of France.

Yves has a decent education. Book learning is not common for a son of peasants, but Yves's handwriting and later working life show some of it. In another way, he is ordinary: like most young men in Brittany, he is pulled to sea. Already the matter of language follows him. Much of Brittany uses the language of Breton. Breton has Celtic roots and is closer to Welsh and Irish than it is to French. A native of Brittany grows up to speak Breton and acquires French as an additional tongue, the official language. But Yves is a little different. Evidence from French archives shows that Yves Le Corgne's parents are newcomers to Brittany, having moved there from the region of Normandy, where French is the dominant tongue. Yves probably grows up speaking French at home and Breton in his schooling. In America, he will continue to shift among languages.

In 1803, news reaches Paris that two-thirds of the men on the flotilla from Brest have been killed in Saint-Domingue, Haiti. Black troops under their commander, Jacques Dessalines, meet the French invaders, who die on the field and in waves of yellow fever, a tropical disease to which the whites have no resistance. Word makes its way to Brest and to the ears of the young Yves Le Corgne that the Caribbean is a death trap. *Les nègres* are killing all our men, and French glory is degraded. By spring 1803, the entire French force in Haiti is wiped out, except for a thousand or so deserters who have decamped to New Orleans and nearby.

Napoleon decides that American colonies, with their slave rebellions and mass graves for whites, are not worth the cost. The emperor will raise money for his European wars by selling the French colonies instead. Diplomats from the United States agree to buy all of Louisiana, comprising one-third of North America, for $15 million. The territory, which was transferred by Spain to France in 1800, is handed by France to the United States in December 1803.

During the Napoleonic wars, at least five men with the name Le Corgne are in the French navy and sailing out of Brest—relatives of Yves Le Corgne. One of them is Yves's uncle, Jean. Jean Le Corgne is said in an indictment against him to be "middle height, with chestnut brown hair." Jean joins the navy during the revolution and serves on a twelve-gun ship called the *Belliqueuse* (Bellicose), which plies the English Channel as coast guard against the detested British. But in 1794, he deserts, walking away from the *Belliqueuse* in some port. The French navy puts out a search for Jean Le Corgne and fails to find him.

Yves Le Corgne seems to follow his uncle's path, both into the navy and out of it. In 1807, Yves is twenty, an age many sailors sign on. War is thrashing throughout Europe, and France wants recruits. What is left of the French navy, half-sunk off of Spain in the Battle of Trafalgar in 1805, is confined around Brest as British ships patrol the English Channel. Eventually a handful of warships get out and reenter the fight for Napoleon. It is April 1809, and Yves may be on board with the fleet. On the west coast of France near the port of La Rochelle, French gunships meet a British squadron in the Battle of the Basque Roads. France does badly, but saves its ships. Two years later, in the Adriatic Sea off Italy, French gunships meet British frigates in the Battle of Lissa, over an island fortress. My aunt Maud's notes say it is this year, 1811, that Yves's ship is captured, and he is taken prisoner by the British. In the story Maud tells, Yves is jailed in England near the city of Bristol, on the River Severn. A British history describes a bastion near Bristol that is fitted out to become Stapleton Prison, which receives French and other captives of Napoleon's half-dozen wars. Yves remains jailed for a period of time before going home to France, probably in a prisoner exchange.

He finds his way back to the French fleet. Now about twenty-five, Yves crosses the Atlantic. I cannot be sure of the circumstances. Napoleon's attempt to reenslave Saint-Domingue has already failed. Haiti has driven out ten thousand or more exiles, half of them white, some of them biracial, some of them black and former slaves. In 1809, these exiles are on the move again, pushed out from their place of refuge on the island of Cuba. They are looking for another French home. Schooners and brigs and frigates and warships collect the exiles, salvage their lives, and take them to New Orleans. This part is conjecture, but it may be that Yves Le Corgne is aboard one of these salvage ships during the last sweeps of the evacuation from Cuba. By this time, back in Europe, the so-called *Grande Armée* of France is giving up the nation's empire. French sailors in the Caribbean hear the bad news from home as Napoleon invades Russia and then retreats; the emperor sends armies to fight in Spain, where the British defeat them. It is 1813. Austria, Prussia, and Sweden declare war on France, and Napoleon meets their armies in a giant battle in Germany, at Leipzig. The French lose again. The glory of France seems to dissolve like a powder. In March 1814, allied armies enter Paris, and Napoleon abdicates.

It is the reversal of his country's fortunes back home, I think, that prompts Yves Le Corgne, still in the Caribbean, to leave France behind. Yves's uncle, Jean Le Corgne, had absconded from the French navy. I suspect the nephew follows this gallant family tradition and decides to take his chances in New Orleans. Yves's method of immigration appears to be desertion, stepping off a French warship and not getting back on. I put the year at 1814. He is twenty-seven.

In New Orleans, Yves is suddenly among many who do not look like Frenchmen. What does this man of warships and exile feel in the presence of black people? Although he probably knows something about blacks as seamen—the French navy recruits black sailors—I imagine that Yves thinks *les nègres* live somewhere outside of civilization.

It happens that a French physician named François Bernier is one of the first to develop racial classification. In 1684, Bernier, who travels for years outside France, to Africa, through Asia, publishes an essay in *Journal des Sçavans*, an early periodical for scholars and a mouthpiece of the new scientific method. Bernier provides an early racist map of humanity. In an essay called "Nouvelle division de la terre, par les différentes espèces ou races d'hommes qui l'habitent" ("A New Division of the Earth, According to the Different Species or Races of Men Who Inhabit It"), he divides the human species into four "races," consisting of the "first race" (Europeans, he says) and three "lower races," namely, Africans and East Asians, plus "the frightful people of the Lapps," the Sámi of northern Scandinavia. Europeans are "the measuring device against which the rest of humanity might be compared."

Fifty years later, a botanist in Sweden, Carl Linnaeus, widens the lens of early science to see and compile species of plants, as well as "races" of people. In 1735, writing in Latin, Linnaeus coins the phrase *Homo sapiens* ("knowing man") in his commanding text, *Systema Naturae*. He names four subspecies for *Homo sapiens*, and gives them traits: *europeaus* ("very smart, inventive"), *americanus* ("ruled by custom"), *asiaticus* ("ruled by opinion"), and *afer* ("sluggish, lazy, crafty, careless").

With Linnaeus, *Homo sapiens* hungers for categories. The attractions of order and genus and species are great. And taxonomy, the idea of different human registers, becomes the path to self-knowledge for knowing man.

Workingmen and sailors with some education, like Yves, do not read Linnaeus, of course, but they would certainly know of the encyclopedia man, *Comte de Buffon*, Count Buffon. He is born Georges-Louis Leclerc but is familiar to France as "Buffon." In the mid-1700s, Buffon starts to publish an encyclopedia, *Histoire naturelle* ("Natural History"), written in common French, and he produces an eventual thirty-six volumes; schools for plain people purchase and teach from them. The books are an *omnium gatherum*, a text of all things, and their contents seep into newspapers. Buffon imports the race program of Carl Linnaeus into *Histoire naturelle* and adds two to the growing scheme. He places Linnaeus's "afers," or black Africans, "between the extremes of barbarism and civilization" and gives the opinion that black people brought to Europe might change their color and become "perhaps as white as the natives."

Buffon's digest of race stresses the high place of whiteness: "We behold the human form in its greatest perfection in Europe." There is a pyramid of humanity, he says. Yet the layers of the pyramid have developed from one source, as the Bible makes clear, the idea of monogenesis. Because blacks and whites have sex and make children, they must be the same creature. Following the fable of Genesis, with Adam and Eve in Eden, Buffon is clear that all humans come from a single root. The *Histoire naturelle* encyclopedia is passed around, and Buffon becomes an authority on the same plane with Voltaire and Denis Diderot. The idea of a stack of races, with whites on the top and people of color on the bottom, spreads through northern Europe. It drifts like sediment into the unconscious of common whites, like Yves Le Corgne, the sailor.

Yves Le Corgne washes up in New Orleans, a town ninety years old. Compared with one-thousand-year-old Brest—rocky, cold, and strict, with a military hardness—New Orleans is new, ramshackle, and steaming. The city counts about twenty thousand, half of them white, half of them people of color. When French colonists come to live in the early 1700s, planting a foot between the Chickasaw and Choctaw, they call the place *la Nouvelle Orléans*. The name flatters the Duke of Orléans, regent of France. A century later, the Americans translate the name as "New Orleans."

People in New Orleans might call Yves a *forçat*, a label for a dubious exile. The word *forçat* dates from the time when many whites in Louisiana are people expelled from France—criminals, beggars, military deserters rounded up and deported. A lot of exiles are boatmen, like Yves. Women who are *forçats* are thrown out from French prisons or hospitals. Yves is doubtful, so are many.

The city is one-half white and one-half nonwhite. In order merely to say that, I am using racial thought, four hundred years old, that divides humans into groups. But to continue: its population is 6,300 white men and women, 6,000 enslaved African Americans, and 5,000 free people of color. Free people of color—"f.p.c." in legal papers, *gens de couleur libres* in French—are a group apart. They are neither white nor black, *pas blanc, ni nègre*. Many f.p.c.'s have white fathers and enslaved black mothers and acquire freedom when their father decides his children should not be his slave property.

Yves Le Corgne has been in New Orleans only a short time when another war comes to his door. Now it is the United States that clashes with Britain, France's old enemy. In the War of 1812, the majority of the fight takes place far from Louisiana—in Ohio, Michigan, Canada, and Maryland—but the final act of the war is closed at New Orleans. It is early January 1815 when several thousand British soldiers and a naval squadron arrive on the Mississippi River at a point five miles south of the city. There they meet an American army of five thousand whites and people of color commanded by forty-seven-year-old General Andrew Jackson. Yves Le Corgne, the new immigrant, might be in the fight, because he probably hates the British and because General Jackson wants veteran sailors to man a handful of gunships, but I find no record. The assault on New Orleans fails, the troops from England leave Louisiana, and the last war that Yves lives through is over.

New Orleans is a murky town for Yves, one swirling with clans. A visitor describes the white men: "They are not capable of violent passions or strong exertions"—in other words, they do not care to work very hard. "They have few men of superior talents. The drawbacks of their character are an overruling passion for frivolous amusements—dance, food—and a tendency for the luxurious enjoyment of the other sex, without being selective of either the black or the white race."

Whether Yves sleeps with black women, or with white, there is no evidence. I have the impression he has little to do with *les nègres*, that he tries to get away from the blacks. He will find a white woman with money, and ask her to marry.

3

Marguerite Zeringue is the woman Yves finds. She is born in August 1798, on a plantation in southwest Louisiana, outside a village called Plattenville. The farm faces Bayou Lafourche, a sluggish stream that peels off the Mississippi, a day and a half by longboat from New Orleans.

Her parents are in the land-and-slave class. Households named Zeringue have run plantations on Bayou Lafourche for generations. On the farm where Marguerite is born, enslaved women and men grow rice that her parents sell. Marguerite's childhood is comfortable—the Zeringues are in the upper five percent—but not extravagant. The family is too fertile. Marguerite has four sisters in the house and twenty cousins within a few miles. Her father, the fourth of ten children, inherits little. And her mother is *Acadienne*, Acadian. By that I mean she is "Cajun," one of ten thousand migrants who come down from eastern Canada with her parents when the English drive out the French.

When Marguerite is seven years old, her parents move away from Bayou Lafourche, take their children and enslaved people, and resettle near New Orleans, buying a piece of land and a house on the Mississippi River, five miles upstream of the city. The new Zeringue plantation has two hundred yards of riverbank and runs away from the water about six hundred yards, ending at the swamp. The family lives in an eight-room house; near it stand four "negro cabins," a corn house, a kitchen house, and a rice mill. Marguerite grows up here, a farm with ten acres of rice in the ground. She is not a *grande princesse*, but she knows black people as the folk who serve her day and night.

The Zeringues do not name their slave farm the way the Americans put labels on land. *Les Américains* call their places all kinds of

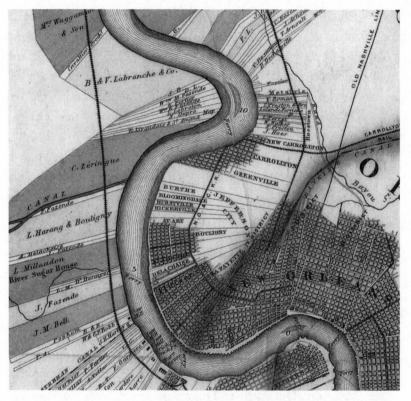

The plantation of Marguerite's cousin, "C. Zeringue," lies
across the Mississippi River from "Jefferson City."

things. The Zeringue plantation is a nameless factory with workers
and fields.

In 1811, Marguerite is fourteen. She steps out to the water, where
she can watch the riverboats. In midwinter, something big happens on
the river, and a lot of blood flows. Thirty-five miles upstream from New
Orleans, on the east bank of the Mississippi, there is an uprising of sugar
workers. As you might expect, for what the people are put through.

On January 8, 1811, near the home of the slaveholder Manuel
Andry, between two hundred and three hundred people form a mob
behind a pair of men. The leaders are named Quamana, an Asante
born in West Africa, and Charles Deslondes, a Creole of color—a
"mulatto," the Americans say. Both men are enslaved on sugar plantations, and so are their followers. The mob seizes the house of Manuel

Andry, where they kill the slaveholder's young son. Armed with axes and farm tools, the troupe makes its way downriver, moving from plantation to plantation, heading south toward New Orleans, picking up recruits. They burn the houses of several sugar planters, then kill a man named François Trépagnier. Going along the riverbank, the army of maybe four hundred comes within a few miles of the Zeringue land, where young Marguerite looks out at the water.

Slaves in Louisiana speak a language of their own; it is not French, not English, but a modified French some call Gombo. In Gombo, you have a saying that fits this occasion—*Même bâton qui batte chein nouer-là, pé batte chein blanc-là*, "The same stick that beats the tied-up dog can beat the white."

Les nègres are cruel and uncivilized, white people say. Like animals, they must be dealt with.

The rebel army reaches a point ten miles upriver from the Zeringues, where companies of whites, armed and mounted, make the attack. Near the sugar plantation of Jacques Fortier, whites chase down and kill forty of the rebels. They capture another sixty or more.

Everyone says the rising is the fruit of Saint-Domingue. Ever since Toussaint L'Ouverture and his armies faced down the French in Haiti and won, blacks have looked for a way to scalp the good white folks of Louisiana.

Marguerite Zeringue, though just a girl, must know something about Haiti. She certainly knows when an army of blacks comes down the river, almost in sight.

After three quick trials, dozens are executed by hanging, more by firing squad. The heads of the men are severed from their bodies and placed on stakes. Within a few days, some one hundred heads appear on tall posts, lining the river. They stand every quarter mile or so, propped up like markers, starting at the riverbank in front of St. Louis Cathedral in New Orleans, going upstream along the river road, ending at the starting point of the revolt.

Marguerite Zeringue is a young woman, just into puberty. When she puts on her fresh linen, stands on the levee in front of her house, and looks across the river, what she sees are fence posts topped with black heads, their faces twisted in the agony of gruesome death.

Yves Le Corgne and Marguerite Zeringue marry and set up house. I find record of a rental where they come to live—*rue Dauphine, #43*—Dauphine Street, where children will be born.

The city of New Orleans looks from the air like a box pushed against the bank of a river. The river washes one side of the town, while a swamp steams up the other. The French use the Native name for the giant river, Mississippi, and so too *les Américains*. North of the town, through five miles of cypress swamp, lies a big lake. The French named it Lake Pontchartrain, after one of their noblemen, the Count of Pontchartrain.

The boxlike settlement between a river and a lake is a little grid, eleven blocks long as you walk beside the Mississippi, seven blocks deep as you walk away from it—sixty-six blocks of three hundred feet each. Yves and Marguerite marry about the time the Americans start to come in droves from the north and east—Tennessee, Virginia, Georgia. Things sprawl. A new suburb, or *faubourg*, appears just east of the rectangle. (The word *faubourg*, or suburb: *faux* / false + *bourg* / city = *faubourg*, "false city.") It is *faubourg Marigny*, named for a man who divides his plantation land and sells building lots. Another suburb west of the old rectangle, *faubourg St. Mary*, is where the Americans move in. That neighborhood has flat façades and English-style windows and sash. Creoles call them *fenêtres à la guillotine*, guillotine windows. They slice up and down and are uglier than French windows, which open like a door into the room.

Both *faubourgs*, St. Mary and Marigny, grow along the river. English is spoken in St. Mary. At some point, the Americans who live there call the older city the "French Quarter," where Creoles and the foreign French live. When they move to Dauphine Street, Yves and Marguerite remain with their people in the *Vieux Carré*.

The new Le Corgne house has problems. It stands a block from the *maisons de tolérance*, the brothels. A half-dozen houses where sex is on sale lie one hundred yards from the newlyweds' front door, just where *rue Douane* (Custom House Street) meets *rue Burgundy* (Burgundy Street). Another problem is the flood. A few months earlier, water fills the streets that lie near the swamp behind the city—Dauphine is one—and most houses sit in water for a time before the flood recedes. A breach in the levee tripped the flood. The levee is the mound of dirt that lines the river and keeps the flow in its banks. Creoles have a word for a levee break, a "crevasse." It happens a lot.

The colored people are everywhere, they own the neighborhood. Yves and Marguerite rent from a woman named Marie Hinard. She is a *femme de couleur libre*, a free woman of color, who owns two houses on Dauphine Street.

I look for the house at 43 Dauphine, but it is gone. A record of the floor plan survives. The property comprised two buildings on a skinny lot—a so-called Creole cottage and, fifty feet behind it, a two-story kitchen house. In the 1800s, the cottage stood right against the street, lined in front by a wooden banquette, a sidewalk made of planks. When they move in, the Le Corgnes occupy the front building, and their wedding present, the enslaved Polly, lives in the kitchen house. The Creole cottage is one-and-a-half stories and nearly square, but Yves and Marguerite have only one side of it; Marie Hinard rents the other side to someone else. The Le Corgnes' half cottage has two rooms downstairs and one room up. It is roomy, until children appear. Behind the cottage, Polly spends much of her life. Her kitchen house is a brick rectangle with a giant fireplace on the ground floor; she sleeps in a room above. Between the kitchen and the cottage, a courtyard. Maybe banana trees, a vegetable garden, a slop corner, bamboo, lizards, and cockroaches, *les cafards*. In the corner, a privy, a hole in the ground with a toilet seat and door. The place looks a lot like a compound in Havana, or in Port-au-Prince, Haiti, two sister cities of New Orleans. Also in the courtyard, a wooden cistern, a big barrel with four legs holding it aboveground. Open on top, the cistern awaits rainwater, used to drink and cook. Many drink from the Mississippi, but only after they let a pitcher of the river water sit for an hour, so that a bed of silt can settle.

Yves stays in touch with his family back home in Brittany. He writes them, they write back. The newspapers tell him when his mail comes. He does not forget his family, but he never goes to France again.

Aunt Maud tells me in her notes that Yves spent his prison months in England in the company of a talkative British officer, and that he learned English that way. It sounds a little twee, and I am skeptical. But I find a directory that says Yves works as *un instituteur*, a teacher in an institute. Probably he gives language lessons. About this time, an English educator named Joseph Lancaster develops a method he calls "reciprocal teaching," and in America, hundreds of academies open to try it. In Louisiana, the method becomes *enseignement mutuel*, mutual learning: American students tell the French things in English, while French tell the Americans things in French. Yves Le Corgne looks on.

Teaching pads the income, but most of Yves's work is on the water. At any time, two hundred schooners, barges, and sloops tie up at the wharfs of the Mississippi. Aunt Maud says that Yves makes his main living as a purser and supercargo on ships in the merchant marine.

Businesspeople in the seagoing trade hire a man known as a supercargo to travel with their goods from port to port. A client in New Orleans ships a load of sugar in barrels to Mobile, Alabama, and Yves goes with the cargo. He sees that it stays dry, and he collects the money. A supercargo brings his own small payload on a ship that hires him, and makes little deals on the side. I suspect Yves takes full opportunity to order around the black men who unload his boat. Back in New Orleans, waiting for the next shipment, he teaches in the institute.

The working hands at home belong to Polly. She is twenty-five in the year 1820. If she has a partner or family, she leaves them behind on the Zeringue plantation, across the river. The place is not far, two hours by foot and ferry. Maybe Polly sees her people two or three days a month, when she can talk her way there and get free of the Le Corgnes. Her domain is the courtyard. She is the factotum who empties the night soil of the chamber pots into the courtyard latrine. She is the laundry worker. She boils water in a vat in the courtyard, dips the madame's white things, the monsieur's shirts, the sheets, uses lye to make them white, hangs them to dry, heats the flatiron in the fire, mixes the cornstarch, damps the wrinkles, flattens them with the iron. Polly does the laundry on Mondays, and it takes all day. She cooks while everything dries.

Polly manages the food, keeps everyone eating. She goes to the covered market on Levee Street at St. Anne Street and returns with *huîtres* and *crevettes*, oysters and shrimp. There is no evidence about how Yves and Marguerite relate to Polly, but in the custom, the three spend ten or twelve hours a day within earshot. When Marguerite and Yves have sex, Polly probably hears them.

Polly wants things, but I do not know many of what they are. She is enchained to the parents of our Klansman. That is what I know about her.

The Le Corgnes' landlord, Marie Hinard, is Franco-African, a French-speaking woman of color. In one important way, Marie Hinard is better off than Yves and Marguerite. She owns real estate. I wonder how her tenants feel about renting from Marie Hinard. To Yves and Marguerite, she is not a *négresse*; she is different from *les nègres*. They may resent her. When Marie Hinard buys another house on Dauphine Street, she owns property on both sides of the Le Corgnes. The colored woman throws shade.

New Orleans is divided into groups. About one in four is white and speaks French; one in four is white and speaks English. One in four is mixed-race and free. One in four is black and enslaved, speaking French or English, and sometimes a dialect of a West African language— Wolof, Mandinka, or Umbundu. Whites have names for nonwhites. "Quashee" is slang that names a defiant slave, a person who says no to her master.

Black people also have names for whites. "Buckra" is a good one. Buckra count their money all the time. Buckra do not tire of taking themselves to church. I want to hear what enslaved people sound like talking about whites, but of course I cannot.

Another name for whites: "ofay." You will not hear the word "ofay" on the lips of the Le Corgnes. Ofay likes it when his Creole women are bright. Ofay wants you to call him *maître*, master. Polly might have such things to say.

Some part of the population, white and black, speaks Spanish, held over from the forty years Louisiana was a colony of Spain. There are also Native Americans, who have survived a century of invasion. Native people number maybe one thousand in the city and live in its margins. The largest group, the Houmas, come to New Orleans to sell goods at city markets before retreating to villages in the western parishes, Lafourche and Terrebonne.

The factions—free white, enslaved black, free people of color, Native—have words for one another. A large number are race terms that whites use to label *gens de couleur*. Yves Le Corgne uses them, these words that fix who and what you are—

A *mulâtre*, or mulatto, is the child of a white man and a Negro or dark black woman.

A *quarteron*, or quadroon, is the child of a white father and a mulatto woman.

A *grieff*, or griffe, is the child of a Negro and a mulatto.

A *sang-mêlé*, or mixed-blood, is the child of a white man and a quadroon.

A *métis* is a mixed-race Native American, with one Indian parent and one white or colored parent.

The words and labels sound strange now, in our world with its "white" and "black" continents of identity. But for Yves Le Corgne, words like "griffe" and "quadroon" are lenses through which he sees his intimates.

Marguerite Le Corgne works, she is not indolent. She helps to run the house and the kitchen, helps to keep everyone in clothes. Many whites, well over half, are workers and tradesmen, people who own neither land, nor people, nor real estate. They live from their sweat. They are *petits blancs*, the little whites. Marguerite and her people, the Zeringues, are a different caste. They are *grands blancs*, big whites. Slavery is the line that separates *petits blancs* from *grands blancs*. About one in four whites is a slaveholder. Marguerite's grandparents, people named Zeringue, had two hundred acres and sixteen slaves. *Grands blancs*. The money trickles down from her parents to Marguerite Le Corgne, despite her marriage to a sailor who jumped ship.

Yves Le Corgne and Marguerite Zeringue make a family, or they try. Their firstborn is a girl, in May 1819. They call her Anne Marie. The child dies soon after birth. Anne Marie is followed by a boy, Yves, named for his father. He is born in January 1820. No doubt the parents hire a *sage-femme*, a midwife. Three years later, little Yves is dead, likely in an epidemic of fever that visits the city in 1823.

Yellow fever is the disease. It killed most of the French soldiers in Haiti, the ones who sailed from Yves's hometown. Whites believe yellow fever is caused by the wetlands behind the city, near Dauphine Street, "the pestilential miasma which rises from the swamps and marshes," as a visitor puts it. In fact, yellow fever—common enough to have a nickname, Yellow Jack—is a mosquito-carried virus of the genus *Flaviviridae*, which also includes the viruses for dengue fever, encephalitis, West Nile fever, and Zika. To Yves and Marguerite, to whites in general, *les nègres* have an unfair advantage. When the fever comes, far more whites die than do blacks. A traveler describes the scene in New Orleans as "the most terrible, when from sixty to eighty persons are buried every day . . . whole streets cleared of their inhabitants, and the city one vast cemetery." It is well-known that "creole, mulatto, and griffe women are the most skillful in the cure of the disease." Experienced white doctors bury hundreds of people, like the three-year-old Yves, while "these old creole women commonly succeed in restoring their own patients."

What is it like, I wonder, to watch your boy die, and see that black people who take care of him, like your own Polly, are doing fine? I wonder if Yves and Marguerite have thoughts like this. The blacks live and live, they brush off the fevers. There is no justice in it. One day, the blacks will be held to account.

In 1824, another girl is born to Yves and Marguerite. Her parents name her Marguerite, hoping her mother's name will carry her. The child dies.

In 1826, Yves and Marguerite have a boy. They call him Yves. He is the second baby they have named for his father. Yves is a seven-pound miracle to his parents, and they write it in his name, Yves *Jean de Dieu* Le Corgne—Yves John of God. The miracle baby is born nine years after his parents marry. Praise God, a boy who lives.

I think of this one as "Yves of God." He receives the love and learning his parents can afford. He is watched by Polly, the enslaved housekeeper. He is looked after by his mother and father. He is a *dauphin*, a prince, growing up on rue Dauphine, Princess Street.

A year and a half later, in 1827, the boy is joined by a sister, named Constance, after her maternal grandmother. She dies as a toddler.

In twelve years, Yves and Marguerite bury four children. It is hard to imagine. Wait a minute. It is hard to imagine Polly and her bitter portion.

Yves Le Corgne, the supercargo, works side by side with black sailors in the merchant marine. Most are free, some are literate. There is a chance that somewhere on a job, in the year 1830, Yves comes upon a little book. It is out of the hands of an African American seaman. The little book is a manifesto: *David Walker's Appeal . . . to the Coloured Citizens of the . . . United States.*

"Search the pages of history and see if any . . . has ever treated a set of human beings as the white Christians of America do us, the blacks, or Africans," writes David Walker.

David Walker is a man of about thirty-three. He is born in North Carolina, and tall. His mother was a free woman of color, his father a slave. He lives in Charleston, South Carolina, for several years before moving to Boston. And there, in fall 1829, Walker publishes his manifesto, the *Appeal . . . to the Coloured Citizens.* Among other things, his little book demands that people like Yves and Marguerite be killed.

"I do declare it, that one good black man can put to death six white men," Walker writes. "I call men to witness that the destruction of the Americans is at hand and will be speedily consummated unless they repent. . . . They have no more right to hold us in slavery than we have to hold them."

David Walker smuggles his pamphlet into the slave cities of the South. He prints three editions in nine months. From his storefront in Boston, he sews the book into the linings of clothing that black sailors wear. Copies of the book turn up in New Orleans in 1830, brought by seamen on cargo ships.

"The whites are dragging us around in chains and in handcuffs, to their new States and Territories, to work their mines and farms, to enrich them and their children," David Walker tells readers. "It is no more harm for you to kill a man, who is trying to kill you, than it is for you to take a drink of water when thirsty."

David Walker's Appeal is one man's attack, a call to ditch white domination.

"The whites have always been an unjust, jealous, unmerciful, avaricious and bloodthirsty set of beings, always seeking after power and authority . . . cutting each other's throats, trying to subject each other to wretchedness and misery . . . deceitful and unmerciful," he says.

The state legislature of Louisiana has an answer to David Walker. After the *Appeal* is discovered on ships at the wharfs of New Orleans, lawmakers outlaw black literacy, making it a crime to teach a person of color to read.

I wonder whether Yves encounters this message in the hold of one of his schooners—

"They (the whites) know well—that there can be nothing in our hearts but death alone for them. . . . Remember, Americans . . . that some of you whites will yet curse the day that you ever were born."

It is summer 1831. The Le Corgne household is full. Yves and Marguerite have a five-year-old son, Yves of God—and now a one-year-old daughter, Ézilda. They have two slaves, Polly and a forty-one-year-old man named Valentin, another human gift from Marguerite's father.

Polly and Valentin keep home and hearth clean and working. And Marguerite becomes pregnant, for the seventh time.

New Orleans during these years is a city of epidemics. In 1832, as Marguerite comes close to giving birth, cholera comes to visit, carried on bad sanitation. The scene looks like a visit of Yellow Jack, as the city empties out. "There is not a breath of air to be felt," a visitor writes. "A deep silence reigns . . . and most of the stores are shut up. No one is to be seen in the streets in the day time except negroes and people of color. And no carriage except the funeral hearse." Those who can leave New Orleans flee, and Marguerite and Yves go to the Zeringue plantation up the river. More than ten thousand in the city proceed to die while pregnant Marguerite is out of town. It is the worst cull of any to date, close to twenty percent of the population.

It is there that he is born, at the old Zeringue place, on April 28, 1832. The boy shows his face in the house where Marguerite grew up, her home. It is the same house where she once saw the heads of decapitated blacks.

She gave her first boy who lived a churchy name, Yves of God. She gives this boy the name of a saint, Polycarp. The Le Corgnes are Catholic, as are most whites; for them, saints are virtually alive. This one, Polycarp, was a bishop during the second century, killed in old age, burned alive, and later sanctified. Perhaps Marguerite and Yves see themselves as long-suffering, or perhaps they expect the boy to die, like their other children.

Polycarp is our Klansman.

The little boy acquires a middle name, from his mother's mother. She was called Anne Constant, and she has been dead five years. It is time to pay her respect.

Polycarp Constant grows into a thin, small boy. He seems to get less attention and receive fewer lessons than his brother, Yves of God. It is a pattern that follows the brothers in life.

The toddler Constant runs back and forth in the house. When he cries, Polly the slave tries to quiet him. His father Yves wants calm, so he can tutor his pupils, but there will be none of it.

4

You release a little breath when you see the birth record of a relative—I mean, one who is dead. It is the sentimental sigh of people who peer into family history. The baptism register where the name "Polycarpe Constant Hypolite Le Corgne" shows up gives me this touch of recognition. *And so, here he is.* (The name is a mouthful. Let me call the boy "P.C.") I feel a flicker of identification with P.C. Even though I know nightmares lie on the horizon, he is still, involuntarily, *one of us.* I want to wish him a good childhood.

P.C. grows up around enslaved blacks. Polly and Valentin live in the kitchen house. They watch him, watch over him. On visits to the Zeringue plantation, P.C. plays with black children. It may seem strange that children of masters and children of field hands keep company, but that is what they do. They are playmates until the black boys and girls start work, about age six.

What comes from the lips of whites is something like this. We love the blacks who are near us, they say. We love them like family. Some of them are so very good.

They also say this: *les nègres* are like a different creature.

P.C. is seven. His grandfather, Jean-Louis Zeringue, is widowed and alone. The grandchildren come around, slave children come around, too. In April 1839, Grandfather Jean-Louis brings some of his people to church to be baptized. P.C. and the rest of the Le Corgnes go to witness the christening of four black children. The service is planned for St. Louis Cathedral, where Yves and Marguerite married.

The *Code Noir*, or Black Code, is the old law that regulates the lives of the enslaved. The law says the church will give its sacraments to people of color, baptisms and funerals, although not marriage. Since the coming of the Americans, the *Code Noir* is a relic, but by custom white Creoles still baptize black children. Jean-Louis brings to church his slaves, the mothers and their babies—Estelle, Frances, Joseph, and Agatha. They are to be blessed and splashed with holy water.

The curate writes in his register.

"Estelle, 14 months, daughter of Josephine."

P.C., at the baptismal font, sees the white clergyman in black cassock and white collar. His name is Father Aquarone.

"Frances, five months, daughter of Henriette. Joseph Adam, three years, son of Rachel and Job."

Rachel's partner, Job, must be on hand for this ceremony. Everyone crowds around as each child is blessed, and the curate thumbs the sign of the cross on each child's forehead.

"Agatha, six months, daughter of Rachel."

They are like family, the blacks. We love the ones near us. But they are so different.

A pause in the rites. It is time for the prayer of exorcism. People know the prayer in the liturgy, and they know the need for the ritual cleansing. There is an epidemic of *voodou* among the blacks. It seems the people who come from Saint-Domingue are especially prone. And the ones who come from Africa—people from Benin, from Senegal, the Fon people, the Yoruba, the Wolof—carry the *voodou* in pure form. Father Aquarone sprinkles holy water on the children to protect them from its curse.

"Almighty and ever-living God, cast out the spirit power of Satan, author of evil, from these children."

The ignorant blacks have their *zinzin*, their power amulets. They have all kinds of *grisgris*, powders and plants and animal parts. They believe their *grisgris* has power to move things in the dark spirit world. The whites know what the blacks believe, and they want to stamp it out. The blacks have their priests and priestesses, the *vodouisants*, servants of the spirits. They live out on Bayou Road, which winds into the swamp behind the city. It is there, in the back of town, that the conjurers draw the blacks to Satan. It is there that the unholy make them believe in diabolical blessings and evil spells.

Father Aquarone prays out the *voodou* curse. He splashes the water. All rise, cross themselves, and the service ends. Little P.C. sits in the pew.

On Sundays it is over to *Place Congo*—Congo Square—to watch the dancing. The maps call it Circus Square, a big, empty field just north of the *Vieux Carré*. Congo Square lies on Rampart Street, where the walls of town once stood. The Senegambians and Angolans, the "Congos," make it their own once a week.

You can hear the thunder from a quarter mile. The square is four blocks from the Le Corgne house, and the sound of drums enters through the windows. The scene takes place the afternoon of the Sabbath. It is diabolical, fascinating, irresistible. Enslaved people start dancing at 3:00 p.m.—not a minute earlier, the city marshals say. When P.C. is a boy, the dancing is Sabbath entertainment for half of the city.

"Every stranger should visit Congo Square in its glory," writes a traveler who comes through in the 1830s, when P.C. is growing up. The sound of bones beating on a barrel starts the dancing. The sound turns to drumming, and there is no break till sunset, five hours later.

Marguerite and Yves and the children make their way down Dauphine Street. Two blocks, then turn left, two blocks along Orleans Street, and there it is. I imagine that their slaves, Valentin and Polly, take a different path. "Going up the street and approaching the corner I heard a most extraordinary noise, like horses trampling on a wooden floor," another white visitor writes in his journal.

When you reach the square, you see five or six hundred black women and men dancing—in dozens of circles—and you see the drums.

The dancers are not *sang-mêlés*. Congo Square is not a place where Creoles of color meet. The Le Corgne landlord, Marie Hinard, is not to be found. The dance is a beautiful thing, but the free people of color feel it is beneath them.

P.C. watches from the edge, with other whites. What he sees is ten or twenty clusters of dance. Inside every circle, drummers pound on pigskin, and two or three dancers command a dirt stage. A white visitor from P.C.'s boyhood named Benjamin Latrobe describes the scene.

"A man sits astride a cylindrical drum about a foot in diameter, and beats it with incredible quickness with his hands and fingers. . . . [Dancers] in their movements, gyrations, and attitudinizing exhibitions, keep the most perfect time, making the beats with the feet, head, or hands, or all, as correctly as a well-regulated metronome."

Latrobe is fascinated by black music, especially black drums, which stun him. "They make an incredible noise," he says. He draws pictures in his journal. The sketches are good. And they should be: Benjamin Latrobe is an architect and well-known, having recently overseen the U.S. Capitol, in Washington, D.C.

"Drums at Congo Square," drawn by Benjamin Latrobe in 1819

The drum of choice is the bamboula. Three feet tall, a cone-like cylinder small on the bottom and wide at the top, the bamboula stands between the knees of a seated drummer. Its business end is animal skin, the bottom left open to amplify it.

Another, larger drum lies on its side. A man sits on it and plays. A third drum, square, looks like a stool. Beat it with a mallet for the deepest bass. For treble sounds there is a rasp, a yard-long bat with lines chiseled along the side that scratch and rattle when raked with a drumstick.

The square has been freshened up, grass and sycamores planted. The *grands blancs* dislike clouds of dust during the city's big show. They want things nicer for white eyes. They also want the festival to continue. The authorities know that Congo Square soaks up the desire and the frustration and the anger of thousands of black people. If they do not have an outlet like this, things could be worse.

Benjamin Latrobe describes more instruments—triangles, violins, jawbones. He is curious about one instrument with strings. It has a calabash for a body, and out from the round gourd a long fingerboard emerges, with several strings held tight by pegs. It is the *banzas*, from Senegambia. In a few years the *banzas* enters white music. It is enlarged and modified, it turns into the American banjo.

The women on Congo Square wear the tignon, a kerchief wrapped and tied on the head. The children wear shifts, neck-to-knee robes of coarse muslin. There are tables around the edge of the square with cotton awnings for shade from the sun. Sellers peddle drinks—ginger beer, lemonade, alcohol. Healers sell amulets and elixirs and *grisgris*.

P.C. sees it all from the perimeter.

The square feeds the devil's work, the churchmen say. Close it down, push out the *vodouisants*. It is grotesque. Sunday belongs to the Lord, and the blacks pollute it.

The bamboula is a drum, and it is the name of a dance in which one man plays star. He flexes to the middle of the circle. The bamboula lets him leap. Around the circle, women sway from side to side, chanting a dirge a hundred times, singing a verse another hundred. The bamboula dancer lures one woman into the circle, drums with his legs, swings her. The calinda is another dance with a man in a circle of women. Calinda dancers wear fantastic ornaments, ropes of cowrie shells, the tails of raccoons, sometimes a hundred feathers.

Congo Square is a place of pleasure and worship for blacks. It is the living heart of barbarism for whites. The trance and delirium. The loincloth over the penis. It is a scene with a double nature. People like the Le Corgnes are attracted, and they are repelled. Some whites move their feet, some are mesmerized. Congo Square is a place of wonderment and of revulsion. It might be that people pretend to be repelled.

It is like a sexual habit, this watching of the blacks in Congo Square. I can picture P.C. Le Corgne making his way with his parents along the banquette, the wooden sidewalk. The little white boy looks at the women who dance. The blacks say, *Bel tignons pas fait bel négresse*, "It isn't the fine headdress that makes the fine negress." The boy looks at the women, and he feels. He puts together emotions about the colored people and who they are. He puts together the feeling of what it is to be white. It is a feeling that depends on a scene that is black. The dancers look to the edge and see the whites.

I think I can begin to see, in Congo Square, a script and a stage, a place where blackness and whiteness meet. The two characters come together. Complications ensue. They move apart. Eventually the script calls for a crescendo. Blackness and whiteness collide, and the ending, for our Klansman, is an explosion.

Benjamin Latrobe, the architect, finishes his drawings.

"I have never seen anything more brutally savage, and at the same time dull and stupid than this whole exhibition," he writes after his day of immersion. Latrobe is absorbed enough to make his pictures, and he is angry with himself for looking. The blacks cannot restrain themselves, the civilized whites who go among them can. The blacks must be taught by the civilized.

At sunset, patrolmen from the city guard show themselves at the edge of Congo Square. Their swords are dangling, their epaulets have a glint of gold. The patrol walks through the square, and the crowd slowly dissolves into the streets, back home to *maître* and *maîtresse*, master and mistress.

In October 1839, P.C.'s grandfather Jean-Louis Zeringue dies, age seventy. His grown children travel out from New Orleans to the plantation on the Mississippi to grieve. Two of his four daughters are dead, two are left. One is P.C.'s mother, Marguerite, the other her sister Mélicent. There is an appraisal of the Zeringue estate. Marguerite and Mélicent have the money and the people to themselves.

The Le Corgnes make a showing, and P.C. is on hand. Slaves are the inheritance of his parents, so they are his inheritance, too.

I look for the probate records. It seems Jean-Louis Zeringue has been busy at the slave auctions. Since his wife died, thirteen years earlier, the widowed patriarch has bought and sold a cabin full of people. He leaves a community of sixteen workers: Josephine, Jules, Seraphim, Henriette, Eugene, Celeste, Rachel, Job, Coralie, Damas, Estelle, Frances, Joseph, Charlotte, Agatha, and Cocotte.

Cocotte—the slattern, in French. Jean-Louis calls his people what he wants. Cocotte is not a name her mother chose, whoever might be her mother. Sixteen, a generous gift to leave for your daughters. The dead man's papers call them "items."

The scene is common in the law, the inspection and appraisal of property. Maybe P.C. goes with his mother, Marguerite, to see the blacks sized up and prices placed on them. Oh, but it was a different time, you might say. You have to accept the dead and their doings on their terms. Do not judge the past by the measure of the present. Yes, I know all of that. And still, it is a nasty business.

It is the buckra way.

Another family member appears. Everyone knows him. He is Camille Zeringue, Marguerite's first cousin. Camille, age thirty-four, lives at his plantation a quarter mile downriver. He is Creole, but he acts like an American. He has named his land. He calls it Seven Oaks, for the old trees around the house. Camille enslaves forty people, but he wants more.

The sixteen slaves must be divided between the two daughters. Yves and Marguerite are set to inherit eight, a windfall. The first thoughts of many white couples in their position would be something like this. Cash them in. Sell them. They are a roomful of living money. Pocket a fortune.

It would be easy to cash in. By this time, the year 1840, New Orleans has become the largest market in the country for people on sale. A new and grand auction house has just opened. It is called the

City Exchange, and it stands on St. Louis Street. The City Exchange auction—slaves, land, anything valuable—occupies a rotunda in the middle of a beautiful hotel. The City Exchange auction house does splendid business in the "nigger trade."

Yves and Marguerite have to decide. City Exchange is just down the street from the house on Dauphine. When they walk past, Yves and Marguerite can see, filing into the side door, a continual stream of black farmworkers and milkmaids, hostlers and carpenters, cooks and porters, nurses and seamstresses, valets and footmen, their hands tied or chained to one another. Inside, beneath the seventy-five-foot dome, people step up onto the block. The auctioneer starts his patter, a few lines in French, a few in English. Sold in two minutes. Prices are good.

Camille Zeringue, the rich cousin on Seven Oaks, distracts Yves and Marguerite from their get-rich dreams. Camille wants the slaves, all of them. He offers an amount lower than the appraisals.

Yves Le Corgne may rationalize. It is for the children. Sell them to Camille so that our children will have something. What can be done with eight people? There is not enough work for them in the city. Where would they sleep? Let Camille buy them. The money they bring is a chance to build something. Camille Zeringue offers $7,200, more or less—$3,600 for Mélicent, the same for Marguerite.

Cousin Camille Zeringue is not the gentlest man with slave humanity. In fact, he has a record at Seven Oaks plantation of people trying to get away from his grip. In July one year, three men steal away from Seven Oaks and take to the swamp. One is named Frank. He is in his early twenties, according to the newspaper, "of middle size, thin, rather reddish, with a black mole on his forehead." Another is Handison, also early twenties, "of middle size, robust and fat." Third is "the mulatto Jarret, about 25 or 30 years, 5 feet 7 or 8 inches high, strong built." Frank, Handison, and Jarret are new to Louisiana and "speak English only," an advertisement says. Probably they were shipped to New Orleans, "sold down the river," as they say, meaning down the Mississippi from some other place. The month of July, when the three escape Cousin Camille, is cutting time for sugarcane. Camille drives his workers through twelve-hour days in crushing heat, and the men do not like it. Camille offers a $75 reward to anyone who will drag the men back to his fields.

Yves and Marguerite decide they will sell half of their "items" to Camille—four people—and they will keep the other four. The transaction is written.

P.C. is nine years old. The items are his, too, in a manner of speaking. They are his inheritance.

The four people Marguerite sells do not move out of their cabins. They stay with Camille at Seven Oaks. The four that Marguerite keeps go back with the Le Corgnes to New Orleans. There, Marguerite will lease them to renters, like real estate. To possess four slaves in the city is like owning four houses to rent. It is like becoming a landlord. It is like you are Marie Hinard, the *sang-mêlé* you resent.

P.C. goes home with his parents. Now he can say something that a few little boys like to say to other little boys. *Nous sommes riches*—we are rich.

Some say the first Mardi Gras parade in New Orleans occurs in the year 1838. If true, P.C. Le Corgne is not yet ten when a delirious procession goes past his front door. It is Tuesday, March 6. He sees masked and costumed women and men, marching and stumbling through the streets of the *Vieux Carré*. Men in harlequin costumes, women as fishmongers or harlots. Men dressed as Turks with a saber and red kepi; women in cheap gowns, playing Marie Antoinette. Papier-mâché figures, like a pig that flies, an alligator that sings. P.C. watches animals walking, but they wear shoes and rabbit fur, and they are not animals. He sees women walking, but they are men who dress as women.

Carnival is a festival that arises in Europe, only to be brought to Louisiana by louche French immigrants. It unfolds over six or eight weeks during winter. Most whites take part in Carnival, as do most blacks. I can see the Le Corgnes in it easily, somewhere.

The festival culminates on Shrove Tuesday, the day before the start of Lent, the austere forty days in the Christian calendar. On Shrove Tuesday, believers can wallow in sin, then confess everything, and still be "shriven," shorn of sin and forgiven. The church gives us the word "carnival" itself: *carne vale*, or "goodbye to meat." Meaning, goodbye to bloody pleasures—and fish only, during Lent.

For many whites during this time, and for many blacks, a month of costume balls and gluttony ends with a blast. It is Shrove Tuesday to the priests and scribes but another name to the crowd—*Mardi Gras*, Fat Tuesday.

A writer in the city when P.C. is a boy describes what he sees on Mardi Gras—

"Men and boys, women and girls, slave and free, white and black, yellow and brown . . . appear in grotesque, quizzical, diabolical, horrible, humorous, strange, masks and disguises. Human bodies are seen with heads of beasts and birds; beasts and birds with human heads . . . mermaids, satyrs, beggars, monks, and robbers, parade and march on foot, on horseback, in wagons, carts, coaches, cars in rich confusion, up and down the streets, wildly shouting, singing, laughing, drumming, fiddling, fifeing, and all throwing flour. . . ."

The flour custom is one that boys fall in love with. A handful of white flour thrown at strangers—to humiliate them, to decorate them. Black men cannot throw flour on whites. That is a privilege reserved for the whites themselves.

I can see P.C. with a bag of flour, powdering the heads and gowns of strangers the whitest white.

The Carnival crowds that stream past the Le Corgnes' door are like rolling theater. Some weave down the street and end the night at a dance hall, packing inside for a bal masqué, a masked ball. On Mardi Gras, the world turns upside down, briefly, without challenging the law. A Catholic priest casts his eyes over the children in the choir and chooses a "boy bishop" to act the role of high priest. The boy climbs into the pulpit and preaches a ridiculous sermon. His text is the same every year. It is Ecclesiastes 1:15, "The perverse are hard to be corrected, and the number of fools is infinite."

Fool societies meet and dress up in foolish costume. A men's club or a workers' guild draws lots, and the winner reigns as king for a day. The pretend monarch in cheap fur gives orders to everyone, whatever their place on the social ladder. He is the "Lord of Misrule."

I wonder whether P.C. sings in the choir at St. Louis Cathedral, where he once was baptized. I wonder whether he plays the boy bishop and contemplates the number of fools.

I am trying to make this thing visible, whiteness. It looks transparent and flimsy, maybe. Some would say it does not even exist. But I am trying to make it conspicuous, as visible and as plain as blackness. I have to keep working at it.

Enter now, from a side door, the scientists. They are coming into the room with an idea. They are holding in hand the idea of race. Let us begin with the first one who enters. He is a man named Samuel Morton.

It is 1840, in Philadelphia. Samuel Morton is a natural historian and a forty-year-old professor at the Pennsylvania Medical College. He teaches for the income, but his real love is anatomy. The first thing to learn about Samuel Morton is that he collects skulls. Bony heads are lined up like sentinels along the shelves of his study at the medical college. This might seem too far from the disposition of whites and blacks in the South, a little remote from the trajectory of little P.C. into the figure of our Klansman. But there is a synchrony between the skulls and the terror of the Ku-klux.

Samuel Morton, who is blond and has a high forehead, is a scientist who wishes to tell the story of human evolution. His chief samples are human heads. Most of the skulls he studies come from the U.S. Army, which is variously at war with the Iroquois, Narragansett, and Cherokee people in the north, and the Seminole, Yamasee, Choctaw, and Creeks in the southeast. As whites push south, southwest, and west over the Appalachians, taking land from Native Americans, seizing captives, and killing some who fight the invasion, officers and physicians in the military gather the bodies of Indians, decapitate them, and send the skulls to Morton. Science feeds on war.

"By the kindness of Dr. Satterlee, of the U.S. Army, I received eight specimens of Menominee skulls," Morton writes in a typical thank-you note for a shipment of heads. Morton possesses more than six hundred skulls. He adds the skulls of African Americans, some of them taken from the death marches of enslaved people through the Appalachian range as they are sold "down the river" to New Orleans. He adds the skulls of whites. The white heads are borrowed from paupers' graves and not returned. Morton builds a family tree of humans with his specimens.

He makes a family ladder of races. "The grouping of mankind

into races has occupied the ingenuity of many of the best natural-
ists of the past and present century," Morton writes in his 1839 book,
Crania Americana.

The tongues of intellectuals have fluttered with race talk for cen-
turies. The innovation of Samuel Morton is not that he coins the idea.
His role is that he uses skulls to extend race backward, into the story
of human origins. Morton develops a fable, the idea that humanity
has many births. The fable is known as "polygenesis." The anatomist
wishes to show that many versions of humanity, which Morton calls
races or "varieties," appeared simultaneously. He measures his collection of heads, and measures them again. "It is proposed," he writes,
"to consider the human as consisting of twenty-two families."

He finds that things like shape, jaw length, and skull capacity, how
much tissue the brain case holds, correlate with places of origin for
humans—in southern Africa, in the Americas, in eastern Asia, and
(he says) in the region of the Caucasus. He determines that there are
five races, with each "born" at a different place and time. Morton says
that the "Mongolian" is a race "ingenious, imitative, and highly sus-
ceptible of cultivation"; the "Malay race" is "active and ingenious";
the "American" race, "averse to cultivation . . . restless, revengeful,
and fond of war"; and the "Ethiopian," clearly "joyous, flexible, and
indolent."

The fifth race, so-called Caucasians, "surpass all other people."
Morton saw Caucasians as peoples in Europe, Central Asia, South
Asia, and the eastern horn of Africa.

After Morton's book *Crania Americana* appears (partly subtitled
An Essay on the Varieties of the Human Species), the idea of polygenesis
spreads from Philadelphia and New York to other enclaves of learning. It streams into the Deep South, where polygenesis receives a
warm welcome. In South Carolina, the *Charleston Medical Journal and
Review* says, "We of the South should consider Samuel Morton as our
benefactor for aiding most materially in giving to the negro his true
position as an inferior race." It spreads to a man named Louis Agassiz,
a Swiss-born ethnographer who becomes Samuel Morton's disciple.
Agassiz, a professor of zoology at Harvard, writes and teaches for fifty
years about the separation of the races in their origins.

Samuel Morton sees himself as an impartial measurer of forms, a hunter who gathers evidence. In fact, he is among the early American philosophers of white supremacy. He is one of the first in this country to recruit the authority of science in praise of whiteness.

The windfall is in, the hoard from the Le Corgnes' inheritance. Marguerite and Yves take some of their money and look for real estate. It is 1839. The couple has five children—Yves of God, Ézilda, P.C., Joseph, and Aurore. Marguerite is pregnant with a sixth. They shop for six lots of land.

The Le Corgnes enslave seven: Polly, Valentin, a new woman named Dinah, and four others. There is nowhere to put everyone in the *Vieux Carré*. The French Quarter boils with people—the porters with their wheeling carts, black and ignorant. The women who spill out of the brothels on Burgundy Street, down the block, loud and lewd. The shopkeepers of St. Claude Street, *gens de couleur*, mulattoes with watch chains and attitude, fops who pretend white style. It is twenty-five years since the Le Corgnes married, and it is time to get off the street of the *sang-mêlés*.

New Orleans is growing east and downstream along the river, also west and upstream. The Le Corgnes look west, to a *faubourg* upstream, or "uptown." There is a suburb there that is new and nearly all white. A rail line is going in, and the train, loud and steam-powered, runs along a road called Nayades. Passenger service brings the uptown *faubourgs* quite close. The places cropping up west of the old city have names like DeLord, Annunciation, Foucher, and Lafayette. Stretches of fields separate them, but the gaps are filling. *Faubourg Lafayette* is booming, its wharfs lined with boats, and shipping companies are hiring. If they head that direction, Yves will have work.

In April 1840, Yves Le Corgne, teacher and supercargo, buys six empty lots uptown for $1,700. It is nearly the amount they pocket from the sale of people his wife inherited. They trade four *nègres* for six pieces of land in a new section of uptown called Bouligny.

A man named Joseph Vincent sells the land to the Le Corgnes.

The empty lots sit on a dirt road called Lyons Street. The river is a block away. Industry and warehouses are moving in. At the end of Lyons Street, on the levee of the river, there is a lumberyard. Next to it stands a big brick factory known as a cotton press, a place that takes a bargeload of raw cotton and compresses it into boxlike five-hundred-pound bales. A family named Dufossat runs a brick kiln nearby, and someone else is building a slaughterhouse. When the Le Corgne boys grow, the trades will be at their fingertips.

Of course, the boys will not be in the trades. They will be *grands blancs*, like their grandparents.

Six lots, one each for the children. Six lots for six houses, six futures. That is the plan. Maybe the Le Corgnes see it as a fresh start, and maybe they see it as moving to get free of *les nègres*. Maybe it is both. The section called Bouligny is a world distant from the cramped, Creole, and colored streets of the *Vieux Carré*. Bouligny and other parts of uptown are white. Blacks, free people of color, and slaves remain crowded into the old city and jammed into a section to the north of it, Tremé. The Le Corgnes move for work, and space, and maybe for the absence of black people.

The *faubourg* is named for Louis Bouligny, the man who owns much of the land and who is selling it piecemeal. Louis Bouligny hires a surveyor named Benjamin Buisson. Like Yves Le Corgne, Buisson is both a Frenchman and a veteran of the *Grande Armée* of Emperor Bonaparte. To honor the great man, Buisson names the main street of Bouligny "Napoleon Avenue" and gives streets on either side of the avenue the names of battles won by the emperor's armies—Valence, Cadiz, Jena, Milan, Berlin, Jersey. The Le Corgnes' street, Lyons (the Americans spell it with an *s*, the French without) marks the city in France where Napoleon, at the end of the empire in 1815, planned his return.

The Le Corgnes are up and out of the French Quarter. While a new house is being built, they rent a place on a nearby street called Terpsichore.

The family has a new baby, Marguerite Eliza, and the house is being built in Bouligny. It is fall 1840 when Yves falls ill.

In Louisiana, when a white man comes down with fever in the fall, his family freezes in fear. You have malaria. You have typhoid fever. Poor sanitation gives rise to typhoid, an intestinal infection that lasts for months and often kills. And you have Yellow Jack. I do not know with certainty whether Yves catches yellow fever in 1840, but chances are pretty good that he does.

Yellow Jack kills a white person in three or four days, and it is violent. The fever starts with chills, moves to agonizing back pain. The skin of a white patient turns yellow. Then comes a crust of black scum on the tongue, and finally, a day of delirium. The killing part is the expulsion of fluids. Diarrhea begins, resembling a syrup, and continues without end. Death is certain as victims curl up with knees to their face. The body seems to expel itself in vomit. The retching is so great that pieces of flesh come from the throat, and vomit appears nearly solid. Patients sometimes welcome death.

Yves Le Corgne does not recover, and he dies November 18, 1840, at fifty-three.

P.C. is a nine-year-old boy when he loses his father. It is an age when a child can be wrecked by the loss of a parent. And does P.C. watch his father die? Almost certainly.

The death of the father is a disaster for most families. Marguerite Zeringue has six children; her parents are dead, and she has only one living sister. The networks of care have thinned. And yet, she enslaves six people—"my niggers," I imagine she calls them. Marguerite's slaves are the reason the family does not collapse. She will rent out her workers for income. Six slaves can run a house, keep everyone clothed, and pay all expenses. They can even comfort *Madame* in her grief. These are the kinds of things a white family asks a community of blacks to perform on their behalf.

Maybe her children say this. Thank goodness Mother has her slaves. She treats them right, takes them to church, gets them baptized. She is good to them.

Marguerite is a new matriarch. In records, the spelling of her name starts to change. The family ceases to be "Le Corgne." It becomes *Lecorgne*. To the law, she is *Veuve Lecorgne*, "Widow Lecorgne."

Once again, an appraiser comes in. This one is named François Laizer. He is just twenty-three and a newcomer to New Orleans. He comes to Louisiana from Cuba, from the city of Santiago, on the east-ern end of that island. Although no one knows it when he walks into the house on Terpsichore, Laizer will play an important part in the life of P.C. Lecorgne, our Klansman.

François Laizer finishes business with the estate, Yves Le Cor-gne goes into his grave, and Widow Lecorgne finishes building the family house. She leases her people. She rents out Eulalie, who is fifty-nine. She rents Anna, forty. She rents Sylvie, also forty. Probably she keeps three people with her, at home, to run her life and raise her six children.

The Lecorgnes are very, very rich next to most black people. They are rich next to most whites. Of the one-quarter of whites who pos-sess slaves, about half of that group, or ten percent of the white popu-lation, enslave more than ten people. The Lecorgnes sit on a soft sofa in a high parlor of white society.

I would also say that is not the way it looks to them. Compared with their cousin Camille Zeringue of Seven Oaks, the Lecorgnes' money is trifling. Cousin Camille is a man with seventy slaves. I have to imagine the Lecorgnes envy him, and maybe they resent him, for his stupendous store of living and breathing capital.

After a year or two on Terpsichore, Marguerite and the household move to Lyons Street, in Bouligny. Their house is a Creole cottage, much like their old one. One-and-a-half stories, four rooms down-stairs and two up, with two front doors facing the street, on the left and right. There is a kitchen house in the backyard and a cabin for the enslaved. The black women run the kitchen. An acre all around for a garden and fruit trees, with room for more houses, when the children grow up.

Marguerite has a new worker, Ovid, named for the Roman poet. Ovid is sixteen, and the record makes no mention of his parents or siblings. Probably Marguerite went to the slave market in the City Exchange Hotel and bought the boy away from his family. It is a guess, but that is the way a nice widowed lady might do things.

P.C. Lecorgne comes of age in *faubourg Bouligny*. He and his brothers and sisters have a mother but no father, and they live in a house where black people are continually present. P.C. knows that "they" are born to work. He knows whites like him are born to be worked for. On Sunday at St. Stephen, the Lecorgnes' new church on Napoleon Avenue, P.C. may hear a sermon from a priest that explains how the world works, how it has all been engineered by the Lord. The priest would share words from the Bible. God's word is full and clear on the subject of slaves and masters. The book of Joshua, in the Old Testament, teaches that there "shall none be freed from being slaves, and hewers of wood and drawers of water."

Widow Lecorgne pays to educate her children: there are no free schools. She sends her girls and boys to academies in town. The girls finish education at age sixteen, or near it; the boys a bit later, except for one, Yves of God. The largest portion of Marguerite's money goes to fill the mind of Yves, her oldest son. Primogeniture is alive and well among Creoles, and the firstborn gets the most.

Yves is a good learner, and ambitious. He wants to get into the law, and he wants to get into the land market that is booming around the *faubourg*. He wants to be a slaveholder, as do almost all whites. These things will happen. P.C., the middle son, is less good at his lessons. It seems his math is poor, and his writing—except his penmanship, perhaps. The evidence is thin, but you can read what survives in reverse. His actions as an adult imply he is not a learner as a child. He wants things, probably; he wants to influence and maybe to dominate the people near him. I am reading again in reverse. He, too, wants to hold slaves. All that he wants will come to him, at least for a time.

I am sure the Lecorgne children see it, at least the brothers do. A new magazine starts up in New Orleans, *De Bow's Review*. It is a little beacon for the mental life of the *grands blancs*. With offices on Camp Street, near the French Quarter, *De Bow's Review* is the creation of a lawyer-turned-journalist, James De Bow. He has the idea of blending social comment with business talk.

The Lecorgnes read the French newspapers, *L'Abeille* (the *Bee*) and *Le Courrier de la Louisiane* (*Louisiana Courier*). They might read the English papers, the *Crescent*, the *Bulletin*, and the *Picayune*. I am sure that some take a subscription to *De Bow's Review*, the magazine for the thoughtful white South. Soon after he arrives in Louisiana—in 1845, from Charleston—James De Bow becomes a thought leader in New Orleans. His *Review* comes out four times a year and is loaded like a barge with economics, history, and argumentative talk. De Bow publishes figures about trade in the region, gives farming advice, and predicts the cotton market. He runs editorials about black people and how to control them. White businesspeople read him avidly. Creoles of color probably leave De Bow on the rack. The majority of black people have no choice in the matter. It is illegal to teach an enslaved person to read. Much of the population is illiterate, by law.

About the time the Lecorgne sons are finishing their education, De Bow decides he must enlarge the minds of his readers by offering them some of the new science. In 1847, he publishes a feature called "The Negro," an essay whose title implies that its author possesses a panoramic understanding of the subject. "When the Caucasian and the negro are compared," the magazine says, "one of the most striking points of difference is seen in the conformation of the head." The writer is a local scientist, Josiah Nott.

"The head of the negro is smaller by a full tenth than the white," Josiah Nott says. "The forehead is narrower and more receding, in consequence of which the anterior or intellectual portion of the brain is defective. In other portions of the skeleton . . . the arm of the African is much longer in proportion than in the white man. . . ."

De Bow's Review is a channel for race thought. It spreads into the city and into the heads of its white citizens. The *Review* takes up scientists like Samuel Morton, the skull collector in Philadelphia. It explains the tribal behavior of whites and blacks and delivers it in pithy summaries. "Negroes are a thriftless, thoughtless people," readers learn, "and have to be restricted in many points essential to their constitutions and health. Left to themselves they will over eat, walk half the night, sleep on the ground, sleep anywhere."

The readership of *De Bow's Review* swells. The thinking men of New Orleans are proud of him, proud of his work. I presume that Camille Zeringue is a subscriber. Everyone knows the truth in what the journal has to say.

P.C. Lecorgne is seventeen when De Bow publishes an essay called "Negro Slavery at the South." Constant may wonder why Valentin holds a hoe in the garden and the Lecorgne boys have textbooks at their desks. The key that unlocks the enigma is here. "Ethiopians," says the magazine—the word is a synonym for black Africans—are a separate species of human. The writer, this time, is a man named Solon Robinson. "The scientific anatomist has demonstrated that the brain proper is smaller in them [in blacks] than in other races of men," Robinson says. "The occipital foramen, the medulla oblongata and spinal marrow, and the nerves of organic life are much larger. . . . The difference in organization is so great that . . . many men believe the Ethiopian race is a distinct species of mankind."

Absorb the basic truths. Intelligent men and women throughout the Mississippi River valley—and hardworking pupils in the uptown *faubourgs*—let them read and learn.

By 1850, the city of New Orleans is home to some ten thousand free people of color. Most of them are the children of white men and black women. Most are *gens de couleur*, French-speaking. Creoles of color are like a third people. Many are educated, many own small businesses. They are carpenters, seamstresses, landlords, bricklayers, tailors, other trades. Their numbers are down by a third from ten years before. Many are leaving, as *les Américains* pass laws that strip them of power. And some, I think, are passing from black into white society.

In 1845, Creoles of color claim a place in race and in literature. Their initial voice is slender, an anthology of poetry called *Les Cenelles*, "The Hollyberries." The book carries verses by seventeen men who identify as *gens de couleur*. The fruit of a hawthorn shrub are *cenelles*. It is a hardy plant that makes sweet berries in harsh conditions— and there is your metaphor. *Les Cenelles* is the first collection of poetry published by a group of nonwhites in the United States. That fact makes it one of the founding texts of black identity.

The year *Les Cenelles* appears is the same year *De Bow's Review* begins publication. I do not know what explains the black and white synchrony. Maybe the poems answer De Bow's trumpet blast.

The compiler and editor of *Les Cenelles* is named Armand Lanusse. He is headmaster of a school for girls of color. Lanusse subtitles his book *Choix de poésies indigènes*, a selection of indigenous poems. "Indigenous"—meaning Creole, meaning native to Louisiana. During the mid-1800s, when nearly all black Southerners cannot read, Creoles of color read, teach, write, and publish poetry.

Are the Lecorgnes aware of *Les Cenelles*? I doubt it. An edition of a few hundred circulates privately in black life, and few in white society notice.

When it comes to public speech, people of color breathe stifling air. Before the Civil War, there is no air at all for black voices. Any speech that summons nonwhite identity is choked, any language that resists the order of race is attacked. The poems of *Les Cenelles* are not political, though in some few verses I detect a disguised politics. The collection of eighty-four poems contains love poetry, pastoral poems, poems about death, and five poems about suicide.

Contributors to *Les Cenelles* are men from the free colored business class. The cigar maker Nicol Riquet is one, and a mason who calls himself Auguste Populus is another. Camille Thierry, the heir to a liquor wholesale business, is a third.

There are odes to the past and poems by men about desiring women; poems about hats (two), about jealousy (two); and pastoral poems, like "Au Bord du Lac" ("Edge of the Lake"). There is an ode to Mardi Gras, "Le Carnaval," which ends on the hopeful line "Tout est permis en Carnaval" ("All is permitted in Carnival"). Would that it were.

The mental world looks out of balance to me. On one side, you have Creoles of color who pioneer black identity with gentle poems of observation. On the other, you have thinking whites who see the world as collections of species. This is the one our Klansman inhabits. I wonder whether it is also the one we inhabit—we among the living.

6

I hesitate to tell this part. It makes me uneasy, because it sounds romantic, and romance does not fit here. But this is the way it happens. In May 1847, a girl arrives in New Orleans on a passenger ship, a two-masted brig, the *Orléans*. She is eleven years old and traveling with her grandmother. The girl's name is Gabrielle Duchemin. She comes from Cuba. Gabrielle Duchemin washes in from the city of Santiago, on the eastern end of the island. She is white. She speaks French and, I am sure, also Spanish. She accompanies a sixty-year-old woman named Eleanor Labarriere. The passenger list describes the grandmother and the girl as "ladies." Eleanor Labarriere and her granddaughter arrive from Cuba to live in New Orleans.

The older woman is doing what she can for the child. Gabrielle has lost her parents and is now an orphan. Eleanor Labarriere and Gabrielle Duchemin plan to move in with a young couple, their distant relations François and Adelaide Laizer. We have met François Laizer before. He is the appraiser who wrapped up the estate of the late Yves Le Corgne. When the "ladies" set foot on the dock, they make their way to the Laizer house, in Bouligny, on Cadiz Street, three blocks east of the Lecorgnes.

The suburb where all these people live has a new name—Jefferson City. The *faubourg* of Bouligny is now part of Jefferson City, which has its own courts, taxes, and sheriff. François Laizer is a thirty-year-old clerk of court in Jefferson City, and he is getting rich in the law.

François Laizer and his wife, twenty-six-year-old Adelaide Bienvenu, have been trying to make a family. They marry in January 1840, and at the end of that year Adelaide has a boy. Ten months later, the child is dead. The following spring Adelaide has a second son. He dies at age two. In August 1843, François and Adelaide have a third boy. He dies two years later, at the end of 1845. I have to lay down some empathy at this. The Le Corgne couple lost their first three children, and now the Laizers.

François and Adelaide Laizer know Marguerite, who got through a string of funerals and has a herd of six. The Laizers look at the Lecorgne household and marvel. No one knows the will of God. How long will our marriage bed be vexed? When Gabrielle Duchemin and Eleanor Labarriere make their way to the house from the *Orléans*, Gabrielle arrives in the role of adopted daughter for the childless Laizers.

Eleven-year-old Gabrielle Duchemin is not Cuban, but French. She is a child from the eastern Caribbean, the island of Guadeloupe. A sugar colony of France, Guadeloupe is a droplet in the Antilles, two hundred miles north of Venezuela, and a place where three-quarters of the people are black and enslaved. It is here, in the capital city of Guadeloupe, Pointe-à-Pitre, on April 25, 1836, that Marie Léonide Gabrielle Duchemin is born.

Her father is Alphonse Duchemin, a thirty-year-old *huissier*, or constable in the French colonial court. He is a cop. Her mother is a woman named Joséphine Perdreau, age twenty-five. Registers give no profession for Perdreau, which is not unusual for women in official pages. Gabrielle's parents are white and unmarried. Gabrielle appears to be a love child, maybe an unwanted child.

At some point early in life, Gabrielle moves with her mother to Santiago, Cuba, five hundred miles west of Guadeloupe. Her father stays in Pointe-à-Pitre and carries on with his life. The name Alphonse Duchemin continues to appear in legal papers in Guadeloupe, while the name of his lover, Joséphine Perdreau, surfaces in Cuban records. Gabrielle's father evidently disappears from her life. Perdreau has family in Cuba. Her parents are there. Joséphine Perdreau and her love child, Gabrielle, move to Cuba and in with them. Their names—Jean and Eleanor Labarriere.

The story is legible, familiar, sad: a woman away from home is seduced by an appealing man. She becomes pregnant, and the appealing man, the cop in Guadeloupe, sends her packing. The seduced and abandoned woman returns to her parents, and the three raise the child.

Cuba is a colony of Spain, but the port city of Santiago, on the eastern end of the island, is home to a large French population. During the Haitian Revolution, tens of thousands of French-speaking whites and free people of color flee the revolt in Saint-Domingue and land in Cuba. The city of Santiago gathers in many because it lies near Saint-Domingue, three hundred miles across a channel. Two of the exiles who make their way to Santiago appear to have been Eleanor Labarriere and her husband, Jean. When little Gabrielle and her mother, Joséphine, move to Santiago from Guadeloupe, about 1840, they arrive at a French enclave on a Spanish-speaking island.

New Orleans may be complicated, but things are more so on the islands.

During the 1840s, Eleanor's husband, Jean Labarriere, Gabrielle's grandfather, leaves Cuba and moves to New Orleans, seemingly to clear a path for other family members to follow. Most of the French exiles in Santiago have already left it. Now, many years after the Haitian Revolution, the remaining few prepare to go. Meantime, Gabrielle Duchemin grows up in the colonial pattern. She attends school and studies French. She takes piano lessons, acquires Spanish. She learns knitting, crocheting, hemstitching, and makes her first communion in the church at the center of town, Santo Tomás el Apóstol (Saint Thomas the Apostle).

In 1845, Eleanor and Joséphine, mother and daughter, are two women raising a little girl, with no man in the house. That year, Eleanor buys a forty-year-old woman named Julia to work as a maid and to help with mothering Gabrielle, now eight. The enslaved Julia ("*una négresse*" in the bill of sale), costs Eleanor 250 Cuban pesos, the going price of a middle-aged woman. For some reason, Eleanor is not available to sign the contract, and so she has her daughter Joséphine Perdreau sign on her behalf and take possession of Julia. An all-female household is complete: Eleanor, Joséphine, Gabrielle, and Julia. They seem to await word from New Orleans about when to leave.

At this point, the paper trail in Cuba runs dry. Something happens to Gabrielle's mother, Joséphine Perdreau, and she disappears from colonial records. Maybe Perdreau falls sick with a tropical disease—malaria or yellow fever are good candidates—and she dies, leaving Gabrielle with her grandmother and Julia. Or maybe Perdreau goes back to Guadeloupe. The result is the same: Gabrielle's mother vanishes, and the girl has no parents. Gabrielle Duchemin is an orphan, left by both father and mother.

When Gabrielle turns eleven, in 1847, she and Eleanor Labarriere board a ship to New Orleans. They do not bring Julia with them. By this time, U.S. law bans the arrival of enslaved people, "the import of slave property," in the vile legal phrase. Grandmother and granddaughter travel alone. As for Julia, she stays behind, maybe at work for a relative of the Labarrieres, or maybe sold away again.

The life of Gabrielle Duchemin is afloat, a piece of driftwood. But Julia is the one handed around like bread at the table.

Gabrielle and Grandmother Eleanor, aboard the *Orléans*, project an image of security and ease. The passenger list describes the two of them, apparently dressed up and mannered, as "ladies, from France." They are neither. It is a pleasing lie they tell.

In New Orleans, Eleanor Labarriere does something white women do. Having left her housekeeper, Julia, in Cuba, she enslaves a new housekeeper. This time it is a child, a girl eight years old, named Lavinia. She appears in the record without mother, father, or siblings. She might be orphaned, like Gabrielle. It is more likely the girl has been sold away from her parents, purchased by Eleanor Labarriere. Lavinia, who goes by the name "Fanny," is assigned to work as a companion and servant to Gabrielle.

That is the way this world works.

Gabrielle and her grandmother land in the house of François and Adelaide Laizer. Jean Labarriere, Eleanor's husband, is already there. I do not know the relationship between the Labarrieres and the Laizers, but they are kin, probably. They know each other through shared family in the Caribbean, but evidence of the link is lacking.

Gabrielle goes through schooling in New Orleans. I see some of the life of Gabrielle Duchemin in another girl. Around this time, a white child named Eliza Ripley is growing up in the city. Later in life, Eliza Ripley writes a memoir about her youth. Let it stand in for Gabrielle, for a moment.

"Every girl had music lessons and every mother superintended the study and practice of the one branch deemed absolutely indispensable to the education of a *demoiselle*," Ripley says. "The city was dotted all over with music teachers." Gabrielle does, in fact, study music. Eventually she will earn an income giving piano lessons.

It is a busy, full household in the Laizer place on Cadiz Street. An older couple, the Labarrieres; a middling one, the Laizers; the wayward and quiet Gabrielle; and a number of enslaved. Five minutes away by foot are the Lecorgnes, and soon the two families are entwined.

P.C. Lecorgne is a teenager in the 1840s, presumably at his books. I doubt he is reading the new black poetry, in *Les Cenelles*. Away from the classroom, he may find entertainment, along with a kind of instruction, in the theater. I would think that now and then P.C. puts himself in the audience at a minstrel theater. During the 1830s and '40s, a form of stage comedy comes up in the Deep South that is based in a kind of tribal drag show. Minstrelsy, so-called. Minstrel theater offers white people who pretend to be black. In blackface minstrelsy, whites cake themselves in black powder from burned cork, then they dance, sing, and tell jokes. Louisiana is a deep source of it, with groups like the New Orleans Ethiopian Serenaders playing to packed houses. A Frenchman named Charles Duprez, native of Paris, has a troupe in New Orleans at this time, Duprez & Green's Minstrels. When P.C. is growing up, the city begins to send out to the North these and other groups of whites who play banjo, "sing nigger," and dance breaks like the ones they try to remember from Congo Square.

It is a performance of blackness that whites want, not the real life of being black. They still want it, I think.

The culture diet of the Lecorgne family, if out for the night, would be a minstrel show. It would not be legitimate theater or opera, both

Poster for an 1847 performance by a minstrel troupe,
the New Orleans Ethiopian Serenaders

of which have a footprint in New Orleans. The tastes of the Lecorgnes have slipped a rung on the ladder from those of the *grands blancs*.
They would find minstrel acts that make their way through jive talk
and jigs at the Varieties Theater, on Gravier Street, or at the Camp
Street Theater, or at a place called Dan Rice's Amphitheater.

When P.C. is sixteen, in 1848, one of the hit minstrel songs is
"Dandy Broadway Swell." It is published that year in *Ethiopian Glee
Books*, a music script for white players trying to make money with
a black act. "Dandy Broadway Swell" is about a ridiculous man who
tries to pick up women. The lyrics, as transcribed by white hands—

Dey may talk ob dandy niggers
But dey neber see dis coon,
A prombernarding Broadway
On a Sunday afternoon.
I'se de sole de-light ob yellow gals,
De envy ob de men;

Ob-serve dis child when he turn out
And talk ob dand-dies den.
For I'se de grit, de go, de cheese,
As every one may tell;
De dark fair sex
I sure to please,
I'se de dandy Broadway swell.

Minstrel acts like the New Orleans Ethiopian Serenaders give white audiences the fun of watching their tribe ridicule another people, as well as (a different kind of pleasure) seeing their own people put on blackness and wear it for a time, like a robe. I suspect P.C. takes delight in minstrelsy, as whites all over America do, as hundreds of millions have done since, and as many do today, in the 2000s. Some things about the minstrel act have never really gone away.

In January 1850, in the city of Baton Rouge, a few hundred gather in front of the new state capitol building to see the inauguration of Joseph Walker, lately elected governor of Louisiana. I do not think the Lecorgnes are in the crowd. Baton Rouge is a daylong steamboat up the Mississippi, and at this point, politics is not their game.

Governor Joseph Walker is a Democrat. The Democrats are the populist party, ever since President Andrew Jackson crashed the working white man into political power, in the late 1820s. On the opposing end from the Democrats are the Whigs, party of the rich and the educated. The Democrats are the slavery party, the Whigs not anti-slavery, but less proslavery. By electing the Democrat Joseph Walker to the office of governor, the white men of Louisiana send a message that they absolutely love their slaves. They love having them in thrall and exploiting them.

Walker takes the oath of office. He places his hand on a Bible and swears, then steps to the podium for his speech. Governor Walker wants to talk about one thing on the minds of a lot of whites, namely, black people.

"The antislavery agitation in the Northern States which has long been a source of irritation to the south has within the last two years taken such a shape that fears are entertained by some that it is about to reach a crisis unfavorable to the stability of the union," the new governor tells the crowd.

Huzzahs and applause.

The governor complains about the abolitionists in the North, the radical ministers and their black comrades. He complains about people like Frederick Douglass. He complains that radical whites and educated blacks want to end the blessed tradition of the South, the "divine institution," as many in these parts call enslavement.

"If, unhappily, the anti-slavery agitations which so long have been allowed to insult our feelings should be carried to the point of aggression upon our rights," Walker says, pausing to stress, "then we are prepared to make common cause with our neighbors of the slaveholding states and pronounce the union at an end!"

Governor Walker predicts that trouble with *les nègres* is going to break apart the United States. He points to the cracks.

Huzzahs and applause.

François and Adelaide Laizer adopt Gabrielle. She now has parents who will not discard her.

The Laizers live a short walk from the Lecorgnes. The two families pass on the street. They nod over the back of pews in church; eyes meet across the aisle. P.C. is seventeen, Gabrielle fourteen. He is finishing his schooling. To judge from his later years, he is a young man with little interest in study. It appears he is learning a trade, spending time in a carpentry shop somewhere in Bouligny. The orphan and the Lecorgne boy meet.

François Laizer, Gabrielle's adoptive father, now makes good money. The *faubourgs* are booming, and he is getting rich with real estate. In five years, Laizer buys and sells nine pieces of land, flipping lots. He buys several tracts in one deal, and for some reason, a seller throws in, along with the land, a slave child, a twelve-year-old girl. Maybe she is a sweetener. Laizer brings the child home, and suddenly, Gabrielle has a black companion, a girl named Caroline.

I do not want to wring my hands again. This is everyday life, customary and familiar in white society. But once again we have a nice family—daddy in real estate, daughter studying piano—buying children. Twelve-year-old Caroline is probably taken from her mother, yanked from her arms. Gabrielle now has parents who want her, and then those parents turn around and seize somebody's girl, tossing her parents aside. Caroline is dropped into the house in front of Gabrielle and handed a bucket and mop.

It is an American pattern, and not just a Southern one. It is familiar in Washington, D.C., in St. Louis, in Philadelphia, and in New York. Slavery is withering. By 1850, it is gone in half the states, but the gist remains even in the "free" North: a black girl is taken from her family and put into a white household, where she is made to serve. It is not just my people who are doing it.

You have a line among the Creoles—black, colored, and white— *Chacun sait ce qui bouille dans sa chaudière*, "Everyone knows what boils in their own pot." Meaning, you know what is going on at home, with your people. You know the hidden things. You know who you are, and you know what your people are. But what is this thing, whiteness? The Lecorgnes know about blackness, or think they do. They look at blackness and make their sense of it. Now they turn to whiteness with something like the same gaze.

In the early 1850s, in Massachusetts, one of the states where slavery has ended, a novelist is musing on whiteness. He has just written a big book. Herman Melville is a writer living in the Berkshires, and he is an ex-roustabout on whaling ships. When Melville publishes *Moby-Dick*, in 1851, he inserts into it a kind of soliloquy—it is chapter 42, "The Whiteness of the Whale"—a stream of images in which whiteness appears to be both appalling and divine.

[T]his pre-eminence [of whiteness] applies to the human race itself, giving the white man ideal mastership over every dusky tribe . . . for among the Romans a white stone marked a joyful day; and . . . this same hue is made the emblem of many touching, noble things—the innocence of brides, the benignity of age . . . [I]n many climes, whiteness typifies the majesty of Justice in the ermine of the Judge, and contributes to the daily state of kings and queens drawn by milk-white steeds; . . . by the Persian fire worshippers, the white forked flame being held the holiest on the altar; and in the Greek mythologies, Great Jove himself being made incarnate in a snow-white bull; . . . yet for all these accumulated associations, with whatever is sweet, and honourable, and sublime, there yet lurks an elusive something in the innermost idea of this hue, which strikes more of panic to the soul than that redness which affrights in blood. . . . the thought of whiteness, when divorced from more kindly associations, and coupled with any object terrible in itself, to heighten that terror to the furthest bounds.

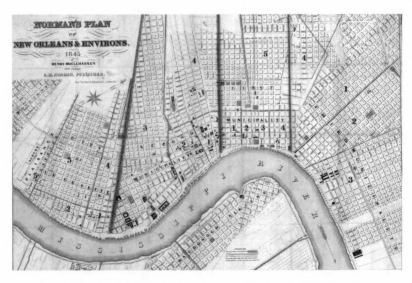

New Orleans in 1845, the Lecorgne neighborhood of "Bouligny" at the upper left

By the mid-1850s, the Lecorgnes spread onto several of the six lots they own. Marguerite, "Widow Lecorgne," lives with her youngest daughter, as well as her slaves, on one lot. Yves of God, her firstborn, has built a house, and Joseph Lecorgne, the youngest brother, is starting another. A single Creole cottage has mushroomed into a compound. We can call it "Lecorgne row."

It looks as though P.C. is the unfavored child. You can see it—he is less bright than brother Yves. He is less good with people, not as oily.

"Lecorgne row"—Lyon Street, between Jersey and "Tchapitoulas"

P.C. is not suited to work indoors at a desk, where you have to show care with what you say. The middle brother makes his way into the trades. He will be an outside man, hammer and plane in hand.

The Lecorgne sisters have their lives. Ézilda, two years older than P.C., lives a few blocks away with her husband, François Fazende. P.C.'s sister Marguerite, fourteen and living with her mother on Lecorgne row, is getting schooled. His sister Aurore marries a man named Numa Leche in 1852, when she is sixteen and Numa twenty-one. Aurore and her husband have a baby and live with their toddler a few blocks away. The proximity of everyone is normal. Anyone of importance to the Lecorgnes seems to live just a few blocks away.

P.C. is twenty and half-made. He earns money for himself in yard-work, advertising as a gardener. A man who gardens for hire makes pretty the houses of the rich, digging the pretty plantings in front of their pretty mansions, which are sprouting along Napoleon Avenue. And here is a crack in the porcelain. Marguerite Lecorgne has raised up her children to aspire to the *grands blancs*. But her middle son is planting hedgerows. It must be galling.

P.C. makes a better living in wood, as a carpenter's assistant. His father, Yves, had a life in the merchant marine. It appears that this experience leads P.C. to the water, to the Mississippi. The trade that he learns is on riverboats. He trains to be a ship carpenter, *un charpentier de navire*, repairing and maintaining barges and schooners that ply the river. Slightly, but only slightly, less galling.

As an apprentice, P.C. is asked to do the hardest work, hewing beams and laying the bottom frames on barges. He cuts the bulkhead and fixes the gunwales, builds the trusses in the hull and lays decking over them. He does not earn much, yet. He jumps to the orders from other shipwrights, takes their wage, hopes for more.

He is not a carrier of water, but he is a hewer of wood.

To judge from written traces, about this time young man Lecorgne discards nicknames. Polycarp Constant Lecorgne is no longer "P.C." when he signs his name to things, he is *Constant* Lecorgne.

In 1853, yellow fever returns to New Orleans in the worst epidemic the city sees in the nineteenth century. A commission to study the disease says that the first cases of Yellow Jack appear at the edge of Jefferson City, among passengers coming off ships and into boarding-houses a few blocks from Lecorgne row. They "die with the black vomit," and the disease spreads. By midsummer, the neighborhood of Bouligny is half-empty, as white people flee once again. I assume the Lecorgnes and at least some of their slaves retreat to the old Zeringue farm across the river, or to Camille Zeringue's place, Seven Oaks. Back in Bouligny, interments at the neighborhood's Lafayette Cemetery rise from 69 in one month at the beginning of the year to 469 in July and 1,177 in August. In six months, one in fifteen people in New Orleans is dead.

The fever consumes several around the Lecorgnes. A cousin dies here, a nephew dies there. Constant's brother-in-law, Numa Leche, is killed at twenty-three. He and his wife, Aurore, have been married for eighteen months, and they have a baby. When her husband dies, Aurore moves with her infant into the back room of the house owned by her brother, Yves of God.

In testimony about the epidemic, a prominent doctor blames it on *les nègres*. "As many have contended," he says, "yellow fever is an im-ported African disease." It is a strange hypothesis. An official report says the fever kills 5,293 white men and 2,475 white women. But it kills only 38 people of color.

In 1856, Gabrielle's adoptive father, François Laizer, goes into poli-tics. He is elected mayor of Jefferson City, the municipality around Bouligny. Laizer is a Democrat, a man of "the Democracy," as people call the Democratic Party. As Mayor Laizer enters office, he appoints a new city treasurer, a Creole named Émile Chevalley. Chevalley lives across the street from Lecorgne row. He is older than Constant, but the two are friendly. In a few years, Émile Chevalley and Constant will find themselves locking arms in a white gang, when together they maraud with the Ku-klux.

Mayor Laizer turns next to Constant's brother, Yves. He is twenty-nine, educated, and unmarried. Laizer gives Yves the office of city clerk, making him a political fixer and functionary. Yves wants a life like that of family friend François Laizer. He wants a sinecure where fees can be pocketed, contracts written up for a charge, and money demanded. Tax money in Jefferson City comes from assessments on businesses, which Yves of God now collects. A dance hall pays $50 a year to operate, while a boardinghouse pays $10. A steamboat pays $25, a pharmacy $20, and a café that sells liquor $100. The money passes through the hands of Yves of God, and he accounts for it in ledgers that he alone maintains. It is a good formula for building wealth.

Constant Lecorgne, journeyman ship carpenter, is betrothed to Gabrielle Duchemin. If this were a piece of romance fiction, they would have been courting for years. The Laizer and Lecorgne households are long entwined. Marriage is promised, if money can be raised. And money is about to fall from the sky.

Gabrielle Duchemin is nineteen, her grandmother Eleanor Labarriere, who brought Gabrielle from Cuba, sixty-eight. Grandmother Labarriere has lost her husband, and her own health is weak. In March 1855, Eleanor falls ill. She seems to know she is dying, because she dictates her will. François Laizer comes to the bedside, Eleanor delivers her testament, and she dies. The funeral comes, Gabrielle grieves.

The will is read, and Gabrielle discovers she is to become an heiress. Not to an estate, but to a person. Her name is Lavinia, or "Lavinia, alias Fanny, a negro girl aged about fifteen years."

Lavinia, or Fanny, is the girl Gabrielle's grandmother bought to serve the house when they first arrived in New Orleans. There is something else in the will. Eleanor Labarriere, on her deathbed, names Constant Lecorgne as Gabrielle's *"tutor ad hoc."* So they have been courting, if that is what power of attorney means.

In Louisiana civil law, a *tutor ad hoc* supervises a minor, a role similar in English common law to *guardian ad litem*. Gabrielle is a minor, younger than twenty-one, and cannot possess or dispose of property—namely, Lavinia, alias Fanny—thus her fiancé is given the power.

Constant and Gabrielle want to marry. Custom calls for white parents with money to endow their daughters, to give them a dowry. In addition to Gabrielle, their adoptive daughter, François and Adelaide Laizer have four children of their own, three of them girls. The idea of endowing a daughter who is not their natural child may be disagreeable. Or maybe Constant, the fiancé, is disagreeable. A gardener and *charpentier de navire* is not a perfect son-in-law for a city mayor. Gabrielle and Constant want to marry, but the bride's dowry comes from elsewhere, namely, the black body of Fanny.

Laizer brings in an appraiser, who says Fanny is worth $600, a sum ample enough for a wedding, with enough left over to buy a little house. It is summer 1855. Eleanor Labarriere is in the grave. Mayor François Laizer arranges a sheriff's sale. Fanny is to be sold on the steps of the courthouse. The proceeds of the sale, minus expenses, go to Gabrielle's *tutor ad hoc*, Constant Lecorgne.

Here is how it looks to Constant. Lavinia, aka Fanny, age fifteen, is the first piece of property he has ever possessed. He looks at the girl and he sees gold.

It is a wretched scene, really. On the morning of October 9, 1855, Lavinia stands on the steps of the Bouligny courthouse, the usual place for estate sales. I have to imagine that Fanny is frightened, sick with despair. Will she be sold, taken away from all she knows? Lavinia turns out to face a crowd of men. They hold cigars. They tilt back their heads, look at her from beneath their spectacles. Sold, for $500. She is yanked off the block and pushed into the hands of a man she has never met. Gabrielle may be able to say goodbye to Fanny, or she may not. I find nothing more about Fanny's life. She is first made motherless and fatherless, then disappears to an unknown fate.

Constant is disappointed. It should have been more. He wanted $600.

The lovely couple move their lives forward. Cash in hand, they can marry.

Gabrielle wants to marry in Cuba. She wants to be with her

first family, in old Santiago. Her grandmother Eleanor is dead. Her mother, Joséphine Perdreau, is either dead or wandering. Alphonse Duchemin, her father, is incommunicado in Guadeloupe. Yet Gabrielle wants to be with the few left in Cuba, from her girlhood.

In early March 1856, Constant and Gabrielle take bags to the New Orleans dock and board a steamship. They have money for Cuba, money for clothes, money for a dinner and gifts. The city of Havana lies on the northwest coast of Cuba and is tied to New Orleans by ship traffic; Santiago lies on the remote southeast coast, twice the distance. After two weeks at sea, they disembark. It has been eight years since Gabrielle left Santiago. She may still have relatives there. I wonder whether the enslaved Julia, who looked after Gabrielle when she was a girl, is on hand. I wonder if she greets the bride-to-be. It is not clear whether Julia would want to greet her.

The church of Santo Tomás el Apóstol, giant and white, dominates the middle of town. On April 3, 1856, Gabrielle ascends the aisle. She is nineteen, a month shy of twenty. Constant is twenty-three, his birthday in three weeks. A priest named Manuel José Muira officiates. He writes the name of the groom in his register: "Don Le Corne Constantino Policarpo."

The sanctuary, as I imagine it, echoes in emptiness. Few remember Gabrielle. Of those who do, many have left Cuba for new lives. There is no sign of her mother. Three witnesses enter their names in the book of marriages. One of them does it as a favor to the priest, a man described as a *clerigo tonsurado*, a tonsured monk. The bride turns from the altar, new husband in grip.

I think I can see myself in these two, the ship carpenter and the love child from Guadeloupe. They are a couple like any, married in the spring. And to me, they are my people. They are my grandmother's grandparents. I pause for a moment to size them up. The Lecorgnes have more social capital than Gabrielle. Constant is marrying down, probably, as his mother sees it. The groom is our Klansman in the making. I take a moment with that fact. Gabrielle has more sense than her new husband. For her part, she also marries down.

Man and wife board the schooner, the *Elizabeth Segar*, bound for New Orleans. The trip must pass slowly, in lust and grasping, to the rhythm of a rocking hull. Gabrielle's mother was free about sex minus marriage: Gabrielle herself is evidence. I imagine Eleanor Labarriere kept a grip on her granddaughter's appetites, and Gabrielle goes to the altar untouched. Not so Constant. His hometown of New Orleans is rich and varied in prostitution. Young white men avail themselves of women for hire, and Constant would be no exception.

The *Elizabeth Segar* draws up to the dock on April 17. The last time Gabrielle set foot on this levee, she was a "lady." Now the passenger list has her as "seamstress." Constant is not a "gentleman," but "carpenter." The young husband is no longer the soft son of one of the rich families in a leafy and growing *faubourg*. He is a craftsman who cuts a hatch between decks and frames a bulkhead with mortise and tenon joints. Things are changed for Gabrielle. She is no more the coddled girl followed around by Fanny, her slave. She is a wage earner. A seamstress can make beautiful things, dresses of silk and shirred bombazine. More often she takes in piecework for slender pay, adding flounces to skirts, cutting necklines, folding cuffs on trousers.

These two working people are not greeted by a black nurse. They sold "our nigger," as Constant would call Fanny. They walk the gangplank into Bouligny.

PART III

TRIBES

I am sure Gabrielle and Constant Lecorgne never see him, never hear him talk. Still, they know the name of Frederick Douglass. Some people spit when they say it.

The Ladies' Anti-Slavery Society of Rochester, New York, asks the abolitionist Frederick Douglass to give a speech to mark Independence Day. Douglass is a newspaper publisher, ex-slave, and black. He agrees to talk about the meaning of July 4. Douglass will be seen and heard by just a few, but in years to come the speech in Rochester is remembered as the most acid description of America as a young slave empire.

From the auditorium stage in a place called Corinthian Hall, in the 1850s, Douglass turns to his audience and calls it "you."

> This Fourth of July is *yours*, not *mine. You* may rejoice, *I* must mourn. . . . What, to the American slave, is your 4th of July? I answer: a day that reveals to him, more than all other days in the year, the gross injustice and cruelty to which he is the constant victim. To him, your celebration is a sham; your boasted liberty, an unholy license; your national greatness, swelling vanity; your sounds of rejoicing are empty and heartless; your denunciations of tyrants, brass fronted impudence; your shouts of liberty and equality, hollow mockery; your prayers and hymns, your sermons and thanksgivings, with all your religious parade, and solemnity, are, to him, mere bombast, fraud, deception, impiety, and hypocrisy—a thin veil to cover up crimes which would disgrace a nation of savages. There is not a nation on the earth guilty of practices, more shocking

and bloody, than are the people of these United States, at this very hour.

Go where you may, search where you will, roam through all the monarchies and despotisms of the old world, travel through South America, search out every abuse, and when you have found the last, lay your facts by the side of the everyday practices of this nation, and you will say with me, that, for revolting barbarity and shameless hypocrisy, America reigns without a rival.

Frederick Douglass talks about New Orleans, the fulcrum of the slave trade. He wants to remind "you" the city is the domestic market that drags nearly a million of *les nègres* across the country, from Virginia and Maryland and the Carolinas "down the river" to auction houses along the Mississippi River.

Take the American slave-trade, which, we are told by the papers, is especially prosperous just now. . . . This trade is one of the peculiarities of American institutions. It is carried on in all the large towns and cities in one-half of this confederacy; and millions are pocketed every year, by dealers in this horrid traffic. In several states, this trade is a chief source of wealth. . . .

Behold the practical operation of this internal slave-trade, the American slave-trade, sustained by American politics and American religion. Here you will see men and women reared like swine for the market. You know what is a swine-drover? I will show you a man-drover. They inhabit all our Southern States. They perambulate the country, and crowd the highways of the nation, with droves of human stock. You will see one of these human flesh-jobbers, armed with pistol, whip and bowie-knife, driving a company of a hundred men, women, and children, from the Potomac to the slave market at New Orleans. These wretched people are to be sold singly, or in lots, to suit purchasers. They are food for the cotton-field, and the deadly sugarmill. Mark the sad procession, as it moves wearily along, and the inhuman wretch who drives them. Hear his savage yells and his blood-chilling oaths, as he hurries on his affrighted captives! There, see the old man, with locks thinned and gray. Cast one glance, if you please, upon that young mother, whose shoulders are bare to the scorching sun, her briny tears falling on the brow of the babe in her arms. See, too, that girl of thirteen, weeping, *yes!* weeping, as she thinks of the mother from whom she has been torn! The drove moves tardily. Heat and sorrow have nearly consumed their strength; suddenly you hear a quick snap, like the discharge of a rifle; the fetters clank, and the chain rattles simultaneously; your ears are saluted with a scream, that seems to have torn its way to the center of your soul! The crack you heard, was the sound of the slave-whip; the scream you heard, was from the woman you saw with the babe. Her speed had faltered under the weight of her child and her chains! That gash on her shoulder tells her to move on. Follow the drove to New Orleans. Attend the auction; see men examined like horses; see the forms of women rudely and brutally exposed to the shocking gaze of American slave-buyers. See this drove sold and separated forever; and never forget the deep, sad sobs that arose from that scattered multitude. Tell me citizens, WHERE, under the sun, you can witness a spectacle more fiendish and shocking. Yet this is but a glance at the American slave-trade, as it exists, at this moment, in the ruling part of the United States. . . .

Fellow-citizens! I will not enlarge further on your national inconsistencies. The existence of slavery in this country brands your republicanism as a sham, your humanity as a base pretence, and your Christianity as a lie.

After matrimony, a cozy home. The sale of Fanny pays for a wedding, but not enough is left for a house. Gabrielle and Constant sort their options and then move in with Gabrielle's adoptive parents, François and Adelaide Laizer.

The house on Cadiz Street is a crowded compound. The middle-aged Laizers occupy one corner of upstairs, while Gabrielle's three teen stepsiblings take another. Enslaved housekeepers and a cook have a cabin behind the main house. There is only so much with in-laws a couple can sustain. But soon after they settle comes good news. Gabrielle has stopped her monthlies. She is enceinte, pregnant. If God wills, the child comes next summer. By then, they want to have a house.

François Laizer is mayor by day and land hustler on the side. Despite their money—tax records say the Laizers are the richest people in Bouligny—Gabrielle's parents do not open their pocketbook. After the Laizers, the next richest is Constant's mother, Marguerite, *Veuve Lecorgne*. Marguerite has her block of lots on Lyons Street, Lecorgne row, and a barracks of slaves for hire.

In the barracks, there is another word on people's lips, "cracker." It is a word that comes with the Americans. Cracker woman will sell a black man in a minute, somebody might say. Everybody knows a slave is walking money.

Marguerite declines to offer land or money to the newlyweds. Constant, it appears, is not the beloved son. He may have a pretty wife, picked like fruit. But something is wrong. His reputation is weak. Nothing is forthcoming.

There is money left from the Fanny dowry to buy a single lot. Gabrielle, pregnant and swelling, eases herself down the stairs at the Laizer house, and the couple makes plans to build. In early 1857, Constant buys a scrap of land, $150 for something on Soniat Street, from a woman named Louise Avart, who is retailing bits of her inheritance. It is two blocks from Lecorgne row. The idea is that Constant can put up a little house before the baby comes.

Time is short, Marguerite steps forward. In her stable of human livestock is thirty-three-year-old Ovid. Marguerite looks forward to the appearance of a grandchild, courtesy of Gabrielle. Constant's mother decides to loan her son the sweat of vigorous and capable Ovid.

Two builders can put up a two-room house in half a year. Constant and Ovid start to work. Ovid is older than his new master, probably more experienced. Constant is still learning the cuts. He knows barges and riverboats, not houses. He knows steamboat men, not joiners and roofers and glaziers. Ovid and Constant take lumber down to the little lot on Soniat. They sweat, raise the studs and beams, frame the roof.

Marguerite has two other sons, Yves of God and Joseph, thirty-one and twenty. The brothers inspect the activity on Soniat Street, and it inspires them. Two months after Constant and Ovid start work, they buy a lot of their own. Their tract lies on Jersey Street, around the corner from Marguerite. Their plan is to put up a house and share it. To buy the land and build, the brothers borrow money from their mother. Marguerite loans Yves of God and Joseph the cash that Constant does not see.

The year 1857 is passing, and Gabrielle is dangerously pregnant. At the end of the summer, the place on Soniat Street is unfinished. The baby comes September 2. The parents name him Joseph Gabriel Numa Lecorgne. Joseph is the name of Constant's younger brother, Numa the name of sister Aurore's husband—the brother-in-law killed by Yellow Jack—and baby Gabriel reflects the glory of his mother, Gabrielle. But the half-finished house molders in the rain.

When the scientist Samuel Morton brought out *Crania Americana*, twenty years ago in Philadelphia, he proved the facts of race variety. Whites and blacks are different species. Now, here at home in New Orleans, as elsewhere, science develops its knowledge.

James De Bow, editor and publisher, keeps up the discussion in the quality journal that carries his name, *De Bow's Review*. For ten years the quarterly has circulated to businessmen and hustlers, slaveholders and would-be bosses. It is the tonic of the intelligentsia in the South. *De Bow's Review* pursues the science of race, beginning in 1847, with a thought piece called "The Negro." It continues in 1849 with "Negro Slavery at the South," an elaboration of slavery's benefits. De Bow runs articles that refine the understanding of whiteness and blackness, both for the good people of New Orleans and for its region.

James De Bow has a comrade in the race theory business. His name is Josiah Nott. Dr. Josiah Nott is a professor of anatomy at the University of Louisiana, the state's sole institution of higher education. (In the future, the school changes its name, to become Tulane University.) A man with blue eyes and straight hair, Josiah C. Nott is a convert to the idea of polygenesis, the fact of the separate origin of the races. During the 1850s, Dr. Nott is an opinion maker on race and identity—what makes a white person white, a black person black. Nott's book, *Indigenous Races of the Earth*, boils down to a few truths about the nature of human identity. Nott is not stupid, however, and he knows that only a few read a fat monograph. So the professor gives public lectures, and the anatomist spreads his ideas in the pages of *De Bow's Review*.

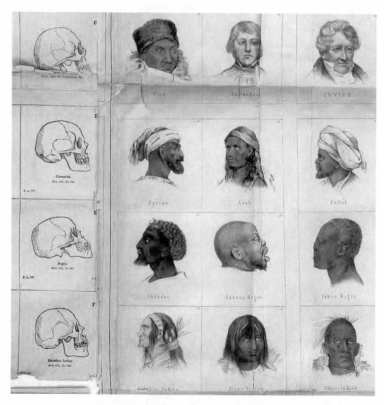

Categories of human, "Races of the Earth," illustrated by Josiah Nott in 1857

Thank goodness Dr. Nott has chosen to work in New Orleans. More like him are needed.

Constant and the Lecorgnes, I feel sure, do not acquire copies of Nott's *Indigenous Races of the Earth*, which is published the year

Numa Lecorgne is born. Yet it is not out of the question that some in the family—perhaps Yves of God, the one with education—may find themselves at one of the scientist's public lectures. In a hall at the university, Dr. Nott fulminates, his charts and drawings and data confirming the absolute rigidity of the racial order, the permanence of the social pyramid. In talks and popular articles, Nott lays out his discoveries in "cranioscopy," the measurement of skulls. He shows that whites, due to the shape of their heads, are close to the "ideal human of the ancients." Whereas blacks, who possess "notably misshaped heads," are not only closer to the apes, but may descend from them.

In "The Monogenists and the Polygenists," Nott explains how different types of human come to exist. He says the varieties arose simultaneously in separate events and on several continents, hundreds of thousands of years ago—the view of the "Polygenists." The "Monogenists" say that all humanity emerges from a single origin—either from Adam and Eve, in Genesis, or from some foundational creature. I can see how this business of polygenesis is soothing. It comforts the insecurity of whites. It explains why whites are conspicuously superior, the high ring in the human chain of being, and why blacks appear to lie somewhere low and abject.

With James De Bow in the role of publisher, race theory burns brightly in New Orleans. "Negro slavery is consistent with the laws of God and with humanity," says Josiah Nott to a roomful in a lecture series in New Orleans. De Bow runs Josiah Nott's essays under headlines like "Diversity of the Human Race." He offers scientific education for the many and makes science subordinate to the needs of exploitation. Josiah Nott, over time, is one of the loudest of apologists for slavery. He knows it can be justified by science. He writes that he wants to "confound the abolitionists" and prove that enslavement is a benign practice. Sometimes, in an aside, Nott calls his discipline of craniology and polygenesis "the nigger business"; sometimes he calls it "niggerology." In the lecture hall, the heads of many nod and smile.

The names Samuel Morton and Josiah Nott are murmured and admired in New Orleans, not in the drunken barrelhouses, but in libraries and cafés, over coffee and beignets, pieces of fried dough with powdered sugar. A third name now joins the discussion, Louis

Agassiz. A professor of zoology at Harvard, Louis Agassiz picks up the consensus on polygenesis and carries it to New England. Agassiz manages to persuade many scholars and sages in the North how whites and blacks represent different species. Louis Agassiz goes further and looks for visible proof. From his rooms at Harvard, Agassiz reaches deep down in the South and brings away evidence. He hires a photographer, a daguerreotype artist in South Carolina named Joseph Zealy. He tells Zealy to photograph specimens of the African race—naked, if possible. The results are splendid, proof positive of polygenesis. The fifteen daguerreotypes of Dr. Agassiz, housed in the Agassiz Library at Harvard, are some of the very few photographs of enslaved Americans that survive.

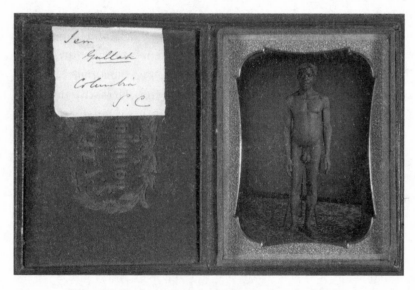

The naturalist Louis Agassiz hired a photographer in 1850
to prove with pictures—including this one, "Jem, Gullah"—the variation
of African "species."

White Creoles, and I think the Lecorgnes are among them, give credit to another writer on race, because he is a Frenchman. He is Arthur Gobineau. A Parisian aristocrat and self-nominated scientist, Arthur Gobineau publishes a long meditation that he calls *Essai sur l'inégalité des races humaines* ("Essay on the Inequality of the

Human Races"). For tribal reasons, any word from France must be listened to in Louisiana, and so it is with Arthur Gobineau, during the 1850s, among a small but influential group of writers and talkers in New Orleans.

I think I can summarize the wordy view of Gobineau by quoting him in one thimble-sized passage—

"I have been able to distinguish, on physiological grounds alone, three great and clearly marked types, the black, the yellow, and the white. . . . The negroid variety is the lowest, and stands at the foot of the ladder. The animal character, that appears in the shape of the pelvis, is stamped on the negro from birth, and foreshadows his destiny." Whereas, Gobineau says, he sees unmistakable "superiority of the white type, and, within this type, of the Aryan family."

Arthur Gobineau is important in part because his catalog of racial difference first puts in circulation the myth of the "Aryan." A linguistic clan set apart by language, the so-called Aryans (from the Sanskrit *ārya*) are said to have ancient roots in northwest India and present-day Iran and to have spread into prehistoric Europe. It is with the help of a French royalist that one of the most caustic formulations of white supremacy is born.

Josiah Nott, the craniologist, is so enamored of Arthur Gobineau that in 1856, he publishes an English translation of *Essai sur l'inégalité des races humaines*. He gives it a sedate title, *The Moral and Intellectual Diversity of Races*, but the contents remain cruel.

Marguerite Lecorgne keeps good appearances. In 1858, she turns sixty. Not everyone has a half block of land and five grown children scattered in reach to look after you. Widow Lecorgne lives high. Not everyone has fourteen *nègres* to call "mine."

Exit Marguerite's house on Lyons Street, walk south one block, and you dead-end at the Mississippi. Some call the road that runs along the levee "Water Street." Here are oyster shacks, barbershops, cafés and barrooms, boardinghouses, pharmacies, clothing shops, barrelhouse beer halls, shoemakers, tobacco shops, furniture stores, and confectioners. The bigger businesses lie on the side of the street that contacts the river. They have wharfs, like the Ocean Sawmill, Constant's haunt, and the cotton press. The cotton press does such heavy business that it sometimes clouds the air with tufts of downy white.

Some call the road that runs along the levee by its real name, Tchoupitoulas. The name has its root in the Choctaw language. Natives who called themselves Tchoupitoulas (CHOP-uh-TOO-las) were the "river people" who lived here and traveled up and down the Mississippi to trade. In good American style, the settler colony drove out the people and kept their name as a remnant.

Jefferson City is bigger now. When the Lecorgnes arrived, fifteen years ago, fewer than five thousand could be found on the streets that branch from Napoleon Avenue. Now thirty thousand live in these parts, three miles upstream of New Orleans. The white suburb whitens more. Immigrants from Ireland, leaving behind the potato famine, have filled in much. Creoles do not like the Irish. They call their section at the edge of Bouligny "the Irish Channel." Germans are coming, too, by the thousand. Creoles like them better, except for their beer.

Despite the Lecorgne family money, I do not believe Constant thinks of himself as fortunate. He leans over a bench with a plane in his hand, bends his shoulders to haul beams. He has an unconscious well in which to collect resentments. The real lucky one is his cousin, Camille Zeringue. When he thinks about Camille, Constant has reason to envy.

Look at Seven Oaks. Camille lives like a prince. He's got all that money. He's got 108 people! The more they cut the sugarcane, the more Camille counts his money.

Constant lays his saw on another eight-foot board and trims it into decking. He cuts a groove down the long edge to receive the bead of the next plank. He walks one more time to Ocean Sawmill, on Tchoupitoulas. He turns to Ovid, his shop man, his mother's loan. Why does a man have to work with a nigger? There is no justice in it.

"Nigger" is a word the Creoles had to learn. *Les Américains* brought it with them when they flooded into Louisiana. Now they use it all the time. It is a sharper word, more useful than the gentle French words for African Americans, like *les nègres*. "Nigger" is nicely caustic and poisonous on the lips.

There is another word the Americans bring with their English, "darkey." It is more mocking and contemptuous, and less aggressive. Nigger is all aggression, but darkey looks down with a smirk. Maybe Constant says something like this. Why does a man have to work with darkies? In fact, he would say *the* darkies. God bless them, they are always making mistakes.

The black population of New Orleans shrinks during the rush of white immigrants. By the end of the 1850s, people of color, enslaved and free, are fewer than one-quarter of the population.

In December 1858, baby Numa is fifteen months old, and the little house on Soniat Street is still not done. It is not clear what goes wrong. But again Gabrielle has stopped her periods, she is pregnant for the second time. There is no more room at the Laizer house, there must be an exit. In January, Constant puts the half-finished cottage on the market. It brings an offer from a widow, and it is gone. Sell it cheap, and say nothing to the buyer. Three weeks later, Gabrielle and Constant have a solution. They buy a cottage on a square lot. The place stands on the corner of Bellecastle and Live Oak streets, in Bouligny, five blocks from Lecorgne row. It is $540, with half borrowed from the seller. All that has to be done is to add a room or two. Ovid can do it, and finally they will have a bedroom door to close.

Gabrielle has Numa on her hip. A young white mother needs to be served. When they move to Bellecastle Street, Constant and Gabrielle take Rachel, a house slave, plus her two children, Frank and Louis. Rachel is thirty-five and one of Widow Lecorgne's people. Marguerite inherited her from her father, and she has been working for nearly twenty years. Rachel had a partner, named Job, but at some point Job disappears. He might have died, or maybe Marguerite sold him. One thing is certain about Rachel, and that is her cost. She is appraised at $900—in other words, more than the new house.

The furniture goes in, the home is made. Rachel and her kids, Ovid, Constant and Gabrielle, plus Numa. In June 1859, Gabrielle has her first daughter. They name her Françoise Mathilde. The house is crowded, but it is away from the in-laws.

Yves of God, the family leader, age thirty-four, goes further into government. He runs for office and is elected justice of the peace for Jefferson City. A census enumerator asks Yves of God his profession, and he answers that he is a "judge." In reality, he writes arrest warrants for drunkenness and fighting, and settles little property disputes. Now he has two jobs, city clerk and justice. As clerk, he manages tax rolls for Jefferson City. Fortunately, the job has a lucrative sideline, which is assessment. As one of three tax assessors, Yves sets property values, more lucrative than punishing drunks. It is not unusual for a tax assessor to accept gifts from businessmen unhappy about their taxes, and to make reductions on paid request.

Constant is a carpenter who can't finish a house. But his father-in-law is still the mayor, and he has a fixer for a brother who works in city hall.

As soon as Yves of God wins election, he gives the youngest Lecorgne brother a job, deputy sheriff. Joseph has been working at a gristmill. There is little to the work: a big round stone in a small, cramped storefront grinds corn into flour. Like Constant, Joseph has not made a move from muscle labor to deskwork. Joseph is engaged to a woman named Estelle Daunoy, and he needs a better job. Deputy sheriff comes with a paycheck and a gun. The job is part-time. Joseph goes out nights to police fistfights in the Irish Channel, or he shuts down the cockfights the city is trying to ban. The pay is good. When there is nothing to do, slaves can always be stopped and roughed up.

The sheriff of Jefferson City is a man named Guy Dreux. Joseph Lecorgne and Guy Dreux arrest whites and blacks in equal number and bring them to the lockup on Magazine Street. The most frequent charge is disorderly conduct—fighting. When they arrest women, the most frequent charge is soliciting—prostitution.

Constant looks stable and reliable. The carpenter has a wife, house, two babies, two slaves. He is a homeowner.

In summer 1860, Constant joins his two brothers in law enforcement. Yves seems to throw him the job. Constant becomes a confiscation agent. It is the lowest kind of work as a cop. People who fail to pay their taxes are shirkers, and the sheriff's office seizes their property. Enter the confiscation man. Sometimes, after litigation, the court impounds the assets of the loser. It might be a building lot, a horse, or an enslaved man. Enter the confiscation man. Yves, justice of the peace, writes the order to impound, which goes to the sheriff, who sends out an enforcer. Constant is deputy sheriff in charge of confiscation.

To seize a man's belongings is neither easy nor safe; nor is selling things on the steps of the courthouse, the last part of the job. None of it is a way to make friends in Bouligny.

In August 1860, Constant runs an item in *The Carrollton Sun*—

"I shall proceed to sell at public auction, at the door of the Court House, the following described property, to wit . . . three lots of ground, bounded by Pearl, Washington, Burdette, and Commercial Streets. . . . This property was seized in the suit of George A. Freret vs. Abraham J. Wright. Terms of sale are cash on the spot."

It is almost an acting role for a cop, a piece of theater. Constant puts on an authoritative look, walks to Magazine Street, climbs the steps of the courthouse. There is a chance of trouble, so he must be armed. I imagine that Abraham Wright, forced to surrender his real estate, turns up at the auction. He must know the sheriff's deputy carries a weapon. He must know that all the Lecorgne brothers do enforcement.

On one occasion, Constant has the pleasure of shaking down a black family for money. It happens in the Third District Court, a venue for debt cases. When a white landlord named Valmont Dufossat sues a free woman of color named Claudine Claude for nonpayment of rent on a house he owns, 642 Rousseau Street, Dufossat recruits Constant to extract the money from the tenant.

Dufossat gets a judge to issue a "writ of seizure," and Constant is sent out to enforce it. He is to drive the woman from her house and collect back rent. It is not clear from the papers whether he uses threats or physically roughs up Claudine Claude. Maybe he does both. He is the righteous fist of the law and does what is required. When he comes back to the courthouse, Constant carries a month's rent in hand, and he has left Claudine Claude on the street. He is a cop and a punisher. The nigger must be put in her place.

They mind their business, they are God-fearing. The Lecorgnes are a few households on a few streets. They have some darkies, that is all, and people envy them. Everybody wants the same.

Leave our tribe alone, they might say. You covet us. It is not so different in your own time and place.

The Lecorgnes marry, they argue about property (the darkies), they have children. They sort out who among them is up, and who down. They work, shuffle houses, guide their children to a match. They praise the Lord, because all blessings cascade from Him.

A new race philosopher moves to New Orleans. He is Samuel Cartwright, from Natchez, Mississippi. A doctor born in Virginia, Cartwright has for years practiced medicine in Natchez. But his intellectual challenge, and his love, is crafting theories of race and behavior. James De Bow has already given Samuel Cartwright many pages in *De Bow's Review* to elaborate his work. In one essay, Cartwright describes a disease he calls *Dysaesthesia Aethiopica*, or "uncomfortable blackness." ("It is a disease peculiar to negroes, affecting both mind and body . . . a partial insensibility of the skin, and so great a lethargy of the intellectual faculties, as to be like a person half asleep," Cartwright tells readers.)

When Dr. Samuel Cartwright moves permanently to Louisiana, the professional men of the New Orleans Academy of Sciences welcome him by sponsoring his first lectures. It is one November, at the end of the 1850s, and the first of the talks takes place at the University of Louisiana, center of mental life in the city.

Cartwright steps to the lectern and speaks. It is a room in which the dignitaries of Southern science smoke cigars and confer.

"There are three principal groups that have maintained the physical traits and mental characteristics unaltered by time for a period as far back as history extends," he says. "Natural historians designate them as the white, yellow and black: otherwise the Indo-European, Mongolian and Prognathous."

The "Prognathous," Cartwright explains, is the human species marked by a lower jaw that projects outward, like that of an ape.

"We behold four millions of the negro race, that group of mankind engaged mostly in agriculture, and under subjection to that other group, called . . . Aryan, Caucasian, or white. . . . The obedience of the negro to the Caucasian is spontaneous, because it is normal for the weaker will to yield obedience to the stronger."

The room is full. Nods of assent are quiet, as the Caucasian is not prone to verbal ejaculations.

"The ultimate limit of progress the negro race has ever made, stops within the confines of barbarism," he continues. "But the white type has ever forced its way and maintained its position in that high order of civilization where moral virtue, clad in intellectual light, rules society."

Between James De Bow and Josiah Nott, and now Samuel Cartwright, New Orleans is a center of race theory. The position of whites is a deserving one, and the scientists who can prove it have a big audience. Samuel Cartwright takes questions, steps down from the dais, and finds the way home. He is a good addition to scholarship in the Crescent City.

Widow Lecorgne has cancer. The record says no more, but breast cancer is one kind that cannot be named. Marguerite lies in bed, her children and grandchildren visiting. The cancer grows, and Marguerite's life drains. It is fall 1859, and her family watches her dying. The pain rises, until relief comes from the pharmacy. It is laudanum, liquid opium, diluted in tinctures for patients to ingest. If Marguerite can drink it, suffering flees for hours.

Constant's new baby, Mathilde, is mewling—she is four months old—when the news comes that Marguerite Lecorgne is dead. She dies November 2, at sixty-two.

Marguerite Zeringue Lecorgne—daughter of planters, mother of five, slaveholder of fourteen, widow to a sailor, grandmother of a half-dozen. The ordinary and predictable life of a Creole woman, fitted to her times. Yet also: the complex and unique life of a Creole woman, full of exceptions. Most people in the South are not French, not white, not slaveholders.

Marguerite dies during the day. That night, there is a wake in the house on Lecorgne row, and the next day comes the service. The Catholic church in Bouligny is St. Stephen. When the funeral comes, I suspect Marguerite's children are not pleased that St. Stephen has assigned an Irish priest, Father Ryan, to bury their mother. The Irish immigrants keep coming. One thing that makes them undesirable, one fact, is that Irish immigrants are known to work with black people. The Irish are not good enough or, maybe, not quite white enough.

The Lecorgnes follow the casket into the sanctuary. Father Ryan utters the memoriam—*Requiescat in pace*—and blesses the body. Marguerite's slaves probably come to see her blessed and buried, or some of them. It is required.

The family meets to divide the estate. Appraisers tally Marguerite's land and houses, but most of the money is in people. At her death, Marguerite possessed more than a dozen, and the inventory lists them:

Anna, age 50	$300
Sylvie, 50	$500
Rachel, 35	$900
Dorothy, 22 & her children	$1,500
Eugenie, 3 and	
Eugene, 18 mos.	
Ovid, 36	$1,200
Jack, 23	$1,400

Louise, 15	$1,000
Frank, 13	$1,000
Edward ("a mulatto"), 15	$1,000
Celestine, 17	$1,000
Caroline ("a mulatress"), 18	$1,500
Eulalie, 69	(of no value)

Marguerite's people come in at $11,300.

Eulalie, the woman "of no value," grew up with Marguerite and served her for sixty years. She was the property of Marguerite's parents. The dead woman inherited her.

Ernest Commagere, the notary, writes up contracts. Constant gets Ovid, whom he already has. Ovid may no longer be *un buck*, a man who can carry a barrel on his shoulder, but he hoists a good load of bricks. Constant also takes Caroline, an eighteen-year-old "mulatress, appraised at $1500." He takes a few pieces of furniture, and he takes an empty lot. He takes his portion.

Yves of God takes the rest of the enslaved. He also takes his mother's house, the furniture, and all her belongings. I look at the estate papers to figure out what happens. It seems Yves keeps the black men and gives the women to his sisters. Each of the Lecorgne women—Ézilda, Aurore, and Eliza—takes command of at least one black woman. The papers are unclear. Some of the outcome must be imagined. After the settlement, it appears that the enslaved women and men continue to live together. But the men are hired out in the city, and the women work for the Lecorgnes in their homes.

Constant has reason to think he has been screwed. His brother, Yves of God, ends up with $8,000 in property and people. Constant comes away with one-third that amount.

Caroline-the-mulatress, age eighteen, moves in with Constant and Gabrielle on Bellecastle Street. Rachel, the cook who cleans and who has worked for the couple since they married, moves out. She and her children go over to Constant's sister Eliza. There is no way to tell, but the possibility is genuine that Constant wants more from Caroline-the-mulatress than food on the table, a clean house, and babysitting for his children. A part of life in the slave South, nearly a fixture of housekeeping, is that mixed-race women find themselves at the sexual mercy of their masters. Does the ship carpenter request Caroline from his mother's estate? Caroline is appraised at $1,500, she is the most valuable. A high price for a young woman reflects her sexual capital.

I am trying to peer into their lives. There is no evidence of what Caroline might meet at the hands of Mistress and Master Lecorgne. And little can be done to protect a vulnerable woman who is dead. Yet she knows, I am sure of it, that she enters a risky new place when she arrives at Constant's house.

The cracker men, you ain't going to know what comes from them till it happens.

As for the whites, they are content, and they are perturbed. Life is good and it is soft. They have what they need, even what they want. But the world is teetering. People seem to know it, black and white.

Yves of God, city clerk and judge, has two feet in politics. In 1860, the political fight grows loud enough to take over almost all public speech. The newspapers are shrill about the threat from the abolitionists in the North. The priests are lecturing their congregations. They talk about the divisions in the country. Father Ryan, the Irishman at St. Stephen, sometimes preaches. Father Ryan says the election this year is dangerous. It could be fatal to Louisiana and to the whole South. The bow is drawn, and our way of life the target.

The Lecorgnes attend St. Stephen and hear all kinds of things. Benjamin Palmer, a Presbyterian minister, is not in the Roman church, but he speaks the truth to his flock in New Orleans. A sermon by Reverend Palmer is passed from hand to hand.

"What is the providential trust of the South?" Palmer says from his pulpit at First Presbyterian on Thanksgiving Day. "I answer that it is to conserve and to perpetuate the institution of domestic slavery as now existing."

Reverend Palmer seems to have been reading Samuel Morton, maybe Josiah Nott. He knows about Arthur Gobineau and does not miss an issue of *De Bow's Review*. Palmer understands the darkies, he says. "Every attribute of their character fits them for dependence and servitude, and thus we are the constituted guardians of the slaves themselves."

Sounds of rustling in the pews, and the God-fearing nod in

agreement. In the big churches, whites sit below, black worshippers in the balcony above. People call the loft where people of color pray "the crows' nest." Up in the balcony, the blacks in Palmer's congregation do not appear to nod.

"The spirit of abolition, the folly of freedom for negroes, is undeniably atheistic," Palmer says. "The negroes belong here with us, in the presence of the vigorous Saxon race!"

Palmer the clergyman points at tribal lines. You have the *Anglo-Saxons*, the English-speaking race, and the *Saxons* of Gaul, of northern France. You have *les nègres*, the benighted and dependent African Americans. The fanatical moralists who do not understand science, let alone the will of God, threaten their balance.

Reverend Benjamin Palmer's Thanksgiving sermon is published in an edition of fifty thousand and sells everywhere in the South. I do not doubt that the Lecorgnes see it, read it, agree with it.

When the French sailor Yves Le Corgne first washes ashore in New Orleans, about 1814, the place is a muddy town, population 20,000. Forty-five years on, in 1860, it is the biggest city in the lower half of the United States, with 170,000 people. New Orleans dominates the states of Texas, Mississippi, Arkansas, and Alabama, and throws shade over the rest of the South.

The city feeds on the giant commerce of the river, and on the sugar and cotton plantations of the Mississippi Valley. Sugar, the first big slave crop, comes to the docks in casks of brown crystal and in five-hundred-pound barrels of molasses, called hogsheads. Sugar rolls out on the new railroad lines that thread the state. The boom in cotton is more important, it builds the city. Cotton plantations start to spread through the South, just as the first Yves Le Corgne sets foot in New Orleans. Fifty years later, more than a million enslaved grow the white fleece on a thousand cotton plantations and send it downstream to New Orleans, where it is weighed, taxed, and sold. Cotton is the biggest U.S. export, sailing out through the mouth of the Mississippi to the world.

Yves of God acquires yet another office, becoming election commissioner for Jefferson City. He counts ballots and announces the result. It is a further good job in politics.

The Lecorgnes—all of them, as far as I can see—are Democrats, and a skinny democracy it is. In Louisiana in 1860, just 83,900 possess the right to vote, white men above twenty-one. Of this electorate, about three out of five vote, which means that seven percent of the population picks the government.

The Lecorgnes are not Whigs. The Whig Party, old club of the thoughtful rich, has vanished, and another club arisen in its place, the Republicans. The Republican Party is born in 1854 in Illinois. Its principles might be summed up in six words: more commerce, more work, and less slavery. The party attracts Christians more than agnostics, city people more than country people, white women more than white men. Though they cannot vote, many women are nevertheless active in Republican politics. Women argue in favor of abolition and against liquor.

When the Mexican-American War ends in 1848, the United States seizes half of the territory of Mexico, and when they arrive, the Republicans take a stand on a new barrier: no slavery in the looted western lands. Whites in the South, poor and rich, detest the Republican Party. To white Southerners, the Republicans are righteous, and they are nouveau riche. More, they do not know the word of the Lord, whose Bible is full of slaves. They do not hear the sound of the money that tinkles in the slave fields.

In 1860, slavery is on the national ballot. The Lecorgnes are prosperous, but they are no longer among the *grands blancs*, the big whites. The family is not influential. They pay attention but do not campaign for things. They know, as everyone knows, the Republicans are for the blacks, and they are traitors to the white tribe.

In May in Chicago, Republicans put up their presidential candidate, a lawyer born in Kentucky who works in Illinois, Abraham Lincoln, a longtime opponent of slavery's expansion, a man who has been in and out of both the Illinois Assembly and the U.S. House of Representatives. By this time, an antislavery line is enough to lift politicians in the North—among some whites but not all. Democrats, both in the North and in the South, call Lincoln the "Black Republican."

Most whites throughout the United States either support enslavement or are indifferent to it. If a newspaper asks five whites living outside the South, What is to be done about slavery?, most of them would prevaricate. Enslavement is too bad for the blacks, one would say. We people have a hard time, too, says another. Things could be better, but slavery is the system we have got in America. The majority white view, both in the North and in the South, is that slavery might be troubling, but it works: just look at the money from cotton. Constant, I think—and his brothers, and probably his sisters—would take a hard line.

Between May and August, the party of "the Democracy" holds one convention, and then another. Democrats name a candidate, John Breckinridge, a thirty-eight-year-old Kentuckian, pretty in the face. Breckinridge threatens that the South will withdraw from the United States and break up the country if slavery is not left alone. Working whites and the middle rich, like the Lecorgnes, side with Breckinridge. A Northern faction of Democrats names a different candidate, Stephen Douglas, bibulous senator from Illinois. A new party, the Unionists, names a proslavery member of the U.S. House of Representatives, John Bell. With all these candidates, the result is a divided field of candidates for the fall of 1860: three proslavery politicians running for president, and one antislavery, Lincoln.

Constant and Gabrielle have two toddlers, Numa and Mathilde. They have Caroline-the-mulatress to serve them, and they have Ovid. The Republicans want to steal Caroline and Ovid. The Constitution lists rights. Guns are a right, slaves a right. If Abraham Lincoln is elected, he and his righteous columns will take away the family's rights.

I do not know what Constant and Gabrielle are thinking. I do not know what they say they are thinking, or what they tell themselves they are feeling. I especially do not know what they actually feel, behind their stated opinions. However, I do know what happens next: they put their man Ovid up for sale.

Chances are good that Ovid, a thirty-five-year-old craftsman, does not want to be sold. He has spent six years with these buckra and done a lot of hard work. I would like to think Ovid has a full life. He lives in a city with a giant and varied black world, churches on one street corner and barrooms on the next, licit and illicit pleasures. Ovid makes love, probably, and he worships. His life might have children in it. His life, possibly, has music and dance. Ovid does not want to be sold, because he knows that to pass through the gauntlet of the slave market is to lose everything. To be sold means to lose your partner and the people you know, lose your home, your pleasure, and go into mourning. Ovid knows that he could end up on a cotton field, five hundred miles distant, with nothing but hoeing and picking and tears in the cruel heat.

Constant does not go to one of the slave traders in New Orleans. With the growth of cotton, the slave market has spilled out of the St. Louis Hotel, and the city has dozens of independent auctioneers, men with offices and showrooms and jails to house their inventory. They cluster on Esplanade Avenue and Moreau Street, at the eastern edge of the *Vieux Carré*. They form a line of storefronts along Gravier Street and Baronne Street, at the western edge of the French Quarter. There are plenty of places to go, but Constant wants to make a private sale, away from the "nigger traders."

He talks to a family friend, a man named Valsin Gourdain. The Lecorgnes and the Gourdains both live in Bouligny. Gourdain is forty-six, and he has been friendly with the Lecorgnes for at least a decade. An appraiser puts Ovid's value at $1,200, and the sale is on. Constant, Gabrielle, and Gourdain make their way to the office of a notary, a man named Amédée Ducatel. Ovid, the property being transferred, is not on hand. Negotiations go badly for the Lecorgnes. Before they sign, Ovid is knocked down to $1,000, a twenty percent discount. The Lecorgnes take the deal.

The handwriting is gentle where "Gabrielle Le Corgne" writes her name. The penmanship is dramatically important where "P.C. Le Corgne" signs.

Ovid might have his own explanation for what is happening—*Bon blanc mouri; mauvais rêté*, "The good white men die; the bad remain." He is taken from the Lecorgne place on Bellecastle Street—in cuffs and chains, or in an agreeable walk, there is no way to know—and marched to the home of Valsin Gourdain.

The timing of the sale of Ovid is suspicious. It might be that Constant and Gabrielle decide to cash in their most valuable possession before the election, in case the Black Republican wins. Or it might be they just want money to buy some bonds, or to smarten up the house.

One month later, on November 8, Abraham Lincoln wins the White House. The three proslavery candidates—Breckinridge, Douglas, and Bell—split the vote of the majority of white people, North and South, who stand by enslavement. That is why Lincoln wins. Lincoln receives no votes at all in Louisiana. That is because election officials in the state have made sure his name does not appear on the ballot. Maybe the election commissioner Yves of God plays some role in the magical act of making a candidate go missing. I think he would enjoy having that influence.

It is time for shooting. November 1860 comes to an end just as rifle clubs and musket gangs take shape in New Orleans and in the rural parishes. Around the state, and around the South, guns come from closets to be lovingly cleaned.

There is little evidence that says what black people think and feel during these events. African Americans are a smaller part of the city population. Some fifteen thousand are enslaved, another eleven thousand free people of color. Life for the *gens de couleur libres* has been worsening for years, and many have left the state. I have to think that both enslaved and free feel competing emotions. One emotion is a gathering dread. What, after all, are the angry ofay going to do?

Another emotion is the feeling of raised expectations. If there is war, it could mean that the vise of white rule might begin to come loose.

The state of South Carolina is the first to withdraw from the United States, on December 20. Louisiana's new governor, a Democrat, calls for a "secession convention" to follow suit. Christmas passes offstage. You have rallies and speeches, marches and mobilization instead.

A lawyer named Judah Benjamin is one of Louisiana's two senators in Washington. He owns a sugar plantation, Bellechasse, with more than a hundred slaves. Benjamin is a Democrat, as are nearly all politicians in the South by this time, and the first Jew to be elected to the U.S. Senate. At the end of December, Benjamin stands in the well of the Senate chamber and gives a lyric and righteous-sounding speech, musing on the war everyone knows is coming.

"You may carry desolation to our peaceful land, and with torch and fire you may set our cities in flames," he says, "but you never can subjugate us." He finishes with the real subject, the presence in his mind of two tribes. "You never, never can degrade us to the level of an inferior, and servile race, never! Never!!"

9

Carnival season starts every year in early January, but in 1861, many pay only desultory attention to the parties and costumes before Mardi Gras, preferring to use their time planning for war. The vote counter Yves of God, for instance, helps with a snap election. A secession convention is set for the end of January, and Yves helps with the recruiting and election of 128 delegates.

Constant and Gabrielle have less room in their heads for the talk of rebellion. At least for the moment, they pay less attention to the masculine theatrics. They are distracted by a very sick baby. Their son, Numa, is three, daughter Mathilde a year and a half. As I imagine her, Mathilde has begun to talk. She has some French, and her parents teach her bits of English, because she has to get along. She starts to walk, teeters across the room. Sometime in January, the wet winter cold, Mathilde falls sick. When a baby is ill, parents burn with fear. In this place and time, one of three children does not reach five years. Mathilde's parents turn inward, preoccupied with nursing their baby. In the third week of the month, she gets worse. Is it pneumonia? Fever? The medical trail is absent, but the disaster is not. The little girl, nineteen months old, dies January 22.

At the service in St. Stephen, a French priest named Xavier Jacquemet blesses Mathilde and sends her to another world. "I the undersigned give to the sepulcher ecclesiastic the body of Françoise Mathilde, daughter of Constant Lecorgne," he writes in the register. She is going to a better place, he guarantees. Because she was christened, she has a key to the kingdom of God.

That leaves Numa. Pray to Mary, let him live.

Two days after the funeral, the secession convention meets in the capital, Baton Rouge, a day upriver by steamboat. Within hours, delegates pass an "ordinance of secession," a one-page bulletin printed in French and English: "The union now subsisting between Louisiana and other States under the name of 'the United States of America' is hereby dissolved," it says. Louisiana exits the country. Crowds of whites swarm down Canal Street, bordering the *Vieux Carré*. A cannon is wheeled to Jackson Square, in front of St. Louis Cathedral, and fires off rounds. The U.S. flag is pulled down from poles. In some parts of town, the white Creoles in the streets sing the Marseillaise, national anthem of France.

It may seem strange to sing the French anthem while breaking up the United States. But the Marseillaise is the best song of revolution.

To my ears, he has a name that sounds like a cake ornament. It is Alcibiade DeBlanc. A lawyer and a Creole, he is a friend of the Lecorgnes. DeBlanc has known the family for decades, probably since childhood. His father acted as witness at the wedding of Constant's parents, Yves and Marguerite. Alcibiade DeBlanc is a delegate to the secession meeting and a signer of the declaration. It may even be that Yves of God helped DeBlanc to get on the ballot. When the secession comes, I suspect that Constant and the in-laws hear about the legal steps of the Southern revolt through their friend *Monsieur DeBlanc*.

Alcibiade DeBlanc makes his home in the town of St. Martinville, in the southwest of the state, where he is a small-town eminence, volatile and loquacious. Maybe the Lecorgnes and DeBlancs see one another in New Orleans, either across the dinner table or in church, because these things are unavoidable. DeBlanc gives speeches at the convention that tremble with anger. He has the skill of heating a room.

The name "Alcibiade" points to a Greek general and orator, of the fifth century B.C.E., Alcibiades, spelled with an *s*. Alcibiade seems to have been christened with the general's name, and later to have dropped the last letter. His surname, "DeBlanc," converts into English as "of white." Together, "Alcibiade DeBlanc" might be rendered "the white tribune." One day, DeBlanc will lead a racist militia in a war on blacks. One day, he will recruit Constant Lecorgne to his ranks. But a dozen years must pass before the ship carpenter will lock arms with the tribune of the Ku-klux.

The rebellion warms up. Before the new president takes office, seven states withdraw from the Union: South Carolina, Mississippi, Florida, Alabama, Georgia, Louisiana, and Texas.

Carnival season comes to a crescendo. On Mardi Gras day—Fat Tuesday, February 12—you have parades and dancing, drinking and masking. Things are made more hysterical by all the war talk. The Carnival club known as Comus puts on the most memorable parade. On Mardi Gras night, a mass of white marchers comes down Canal Street. All are wearing blackface rather than masks, as though they are in a minstrel show. The men of Comus who wear blackface carry an effigy of Abraham Lincoln, a man whom they hate. It is a big puppet of Lincoln. The puppet rides a fence rail that has just been split in two—the country divided. *Le Républicain noir*, the Black Republican, has not yet taken office.

Constant is twenty-nine, Gabrielle twenty-five. One child taken, one living. They mourn.

Troops are being raised. In Jefferson City, hundreds join a new unit, the Lafayette Rifle Cadets. They drill on Napoleon Avenue through Lawrence Square, the center of Bouligny, with guns brought from home. The men march back and forth, stop to listen to speeches, march some more. No one has a uniform because none yet exist. Women like Gabrielle, the seamstress, are designing them in their sewing rooms.

Lincoln is inaugurated March 4.

Another militia forms, the *Tirailleurs d'Orléans*, the Orleans Sharpshooters. *Tirailler* is "to skirmish." The "Skirmishers" sounds clumsy, but it captures the self-regard. They feel like bandits and guerrillas.

The war begins eight hundred miles east, in Charleston, South Carolina, on April 12. Shots are fired on Fort Sumter, in Charleston Harbor. Right away, the Lecorgne brothers join the movement. Joseph, the youngest, is twenty-five. His wife, Estelle Daunoy, is six months pregnant with their first baby. From their bedroom on Jersey Street, Joseph and Estelle can hear the marching on Lawrence Square. Joseph signs up.

Yves of God, the oldest brother, thirty-four and unmarried, looks for a gainful angle. He does not want to fight, but maybe he can profit from the war. Yves pleads he is too old and offers himself as a recruitment agent who will sign up soldiers.

After the attack on Fort Sumter, the rest of the Southern states secede: Virginia, Arkansas, North Carolina, and Tennessee. The rebels have a name for their new nation, the Confederate States of America. Men in the militias are "Rebs," a label used with a smile by the rebels themselves. Their enemies in the North are "Yankees," said with disdain. Yankee is what the British called the Americans at the time of the Revolutionary War.

Yves of God helps out his middle brother. In May, Constant is named a captain in the Eighth Regiment, First Brigade, First Division, Louisiana Militia. The rank of captain is high, considering he has no military experience. But the newspaper explains: he is signed up and ranked by "Yves J. Lecorgne."

Across the Mississippi is Camille Zeringue, the Lecorgne cousin, an exception to the family pattern. Cousin Camille does not want secession, and neither do some of the other rich sugar planters and slaveholders around New Orleans. Camille is no abolitionist. He worries that a breakaway South will be disastrous for his business. But Camille's son, Fortune Zeringue, joins a militia.

In Washington, President Lincoln calls his generals around and devises a strategy. The North will starve the South. The North possesses a navy, the South none. The U.S. Navy will encircle the Confederate States like a snake and choke it off in a big blockade, starting with the most important port, New Orleans. The mouth of the Mississippi is sealed by summer 1861.

Joseph Lecorgne joins the same regiment as Constant. He pulls a rank of second lieutenant, far down the officer ladder. Yves of God himself takes the rank of captain, though he has no plan to command anyone. Captain Constant Lecorgne is given the assignment of recruiting privates from a square-mile section of Bouligny. A private is the lowest rank; he is cannon fodder and knows it. Yet men line up all day to enlist. Constant drills them on Lawrence Square, shouting orders. He shouts up marching orders in French, shouts them down in English.

The militias grow. By June, more than twelve thousand men in the state sign up. At the end of the summer, it is twenty-one thousand, or one in five white men in Louisiana.

Two weeks after he is appointed captain, Constant is demoted. He falls from his rank as captain to the rank of second lieutenant. A newspaper announces the change but gives no reason. Is it misconduct? Incompetence? Constant appears briefly to be a man with skills and command. Then he seems to screw up. It is a pattern in his life. He is not a leader but a follower.

A better-educated man, whom he knows, replaces Constant as a recruiter. He is Émile Chevalley, a young lawyer who lives across the street from Lecorgne row. The ship carpenter may look at the lawyer with skepticism. A few summers later, however, when this recruitment business is a memory and the war is over, a time will come when Émile Chevalley and Constant are again friends. They will sign on together with another militia, known as the Ku-klux.

Gens de couleur libres, free people of color, are under terrific pressure. The state has throttled them with higher taxes, a ban on dying slaveholders giving freedom to their children of color, and a prohibition on leaving and then returning to Louisiana. A few hundred free people hold a meeting. They decide that the best defense, in their impossible situation, is to put on a performance. They will pretend to support the white man's revolt. African American craftsmen and small businessmen come together to form a militia. They call themselves the Native Guards. It is a survival tactic, a piece of theater. The 1,500 volunteers march and drill like the whites. It is a charade to keep them and their families safe. The rebel governor of the state, Thomas Moore, instructs the Native Guards to remain in New Orleans, because white Rebs make it clear they will quit the movement if a colored regiment is given anything to do.

———

Feeling his demotion from captain to second lieutenant is unfair, Constant quits the Eighth Regiment and finds another unit. He joins the Third Regiment, Fourth Brigade, and persuades the command to bump him up a half step to first lieutenant. The rank is common for a mason or carpenter with a thin education. Within a month, he is transferred to yet another unit, Company B of the Jefferson Cadets, a hometown corps. To judge from the roster, the Cadets are full of family and friends. He has a cousin in the ranks, Fortune Zeringue, son of Camille Zeringue of Seven Oaks, and an in-law, François Fazende. The roulette wheel finally stops when the Jefferson Cadets merge into the regular rebel army; the unit becomes Company B, Fourteenth Louisiana Infantry.

Constant makes friends in Company B, four in particular— William Zimmerman, Jules Michel, Peter Duffy, and James Hetherton. I cannot say how well they all do as rebels. After the war ends, however, they perform vigorously, as these four join Constant in a branch of the Ku-klux.

The first battles come. In June, in western Virginia, at the town of Philippi, the rebels lose in a first clash. A week later, twenty are killed on the Chesapeake near a church known as Big Bethel. The Yankees lose that one.

In New Orleans, Constant is inducted into the army with his unit at a ceremony in front of city hall. When she turns out to say goodbye to her husband, Gabrielle is round at the waist, six months pregnant. Gabrielle knows, I think, that she got the baby just before she buried her toddler, Mathilde. A pregnant woman sends her husband into a fight, and the killing has already started. Feeling is high.

At the send-off, Constant hears a politician tell the Fourteenth Infantry that they are part of a noble experiment. You are the bone and sinew of a new nation, he says. You are ordinary men, but your cause is great, and glory is yours to take. It is a scene repeated in cities and towns around the South—in Savannah, for instance. During a speech in Savannah, Georgia, in front of a similar crowd, Alexander Stephens, vice president of the infant Confederate States of America, sums up the rebel cause and names the high ideals of the rebellion.

"Our new government is founded upon exactly this idea," Stephens tells his audience with new soldiers. "Its foundations are laid, its cornerstone rests upon the great truth, that the negro is not equal to the white man; that slavery—subordination to the superior race—is his natural and normal condition. This, our new government, is the first, in the history of the world, based upon this great physical, philosophical, and moral truth."

It is inspiring, a thought to raise the morale of young men as they march off to die. The teachings of science, race difference, and species difference are in rich harmony with the teaching of politics. They seem almost interchangeable, and not for the last time.

At twenty-nine, Lieutenant Constant Lecorgne is an older soldier. He and the other men of the Fourteenth Louisiana raise arms for their oath of allegiance, and they are gone.

Company B travels by train a hundred miles northwest, to the town of Amite. They make camp. Amite is a staging area where thousands of soldiers from around the state get ready to ship out to fighting in Virginia. The order comes that the Fourteenth Louisiana is going east. With a thousand men, the regiment must travel on two trains, as railcars come available. Company K of the Fourteenth leaves on one train, Company B follows a few hours later.

As I remember it, my aunt Maud Lecorgne pauses at this point in the story of our Klansman. Her words, which appear in one of her genealogical notebooks, are restrained. "My grandfather Constant joined one unit, but he did not like it much, apparently." It is a diplomatic sentence that hides more than it discloses. Because what happens next to Constant's unit is the subject of a court-martial.

Constant's train moves slowly, easing into Mississippi before turning north to head toward Tennessee. At every stop, groups of men from Company B get off to buy liquor, then climb back in the car. There are many stops. When the train reaches Grand Junction, Tennessee, just over the Mississippi line, much of the unit is drunk.

It is night in Grand Junction, time to make camp. In a field near the train stop, the men of Company K have already pitched tents and built fires. They arrived hours earlier. Half of Company B leaves the train to join Company K in camp, half stay behind at the station to drink. In the middle of the night, the drinkers finish their bottles and stumble into the campsite to discover that no dry place on the grass is cleared for them. Some of the men pick fights about the noise, and about the tight space, and soon a hundred men are swinging fists and tent poles.

It is unclear from the military report whether Lieutenant Lecorgne is among the drinkers who crash the campsite, or he is with the defenders who lunge at them, teaching the drunks a lesson.

A lieutenant named Myatt, in charge of the camp guard, has the task of keeping order. Lieutenant Myatt and several guards manage to arrest two dozen of the brawlers—the drinkers are incapacitated—and start them marching back to the town center. Myatt plans to lock up the group at the Percy Hotel, in the middle of town. On the march, a few prisoners bring out knives and attack their guards. Myatt's men have guns but no bullets. The guards fight back with bayonets and rifle butts.

Lieutenant Myatt sends a runner for reinforcements and to alert officers. The upper ranks have rooms at the Percy Hotel, the would-be jail. The prisoners are enraged that they are to be dressed down, and the drunks chase their captors to the Percy Hotel. A few in Company B rush around the yard to collect kindling and wood. They are mad enough that they will burn down the building.

A fire is growing on one side of the Percy Hotel when Colonel Valery Sulakowski, commander of the Fourteenth Louisiana, rides up on his horse. Colonel Sulakowski is a military man from eastern Europe. Born in Poland, age thirty-four, he is a former officer in the Austrian army, the experience of which has given him both a volatile temper and the habit of wearing a sword. A revolver in each hand, Sulakowski forces his horse into the boiling crowd. He shouts an order that every soldier must return to camp or expect to be shot. When one refuses, Sulakowski shoots him. Eleven men from among the drinkers of Company B are shot, almost all of them by their Polish commander.

I do not believe that at this point Constant sleeps peacefully in a tent at the campsite a quarter mile away. I believe he is in the middle of the chaos. Later in life, he will show his taste for a good riot and hand-to-hand fight that spills a good gallon of blood.

In all, seven are killed, nineteen wounded. When Sulakowski shrieks the order to put out the fire, some soldiers obey, and the Percy Hotel is saved. The injured and dying are put up in vacant rooms. Morning comes, camp breaks. Colonel Sulakowski gives orders to handcuff the worst fighters, who are to be charged with mutiny. Constant appears to be one of them. But the trial must wait until the trains reach Virginia.

The deadly riot is news both South and North, as stories about rogue Company B—"a Confederate mutiny"—run in all the papers.

Company B again boards a train. Sulakowski telegraphs ahead to Knoxville, Tennessee, four hundred miles east, the next place he plans to camp. He leaves word for Captain David Zable of Company K. Sulakowski tells Zable, whose company will arrive first, to see that all the taverns and barrelhouses in Knoxville are closed when Company B rolls into town. The train pulls out of Grand Junction. Constant and the mutineers are on board, hungover.

The Fourteenth Louisiana wants a fight with Yankees. The battle of Manassas—twenty-five miles south of Washington, D.C.—has already taken place. Nothing else looks imminent, and that is a disappointment. A man feels cheated if a war does not hold a seat for him.

Constant's first experience of war is also a disappointment. He dodges friendly fire, as Colonel Sulakowski shoots his own troops, and he is looking at punishment for misconduct.

Company B rolls east toward Bristol, Virginia. The Rebs in Bristol have heard what is coming, and the liquor stores been warned. Drinking is avoided till the train gets to Lynchburg, another two hundred miles along. By the time the transport reaches Lynchburg, a number of men have straightened up. The sober group marches to a fairgrounds to drill with other companies. But a hard core holds back, stays in town, and finds seats in a barroom.

Constant's company again climbs aboard. The transport arrives in Richmond, capital of the Confederate States of America. Company B is sent to a depot on the south side of town. Colonel Sulakowski summons an armed band of military police to pull twenty men out of the group, the ones to be prosecuted. The Polish colonel and his superiors decide to break up the unit. Company B is dissolved, and many of its soldiers—the ones who escape arrest—are swept into another battalion. The rest are court-martialed.

At the trial in Richmond, convictions of the worst rioters are swift, and the men are sentenced. They do not face the common punishment for mutiny, hanging. Instead, the sentence is public shaming. The rebels are to have one-half of their scalps shaved clean. And in a public ceremony, they are to be cashiered. They are to have their stripes of rank ripped from their uniforms before being expelled from the army.

Military records say the riotous officers and men "resign." The record of Lieutenant Lecorgne states that he "resigned" the same day his unit is expelled from the Confederate Army. It looks like he was allowed to flee, rather than face prison. During the first week of August, he is kicked out and told to go home to Louisiana.

New Orleans lies a thousand miles southwest of Richmond, Virginia. The usual route would be to take a steamship from the Virginia coast, around the tip of Florida, across the Gulf of Mexico, and up the Mississippi. But the ports are sealed by the Yankee blockade. Constant and his disgraced comrades are taken back to the train, and they retrace their abject journey in practically empty train cars, the transports going to Louisiana to fetch more men. He is home by the end of the summer.

When Constant sees his wife, Gabrielle, she is large and round, eight months pregnant. She must be surprised. He has a haircut that makes him half-bald. Her husband is home, and he is a disappointment. Men disappoint.

Disgrace trails him. The Lecorgnes and the in-laws know, and everybody knows, what has happened. I am sure that many laugh behind his back, or deride him to his face. *Les nègres* know, and as the race philosophers will tell you, blacks laugh louder than anyone. He is a failure as a soldier. His father was a failure, too, as a soldier. It cannot be hard to remember that fifty years back, Yves César Le

Corgne, sailor in Napoleon's navy, made port in New Orleans and quit the French fleet. Of course he did, people say, yet there is a difference. Constant does not desert the service, he is thrown out.

About three weeks after he reaches home, on September 1, Gabrielle gives birth. They name the boy Louis Constant.

Louis Constant Lecorgne is a great-grandfather of mine. My mother used to talk about Louis Constant, her grandfather, whom she knew well. He became a carpenter, like his father, and then a contractor, building houses in uptown New Orleans. My mother lived in the same house with Louis Constant when she was a girl, growing up at the edge of Bouligny. Louis was an old man then. He liked his game of bridge. None of this is long ago, when you think of it.

10

The war warms up, people die. But the sugar still comes in from the bayous, and the slave markets are still open. On Esplanade Avenue, in the sale rooms, handlers rub oil on the field hands and cooks to make their skin shine. They hand out jackets and dresses for *les nègres* to wear on the auction platform. Outside, herders line up women and children for sale on the banquette, like living mannequins.

The newspapers are discouraging. The blockade grows at the mouth of the river—ten gunboats, then fifteen. Word comes that the U.S. Navy has intercepted a dozen barges and schooners in a day, seizing their loads of cotton and sugar. In October, Governor Moore issues a proclamation that bans the shipment of cotton to New Orleans, to keep the golden crop out of the hands of the Yankees. The stream of money to the city ceases.

Constant tries to protect his wounded pride. All the men younger than thirty-five have signed up and left. Except his brothers. Yves of God, with his important airs and shirker's job as a recruiter. And brother Joseph, who is camped in town with his battalion, the Thirtieth Louisiana Infantry. Joseph's regiment is assigned to defend the city.

If Constant were to make a show of support for the rebellion, it might be better for him—and for Gabrielle, Numa, and little Louis. If he were to make a gesture, a symbolic act, it might take him off the list of losers and laughingstocks. An opportunity comes. The Confederate States of America wants cash, because the rebellion is expensive. To raise money, the government in Richmond is selling bonds. From family tradition, I learn that Constant and Gabrielle invest a lot of money in the Southern cause. I look at the evidence in property records, and something I find tells me that in fall 1861, Constant puts down everything he has. If the Lecorgnes can sink a big sum into the fight for slavery, and they can let this be known, then the shame of the mutiny, the family stain that sticks to the ship carpenter, might be whitewashed.

Constant has been home just a month. Louis gurgles at Gabrielle's breast. The parents decide they can sell their house to raise cash. They make a deal with a man named Thomas Savage to sell him the house, and then rent it back. On September 28, 1861, Thomas Savage pays $1,500 for the house on Bellecastle and Live Oak streets and the big lot on which it stands. The Lecorgnes stay put, now as tenants, paying rent. They have money left over from the sale of Ovid. Add this to the fat envelope of cash from the house sale, and they can put down a good stake. They will invest in the rebellion, and this may open a path to redemption for the disgraced soldier.

It is important to make a show of paying for the war. In the winter, the rebel government sets up its first funding scheme, a bond issue. The idea is to borrow money from the good white people of the South. New Orleans is the richest city in the Confederacy, and so it is no surprise that nearly half of the war loan, or $6 million in bonds, is raised in New Orleans. Constant and Gabrielle decide to buy.

Downtown near city hall, the bonds can be viewed in banks, spread out on tables. It is money that could soften a family's nest, money that could educate the children. But a patriot has to think of his country. If the rebel army is wanting, the Yankees will soon be at the door. Constant and Gabrielle, once a prosperous young couple, mortgage family and future to the great philosophical and moral truth of the superior race. Now they have no security. Their hope to remain a nice middle-class family is that the South wins the war, the Confederacy pays its debts, and slavery stays alive.

Meanwhile, Yves of God is determined to remain rich. He has no desire to squander his own family's future. Yves of God keeps his money in specie, gold and silver, and does not buy Confederate bonds. Because the rebellion is not a sure thing.

The bombastic name for the Yankee army is the "Grand Army of the Republic." To avoid having to say all of it, and because the fight will decide whether the United States stays in one piece, everyone calls the Northern army "the Union."

In early 1862, General Ulysses S. Grant captures Fort Henry, in Tennessee, and then nearby Fort Donelson. The Union command looks south, down the Mississippi Valley, contemplating New Orleans. In February, Union gunboats take possession of Ship Island, a big sandbar in the Gulf of Mexico, off the state of Mississippi. Ship Island is a stepping-stone to Louisiana. From Ship Island, the Union looks north, again to New Orleans.

The siege of Louisiana takes shape. Two Yankee officers, Captain David Farragut and General Benjamin Butler, arrive at Ship Island and collect their tools. Farragut brings forty vessels fitted with guns, and General Butler an infantry of 10,000.

In April comes a prelude, a slaughter in Tennessee. Far to the north of New Orleans, around a nondescript farm town called Shiloh, 10,000 Yankees meet 10,000 rebels for two days of shooting. The fight kills 3,500 and wounds 16,000. Nothing of this scale has been seen in North America; the entire Mexican War killed 2,000 U.S. soldiers. Black Americans see routine cruelty in the sadism of slavers, but whites have reserved some of their finest viciousness for one another.

The Union claims victory, and for the next few days, trains full of Louisiana soldiers roll down to New Orleans and into the station on Basin Street. The railcars are loaded with the bodies of dead rebels and with the groaning and gangrenous wounded. White families swarm the train station to look for their men, to see the freak sight of the war come home, and to mourn. Constant and Gabrielle may well join the crush on the train platform. They no doubt know men in these units.

The fight at Shiloh is the first strike of the Union campaign to strangle Louisiana and to shut down the rebellion in the Deep South. Ten days after the battle, the Confederate Congress in Richmond hands down the Conscription Act, creating the first army draft. Until now the rebel military has relied on volunteers. The Conscription Act requires uniformed service for white men aged sixteen to thirty-five.

Twenty-nine-year-old Constant is back on the hook with the draft. He must find a way to reenter the war.

Brother Yves of God is a Confederate patriot. But if he joins a fighting unit, he risks losing his nine slaves and his nest egg of $8,000. Fortunately, at thirty-six, he is a year older than the upper age of the call-up. Yves of God can breathe a sigh of relief that he will not be drafted. He remains on light duty, drilling on Lafayette Square during the weekend, recruiting new men.

The Union invasion cannot reach New Orleans by land. The swamps are impassable and the dry causeways that run through them easily blocked. A river route is the only military path. If an army can come down the Mississippi from Tennessee, or a flotilla can travel up the river from the Gulf of Mexico, the city is a prize.

Half of Louisiana's white men have already left for the war. The defense of New Orleans consists in two forts that lie downriver, plus three thousand men in the Thirtieth Louisiana, the unit of Second Lieutenant Joseph Lecorgne.

The two forts, St. Philip and Jackson, lie seventy-five miles downstream, facing each other on opposite banks. The Confederate general in command, Mansfield Lovell, orders crews of enslaved to build a boom across the river near the forts. It is a bitter drink for an enslaved man to work on behalf of the rebel defense. But to resist is to face brutal punishment. The crews contrive a string of cypress logs, each sixty feet long, chained together by cables and anchored at points on the river bottom. The line is meant to stop ships coming upstream.

Brother Joseph Lecorgne is stationed in New Orleans, but the main events take place downstream. Constant lies low.

In early April, a flotilla of Union gunboats commanded by Captain David Farragut leaves its launch on Ship Island and enters the mouth of the Mississippi. The flotilla wends upstream, moving at night, lights out. Gunshots come from the levee but no artillery. The Yankee ships reach the forts, St. Philip and Jackson, the last defense of the city against invasion. At night on April 17, the federals pull up abreast of the forts and begin bombardment. The rebels set fire to barges loaded with pitch and timber and send the flaming hulks downstream. Union men hook them with lines and tow the fire rafts to shore to burn out. A Confederate squadron arrives from upstream. The Yankee gunboats kill some sixty rebels. The shooting continues for days, with the federals firing thirteen thousand shells. In the middle of one night, Union scouts cut through the chains of the boom across the river. On the night of April 24, Captain Farragut puts his flotilla in single file to pass in front of the forts. Two hours later, hit by cannons, the Yankees have a hundred dead, and they are steaming to New Orleans.

Whites in New Orleans feel panic, but no source that I can find names what three hundred thousand enslaved people in Louisiana feel, think, or do during these days. Are black people watchful? Is it the end of something? Are African Americans jubilant, or are they worried about reprisal? I imagine it is all of these things.

From Ship Island, in the gulf, the army of General Benjamin Butler, numbering fifteen thousand, ships out toward the city.

The city government gives orders to merchants to destroy the goods in the warehouses to keep them out of enemy hands. Storerooms are emptied onto the street and made into bonfires. Arson teams sent out by the mayor burn fifteen thousand bales of cotton that lie strewn along the levee. Gangs board empty steamboats, set them on fire, cut their moorings, and send them downstream.

There is no evidence Constant joins the marauding. But as a soldier from a delinquent unit, the ill-fated Company B, capable of menace, Constant is comfortable in the role. He is available to plunder and knows what is required.

On April 25, in a rainstorm, the city watches the Union fleet pull up and drop anchor. The level of the river is higher than the streets of the city. Captain Farragut points cannons down at the *Vieux Carré*. Joseph Lecorgne's superior, General Lovell, the Confederate commander, gives the order to his troops to evacuate the city and take what supplies they can carry. The Thirtieth Louisiana packs ordnance, stores, and the city's archives. Joseph Lecorgne helps to load the trains.

The regiment makes its way to the station, boarding the same boxcars that brought in the dead from Shiloh. Constant and Yves of God must say goodbye to their younger brother, then Joseph is gone.

His train heads toward Camp Moore, a military depot eighty miles north.

The mayor surrenders New Orleans on April 29.

For Constant, it is an occasion for disgust. It is also the day after his thirtieth birthday. The invaders run the United States flag up the pole in front of the main federal building, the U.S. Mint, where metal currency was once stamped before the war.

General Butler's waterlogged army arrives after dark on May 1. The Grand Army of the Republic enters the city, marching in thousands behind a drum corps that plays "Yankee Doodle." They meet jeering and curses from gangs, spitting and high noses from white women. They hear people yell at them that the sooner the Yankees die from Yellow Jack, the better.

I can see Constant in the mob. I cannot see Gabrielle. She may be nursing, she may not be such a rebel as her husband. The week New Orleans is occupied, the little boy Louis Constant is eight months old. Caroline-the-mulatress hovers over him.

Most whites are furious at the rebel military. Most blacks, I think, are the reverse—gleeful might describe it—but unsure about what is coming. It is a season of revulsion for the Lecorgnes and one hundred thousand other whites. It is jubilee, maybe, for the city's twenty-five thousand slaves.

For the first time in 150 years, the auction houses empty their jails, and the slave traders cannot be found.

These are some of the thoughts good Creoles like the Lecorgnes might have—

The Yankees are godless and despicable. All you need to know can be seen in the eyes of the blacks. Les nègres are happy, and so are the gens de couleur. And now we fall under the heel of the race traitors.

Most of General Benjamin Butler's troops camp outside of town, but 2,500 patrol the streets, where crowds of whites heckle them. Butler is irritated that white women are among those who show their contempt. When Union soldiers step onto the sidewalk, women pull tight their bareges, the long scarves on their heads, step off the banquette, and show their backsides. Two weeks into the occupation, a white woman spits in the faces of two officers, and Butler issues General Order No. 28, the so-called Woman Order.

> As the officers and soldiers of the United States have been subject to repeated insults from the women (calling themselves ladies) of New Orleans, in return for the most scrupulous noninterference and courtesy on our part, it is ordered that hereafter when any female shall, by word, gesture or movement, insult or show contempt for any officer or soldier of the United States, she shall be regarded and held liable to be treated as a woman of the town plying her avocation.

Most white women of the city do not wish to be likened to prostitutes. Newspapers cry outrage, calling the decree an invitation to rape. Resentment washes through town, and fear. It is a rhetorical coup: in one paragraph, the Yankee general intimidates tens of thousands. The Woman Order becomes national news, then international, with newspapers in Europe running stories.

And the drama has a familiar racial smell. Far from the streets of the *Vieux Carré*, in distant London, the British prime minister Viscount Palmerston denounces General Butler for his attack on the white tribe. Rising in the House of Commons, Palmerston says that the Woman Order in New Orleans is a disgrace. "All good English stock must blush to think such an act has been committed by one belonging to the Anglo-Saxon race," says the prime minister.

Gabrielle Duchemin does not write down her feelings, or if she does, no papers survive. But a woman whom Gabrielle resembles does write some things, in a diary. Her name is Julia Le Grand, and she lives on Prytania Street, at the edge of Bouligny. Julia Le Grand was raised on her father's plantation in Mississippi, Millican's Bend, and at the age of thirty-three, she runs a school for white girls in New Orleans.

"I do hate those bloody wretches who have made war upon us," Le Grand writes. "Theirs is a most cowardly struggle—and I glory in our Southern chivalry."

Julia Le Grand is of French descent, like Gabrielle, though seven years older. And like Gabrielle, she was brought to New Orleans in childhood. Both women are white slaveholders; each lives in comfort but not luxury. Each sees the world from a house in the same *faubourg*.

"It is rumored that we are to have a negro insurrection," Le Grand says, voicing a fear that runs through the white world. The Yankees are "inciting them by every means to rise up and slay their masters. Some of the Federals preach to the negroes in the churches, calling on them to sweep us away forever. I feel no fear, but many are in great alarm. It may come at last. Fires are frequent and it is feared that incendiaries [arsonists] are at work."

Le Grand points out, and I think Gabrielle would say the same, that in the presence of black people, the Yankees are not the loving souls that many Northerners believe themselves to be.

"The generality of the Yankee soldiers hate the negroes and subject them to great abuse whenever they can," Le Grand says. "This poor silly race has been made a tool of, enticed from their good homes, and induced to insult their masters. They now lie about, destitute and miserable, without refuge and without hope."

Gabrielle and Constant do not regret they sold their man Ovid. He brought them a windfall, now sunk into Confederate bonds. Ovid lives across town, where he works for the family of Valsin Gourdain. Gabrielle and Constant do not regret that they sold Ovid, especially because he is suddenly worthless to the Gourdains.

Caroline-the-mulatress is the Lecorgnes' last worker, their final slave. She must wonder, is it time to leave?

Whites normally fear a black uprising. The invasion brings a reversal of expectations, as the Union Army worries about a white uprising. General Butler bans all public gatherings but church services. No more than three whites are allowed to meet on the streets.

The invaders control New Orleans and its swamps, a radius of twenty miles. And they control the river, as far north as Baton Rouge. Outside of town, the rebels have rural, wet Louisiana—the Acadian parishes in the southwest. Rebels own dry parts, too, the cotton parishes north of Baton Rouge. A rebel camp appears a hundred miles northwest of New Orleans, in the French-speaking town of New Iberia. There, a few hundred men retrench under the Confederate commander General John Pratt. Some come in after the evacuation of the Thirtieth Regiment, though not Joseph Lecorgne, who is sent east. General Pratt wants more soldiers to sneak out of the occupied areas and regroup on the rebel side. He writes a one-paragraph plea, gives it a headline, "Militia Men," and sends the bulletin to a printer. When one thousand sheets come back to hand, Pratt gets them smuggled into New Orleans, where they are spread around—

"The country is not yet lost. The enemy may be checked and the insolent invaders of our soil will be ignominiously driven back from where they came.... Let every true and patriotic man capable of bearing arms rush to fight and all will be safe. There is no alternative. —John G. Pratt."

Whites in New Orleans pass the message hand to hand, like pornography. If a Union soldier finds it, reprisal comes. Constant gets his hands on one of Pratt's fliers. At least I imagine this is true, because his next step is to try to get to New Iberia. He will rejoin the fight there, and go rebel again.

The Yankee general Benjamin Butler is bald, squat, and orotund. He has a face that looks like a bullfrog's. The general hangs a man accused of pulling down the U.S. flag, a deed that gives him a nickname, "Beast Butler." Having made a martyr, Beast Butler raises the pressure. He orders all white men in the city to take a loyalty oath to the United States or to register with the Union Army as an "enemy of the state." The U.S. Congress passes the Confiscation Act in 1861 and follows it with a stronger law in 1862. If whites in the occupied areas do not declare loyalty by signing an oath, the hammer falls. The

Union can seize a house, a bank account, a piece of land. Fearing confiscation, almost all whites in the city, upwards of seventy thousand, put their names to a piece of paper that states they will be nice to the blacks, from now on—

"I solemnly swear in the presence of Almighty God that I will . . . faithfully support all acts of Congress passed during the existing rebellion with reference to slaves . . . so help me God." At this point, enslaved people remain slaves.

The Yankee army is "Anglo-Saxon," like the rebel government it replaces. Beast Butler does not ask for a loyalty oath from the enslaved, because he knows every person of color prefers the Union Anglo-Saxon to the rebel. The plantations north and west of the city, where eighty percent of the state's black people live, are in rebel hands. At night, thousands of workers escape them. They head for the city and its Union forts. Camp Parapet, seven miles upriver from New Orleans, is one; Fort Jackson, just downriver, another. By fall, ten thousand black people have freed themselves by stealing away from the bayous. At Parapet and Jackson, they are refugees. Union commanders put black people to work, digging trenches and cleaning tents, cooking for white soldiers and building fortifications. In return, they have housing, food, and pay of about $10 per month. The wages must stun the thousands who free themselves. None has ever been paid for work.

At the end of summer 1862, Beast Butler tells the banks in New Orleans to stop circulating Confederate money. He also tells them to burn their rebel bonds. When that happens, Constant and Gabrielle's status as people of means suddenly disappears. Deep in debt to the Southern cause, they watch their money vanish.

Fearing a guerrilla movement, Butler orders citizens to surrender their firearms, and the Yankees start to collect guns that whites have at home. Constant probably sees this as theft. When a man gives up his gun, he feels the clothing being pulled off his body.

The Yankees keep coming. In Maryland, along Antietam Creek, near the Potomac River, two armies like giant beasts turn the water red. In the Battle of Antietam, more than five thousand men are killed in one day, September 17. The scale of killing is the highest for a twenty-four-hour period in any U.S. war, before or since. Constant knows from newspapers about the slaughter. He knows that some of his comrades, men from the Fourteenth Louisiana, are among the dead.

The slaughter is taken as a Union victory. It opens the door for Abraham Lincoln to make an announcement. After Antietam, the White House issues a draft of a document called the Emancipation Proclamation. It promises a mass act of freedom on January 1. The text circulates in the newspapers, and it is a little astonishing. Despite decades of agitation by abolitionists, few expect to see black people, in this life, walk out of enslavement. President Lincoln, when he writes the Proclamation, adds a sweetener for Southern rebels. It is a promise of compensation, money for people. If slaveholders release their workers, they will receive payment, reimbursement for human property.

At least one man in science, Louis Agassiz, the natural historian at Harvard, is worried by the idea of emancipation. Agassiz is one of the American tribunes of race thought. He holds tight to the theory of multiple evolution, the idea that races are different species and must be seen in rank. Agassiz writes to the American Freedmen's Inquiry Commission, set up by Lincoln with the Emancipation Proclamation. The scientist wants to warn about the dangers of freedom for the tribe or species of black people.

"Social equality I deem at all time impracticable . . . flowing from the character of the negro race," Agassiz says. Blacks are "indolent, playful, sensuous, imitative, subservient, good natured, versatile, unsteady in their purpose, devoted, affectionate, in everything unlike other races, they may but be compared to children, grown in the stature of adults while retaining a childlike mind."

Louis Agassiz says he is especially worried about interracial, or interspecies, sex—

"The production of halfbreeds is as much a sin against nature, as incest in a civilized community. . . . Far from presenting to me a natural solution of our difficulties, the idea of amalgamation is . . . a perversion of every natural sentiment."

For Constant, the news that enslaved people might be free if the

South loses is the worst insult, unthinkable and possibly as disgusting as it is for the distinguished scientist. The Lecorgnes have lost too much already. Constant still has one worker, and his siblings hold another ten or twelve people. And there is no earthly reason for a government to take away a man's property.

The Emancipation Proclamation has a loophole. It frees people only in areas of the South that are in rebellion at the time it is issued. Areas occupied by the Union Army are exempt. Which means that for now, it is symbolic and unenforceable. In Louisiana, rebels will not voluntarily free the 250,000 black people who live behind Confederate lines, and the 50,000 behind Union lines remain enslaved.

Caroline, the Lecorgnes' last slave, is twenty. I imagine that when she hears of the freedom plan, she wonders hard what will come. It is not likely the Lecorgnes will let her go. Maybe that line in Gombo runs in her mind: *Ça va rivé dans semaine quatte zheudis*, "That will come to pass in a week with four Thursdays."

Enter now two men of color. One is Paul Trévigne, the other, Nelson Fouché. Paul Trévigne is an educator, a free African American, and prosperous. For twenty years he has been teaching at a school for Creoles of color. In September 1862, Trévigne starts to publish a small weekly newspaper. He calls it *L'Union*, "The Union." The paper is in French, and the first issue appears soon after the Proclamation. Trévigne hires a Creole of color, Nelson Fouché, as editor.

Les Cenelles, the poetry collection, is a birthplace of black American verse. *L'Union* is the birth of African American journalism in the South, the first "black newspaper" south of Virginia. It is a beginning for black public speech. The presence of the U.S. Army makes it possible that Paul Trévigne and Nelson Fouché can publish anything at all. New Orleans is occupied, and in the absence of the Yankees, the white city would not allow a black man to print anything but gentle poetry. A black newspaper would be torched.

The so-called Native Guards, people of color who sign on with the Confederacy, come out of hiding. A Union soldier on every street corner means the game of pretend is over. Officers from the Native Guards pay a visit to General Butler and ask whether their company might be useful to the occupation.

Beast Butler likes the idea. He wants to recruit black men as Yankee soldiers. At the end of September, about one thousand *gens de couleur* are mustered for the Union—the First Regiment Louisiana Native Guards. That is their Yankee name, but they call themselves something different—*Chasseurs d'Afrique*, African Hunters. The name nods both at their blackness and at their identification with France.

The *Chasseurs d'Afrique* are a break in the mold, one of the first black regiments in the U.S. Army. They are paid the same as white soldiers. Eventually Louisiana will send twenty-four thousand blacks in uniform to fight for the Union, or about half of the black male population of military age.

Constant plans his return to the fight. It is one mess after another, and the *Chasseurs d'Afrique* are the last insult. Black soldiers who change sides prove that the most devious of fighters are niggers.

He has a friend in New Orleans named Charles Gauthier, whose family runs a brick manufactory just downriver from Bouligny. At twenty-four, Gauthier is younger, but he and Constant have something in common. Gauthier also has a botched tour in the war. He enlists in the Thirtieth Regiment, Joseph Lecorgne's unit. Although Joseph escapes when the Yankees come, Gauthier's company is captured, and he spends time in a prison camp. When Beast Butler orders the release of the rebels, Gauthier is paroled and goes home in shame.

Gauthier and Constant share frustrations. They talk about the war, and they talk more about the war, until one day, they disappear. Sometime in October, Gauthier and Constant say goodbye to their wives and children, and they sneak out of town. They cross Yankee lines and break out of New Orleans together.

I remember my Aunt Maud on this story. Her version of the tale makes it an adventure. She writes about it in one of her family history ledgers. What she says sounds like this.

—My grandfather, Constant Lecorgne, did not like the first company he enlisted in. Not very much. He had a bad time of it, and he resigned. Eventually he joined another unit. In the middle of the war, he walked up the Mississippi levee for fifty or a hundred miles and made his way to another company, where he signed up again. He liked that unit better, so he stayed till the end of the war.

Aunt Maud's story overlooks the mutiny, the court-martial, the haircut. But she is right about the rest.

Constant and Charles Gauthier leave the city at night. The levee along the Mississippi is the only way north; the roads leaving town are guarded and patrolled. A few miles upriver, hard by the levee, lies the federal bulwark, Camp Parapet. The Yankee fortress is a garrison and a giant refugee camp for slaves, with several thousand people living in a tent city. Constant and Charles have to avoid Camp Parapet, so they must cross the river to the western bank. They take a ferry, or maybe steal a boat. On the west bank of the Mississippi, they resume walking north, atop the levee.

Their destination is New Iberia, the place where General John Pratt, author of the call-up plea ("there is no alternative"), sits in a tent-and-campfire village, gathering in a resistance army. If they could fly to it, New Iberia would lie one hundred miles west of New Orleans. But the town is really two hundred miles by swerving waterways and boot steps down meandering swamp paths.

Charles and Constant are runaways. If they were enslaved, there would be advertisements about the escape, patrols to capture them, and a price on their heads.

They walk night and day, until the town of Donaldsonville, probably, a distance of sixty miles, where they turn south. In Donaldsonville, they find a nasty scene. A month earlier, the Union sends gunboats up the river to bombard the town, and then burn it. The scorched earth is retaliation against rebel snipers who have been hiding here and shooting at Yankee boats.

Western Louisiana counts four big streams that run north to south: Bayou Lafourche, Tensas Bayou, the Atchafalaya River, and Bayou Teche. Go west from New Orleans and you cross the four waterways one after another. These slender and sometimes hidden rivers cut through swamps, open into rich bottomland, and return to swamps.

At Donaldsonville, on the Mississippi, Constant and Gauthier reach the first stream, Bayou Lafourche, and turn south to follow the current. The men get into a boat, borrowed or paid, to ease down the bayou. Bayou Lafourche is family ground for Constant. His mother was born on a plantation here, so he knows his way through the half land, half muck of the watershed. They come to a canal that leaves the bayou and cuts west through the swamp, ending at a place called Attakapas Landing. Here it is back on foot. A few miles through woods, then into the water again. The streams meander and shrink. Constant and Gauthier probably find themselves in a canoe. In Louisiana, a canoe is a "pirogue," a dugout log made for shallows. Edging a pirogue along the creeks, the runaways come to Tensas Bayou, where they trudge again a few miles through mud, then cross over the Atchafalaya River, thread down more streams and rivulets, get up onto land, and finally reach Bayou Teche.

It is known as "the Teche," a languid, narrow river that winds past a hundred or more sugar plantations. The Teche is the sugar bowl of Louisiana, for its plantations. It is the thickest black belt in the state, home to tens of thousands of enslaved. The rebel camp at New Iberia is huddled on Bayou Teche, and it is seething. Since the call for recruits, the camp is doubled in size, thanks to new joiners and to a rebel commander who just turned up. He is General Richard Taylor, lately fighting in Virginia, called to New Iberia to do the same in Louisiana. General Taylor has orders to make a fresh killing force west of the Mississippi, to fight the Yankees up and down the river, and to try to take back New Orleans.

It is mid-October. Constant and Gauthier look like ghosts as they stumble out of the woods and into the encampment. They have been slogging toward New Iberia for a week or more. They come at the right time. General Taylor wants warm bodies, and his minions are signing anyone who can walk.

There is no record of it, but I imagine a conversation something like this.

—What is your name?

—*Terrance. Terrance Lecorgne.*

—Previous service?

—*None.*

—Terrance Lecorgne, you are now with Company K of the Yellowjackets.

The "Yellowjackets" are the Eighteenth Louisiana Infantry. When Constant and Charles Gauthier join, Gauthier puts his name on the rolls, but Constant does not. Instead, he uses an alias, "Terrance." By this time, the mutiny in the Fourteenth Louisiana is notorious. Confederate commanders do not want the drunks and dregs of Company B, Constant's first unit. The name Terrance Lecorgne appears nowhere on a blacklist, and there are enough Lecorgnes in the service that "Terrance" is a plausible fake. Constant picks the name out of the air and dodges suspicion.

He is assigned to Company K as a sergeant. In his last berth, he was Lieutenant Lecorgne. To enlist as a sergeant means another demotion; it is a fall of six or seven ranks from the middling height of lieutenant to the low shelf of sergeant, just above the grunt's rank, corporal. The long slog from New Orleans is a heroic show of devotion to the cause, and another man might have parlayed it into an officer's status. But Terrance Lecorgne is a man who makes a poor impression.

A pattern is visible. Through friends and family, Constant finds his way into a nice position, one with authority—as captain or lieutenant, as a recruitment officer or sheriff's deputy. But his superiors find a man different from the one they thought they had in hand.

Two weeks later, Sergeant Terrance Lecorgne goes into battle, his first. It takes place around a town called Labadieville. Beast Butler, down in New Orleans, wants to extend federal control in the state. Butler plans an invasion along Bayou Lafourche, the plantation nest closest to the city and the homeplace of Sergeant Terrance's mother, Marguerite. Butler names a commander, a thirty-year-old German immigrant, Brigadier General Godfrey Weitzel. The plan is for Weitzel to take a flotilla up the Mississippi, seize the town of Donaldsonville at the mouth of Lafourche, then move down the bayou, destroying its rice and sugar plantations and unlocking the chains of slavery from thousands. Four gunboats and three thousand men make up the force. Some of the infantry are the *Chasseurs d'Afrique*, or First Regiment Louisiana Native Guards, the first black unit in the federal army. It is their first fight, too.

Sergeant Terrance and the Yellowjackets cannot believe the vileness of the facts. A German interloper is set to plunder their French homeland. And worse, armed blacks are going to assist.

Union troops reach Donaldsonville on October 24. Hearing of the landing, the Yellowjackets make their way to the town of Thibodaux, far down the Lafourche stream. Two French Creoles command the rebels—Alfred Mouton, a man popular with rank and file, and Leopold Armant, a highborn twenty-seven-year-old colonel. Sergeant Terrance shares the French language with these men but little else. He is well below them, socially as well as mentally.

It is at the peak of sugar grinding season on Bayou Lafourche. Every worker on every plantation is cutting sugarcane, feeding it into the stone teeth of grinding machines, and boiling the sludge in churning cauldrons to make cane juice. Up and down the bayou, black smoke traces the air from the fires that feed the boil.

The day of the fight, October 27, is supremely cold, with frozen cane in the fields and a coat of ice on the cypress trees. The two thousand Yellowjackets move upstream from Thibodaux toward Labadieville. They stop at a choke point with impassable swamps on one side and the water of Lafourche on the other. Here the Yankees must push through a narrow field. Terrance Lecorgne's Company K is placed at the center of the Confederate line, on a dirt stretch of Texana Road. According to the memoir of one soldier, as the Union column advances down Lafourche, enslaved people abandon the fields, flee the plantations, and join their line.

At about 11:00 a.m., a Union advance squad comes to a wood where Colonel Leopold Armant commands two hundred men, Sergeant Terrance among them. The Yankees attack the rebel line and are met with rifle fire and artillery. Ten men fall dead. Another wave of white Union men is slowed by a thicket.

The black unit, the *Chasseurs d'Afrique*, is a few miles away in another branch of the fight. Sergeant Terrance does not face them. The moment when a black company with guns faces a rebel company with him in the ranks will come, but not today.

The Yankees fire artillery, Colonel Armant's right flank disintegrates, and the fight turns against the rebels, shot and falling. A Union charge, Armant's line breaks and runs. Sergeant Terrance's company flees "like panic-stricken sheep," as one soldier who witnesses the scene puts it.

Union troops chase the retreating Yellowjackets for miles. By the next day, Company K has lost half of its men, killed, wounded, or captured. But Terrance is unharmed.

The Yellowjackets make their way to the town of Opelousas, one hundred miles northwest. Then they withdraw another seventy miles, to Alexandria, Louisiana. A Yankee corps follows them, until finally, hunted like prey, the Yellowjackets retreat to Natchitoches, sixty miles further north.

The Union goaded him back into the war, now *les nègres* chase Sergeant Terrance from pillar to post.

The Emancipation Proclamation is affirmed January 1, 1863, with a big change. The line about money is gone. Congress will not pay off slaveholders. Washington does not care to ransom four million captives.

In New Orleans, the Lecorgne women hold things together. Constant's younger sister, Eliza, goes to work as a schoolteacher. She is thirty and unmarried, and she lives with Yves of God. Eliza gets a job teaching in the boys' department of the public schools in the city's Second Ward, two miles east of Bouligny. She is one of twelve women in the neighborhood who teach, all of them white, all unmarried but one. Eliza earns $360 per year, about fifty percent more than the income she can take in by renting out her enslaved cook, thirty-eight-year-old Rachel.

New Orleans has no fewer than 140 private secondary schools, plus 44 public schools—for whites. None admits blacks or *gens de couleur*. Half of white children attend public schools, half attend private academies or parochial schools run by the church. People of color who have money enough send their children to be educated in a convent for black nuns downtown, for good fees. The corridor to literacy for nonwhites is narrow.

Eliza Lecorgne's students are white, and I imagine she would not have it otherwise. When Eliza starts teaching, the Yankee occupiers are trying to smash open the education system, starting seven new public schools for blacks. By October 1863, New Orleans has 1,700 black students enrolled, with 20 teachers on staff. Most of the teachers are white women from the handful of families that support the Union.

Most whites ostracize them. Eliza Lecorgne does not care to be ostracized, and she does not care to teach pickaninnies.

Constant's twenty-seven-year-old wife, Gabrielle Duchemin, keeps the faith. Her husband is off in the fight. Her sons, Louis and Numa, are one and four years old. With Ovid gone, she leans on Caroline.

Gabrielle watches the city fill up with blacks from the parishes, and the diarist Julia Le Grand writes down thoughts—

"The suburbs and odd places in and about this city are crowded with a class of negroes never seen until the Federals came here, a class whose only support is theft and whose only occupation is strolling the streets, insulting white people, and living in the sun," says Le Grand. "This is really the negro idea of liberty."

It is a disaster, as the women see it. Their right-thinking men are gone, the ghastly Yankees are in the streets, and the repellent blacks fill the gaps.

Butler issues more abuse. He lets black people testify in court against white people, for the first time, and he integrates public transportation. There had been separate streetcars for people of color, ones painted with a big red star that is visible from a block away. Butler does away with the "star cars."

At a distance of 150 years, all of it seems mild, obvious, normal, and correct. To Gabrielle and family, it is one abomination after another.

I hear the mind of Gabrielle in the thoughts of Julia Le Grand—

"I once was as great an abolitionist as any in the North and in my unthinking fancy placed black and white upon the same plane. My sympathies blinded me. My experience with negroes has altered my way of thinking and reasoning. It was when we owned them in numbers that I thought they ought to be free, and now I think they are not fit for freedom."

The darkies walk the streets, and the white women commiserate. Good women take up the program of race thinking where the men left it off. Julia Le Grand shares her philosophy of color, one that is spun in rooms of thought much like the ones Gabrielle inhabits.

The negro is the only race which labor does not degrade. We all know that white men and women are very different. The white race is distorted by labor; hair, features, complexion and shape all tell the tale of hardship and labor. Not so with the negro; they live so easily. White men generally struggle up to something higher, but not so the black man. They have no cares but physical ones and will not have for generations to come, if ever. The free black man is scarcely a higher animal. He has sensation, but his sensibility is not well awakened; he does not love or respect the social ties. His wild instincts are yet moving his coarse blood; he is servile if mastered, and brutal if given license; he cannot, either by force or persuasion, be imbued with a reverence for truth.

The house on Bellecastle needs cleaning. Caroline is told to clean it. Julia Le Grand wraps her theory of race with musings about the difference between species, and how each must find the proper level—

"What place is there in the scale of humanity but one of subjection for such a race as blacks? Slavery indeed cannot be considered a good school for the white man, but it should be remembered that we found these people mere animals in Africa."

There is at least one thing in her diary, a lament, which sounds about right. "America seems perishing of madness," she says.

Sergeant Terrance Lecorgne spends two-and-a-half years with the Eighteenth Regiment. He and the Yellowjackets swarm around the state, going from fight to fight in a moving hell. They march over cratered and washed-out roads, often underfed, cut off from supplies, and underdressed. Occasionally their supply lines work, or they empty a smokehouse full of a farmer's meat and leave a piece of paper with a word, "Requisitioned." Sometimes the numbers of the Eighteenth go up to nine hundred; then they drop to seven hundred when the corps passes a town that men call home, and the desertion begins.

In January 1863, Sergeant Terrance and the Eighteenth cease their wandering and return to camp. They make winter quarters at a place called Fausse Pointe. There is not much firm land around the spongy ground at "False Point." The camp lies just east of New Iberia on Bayou Chêne, Oak Bayou. A hundred miles west of New Orleans, Bayou Chêne is out of reach of the Yankees. The Yellowjackets take February and March to sit still.

The Yellowjackets call their winter encampment "Qui Vive" (Those Who Live), a redoubt in the Atchafalaya Swamp. Qui Vive has amenities, like mail. Despite the war, the post still comes up the Atchafalaya River. Despite the war, a man can get a letter to his wife, who waits behind enemy lines in New Orleans, and he can get a letter back.

Colonel Alfred Mouton, Creole commander of the Yellowjackets, wants to please his men. He arranges for wives to come visit—at least wives with money to pay the way. Colonel Mouton is keen to bring wives to Qui Vive in hopes of cutting down on prostitutes, the camp amenity that causes more problems than it solves.

In New Orleans, Gabrielle hears word from her husband, and she makes arrangements. It is easy for a woman to get out of the occupied city. A rebel woman does not alarm the Yankees as much as a man. Gabrielle leaves her children with family, books passage to Atchafalaya, and leaves Caroline alone.

Qui Vive lies deep in Acadian Louisiana, in the watery west of the state. Gabrielle boards a steamer. The boat powers down the Mississippi, out into the Gulf of Mexico. I imagine other wives of soldiers on the deck with Gabrielle. A starboard turn, and the steamer edges along the Gulf coast as far as the mouth of the Atchafalaya River. Turning north into the river, the boat pushes upstream, fighting the flow as far as Bayou Chêne. Gabrielle may get off here and board a flatboat, because the Chêne is shallow. A portside turn into the bayou and a straight run to Fausse Pointe.

Gabrielle steps off. She is with him again, her fighting man, in the tents of the camp. Accommodations are thin, but she and Sergeant Terrance find a way to be alone. Her husband must know from her letters—Gabrielle is enceinte, pregnant. They made the baby in New Orleans last September, when Constant came home from the mutiny and court-martial. They must talk about it, and they must plan. Gabrielle is seven months along. She can deliver with her husband at her side. As armies clash, a soldier and his wife reunite, and together they can be redeemed by a birth.

The Eighteenth Louisiana has not moved in two months. From New Orleans comes word that the Union is sending gunboats and thousands of men up Bayou Teche, to the east. If the Yellowjackets do not cut them off, the Yankees will slice through the state. The war warms up, the first fight is expected in days. It is a pastoral picture, two parents who plan to share a birth in wartime, and now it dims. Gabrielle and Sergeant Terrance improvise. They make their way a few miles north, up to the town of St. Martinville. Compared with other places, St. Martinville, one of the old and pretty French towns, is an island of calm. Here are boardinghouses and doctors, churches and priests, slave nurses and midwives. Gabrielle is to have the baby in St. Martinville, while Terrance goes back to the front.

In April 1863, Gabrielle is thirty-nine weeks pregnant, in a war zone with her husband. And then she is alone in St. Martinville.

Sergeant Terrance leaves to join the Yellowjackets. Colonel Alfred Mouton, the rebel commander, has pulled together four thousand men for the battle, and still he is outnumbered. The rebels line up along the east bank of Bayou Teche at a garrison called Fort Bisland. Sergeant Terrance takes his position. Here the rebels will stop the Yankee advance up the bayou. As they wait for the attack, the Yellowjackets receive an unexpected gift. The command has arranged a surprise delivery, a cargo of fresh uniforms. It is the first set of new clothes that many have had in a year. The uniforms go on their backs, and they look like new recruits.

The fresh-looking regiment prepares to die. On April 12, the Yankees arrive, with artillery. In twenty-four hours, the rebels lose 450 in dead and wounded. The Union has casualties of 230. Terrance is again untouched.

The next day, the Union swarms Fort Bisland. About noon, Company H of the Yellowjackets is surrounded and surrenders. Terrance's unit, Company K, is pushed into the cypress woods beside the fort, where some of them fight hand to hand, with fixed bayonets. When night falls, Colonel Mouton sees that a Union company has reached the back of the fort and that his men are going to be cut off. He orders them out. Terrance flees with his company to the town of Franklin, five miles upstream. He survives another fight in which he sees many of his comrades killed.

A few miles north, in St. Martinville, Gabrielle goes into labor. The Yellowjackets make a slog back to camp. They arrive at Qui Vive on April 15.

On the same day in St. Martinville, a midwife helps Gabrielle through the birth. She delivers a little girl. Gabrielle has two young sons, Numa and Louis. Her daughter Mathilde is two years dead. The girl is her fourth child. Making his way from Qui Vive to St. Martinville, Terrance is one day late to his wife's childbed. I imagine Gabrielle waits until he arrives before the two decide on the name for the baby. He turns up unscathed, a blessing for his wife. The parents call the girl Marie Estelle.

They have a few days with their newborn. They take her to be christened. Estelle is baptized at St. Martin de Tours, a drafty and majestic church in the middle of St. Martinville. A week later, Sergeant Terrance is called back to the fight, and he is gone.

Gabrielle retraces her steps to New Orleans, Estelle at her breast. She and the baby board a steamer downstream, out to the Gulf, and up the Mississippi.

I feel empathy for them. Every discovery about their lives is a little piece of tile, and the bunches of detail collect into a mosaic. Their lives look hard. One child dead at nineteen months, a father who loses his work to war. A woman who crosses enemy lines to be with her man and have their baby, a soldier who pushes through muck and watches hundreds die around him. Their trials are awful. And for what? So that Cousin Camille can keep his slaves at Seven Oaks? So that Sergeant Terrance can go home to see Caroline-the-mulatress?

In spring 1863, the Yankees get approval from Washington to enlist blacks in Louisiana. The *Chasseurs d'Afrique* are already in uniform, but they are only one thousand, a small group. The recruitment comes in like a tide. In six months, the Union Army raises ten thousand black troops in eighteen regiments. Some are former slaves who have fled to the Union side, and some are *gens de couleur.*

The first combat by the recruits is an attack on the town of Port Hudson, just north of Baton Rouge. It is late May, and thirty-two are killed. One of them, Captain André Cailloux, a cigar maker, is taken up as a hero by African Americans in New Orleans. After the Battle of Port Hudson, Creoles of color around Paul Trévigne and his newspaper, *L'Union*, agitate for the right to vote. The occupation army in New Orleans talks about holding an election for governor, sometime soon. The first meetings take place in June 1863 at an auditorium called Economy Hall, and the editor of *L'Union*, Nelson Fouché, serves as chair. At the meeting, several stand up to make the argument that illiterate white men can sign a voting register with an X and cast a ballot, but educated Creoles of color, like the martyred Captain André Cailloux, and like the poets who contribute to *Les Cenelles*, are prohibited from voting. It is unfair.

At the rally, one of the colored soldiers in the crowd, Captain Pinckney Pinchback, puts the argument plain. "We do not ask for social equality, and do not expect it," Pinchback says, "but we demand political rights." Outside of the Yankee-held part of the state, in rebel or Confederate Louisiana, enslaved people are still captive workers. Rebel whites are hearing none of the Emancipation Proclamation. Within occupied New Orleans (and this part may sound weird), enslaved people also remain slaves. But with the Union Army running things, the policing of black people is a lot less harsh, and everybody knows the locks are eventually coming off.

I do not know exactly when it happens, but it appears that Gabrielle reaches the city and arrives at the Lecorgne house on Bellecastle, where she finds that Caroline is gone. Circumstantial evidence tells the story. Caroline disappears from the record during the war. It seems she uses the absence of "Missus Lecorgne" and the presence of the Yankee army as two good reasons to leave. She merely follows the example of thousands in New Orleans who do the same. Caroline is not heard from again.

When Gabrielle finds that her indispensable woman of color has fled, the diarist in the neighborhood, Julia Le Grand, again opens a window onto her mind—

"A relative saw my slave in the street today. She did not speak but watched her closely. She left during the summer, having stolen money from the box. We had so spoiled her that she would not take the trouble to answer unless she pleased. She pouted always, and passed all of her time in the street. She had been with us a long time and was consequently associated with much that is past and dear."

Caroline, at twenty-one, has worked for Gabrielle and her husband three years before she vanishes.

"The day she ran away was as unhappy a one as I ever passed," Julia Le Grand says about her own experience as a white mistress. "We made every effort to bring her up as a high-toned woman, but she preferred lying to confidence, stealing to asking, and a life of vagrancy to a comfortable and respectable one. I have learned this lesson— negroes only respect those they fear."

If she does what many enslaved in the city do, Caroline leaves and walks upstream on the levee for five miles, as far as Camp Parapet. There, a general named John Phelps runs the U.S. Army camp. Phelps is a white soldier who is antislavery, which makes him more militant than most of his Union comrades. He keeps the camp gate open for "runaways," people who emancipate themselves. The army calls the refugees who come to Camp Parapet "contraband," as in pilfered property. And Parapet is one of the first "contraband camps."

Sergeant Terrance and his comrades march for months, covering hundreds of miles, crisscrossing the state. They pass through towns with Old World names, like Alexandria and Jena; towns with Native American names, like Coushatta and Natchitoches; towns named for politicians, like Winnsboro and Monroe. One officer on the march describes the path of the Yellowjackets as "incomprehensible wandering." The new clothes from Fort Bisland come to grief. In June, an officer in another unit sees the men and says that "they have lost their clothing and their tents, and their shoes have worn out. Many have no pants, others no shirts."

After one skirmish near the town of Brashear City, Terrance's unit seizes a store of Yankee uniforms. They discard their tattered gray and put on the dark blue. Now they must be careful not to get shot by their own side. In 1864, rebel companies in a state of desperation, like this one, are typical. For Sergeant Terrance, the war moves in sick rhythms. A day of terror, then weeks of boredom. A ten-mile march to a plantation, corn scraps in a barn for dinner. A morning bath in a stream, an afternoon of fear, and a night under tarred canvas in rain.

In November, the Yellowjackets go up the Atchafalaya River to the town of Alexandria, on the Red River. In December, they leave for Monroe, one hundred miles farther north. On New Year's Day 1864, the men march up the frozen Ouachita River toward Monroe. "For many of the men it is the first time they have ever set foot on ice," a veteran remembers. Barefoot soldiers leave bloody footprints as they cross the frozen ground. When a Confederate supply train rattles past, bound for another camp, General Alfred Mouton confiscates it for his suffering men. When they reach Monroe, Terrance and the others build cabins to make winter camp. Sergeant Terrance's hand in carpentry and millwork make the quarters tight and dry.

In the spring, three hundred miles northwest of New Orleans, a Yankee army numbering thirty thousand moves along the Red River, a tributary to the Mississippi. The Eighteenth Regiment marches in to meet them. On April 8, the Yellowjackets approach the village of Mansfield and a cotton farm known as Moss plantation. The place has a columned mansion in Greek Revival style and a complement of slave cabins.

By this time, General Alfred Mouton's brigade is broken. Of 2,200 men once in his command, 760 have been killed or wounded. The rest prepare to face the Yankees in the bloodiest campaign of the war in Louisiana.

At Moss plantation, the Yellowjackets trade back-and-forth charges with the Union, and the first dozen fall dead. Two hours into the fight, Mouton throws his forces against the enemy center. He chooses Sergeant Terrance's unit to make the charge and tells them that as commander, Mouton himself will lead it. For this kind of thing, Mouton is a hero to his men. The attack turns into slaughter. The Union line gives way in the charge, but Colonel Leopold Armant, commander of a pair of French companies, is killed. The rebel rank and file turns disgusted and angry. Some Yankees drop their rifles, some flee, some try to surrender. The charge continues, and mayhem with it. A Yankee soldier shoots General Mouton off his horse, dead. The rebels now have two of their commanders motionless on the ground. The rebels are enraged, especially the Frenchmen.

The Yellowjackets begin to kill the surrendered and fleeing Yankees. When all is done at Moss plantation, the Eighteenth Regiment counts 19 of its own dead, 75 wounded, 1 missing. The Union counts 113 killed, 580 wounded, and 1,540 captured or missing.

Paper evidence puts Sergeant Terrance Lecorgne in the middle of the revenge killing. He is with his company during the hours and at the location of the highest number of deaths. There is no proof that he shoots captured soldiers, and no sign he does not. Yet he is a veteran of one lawless gang, the soldiers' mutiny.

What is happening to this thirty-two-year-old work-for-hire carpenter? The war gives a man who feels he is abused by *les nègres* a path to cathartic relief by attacking the scapegoats in front of him. It provides a man with a habit of resentment a way to get back his lost pride using the enemy's blood. The war gives the drunken swill of vengeance. It is Constant's first experience of a massacre, and not his last.

I have, like a reflex, a few questions. What would we do, in the impossible event that we lived at that time? How would we act? We would behave differently, of course. Because we fly high above the carpet of ignorance that so obviously covers this man and his comrades. We would make righteous choices, because we share nothing with these people. We live so far from their benighted world. The society they inhabit, the one that puts people in chains, is vicious and stupid. Whereas we are humane. To go and fight for the slave power is a decision of unusual cruelty. To kill captive soldiers in war is an act of sadism. It is what we call a "war crime." Leave aside for the moment that war itself is ordered criminality. Within war, there are crimes more criminal, so-called war crimes. And here is one. We would be different, because we are not capable of this thing.

I look around the life of Constant and find that there are few places from which to observe him that are not above the man and superior to him. There are few places that do not look down upon the past from the height of condescension. It is comforting to glide over history at the moral altitude of the birds. What is wrong with this petty and un-educated failure of a man, this hewer of wood? He clearly hates black people. And we—I mean, we white folks—are more evolved than to wish anything but happiness and wealth for African Americans. If we were alive then, we would do it all differently.

It is a false question, *What would we do?* The self of a white ev-eryman or everywoman, such as can be found in the United States of the twenty-first century, is not a self that appears in the Deep South of the old slave empire. A thought like this—*I would not be a woman like Gabrielle who sells a man like Ovid*—is incoherent. It as-sumes that a modern white woman might be transplanted to another generation, where she makes choices from ethics that have hardly been thought. It supposes we gentle moderns would be among the one in ten thousand who refuse to act in the pattern of an ungentle, early, and malign white supremacist. Can we afford the luxury of this self-portrait?

The promise of the thought experiment, the consolation of what-would-I-do, no-doubt-I-would-do-better, dissolves along the way. I wonder how I would behave in a firefight on a battlefield during the Civil War. The reality is that "I" cannot inhabit the war of Sergeant

Terrance Lecorgne. Only he and other young white Creoles can inhabit it. But here is a different appraisal. Suppose the hypothetical was not impossible, and "I" were such a person, a young white Creole. The chances are better than half that I would shoot captive Yankees as they are rounded up.

12

Camille Zeringue, the enviable Lecorgne cousin, the sugar baron, tries to hold on to comfort at his manse, Seven Oaks. Since the occupation, his cloud of black workers has thinned to a wisp. Two-thirds of the workers on Seven Oaks have walked off. General Benjamin "Beast" Butler has been reassigned to Virginia, and the new commander of the army in New Orleans is another general, Nathaniel Banks. Cousin Camille complains to him.

"After the occupation, a state of tumult and malaise attacked my negroes," he writes Banks in February 1863. Camille's workers leave the plantation and move to the army's refugee site, Camp Parapet. But when the Emancipation Proclamation is announced, in January 1863, most of the seventy workers return to their cabins at Seven Oaks, "anticipating that they would be treated as free and independent," as Camille puts it. Somehow the army makes clear that black people are not free if they happen to be enslaved by planters who claim to be loyal to the Union. Camille has signed the oath, he claims to be loyal. When the workers at Seven Oaks learn this, the same group leaves the plantation again, heading to Camp Parapet. Which is easy to do, since the contraband camp is a fifteen-minute boat trip across the Mississippi.

Camille is disgusted. "It is a fact that *les nègres* are grown children," he tells the army chief. "It is necessary always to direct, surveil, and control them. They live with only the care that they are fed, housed, and cared for when sick. The future doesn't exist for *les nègres*. They live only in the present—to drink, to eat, to sleep, and to maraud."

Gabrielle, across the river in Bouligny, and nursing Marie Estelle, probably sees things like this. Poor Cousin Camille, he is in a bad predicament. It is unfair what they are doing to him. He was the one in the family who did not want secession. Let him keep his coons with their hands on the sugarcane.

An army surveyor comes out to Seven Oaks and writes his report, scribbling on a survey form that "the number of niggers present" on Camille's place is forty, whereas "niggers ran away" number seventy. The surveyor is a Union soldier who is not particularly antislavery.

The enviable Camille, the cousin with all the money, gets his comeuppance. Two weeks after Camille complains to the army, he looks out his front door and into the barrel of a gun.

It is early March. Six of the remaining sugar workers have armed themselves with guns. It is not clear how they acquire their pistols or how they pay for them. Perhaps a sympathetic army officer is involved. The armed guerrillas take themselves to Camille's house, the house with the sixty-foot columns on each of its four sides. The rebels—they are black rebels, this time, and the report does not give their names—shoot into the windows and through the doors of the house. No one is hurt. Perhaps Camille is hiding beneath the stairs. The house is shredded by bullet holes. The men make it plain that they want an audience with Camille, the man who claims to own them and their sisters and brothers and children.

Camille emerges and makes himself available, without enthusiasm. Once they have him, the armed workers say that they will not work and will not leave the place until Camille "gives them their freedom papers," as the report says. Camille begs for time to consider. He talks his way through the ultimatum, saves his own life. I think of his likely words.

—Look around, it is good here. The farm works for everyone. Things are changing. It will be better when the war is over, it will be less hard. About freedom papers, it requires some thought. These things take time.

Fortunately for Camille, the rebels do not shoot, and they leave him to think.

Sergeant Terrance, far off in north Louisiana, does not hear about the events at Seven Oaks. However, if he could see the empty cabins behind the house, if he could witness the hostage taking of Camille, I imagine he would feel a bit of schadenfreude.

Camille Zeringue knows the hairsplitting terms of the Emancipation Proclamation, namely, that enslaved people within the Union lines remain enslaved. The law is on his side. He calls out the U.S. Army. The occupiers are his defenders, they will put down defiant blacks. A Yankee squad rides out to Seven Oaks. In the lead is the Union provost marshal, chief of the military police force. The army comes with officers from the Jefferson Parish Police, local men who are ex-rebels. The police detest the Yankees, who look down on them. The police also detest the black rebels.

The army marshals seize and disarm the six black rebels. They hand the six to the local police. Jefferson Parish lawmen are no friends of abolition. They consult with Camille, and a solution is determined. They will whip the perpetrators for their insolence. The men are stripped and tied to the ground. With a long whip, apparently borrowed from Camille, the police lay on "twenty-five to thirty lashes," according to the army report. Union soldiers in the group stand aside to watch. They are curious. They want to see how the South's Anglo-Saxon does his business.

If this scene were in a novel, it would turn into a moment of revelation and despair. The black men who push back at their confinement, who demand a key to full humanity, freedom papers, discover another false promise. They learn how whiteness must prevail, despite the Proclamation, despite army men come to end the old ways.

That will teach the bastards.

Work resumes at Seven Oaks.

After New Orleans falls, in summer 1862, and after the Emancipation Proclamation of January 1863, the South starts to lose its way through the Civil War. The giant Battle of Gettysburg, Pennsylvania—7,000 dead, 11,000 missing, 34,000 wounded—ends with Union victory on July 3, 1863. Vicksburg, Mississippi, falls to the Yankees the same week, putting all of the Mississippi River in Northern hands. By this time, many in both the North and the South act as though it is a black and white war. In July 1863 in New York City, thousands of white men and some women riot against the Union's military draft, marauding in black neighborhoods for nearly one week and killing hundreds of African Americans. If you put the question, few whites in the North would say they want to fight to free the enslaved. The war is the fault of the blacks, says the workingman, he who is a "wage slave."

At twenty-seven, the youngest of the three brothers, Joseph Lecorgne is a second lieutenant with the Thirtieth Louisiana Regiment, a few ranks above his older brother, "Sergeant Terrance." In three years of fighting, he sees less blood than his middle brother but far more than their older one, Yves of God, the homeboy who escapes the war altogether. Joseph's Civil War is dramatic enough. Black Yankees nearly kill him, and he ends up in a lice-infested prison camp.

It is July 1863, and Sergeant Terrance fights with the Yellowjackets in upstate Louisiana. Joseph, meanwhile, is in Jackson, Mississippi, defending that city against a Union siege. The rebels have lost Vicksburg, fifty miles west. The Thirtieth Louisiana wants to keep Jackson, the state capital. But the Union Army seizes the city in a week, and the rebels flee. Joseph and his regiment escape farther south. Through the fall of 1863, five hundred miles away, big, cruel battles grind at Chattanooga and Knoxville, Tennessee. In the winter, Joseph garrisons at Mobile, Alabama, with his unit, Company F of the Thirtieth. When spring comes in 1864, he and Company F are ordered to Georgia. That is because a giant army under the Union general William T. Sherman has marched out of Tennessee toward Georgia, aiming for Atlanta. Joseph and his comrades pass months of fighting near Atlanta. In July 1864, he is among tens of thousands of rebels who range around southeast of the city, trying to block an invasion. General William T. Sherman has brought his swarming army of 55,000 to take Atlanta, and the fight is a charnel house. Sherman's legion loses 3,600 in dead and wounded, the rebels 5,500. Atlanta is kept from capture, for a time.

Joseph survives several battles untouched and falls back with comrades to a few days of rest. He seems to have the same luck or skill as his brother, Sergeant Terrance, in dodging flak and rifle fire. He misses all of those flying "Minié balls," as bullets are called. Bullets in this war are named for their French inventor, Claude-Étienne Minié.

West of Atlanta, Joseph finds himself in a fight near a chapel, Ezra Church. This time, General Sherman's mob nearly slaughters Joseph's regiment. At Ezra Church, three-fourths of the men in the Thirtieth Louisiana are killed or wounded. But Joseph stays clean. The Yankees can no longer be kept from the city, and what is left of Company F slouches away in a ragged column, heading toward Tennessee. Its officers are dead, and Atlanta burns behind them.

Joseph is married and a father. In New Orleans, his wife, Estelle Daunoy, watches the newspapers and the mails, hoping for good news, which declines to appear. Estelle minds the couple's three-year-old daughter, Alice. The girl has no memory of her father, whom she has not seen for two years. I have to wonder whether Alice and her mother, Estelle, visit Gabrielle and her children. The two war wives, five blocks from each other in Bouligny, compare lives. They talk, their children play. They tell the children about their daddies, far away at someplace important.

Like the other Lecorgne mothers, Estelle employs enslaved people. She has on hand Frank, eighteen, and Edward, nineteen, two men inherited by her husband. Estelle may also have a woman who runs the stove, scours the house, and stays awake at night when little Alice is sick. To enslave such a person would be *comme il faut*, how things are done, correctly.

If Joseph is like other infantrymen, now and then he writes his wife a letter. The news he sends softens the disaster he is living. If Joseph is like the others, his letters declare his love for Estelle and Alice, and he sends deep embraces. He names the Lecorgnes whom he misses, but he says nothing about the black people all around them. They are invisible, like ghosts in the corridors. Edward and Frank, the young black men at his wife's side, whom he knows well, would fail to appear in Joseph's letters. Now and then such a letter, scribbled at night in a tent lit by a candle, might make its way back to New Orleans.

The slaves are to blame for this wretched war, Joseph knows, though he is unable to say just how. If not for them, none of it would have happened. The Lecorgnes would be together, if not for them. We would be at peace, at home, and in good money, if it were not for the godforsaken darkies.

In February 1864, two Creoles of color take a steamship from New Orleans up to the Northeast. They are Jean Baptiste Roudanez, a mechanical engineer, and Arnold Bertonneau, who sells wine for a living. This is a lobbying trip. Their destination is the White House, where they have arranged a meeting with President Lincoln.

Bertonneau and Roudanez are leaders in the black bourgeoisie of New Orleans. They are close to Paul Trévigne, editor of *L'Union*, as well as with the French-speaking African Americans who write for the paper. Bertonneau and Roudanez carry a petition signed by several hundred prosperous *gens de couleur*. It is an appeal for the right to vote among people of color. The wine merchant and the engineer plan to present the petition to the president.

The two get off their steamship in New York, where they visit with Frederick Douglass and other abolitionists. Then they go to Boston, where they meet William Lloyd Garrison, white publisher of *The Liberator*, an antislavery newspaper. They leave for Washington, and on March 12, they go to the White House. About one-half of Louisiana is under occupation—Union territory—and one-half is in rebel hands. Lincoln receives the gentlemen of color from New Orleans into his office when he is wondering what to do with this biggest piece of Southern turf in Yankee hands. Is Louisiana back in the Union de facto, and should elections be held?

Bertonneau and Roudanez enter Lincoln's office. They are here to share words—*Causer, c'est le manger des oreilles*, "Conversation is the food of the ears." They give Lincoln their petition. It has the signatures of a great many moneyed and literate Creoles of color. The two argue with the president that people who are not white should have the vote. They listen politely to his prevarication, and then pick up their hats and withdraw. The president is moved. He does not leap to his desk to write a proclamation of universal manhood suffrage.

The next day, however, Lincoln sends a letter to the new governor of Louisiana, Michael Hahn. He mentions his meeting with Roudanez and Bertonneau and recommends that Louisiana try to give voting rights to educated and prosperous blacks. They are, after all, just like the white tribe.

In New Orleans, Paul Trévigne writes an editorial in *L'Union*. Voting is "the rightful capacity of all native and free born Americans, by virtue of their nativity in the country, irrespective of national descent, wealth or intelligence." *L'Union* is read by Creoles of color. No whites pick it up, let alone advertise in it. Most African Americans speak only English. The paper struggles for two years. Paul Trévigne and his editor, Nelson Fouché, do not think they can continue in business. What is more, threats come from whites, anonymous threats, violent threats. In 1864, Fouché and Trévigne decide to shut down *L'Union*.

An angel of the press steps forward. He has a familiar name— Louis Charles Roudanez. He is the brother of the petitioner, Jean Baptiste Roudanez, the one just back from the White House. The angel of the press is well-known in the French Quarter. Louis Roudanez is a physician, he is rich, and he is a man of color. When Paul Trévigne folds *l'Union*, Roudanez takes out his wallet.

Louis Roudanez (pronounced *Roo-dah-ney*) has his office on Conti Street, a few blocks from the first Lecorgne house, on Dauphine. When *L'Union* closes, in early July 1864, Louis Roudanez buys the paper's physical plant and reopens the shop. As publisher, he wants to put out a different newspaper. It is to be bilingual, so as to double its reach. Roudanez gives it a new name, the *New Orleans Tribune* (in French, *La Tribune de la Nouvelle Orléans*). The new publisher has deep pockets and plans to lose money, like a good angel.

He is born in 1823, the son of two free people of color. Louis Charles Roudanez is a young man during the 1840s, when he lives in the *Vieux Carré* as a bond trader dealing in municipal securities. He is one of a small group of men of color—maybe there are five hundred in New Orleans—who make serious money in business before the Civil War. In the late 1840s, cash in pocket, Roudanez takes himself to Paris. He stays for several years and studies to be a physician, taking a degree at the Faculté de Médecine de Sorbonne Université.

Roudanez returns to New Orleans during the 1850s and marries a free woman of color named Célie Saulay. He opens a medical office that serves both blacks and whites. When the war comes, Roudanez decides that treating the venereal infections of white businessmen and the diarrhea of colored children is not satisfying enough. His friends are getting into politics, and he does the same.

The *New Orleans Tribune*, Roudanez's newspaper, calls itself an "organ of the oppressed" and advocates the radical idea of a nonracial democracy. The paper calls for a fair deal for people of African descent. Roudanez says in print that he will "spare no means at our command" to take the momentum out of white supremacy.

The *Tribune*'s first issue appears July 21, 1864. An editorial reads—

"The old plantation system should be summarily abolished, the plantations divided into five-acre lots, and partitioned among the tillers of the soil. [Black people] should be armed [and] educated as fast as possible, taught to honor the flag and to hate their former rebel masters."

Do the Lecorgnes read the *Tribune*? I do not know, but I doubt it. Do they hear about the paper? They must. What I believe they feel is that the newspaper is a rich black man's disgusting trick.

The *Tribune* starts publishing three times a week, Tuesdays, Thursdays, and Saturdays. It runs two pages in French, two in English, and sells for five cents. African Americans read it, and a few whites. By October, the *Tribune* becomes a daily. The paper becomes the strongest voice of the black South. The idea is surprising: during the Civil War, deep in bedlam, in a state that is fighting to keep slavery, it is here that a black newspaper is born.

In 1864, occupied Louisiana writes a new state constitution. It is a step in President Lincoln's so-called ten percent plan for restoring the United States. He laid out the scheme in a December 1863 statement, the Proclamation of Amnesty and Reconstruction. If ten percent of the state's voters take an oath of allegiance to Washington, and a new constitution is produced that bans enslavement, Louisiana can return to the Union. In New Orleans, a constitutional convention is arranged, with delegates elected under pressure from the U.S. Army. Whites behind the rebellion, the big majority, stay away

Louis Charles Roudanez, physician, Creole of color,
founder of the *New Orleans Tribune*

from the polls, not least because many are off in the war. But at least
ten percent of the white men still in town make their way to voting
stations.

The capital city of Louisiana has moved back to New Orleans, its
old seat, from the town of Baton Rouge. The governor's office, the
legislature, and functions of state again inhabit the Crescent City. But
the government center is not a white, classical building with columns
and pediment. It is an ad hoc statehouse, a brown brick meeting hall
known as the Mechanics Institute.

The constitutional convention—ninety-four white men—meets
at the Mechanics Institute. When the work is done, the 1864 constitution contains a provision for the abolition of slavery and a promise
of public education for both whites and blacks in a dual system of
separate schools. Emancipation becomes the law—the demand from
Washington—but the constitution does not create a mechanism to

fund the black schools, only the white. It is a clever omission. Most of the black schools that open in Louisiana are funded by the Union occupation and by charities in the North, so-called freedmen's aid societies.

The Lecorgnes have schoolteachers in their ranks, like Constant's sister, Eliza Lecorgne. I do not think Eliza would be interested in work at a black school, like the ones the new law proposes. When Eliza hears of the Constitution, she must give it thought. It is not likely she applies for a new teaching job.

The armies of the South, defending the Confederate capital at Richmond, Virginia, have victories through the hot summer of 1864, at Spotsylvania, Cold Harbor, and Petersburg, Virginia. But toward year's end, the outcome of battles tilts to the North—in September, the fall of Atlanta to the Union; in October, the Yankee control of Virginia's Shenandoah Valley; and in December, the end of General Sherman's so-called March to the Sea, with the fall of the city of Savannah, Georgia. Along the way, in mid-November, President Abraham Lincoln is reelected.

Two weeks before Christmas 1864, Joseph Lecorgne is in central Tennessee, along with thirty thousand other rebel soldiers. The multitudes are sent by their commanders to attack Nashville, a Southern city in the hands of the Union. It is another giant, wheeling fight. Joseph's company is attached to the Army of Tennessee, which is thrown against fifty-five thousand Union soldiers in and around Nashville.

Joseph and the other rank and file of the Thirtieth Louisiana are not happy when they learn that their beast of an enemy has brought to Tennessee no fewer than eight regiments of U.S. Colored Troops. To fight against eight thousand black soldiers is not the first choice of Joseph Lecorgne or other plain men of the Confederacy. It is especially not the pleasure of one rebel general, who rides toward the battle as the fight begins. His name is Nathan Bedford Forrest. General Forrest's cavalry division is going to Nashville to try to save the city.

For two days, Joseph's detachment, Company F, meets clouds of grapeshot and a rainfall of artillery. Grapeshot is a cluster shell, a bundle of metal slugs packed together in a canister and fired from cannons. And again, Joseph escapes injury. The Confederate general Stephen Lee commands Joseph Lecorgne and one thousand other men. On December 17, the corps is seven miles south of Nashville, dug into trenches, fighting against white troops, when suddenly a line of black soldiers appears to their left. The black unit is the Thirteenth U.S. Colored Troops. The Thirteenth Colored attacks the hill called Peach Orchard, which Joseph is helping to defend. The Thirteenth Colored overruns the rebels, the Yankees losing 220 officers and men in one afternoon. It is the first time Joseph has fought against black soldiers. With buckets of blood, they have the victory and Joseph the defeat.

The rebel defense of Nashville breaks down, and a column of the Army of Tennessee forms to march a retreat south. Union runners chase them along a turnpike that leads to the town of Franklin. Somewhere in the disarray, Yankees surround Joseph's detachment and capture some two thousand rebels. Joseph's luck runs out, and he is made prisoner.

The Thirteenth Colored is among his captors. He is stripped of his gun and led away. When Joseph falls into black hands, it is as though he has entered a twisted world. At home in New Orleans, Joseph knows many black people, but this is the first time he has taken orders from a black man. He has never heard a black sergeant tell him to get up and move. Many of his captors, Joseph knows, were slaves the year before. They have been unlocked from plantations and signed on to help the Yankee cause. To be made prisoner by black soldiers bends belief.

It is wrong, madness, and unforgivable. This day is one to tell to the grandchildren, to bewitch them with the story of how the order of things failed. The day Joseph is taken prisoner by a coon will have a red letter marked on the calendar. I would like to have seen Joseph when his hands were tied by a black sergeant, when the light went out in his eyes. I feel empathy for him, because he must have been in psychological torment.

A memoir by a Confederate soldier named John H. King, made

prisoner like Joseph, has something to say about the experience of being handled by black soldiers.

"We are thrown into the gloom of abject dejection, greatly increased by the insolence of the negro soldiers," King writes. "They with insulting injunctions are not slow in letting us know that they are now our masters."

The day after Joseph's capture, the cavalry of Nathan Bedford Forrest arrives. General Forrest is a notorious figure, a man hated by the Union Army for a massacre of Yankee troops, which he supervised. In May 1864, two hundred miles west of Nashville, Forrest and his regiment took possession of Fort Pillow, a Union outpost on the Mississippi. When the black soldiers in the fort surrendered, instead of taking them prisoner, Forrest and his men executed some three hundred. Every man in the Yankee rank and file knows and remembers this event. It was only six months ago. The Thirteenth Colored remembers better than any.

General Forrest tries to protect the rest of the rebel retreat from Nashville as it swarms south. Joseph Lecorgne does not see the chisel-faced Forrest, who appears on the scene after his capture. But the sinewy General Forrest will come back to our story, with the Ku-klux. Three years later, when this battle is in the past, ex-general Nathan Bedford Forrest will be found in a nearby part of Tennessee, seething—a Confederate loyalist, his war lost, a man sunk deep in resentment. Out of a well of anger and disgust, Nathan Forrest will help mobilize a new rebel force, a second uprising. His resistance army, raised during the peace after the war, is that militia with a mysterious name, the first wave of Ku Klux Klan. And it is the Ku-klux that will put to right the deformed world in which blacks give orders to whites.

The Yankees keep Joseph and one thousand other prisoners on hand for several days near Nashville. He is processed as a prisoner of war, boards a train with his remnant of Company F, and the men are sent to Louisville, Kentucky, where they arrive January 2, 1865. At Louisville, Joseph's prison gang crosses the Ohio River on a ferry, armed sentries all around them. They climb into railroad cars and the next morning find themselves in Cincinnati. Rebel prisoners pass through Cincinnati often enough that their appearance is a local attraction, like captured animals arriving to populate the zoo. In the Cincinnati terminal, as John King describes it, "we are surrounded by a rabble of men, women and children who with jeer and gibe insult us in every way their filthy language permits."

From the taunting crowd, Joseph learns that he is going one hundred miles northwest to a place called Camp Chase, near Columbus, Ohio. A jail for ten thousand war captives, Camp Chase is a place "looked upon by both North and South as being the hardest on Confederate prisoners of all the federal prisons," as one veteran sees it. At Cincinnati, Joseph gets on another train, and a few hours later, shy of the city of Columbus, he steps off. Company F marches at gunpoint through some woods, crosses a turnpike, and arrives at the stockade walls of Camp Chase.

The prison covers five acres. A palisade wall fifteen feet high forms a giant rectangle, and guards patrol the parapet that sits atop. When Joseph walks through the gate, he steps onto a naked grass yard and faces another wall, the footprint of a second rectangle inside the first. A walk through the spiked gate, and he is in the first prison yard.

Camp Chase has three separate jails, three prison yards, their occupants determined by rank. Commissioned officers go in yard #1; junior officers in yard #2; and common soldiers in yard #3. Second Lieutenant Lecorgne goes in #2. Once inside, he sees the "dead line" that runs along the yard perimeter, ten feet from the wall. If a prisoner comes up to the line, a guard yells from the parapet above, "Fall back!"—before he shoots. Yard #2 has two rows of wooden barracks with a center street running between. Eighteen identical barracks, each long, skinny, raised up on brick piers. Within every building are eighty bunks made from naked planks, two men in each bunk, the bunks stacked three high for the length of the room. On the long wall are three windows—wood casement, no glass—and on the narrow end of the building, a single door. Against the Ohio winter, two box stoves, one at each end.

Joseph is put in barracks #15, with 140 other men. The prison detail is white. Everyone is aware that if the jailors are black, rebels will turn defiant and unmanageable.

Camp Chase, Ohio, 1864

It is winter when Joseph Lecorgne arrives, and dead prisoners are a common product of Camp Chase. A prisoner named William Duff remembers the scene—

"There was much sickness and many deaths. . . . When a man died, his comrades would get a coffin from under barracks no. 19 and put him in it, then notify the authorities about him. A dump cart would be sent and the dead would be taken away. Sometimes it happened that the coffins were too short. The foot piece would be knocked out, and the man's feet would be exposed."

The straw bedding on which prisoners sleep in the barracks is filled with lice. But merely to have a roof and door gives Joseph a living situation better than some of his Yankee enemies. On the other side of the fight, many Union captives of Confederates are jailed at Andersonville Prison, 125 miles south of Atlanta. At Andersonville, some forty thousand soldiers are held outdoors in a vast pen. During 1864, the year Joseph is at Camp Chase, thirteen thousand Union men die of dysentery and starvation at Andersonville.

By contrast, Joseph Lecorgne is housed and fed. In early March, he signs a piece of paper to confirm that Yankee jailors are giving him a new shirt and pair of socks. He stands in line for the clothing hand-out with a friend from New Orleans, a man apparently captured with him in Tennessee. The friend signs his name "M. K. Chandler." He is

Kendrick Chandler, from Bouligny. Joseph and Chandler know each other from back home.

Joseph Lecorgne and Kendrick Chandler put on their new shirts. In a few years, Chandler will once again become a fighting comrade of the Lecorgnes. He and Joseph's brother Constant will join arms as raiders with the Ku-klux.

A soldier with the Yellowjackets reports that by March 1865, "disasters befall our armies" on a daily basis, and "a gloom settles upon our minds." Confederate money, when the men are paid, is worthless. Desertions empty the ranks. During one week, Sergeant Terrance Lecorgne's regiment, the Eighteenth Louisiana, loses 150 men to desertion. The men leave all at once, walking off *en masse* to make their way home.

Terrance, for his part, is not one to let go. To his commanders, he has grown into a good soldier. He listens to orders, no matter that they may be suicidal. His commanders know that when his wife lies in her birthing bed, Terrance joins a gruesome battle, rather than steal away to be with his newborn son. Strangely, as his officers must also see, Sergeant Terrance always gets out unscathed.

He is no longer the unstable recruit who stumbles through a mutiny. He runs ahead into every fight. At the battle of Mansfield, the Yankees are shot as he takes them captive. He is hardened, effective, and a killer.

The biggest of the Southern armies surrenders in Virginia on April 9. Less than a week later, President Abraham Lincoln is killed in Washington, D.C., by a man named John Wilkes Booth, a stage actor. In Louisiana, at the far western end of the South, I suspect the remaining men of the Eighteenth Regiment greet the news of Lincoln's death with a bitter smile.

The Yellowjackets are part of the so-called Trans-Mississippi Army, a group of battalions to the west of the great river. Two weeks after the surrender in the east, word comes that the commander of the Trans-Mississippi, General Kirby Smith, is negotiating terms for his army. The war really is over. When the curtain comes down, the Eighteenth is camped in the town of Natchitoches. The men who are left refuse to give in. Sergeant Terrance and his comrades defy the order to hand in their weapons. They refuse for many reasons—maybe from stubbornness, or from fear; from exhaustion, or for masculine show; from delirium caused by too much death and not enough food. Other units in the Trans-Mississippi unload their rifles and throw them onto a giant pile, turn and look for a way home. The Yellowjackets stay in Natchitoches, holding out, loaded guns in their laps.

The standoff continues for two weeks. The governor of Louisiana, Henry Allen, travels to Natchitoches to visit the insubordinate men. He tells the shrunken battalion that the war is over and that they must surrender. They are die-hards for the rebellion. The men listen and shake their heads.

Finally, on May 18, their discipline breaks. In an explosion of anger, the holdouts seize the regiment's wagons, mules, and supplies. "The division became a mob and rabble," an officer reports, "disregarding the authority of their superiors and governed alone by a spirit of lawless plunder and pillage." Accounts differ about when Sergeant Terrance's unit gives up. It appears that the eighteenth never hands over its guns. Instead, the unit disintegrates as a few at a time leave camp in pilfered wagons. Sergeant Terrance is one of the last to go.

When he leaves, the sergeant takes back his name. He is once again "Constant."

"Polycarp Constant Lecorgne is honorably discharged at Natchitoches on about May 28, 1865," an officer in the battalion writes. The date means his company is among the last two or three Confederate units to surrender anywhere in the South.

Constant, hard and intransigent, gets on a barge and drifts down the Mississippi to New Orleans, where Gabrielle and the children are waiting.

The Northern war prisons are emptied. On May 8, 1865, the secretary of war Edwin Stanton issues General Order No. 85, which releases all

Confederate prisoners on condition they take an oath of loyalty to the United States. In Ohio, Joseph Lecorgne is let out of his prison camp, after five months. In May, two thousand men leave the jail at Camp Chase. Joseph takes the oath May 13, is released, and walks out of the prison yard.

The prisoner-of-war camp stands on the Scioto River, which drains into the Ohio River, which drains into the Mississippi. The water route home to New Orleans is a weaving trip of 1,500 miles. Newspapers describe the line of steamboats that brings home prisoners of war.

Louisiana sends fifty-five thousand white men to fight. More than half are killed or wounded, or die of disease.

Joseph Lecorgne comes down from jail in Ohio. His brother Constant comes down from insolence in the town of Natchitoches. They reach the wharf in New Orleans at about the same time.

It is a nauseating and lurid war. Four years of suffering and defeat. At home, the good order of things crumbles to nothing. Caroline-the-mulatress frees herself, and the Lecorgne family is forced to answer to the invaders. New Orleans is saved but conquered. The eyes of a soldier see a hundred friends killed by guns, a hundred more by gangrene. The waste of it. And meanwhile, all of *les nègres* are doing just what they want. The world is turned inside-out. The shame of it, the goddamn shame.

The crackers are not content. That is how they look.

Joseph and Constant step onto the levee of the river at the edge of New Orleans. The brothers seem to appear from nowhere. They are famished and sick from exhaustion. They reek with their dirt. They look down at the city. It is a new sort of place. The blacks are in the street. The tribe swarms in uncountable numbers, many more than before the war. Emancipation comes, finally, for the three hundred thousand enslaved in the state. The city seems to be seething. Constant and Joseph see the niggers in the streets. Their celebration is vile. And the Lecorgne brothers are touched with rage.

PART IV

INTRODUCTION TO AN ATROCITY

Les nègres look happy. They wear polished shoes and low-cut dresses. They stay out late, restless. They stream out of the country parishes, flow in thousands to the city. They look glad to be alive, at least the ones not begging for bread.

It is summer 1865. Constant Lecorgne does not appreciate seeing a happy colored man. They copy their betters, and it is disgusting. They are the reason everything has come to grief. The blacks are the root and branch of the disaster.

Before the war, a nigger does not smoke. Now the men stand on corners and bring out cheap cigars. Look at them on display. Before the war, a black man does not go out to drink. He keeps it in his shack, he never drinks on a white street. Now they walk the roads in a posse, sharing a bottle. They make noise. The streets are quiet before the war, because the blacks do not want the patrol to shut them down. Now you cannot take a streetcar down a black block for the din. They stand on the corner with their banjos from the jungle and howl their stupid songs.

Constant, Joseph, and uncountable more returning from the fight do not like what they feel. The traditional and wholesome awe of the white race that has kept *les nègres* in subjection is gone. In the aftermath of the war, whites feel the great perversion.

New Orleans doubles its black population between 1860 and 1870, and the number of whites dwindles. Ten thousand rebels come home in coffins. Another ten thousand whites decide to get out and leave for Texas and Mexico. Things are freer out west, freer farther south. A man can make a life there that looks more like the old. Some two thousand men and women leave North America altogether, for Brazil.

Slavery lives on in Brazil, thank the Lord, and a sugar planter there can do the things he knows how to do with the blacks.

President Lincoln is dead. It is good he went down. The assassination is a gift. Let the nigger-lovers grieve, for a change.

The ex-rebels do not like what they see: black soldiers on patrol, a special insult. When the Union brings in African Americans, the occupation army fills up with black recruits. In New Orleans, a thousand ex-slaves patrol the streets with guns lowered. Everyone knows that a black man is supposed to wear torn pants and a belt made from a piece of rope. Instead, he struts with a rifle, in a blue jacket with brass buttons.

The editor at the *Louisiana Courier* is having none of it. "We would have received white troops with kindness and respect," the paper says. "Instead, our people are jostled from the sidewalks by dusky guards, halted in rude and sullen tones by negro sentinels. To see our own slaves freed, armed, and put on guard over us is a deliberate, cruel act of insult and oppression, an exercise of tyranny."

Constant the veteran, thirty-four, is weary like a much older man. Gabrielle and the three children see a withered father. Numa is eight years old, Louis is four, Estelle two. For three years, Gabrielle Duchemin is a single mother, income gone, less to eat, and Caroline-the-slave out the door. Gabrielle does the housework, for a change, cooking and minding the children. She is not used to it, and she is exhausted. She turns to the good help of her in-laws, but her husband's sisters and brothers have also lost their workers. Except Yves of God. He is always the exception. Yves has managed to hold on to one or two of "the help."

What Gabrielle knows, when she thinks about it, is this: at least they do not come after her with guns, like they did to cousin Camille, at Seven Oaks.

The reunion when the veteran returns is sharp and disappointing. Gabrielle last saw her husband two years ago, outside a Confederate camp, when she gave birth to Marie Estelle, and then retreated with the baby back to New Orleans. Now the rebel pageant has come to dust, and women like Gabrielle have questions. Where have you been? Most of the men fight a thousand miles away, but Constant has stayed in the state, on the bayou, eating étouffée and boudin and doing God knows what with the camp women. His wife knows that a good commander provides his men with service from a *maison de tolérance*, a brothel.

Some of the bitterest rebels come home to find wives who do not care for their touch. The touch is the hand of a man who has wrecked the family.

Constant looks up and down the street. His house is still beautiful, the big cottage with a wraparound porch and ample rooms, but they do not own it anymore. And what is more, the black people are moving in. Five years ago, all the neighbors are white—Creoles, Germans, maybe an Irish family. Bellecastle Street is turned black. Colored families live in five houses on the block. The people next door are French, name of Porée, but they are *sang-mêlés*, mixed-race. Next to them, another mongrel family called Dejoy, griffes or mulattoes, you hardly know anymore. After that, the street is black all the way down. Constant sees on the block one other white address, belonging to the Bouche family. The Lecorgnes and the Bouches are like white bars of soap floating in brown water.

Frederick Douglass, abolitionist and publisher, living now in Washington, D.C., describes what he sees when four million African Americans, a third of the population of the South, leave enslavement—

"The government leaves the freedmen in a bad condition. . . . He is free from the individual master, but the slave of society. He has neither money, property nor friends. He is free from the plantation, but he has nothing but the dusty road under his feet. He is free from the old quarter, but a slave to the rains of summer and to the frosts of winter. He is turned loose, naked, hungry and destitute to the open sky."

The war causes the deaths of 750,000—about one in ten white

men, North and South. It is not a death toll, it is more like a cull. In the South, about half of white men younger than thirty are killed or maimed. Add to the roll of decimated the half-million women who might have chosen to marry, but who live their lives single, because the men have vanished.

Andrew Johnson, Abraham Lincoln's vice president, moves into the White House. Lincoln was an Illinois Republican, Johnson a Democrat from Tennessee. He is a former slaveholder—a minor master, like the Lecorgnes. He comes from the white South and understands it. The ex-rebels are lucky to have him. The idea of "reconstruction," making a new union, falls into his hands.

Lincoln's hope was to set up new governments in the eleven rebel states with the ten percent plan, building out from a tiny white minority that would accept an end to slavery as the ticket to rejoin the Union. Eventually this might start to drain some of the pure whiteness from around institutions of power. With Lincoln dead, President Johnson's hope is to dissolve slavery but keep white domination, no adjustments needed.

Louisiana has a new governor, James Madison Wells, a rich planter and former slave master from Rapides Parish, in the northwest of the state. Wells is for the Union and for mending the nation but not too much. He knows who his constituents are, the men coming home from the war.

A month after Lincoln is killed, Governor Wells goes to Washington to see President Johnson. The men, both fresh in power, sit across a table to talk. Johnson is pleased with a man like Wells, a prince of the old plantations. Andrew Johnson never owned a village of slaves, and the idea of it seems majestic. Governor Wells and President Johnson have drinks and get along smartly. Each is conservative. Each wants to go soft with the ex-rebels, treat them easy. Johnson does not want slavery to return, but he wants things to feel familiar, coloreds below, whites above. Johnson does not want reconstruction, he wants what he calls "restoration."

President Johnson retreats to his office. On May 29, 1865, he signs an order to give amnesty to Southerners who fought. It is the first of several amnesty decrees. Constant and a million other men put on gray jackets and tried to overthrow the government. To escape reprisal and regain the vote, a rebel must sign an oath that states how he accepts both allegiance to Washington and the ban on enslavement.

For Constant and the Lecorgnes, it is easy to sign. They signed a similar oath during the occupation and will sign more oaths after this one. As they see it, oaths buy a voice. Freedom for negroes may be wrong, but it is the future. Emancipation is a legality, a status change, like going from married to widowed. A man may miss his wife when she dies, but life continues.

Constant finds himself downtown on Carondelet Street near the seat of city government, a block called Lafayette Square. Thousands of men jam the streets. He heads to the office of the army's provost marshal. The provost marshal handles amnesty papers. A crowd of ex-rebels wants to sign the oath and get the amnesty. It takes all day, but finally he reaches the office, and everything is settled.

It may be a charade, but it means you will not be prosecuted for treason, and it means you can vote in the next election. The blacks do not vote. If the world is sane, they never will vote.

The new Louisiana state constitution says black people are free and there must be public schools for blacks as well as whites. But it says nothing about citizenship, and it is vague about the vote. In 1865, black people are not citizens, neither in the South, nor the North, nor the West. The Supreme Court with its neutral majesty ruled in *Dred Scott v. Sandford*, in 1857, that people of color "whose ancestors were imported . . . and sold as slaves" are "beings of an inferior order, and altogether unfit to associate with the white race, either in social or political relations; and so far inferior, that they have no rights which the white man was bound to respect."

After Emancipation, the thought of black citizenship is strange, and the idea of black suffrage radical.

Constant and Joseph Lecorgne, plus their many cousins who fought, plus thousands more white men who detest the presence of the Union Army in the South, fill the new voting rolls. All are Democrats, followers of the old proslavery party. When the election comes in August to set up a new state legislature, they are the only people who vote. Faced with a ten-to-one rout, the Republican Party boycotts the election, and so do the very few whites who support the Union.

Constant knows the man with the flowery name, Alcibiade DeBlanc. He knows the flamboyant lawyer from old family connections on Bayou Lafourche. He may also know DeBlanc through the channel of his brother, the Lecorgne in government, the justice of the peace Yves of God.

Alcibiade DeBlanc is forty-four years old, with a strong jaw and bushed eyebrows. He is an attorney and a sophist, a man known in court and in the newspapers as a mellifluous talker who can move a jury and persuade a room of people to do anything. He rose to the rank of colonel during the war and commanded a regiment. In summer 1865, DeBlanc is back from the fight and in his hometown, St. Martinville. He is brooding and angry. He writes an essay for the local paper, *The Courier of the Teche*, and the editor publishes it as DeBlanc's "Address to the People"—

"I write from the illustrious ruins of our departed Confederacy," DeBlanc says. "I think now as I did on the day I enlisted as a soldier. Our cause was a just and sacred cause, and there is nothing of the past that I would repudiate. Had we been successful, the whole world would have courted our friendship . . . but we have failed, and we are now seen as criminals and traitors!" It is defiant talk. DeBlanc says that since the surrender, he has taken the loyalty oath and reluctantly "aligned" with the United States. Yet "I am loyal as long as the cost of that allegiance shall not be the degradation of our race."

DeBlanc says that the abolition of slavery is illegal, because slavery appears in the Constitution, and it is incontrovertible. Abolition is also irrational, he says. The end of slavery "is nothing less than the abolition of labor, and will convert our laborers into hordes of vagrants, useless to themselves, their families, and the state."

The Lecorgnes look up to DeBlanc. He is one of their betters, a nobler version of themselves—a high officer, a lawyer, even a writer.

The Lecorgnes are also disappointed by the war. DeBlanc is a man who diagnoses their malaise. His "Address to the People" is passed hand to hand in New Orleans.

Alcibiade DeBlanc is a man to follow, and soon Constant will walk in his footsteps.

In New Orleans, Louis Roudanez, publisher of the *New Orleans Tribune*, the black daily paper, answers DeBlanc's bulletin. He runs a sardonic editorial about whiteness and its virtues. The *Tribune* quotes DeBlanc on the "degradation of our race" and continues:

> *LA TRIBUNE DE LA NOUVELLE ORLÉANS*
> 21 juillet 1865
> Jusqu'à la 'dégradation de notre race,' je regrette beaucoup que M. DeBlanc ait employé ces mots, car il me met dans la né-cessité de lui répondre que malheureusement, depuis quelques années, la race blanche généralement a pris sois de se dégrader elle-même par l'immoralité. . . .

> *NEW ORLEANS TRIBUNE*
> 21 July 1865
> As far as the 'degradation of our race,' I very much regret that Mr. DeBlanc uses these words, for he puts me in the position of answering that unfortunately, for some years now, the white race has generally been degraded by immorality. It has been degraded by . . . first-degree crimes committed in the cities, in broad daylight, on white abolitionists; by the mass killings at Fort Pillow . . . and that is not to mention the slaughters that haven taken place on the boulevards, without any repercus-sions, sometimes even without burials. Is that the sublime race of Mr. DeBlanc, the one that cannot suffer degradation, the one of which he is so proud?

A white lawyer named Thomas Durant is making speeches about black people and the right to vote. He favors it, which makes him unusual. A journalist calls Durant, who is forty-eight, "tall, thin, sal-low, and cadaverous." Durant has lived in New Orleans for thirty years. He is the former U.S. Attorney for Louisiana, appointed by President Lincoln, and the head of the so-called Free State Party, a small group of whites loyal to the Union. The white newspapers call him a "negro-worshipper."

The Republican Party forms a branch in New Orleans in 1863. After the war, it consists of a few hundred whites who withstand the experience of being shunned, "traitors to their race." Thomas Durant pulls together a few Republicans and forms the Friends of Universal Suffrage, a group to agitate for "the negro ballot." Members are some blacks, some Creoles of color, and some whites. Durant calls a rally at the Carrollton Train Depot, near Bouligny, and a crowd of some thousand turns out to shout for the voting rights of black men.

The house on Bellecastle Street is not far from the rally. If Constant does not quite hear the cheers and drums and speeches, he certainly hears about them. I imagine he has a thought—*Où il y a charogne, il y a des busards*, "Wherever there is dead meat, there are buzzards."

The Lecorgne in-laws are the first to react.

Paul Fazende, a cousin as well as an in-law, owns a sugar plantation across the river from Bouligny, in the village of Gretna, near Camille Zeringue's Seven Oaks. He used to own his farmworkers; now he pays them $14 a month. He does not like the change. Seventeen farmhands live on the Fazende place, along with their twenty-six children. These forty-three were once like money in the bank that paid interest in the form of new children every year. Now the asset is a liability. Fazende detests giving people wages; there is no justice in it.

One day, Paul Fazende is out of his house, walking a field of vegetables and fruit, carrying a gun. Before the war, a man walking his garden did not carry lethal force. Now, some whites wear holsters, and they are angry. Near the strawberries, Fazende encounters a black man, Lew. He is a former slave, and he is foraging. Fazende does not like trespassers. He lifts his gun and shoots Lew. Fazende tells a judge he thinks Lew "was stealing my watermelons."

A government agent files a report that says Paul Fazende is "in the habit" of shooting at blacks who come near his house. Lew, the foraging man, is hit and wounded, but he will recover. It is assault with intent to kill, perhaps, but the referee in the case, a Justice Nandain, who is white (there are no black judges), does not jail Paul Fazende for attempted murder. He jails Lew for attempted theft. The judge puts the injured man in jail for three months and schedules his trial for larceny. Fazende leaves the courthouse and goes home to Gretna.

The story of Cousin Paul Fazende and the pilfering Lew is heard around the Lecorgne dinner table. Let them learn where they belong. A little gunplay is not too much to show them.

In hindsight, the prosecution of Lew and exoneration of Fazende looks to be an example of an American judicial rule that whites get off, and blacks pay.

Judge Yves Lecorgne would defend this principle. About the time Lew is shot, the Freedmen's Bureau, the new federal agency with the assignment of helping ex-slaves, issues a report about the judicial temperament of Judge Lecorgne. The Union captain A. Morse calls Yves of God intransigent and biased on the bench. Lecorgne, he says, will not hear the testimony of black witnesses in court, only white. The Freedmen's Bureau recommends Judge Lecorgne be removed from office. He disappears from the job, at least for a time.

Veterans stream back to New Orleans from the war. Among them is a rebel colonel, Frederick Ogden. During the fighting, Fred Ogden is a young commander, officered at twenty-seven and head of a cavalry regiment. Ogden and his mounted troops surrender in Alabama at the end of the war. He returns to Louisiana and hangs up his sword.

Fred Ogden is like Alcibiade DeBlanc. They are both commanders who do not lose their anger. Both remain hungry for the fight. Constant is an infantryman, a foot soldier. He does not know Fred Ogden. In time, they will meet, and Constant will follow Ogden into new battles.

In fall 1865, Colonel Fred Ogden enters New Orleans politics. He summons a band of veterans, calls them the Young Men's Democratic Association, and puts himself at the head of it. The first election in which ex-rebels can vote is set for November. Ogden and his gang want to fix the outcome. The Lecorgne brothers know about Ogden and the Young Men's Democratic Association (YMDA) and probably know some of its members. But I do not think the Lecorgnes join, in part because the YMDA is full of *les Américains*. The brothers prefer their French company, people like Alcibiade DeBlanc.

In early October, members of the Democratic Party, plus the YMDA, come together to plan. They meet at a neoclassical jewel of a building, the St. Charles Street Opera House. The ballroom hangs heavy with red velvet, cigar smoke obscures gold paint. The Democrats pass a resolution that denounces the 1864 state constitution, which had abolished slavery and promised schools for black students. Party leaders proceed to write a platform for the fall campaign. Colonel Fred Ogden helps to draft the text, which begins—

"Resolved, that we hold this to be a Government of White People, made and to be perpetuated for the exclusive political benefit of the White Race. . . . [We hold] that the people of African descent cannot be considered as citizens of the United States, and that there can in no event nor under any circumstances be any equality between the White and other Races."

Lincoln has been in the grave five months. Black people have been away from the lash long enough to start new lives. And white supremacy is the central plank of the state's Democratic Party.

Around the state, things are looking good for whiteness. In St. Landry Parish, west of Baton Rouge, authorities pass an ordinance that bans black people from owning or renting a house: "No negro shall be permitted to rent or keep a house within said parish," it reads. St. Landry Parish is an area of 920 square miles. Blacks, by law, must live on white-owned property and carry work papers: "No negro shall be allowed to pass within the limits of said parish without a special permit in writing from his employer."

The Republican Party is the party of the victors. It is the party that promises some equity of black with white. New and frail, the party stages rallies where a few whites run the proceedings and blacks by the thousand attend. Maybe one in a hundred whites in Louisiana defends the Republican program of integration and economic development. The state has a slight black majority, but no African Americans can vote.

Facing a big defeat by the Democrats, the Republicans sit out the election. Democrats run unopposed in most districts, and when the voting ends, ninety percent of the Louisiana Assembly is Democrat. Newspapers pin a name to it, the "Rebel Legislature."

In a few weeks, the Rebel Legislature passes the Black Codes, and the governor signs them. A lawmaker named Duncan Kenner writes most of them. Once a rich slaveholder, Kenner loses his fortune to Emancipation, which makes him unhappy. One provision of Kenner's statute gives the state authority to seize black children whose parents "cannot or will not support them" and place them in "apprenticeship" as servants or farmworkers—a form of legal captivity. Another requires black adults to sign five-year labor contracts with employers and allows their "recapture" if they leave a job. A third gives police the power to arrest "vagrants," adults who make the mistake of being on the street without job papers. Convicted vagrants are to be "leased" to work for landlords and businesses. The Black Codes revive the old world.

The Lecorgnes feel good about the Black Codes. Some take advantage, like the family of Gabrielle Duchemin. Constant's wife of nearly ten years, Gabrielle is also a good stepdaughter. She and her husband still see her adoptive parents, François and Adelaide Laizer, who live a few blocks from the house on Bellecastle. François Laizer is no longer mayor of Jefferson City. But like Yves of God, Laizer has managed to protect his money, and he is making a good living by speculating in land.

In early 1866, one month after the Black Codes become law, Laizer picks up a black child from the street and forces him into work. A court in Jefferson City "delivers to F.J. Laizer" a boy named Randall, "orphan of Mrs. Baker." Randall, who is twelve, "is to serve Laizer for the term of nine years," in exchange for food and a roof, but no wages. Although the arrangement is "an indenture," it smells like enslavement, with this difference: Randall "shall receive sixteen weeks of schooling per year." It seems to me now, 150 years later, that the slave days in which my people played a heavy role do not want to end.

———

Sometime in 1866, a few ex-rebels come together to drink. Reunions of soldiers happen around the South, but this one is different. The nighttime toast takes place in Tennessee, in a town called Pulaski, south of Nashville. Six men turn up, all of them ex–junior officers in the rebel army. They are not rural people but educated young men—three lawyers, a newspaper editor, a cotton broker, and the twenty-year-old son of a rich farmer. They come together in a small-town office to laugh and to drown their resentments. If the men's group follows the common pattern, the veterans pour their bourbon and their beer, complain about the lost war, smoke cigars and pipes, and say vituperative things about the niggers.

It is a tribal meeting, and a theatrical one. From their college years, these six ex-rebels in Tennessee remember touches of performance. Some have been members of Greek societies—fraternities, as they become known. They know a smattering of Greek. They know about secret handshakes, and they may have taken a few oaths in their time. No notes survive from these nighttime drinks in the office of a lawyer in Pulaski. But I imagine that someone throws in a few lines of self-congratulation.

There must be a higher purpose to cursing and complaining, one might say. There should be a name to our thing. A lawyer in the room pulls a fraternity word from his memory and suggests a name for their bitching society. It is *Kuklos*, or "circle" in Greek. Things are under way.

James Crowe, a lawyer, is one member of this first *Kuklos*. In a letter written years later, Crowe remembers that the *Kuklos* takes shape in the winter of 1866. Crowe says that at one bullshitting session, a man in the group named John Kennedy suggests that another *K* be added to *Kuklos*. Kennedy offers the word "clan," but intentionally misspelled as "Klan," because it looks better. I imagine there are laughs around the room.

It is not long before *Kuklos*, aided by drink, degenerates into "Ku-klux."

Sometime later comes the distinctive term, "Ku Klux Klan." But for now, the little cell in Tennessee, the bitter men who like to remember and console one another, men seething about the way things have turned out, are just the "Ku-klux," with the nonword "Klan" sometimes attached for emphasis.

A boastful letter about the Ku-klux written by one of the group's founders mentions that its first members are all Protestant. "We are three Presbyterians, one Episcopalian, and two Methodists," says James Crowe. By this time, most of the South is Protestant, the main exception being Louisiana. James Crowe stresses the Protestant identity of the Ku-klux pioneers, because it is thought to demonstrate a kind of purity. To be Protestant means to have family with roots in northern Europe—excepting Ireland and France. It means not to have roots in southern Europe. To be Protestant means to be from among the chosen people, the ones who belong to the inner circle, the *kuklos* of whiteness.

The Catholic Church dominates the lower half of Louisiana, south of the city of Baton Rouge. When Ku-klux gangs spread through the South, which soon occurs, they do not thrive in southern Louisiana. It is not that white Catholics believe themselves to be less chosen than the other chosen people, white Protestants. But French Creoles in Louisiana, all Catholics, feel less a part of the *Kuklos*. In the end, they set up groups identical to the Ku Klux Klan but differently named. The Protestant Ku-klux does not shun the Catholic movement. But the Ku-klux militias and the Creole militias keep apart, dividing up the work of white domination.

If they were characters in the theater, the six men in the dreary office in Tennessee would say portentous things to one another. They would talk of the bloody glory that comes to the vigilant. This is a time when the crooked places will be made straight. We will raise the lantern and erase the shadow the blacks throw over us. In years to come, the men in the dreary office will be called "the holy six" by millions of grateful and admiring whites. That is what happens. It is not from a script for the stage.

The birth of the Ku-klux in Pulaski, Tennessee, makes no rapid impression in Louisiana. Few in the South in 1866 or 1867 hear that a ritual-loving sect is formed. Few, for the time being, know that a rite-heavy fraternity has come together to anoint and to defend the white tribe.

Here is the place where the firemen enter the story. Their appearance is unexpected and seemingly benign, but murderous.

Every few blocks in New Orleans you see a firehouse—a brick building with a carriage door, and inside, a water truck, hoses, and ladders. Six fire companies have station houses within walking distance of the Lecorgnes in Bouligny: Home Hook & Ladder Company, Vigilant Engine Company, Pioneer Engine Company, Perseverance Engine, Lafayette Hook & Ladder, and the Creole Engine Company. You have many squads, more than needed.

The fire companies are all white. Whites own almost all the real estate, and the thinking is that the other tribe, people of color, are inclined to use arson as a weapon. Politicians and priests point to mysterious fires as evidence that African Americans avenge themselves on whites by burning buildings. It is said and believed by many that during the slave years, the fire companies arise as a line of defense against black arson. They exist to protect whites and their property. That is not the end of it. Added to their practical and policing value, the firehouses are clubs for men and factories of social identity for their families. Most of the Pioneer Engine men are German immigrants. Most of the ranks of Home Hook & Ladder are French Creoles, like Constant Lecorgne.

I am interested in the details, like the money, which is important. Taxes pay for courts and judges, streets, and the police, but the fire companies are volunteer. Firemen do not work full-time or for wages; they run from home to a blaze at the sound of a fire bell, out of civic duty. The fifty or more companies in New Orleans are linked to a private group, the Firemen's Charitable Association, which has a pot of money refreshed by fundraising. Every company has a meeting hall and runs banquets, concerts, picnics, and dances to feed its budget. The fire companies are a big public enterprise but outside of government.

In Bouligny, Home Hook & Ladder keeps a station house on Jersey Street near Napoleon Avenue, two blocks from Lecorgne row and four blocks from the cottage on Bellecastle where Constant and Gabrielle live. Evidence is good that for a number of years Constant is attached as a volunteer. He seems to be a back bench member, not a leader.

The Lecorgne company, Home Hook & Ladder, is one of the better-financed squads. It has a pretty Romanesque building, kept immaculate, the façade clad with stone on the first floor and red brick on the second. Their clubhouse is busy enough with social events that the company stores its firefighting gear in a separate "truck house" on Marengo Street. It is there that Constant and his comrades keep the nickel-plated fire truck polished to a mirror shine.

In 1861, at the start of the war, the men of Home Hook & Ladder disband the company to form a militia, the Jefferson Cadets. Constant is named a captain of the Jefferson Cadets but soon demoted to lieutenant in favor of another Home Hook & Ladder man, Émile Chevalley, a friend who lives across the street on Lecorgne row.

The firehouses play a big part in the tale of the Ku-klux. Home Hook & Ladder comes back together at the end of the war. In 1865, it has thirty-two volunteers, most of them older than forty. They elect as their fire chief Émile Chevalley. By 1866, something has happened, and Home Hook & Ladder has a roster of eighty-five, many of them young recruits. Eighty-five men in one company are far too many for the job of putting out the occasional kitchen fire in a radius of half a mile. Veterans swamp the station house.

In November 1866, Home Hook & Ladder has its portrait taken by the photographer Theodore Lilienthal. The picture has gone missing. Another portrait that the same photographer makes on the same day (of the Jefferson Steam Engine company) gives an idea of what Constant's gang of well-dressed ex-rebels looks like.

The seventy-six-member Jefferson Steam Engine fire company, 1866

The city's fire companies balloon with new volunteers, all of them veterans. They look like and behave like military units. The men wear uniforms. Home Hook & Ladder puts on blue shirts trimmed with white piping, and black pants. They stage parades. After the war, a parade of ten companies and five hundred men marching the streets is common. The men show off equipment, the hoses and the water trucks, the horses and hatchets and ladders. Firemen's parades weave through town, stopping at Creole cafés for draughts of wine, or at German barrelhouses for pitchers of lager. On the route, women toss the men bunches of flowers. The men carry banners embroidered with the company's name and motto. For Constant's company, the motto is "Ready for Duty."

At parade's end, Home Hook & Ladder returns to its meeting hall for a night of toasts and curses about changes the war has brought.

On orders from the Freedmen's Bureau, the court removes Yves of God, the judge who admits no testimony from blacks. But the oldest Lecorgne brother outmaneuvers the enemy and lands another sinecure. He is appointed comptroller of Jefferson City. The job makes him a town prince and opens the door to favors. It is a rare money handler who turns down bribes for city contracts or fails to reward friends.

Yves of God keeps the accounts of Jefferson City for two years. He files money reports and shows up in notes of the city treasurer. He is not very clean about the business. One newspaper says Yves is a bad bookkeeper ("derelict in his duties . . . with little or no system") and that he fails to block fraud ("parties who forge cash warrants" are taking public money). Another paper makes charges against Yves's partner, the city treasurer Felix Lagroue. Lagroue is close to the Lecorgnes. In a year, his brother plans to marry Yves's sister, Eliza. Felix Lagroue is said to take cash from city coffers for himself. When Yves keeps the books, Lagroue cannot account for the whereabouts of $16,595, an amount equivalent to building fifteen nice houses.

I do not know how they find a home, or where they go, but in 1866, Constant and Gabrielle and their four children move out of the place on Live Oak and Bellecastle streets. Probably they rent a cottage in Bouligny. The move begins a phase of churning in their home life, of leaping from house to house. According to city directories, during the next seven years they move nearly every year, again and again.

The reason people move is money. Constant and Gabrielle are tenants who cannot pay the rent.

In New Orleans, the economy moves at half its former speed. Many plantations are back in business as sharecrop farms, as enslaved people go back to the fields for wages and some of the crop. But the cotton harvest upstate fails for two years, leaving the city thirsting for the old river of money that cotton once brought. Constant gets little work, because little is on offer.

The U.S. Congress passes the first Civil Rights Act in March 1866. The law defines birthright citizenship, the idea that anyone born in the United States belongs to the nation. It conveys citizenship on the nearly ten percent of the American population once enslaved, whose legal status is still *persona non grata*, alien invader. The Civil Rights Act makes clear that blacks can own property, sue or be sued, make contracts and enforce them, give evidence in court—ordinary things that whites think are natural.

It is the first law of its kind. Yet the Civil Rights Act is a gesture at symbolic equity. It is not a material answer to 246 years of enslavement, and not at all an attempt at restitution. The army experiments with reparations after the war, trying land distribution in South Carolina, the origin of the phrase "forty acres and a mule." But the Johnson government shuts down the program, and Congress does not revive it. Congress rejects financial reparations, and President Andrew Johnson and the Democrats are appalled by any equity, symbolic or real.

The Civil Rights Act passes Congress over unanimous Democratic opposition. Johnson vetoes it, saying the law helps the wrong people. "The bill is made to operate in favor of the colored and against the white race." Johnson speaks for the *petits blancs* of Louisiana. He speaks for the Lecorgnes and for millions of like minds.

Ofay, as a general matter, dislike race parity.

The Republicans override the president's veto.

In June, the U.S. House drafts an amendment that puts citizenship in the Constitution. By this time, the Thirteenth Amendment, which outlaws slavery, has been ratified, with Southern states accepting it as the price of being let back in the Union as states. The Fourteenth Amendment, about citizen and civil rights, goes to the states for a vote. But whites, as a rule, have trouble with civil rights.

Memphis, Tennessee, population forty thousand, sits on the banks of the Mississippi, four hundred miles north of New Orleans. Like Charleston, Atlanta, and elsewhere, Memphis is filled with black people who leave the plantations for new lives in town.

On May 1, 1866, the telegraphs in newspaper offices rattle with word that white mobs are marauding through black streets in Memphis. When a white policeman tries to arrest a single black man, and he resists, gangs of whites come together and start to attack African Americans. The "race riot" kills forty-six, and many women are raped. All the victims are black. Union troops take three days to put an end to the so-called Memphis Riots.

If you look at this episode, you may begin to think violence is a white monopoly.

Black people in the South have seen much blood, typically as the people who bleed. Millions of slaves endure routine beatings and rapes. A culture of self-defense could not grow, because to fight back under slavery meant deadly reprisal. Over time, physical violence comes to be regarded as a white prerogative. In the slave days, a black person who strikes a white is often maimed or killed, and when slaves manage to put together a band of guerrillas, the attempt always ends in slaughter.

After Emancipation, thousands of blacks join the Union Army. They grow familiar with tactical violence. But blacks in arms and uniform and in control of social space are the exception to long and deep tradition.

By contrast, about a million white soldiers come home from the Civil War with advanced degrees in gang violence. Rebel veterans know how to kill people with guns, large and small. They can move a squad in the woods, ambush, stalk, and run raids. At least half of white men younger than forty have seen and done these things.

There is also a flood of guns after the war. Gunmakers like Winchester, Remington, and Colt churn out weapons during the fight, earning a river of money from long guns and revolvers. Guns are supposed to be surrendered with the peace, and many rifles are. But handguns less so, and many return to closets.

The explosion in Memphis in May 1866 is both a rage and a backlash. It is the first retaliation against a new world that is trying to be born. The next strike comes in Louisiana, and Constant is on hand.

———

The ex-rebels with the vote elect a mayor in New Orleans, John T. Monroe, a Democrat who regards whites as a mistreated minority that is to be lifted up again. Mayor Monroe learns of the killings in Memphis and, seemingly inspired, takes a series of steps. Monroe tells the New Orleans police not to interfere with "respectable persons" who carry concealed weapons. The army has tried to collect guns from the hands of ex-rebels. No more, says Monroe. Armed citizens may be called on to help the police if trouble hits the street. Next, the mayor doubles the all-white police force. He appoints a commissioner to hire five hundred officers at an exorbitant salary. The new cops are to receive $80 per month, four times the pay of a workingman. There is a stampede at Gallier Hall, seat of city government. One in three white men in New Orleans applies for a police badge.

I do not know whether Constant and his brother Joseph are among the men who clamor for the job of richly paid cop. I suspect they are, but I have no evidence. Yet Constant has a friend from Bouligny, Seymour Rapp, who is hired as a new officer.

Seymour Rapp is thirty-seven, a veteran and a fireman, part of Home Hook & Ladder.

Mayor Monroe is not finished. He appoints a sheriff, named Harry Hayes. Hayes is a leader in the city's Carnival, head of the Krewe of Comus, the men's club that sends out a rich parade on Mardi Gras night. An ex-rebel general, Hayes names dozens of men from his old regiment as deputies. They are there to help when trouble comes with the blacks.

The elections of November are past. White voters in states around the South follow the pattern of Louisiana, setting up their own rebel legislatures that pass versions of the Black Codes. President Johnson likes this outcome. He declares that the Union is restored. Meanwhile, there is a rise in seemingly random attacks on blacks. The Freedmen's Bureau adds up the number of violent attacks by whites against blacks during the period since the end of the war and reports that 86 freedpeople are killed in Louisiana and 230 injured in assaults, with no one convicted. In the same period, one white person is killed by a black man, who is hanged. It looks like a white monopoly.

It is summer 1866. Constant may have trouble making a living, but he feels wanted and needed at the firehouse, between its drills, banquets, drills, concerts, drills, and drinks. The three children are growing; Numa and Louis are in school. Despite the legal mandate, public schools remain racially separate. A handful of schools open for the giant number of never-educated black children. Dozens of white schools reopen and fill their classrooms.

The *Tribune* publisher Louis Roudanez calls again and again for blacks to have the vote. At some point, he and comrades see a path to the ballot. A clause in the 1864 constitution allows delegates who wrote the document to meet again for more deliberations. Maybe a recall of the convention would do something. Most blacks and a tiny number of whites want the vote for black men. Probably ninety-five percent of whites do not. The newspapers say that black voting rights will mean "negro domination." The *Picayune*, the *Times*, the *Courier*, and the French paper, *L'Abeille*, run nasty pages on "mixed marriage" and the disaster of "social equality," two horrors that black voting would bring about.

The position held by all the newspapers, except Roudanez's *Tribune*, is that black people are monstrous. They are ignorant. They cannot hold any power, cannot be turned into leaders who tell anyone what to do. The position held by the newspapers is that whites are a wounded people who need to be nursed and healed.

On June 23, an invitation to meet goes to ex-delegates who helped write the 1864 constitution. Ex-rebels in the government, the fire companies, and the police all see a threat. If blacks get the vote, white power is lost. Louisiana is one of two states with a black majority, the other being South Carolina. The papers say that a coup is in the making. If black people vote, the suffering that whites now endure will be made permanent.

The convention is set for late July, in the statehouse. The brown brick Mechanics Institute stands outside the French Quarter, on Dryades Street near Canal Street. The governor's office is here, and

The Ku-klux in Louisiana, aided by police and firemen, conducted a
first massacre at the Mechanics Institute in New Orleans.

the Rebel Legislature meets in its auditorium, known as Mechanics
Hall. The hall is booked for the end of the month.

The ex-delegates are white, their popular support is black. Whites
like the Lecorgnes regard the authors of the constitution as traitors to
the state and to their race. On Friday, July 27, delegates to the meeting stage a nighttime rally, and some five thousand attend, most of
them freedpeople. Speakers call for political equality between whites
and blacks, and the last man on the platform closes with a blast, shouting, "The decree of God has gone forth that there shall be universal
freedom and universal suffrage throughout the South."

I am picking through the evidence. It is thin and circumstantial,
and yet it seems to me these are the days that radicalize Constant.
The trauma of the war affects him. His marriage may be under pressure. He has lost the house he built and seems to work hard to lose
much of his income. And now the blacks are grasping.

Les nègres are the cause of all that is wrong, really. They are to
be blamed. If the blacks get the vote, they will flatten us. Let them
make one wrong step, and they will pay.

White fear of people of color is not a new fear. It is as old as the colonial settlement of America. It is so old and so established that it lies like an animal asleep in the mind. When the idea gets around that a new convention is coming together to change the constitution and spread the franchise, the beast of fear awakens.

The delegates have a plan. They will come together in Mechanics Hall and issue a proclamation that calls for universal suffrage. Louis Roudanez has already printed the decree at the offices of the *Tribune*. It is stacked and ready to hand around. The first meeting is scheduled for Monday, July 30, at noon. Maybe forty delegates, all white. Maybe two hundred supporters, most of them black. The plan is to talk voting rights for two hours, and then adjourn.

In the months after these events, the U.S. Congress will conduct an investigation. A committee will take testimony from dozens of witnesses, black and white, and publish the six-hundred-page *Report of the Select Committee on the New Orleans Riots*. It provides an hourly account.

During the weekend, after the night rally, bunches of men are overheard on street corners talking over the "nigger meeting" and how to deal with it. I do not know whether Constant is one of the men in a huddle on the street. He does not need a street corner on which to huddle. The firehouse of Home Hook & Ladder is a better place to lurk, a den close to home.

On Sunday, July 29, Mayor John Monroe and Sheriff Henry Hayes meet to discuss. The decision is taken to mobilize the police and to arm Hayes's new deputies. The decision is also taken to mobilize the fire companies. Mayor Monroe tells his staff to "let all the fire companies assemble to monitor events," according to the congressional report. At 5:00 p.m., the mayor and chief of police send out an order by telegraph that all police are to report to their stations the following morning, armed. Another bulletin goes to the city's firehouses, telling them to "come out in force" when they "hear the strokes" of the fire bell. Two witnesses at Congress testify that members of every fire company are visible at the scene.

Firemen across the city, on orders from their chiefs, meet at firehouses to plan their action. The chief of Home Hook & Ladder is Émile Chevalley, Constant's neighbor and friend. Constant is also in touch with his friend on the police force, Seymour Rapp.

Union soldiers are the blue line that protects, at least some of the time, black activists in politics and their handful of white allies. But the companies of Yankee soldiers are at their military base, Jackson Barracks, which lies three miles downriver.

On the morning of Monday the 30th, the firemen turn out. They are milling about, not close to Mechanics Hall, but within sprint distance. Some have pistols in their belts. One man walking to Mechanics Hall—he calls himself "colored" but appears to be white, like many Creoles of color—is stopped in the street by an ex-rebel. The rebel says, "The police are coming, and we are going to have some fun. We are going to have all these niggers and half-niggers wiped out."

Before noon, at the eastern edge of the French Quarter, in *faubourg Marigny*, some three hundred black men and women meet for a parade to Mechanics Hall. Most of the marchers are Union Army men, some still in the service, some out. With drums and banners and a U.S. flag, they start on Bourbon Street near Esplanade Avenue and make their way west through the French Quarter. Mechanics Hall lies a mile distant. The procession is defiant and singing. Crowds of whites watch. They jeer. They spray spit.

The circumstances seem to say that Constant goes with his friend Seymour Rapp to the scene of the meeting. Constant and Rapp are comrades from Home Hook & Ladder. And Rapp, as a police officer, has orders to show up.

The black parade moves through the *Vieux Carré*, the old neighborhood of the Lecorgnes, twenty-five years back. It passes near the family's old house address at 43 Dauphine Street. It drums down the blocks where Constant played when he was a boy. That was before the Lecorgnes moved out to the white suburb of Bouligny. A parade like this is equal and free, a celebration. A procession like this is an expression of power and community. The marchers come up Bourbon Street.

At Mechanics Hall, now a half mile distant, the scene is menacing. Several hundred supporters of the convention, most of them black, turn out to watch the delegates enter the building. The number of delegates is small; many back out in fear. Angry white faces gather at the edges, surrounding the black crowd. The delegates pass through a gauntlet, a heckling mob of whites, a cheering section of blacks.

As the parade comes out of the French Quarter, a white man pushes a black marcher down on the street. He fights back, and the white man pulls a pistol and fires. The bullet misses, no one is hit, but the day moves to its lethal stage.

The delegates and two hundred or more black supporters make their way inside, climb the stairs to the second floor, and enter Mechanics Hall. The room is 75 x 120 feet, and high-ceilinged. At one end of the hall is a platform, in the middle are rows of chairs. At 12:00 p.m., the chairman gavels the meeting and starts roll call.

It is a little past noon when the black parade arrives in front of the building, followed by a seething crowd of whites. It is a little past noon when the fire alarm bells ring down the street.

Fireboxes stand here and there around the city, a network linked by electric lines, with bells that clang in unison. The system uses simple signals to point to the location of a fire. Two strikes of the bell mean a fire in the city's District 2, four strikes in District 4. But just after noon on this Monday, the fireboxes throughout the city all sound an alarm of twelve bells, more than the number of city districts. The signal of twelve bells has been used only once, during the Civil War, when Mayor Monroe had his first term in office. Then, the sound of twelve bells signaled not a fire but an invasion, a warning that the city was under attack. Five years have passed, but everyone remembers the meaning of the bells, not least the men in the fire companies.

Twelve bells signal the start of killing.

I do not know with certainty whether Constant Lecorgne is among the marauders, but I believe he is. The membership in a fire company, the alarm calling all firemen. Yet the newspapers publish no lists of killers. There is no honor roll of volunteers who claim to have joined in the attack that historians refer to as the Mechanics Institute Riot. And I have no photographs or letters about the day. Still, the preponderant clues say that Constant is in the streets with the other firemen, who help the police to kill dozens of black people. I cannot escape the conclusion that the Mechanics Institute massacre is a blood baptism for him.

Lines of police appear, spilling out from their stations and marching in columns toward Mechanics Hall. The police wear regulation hats with badge numbers on them, each officer's number sewn onto a hatband. Witnesses notice that the badge numbers are reversed, turned upside down, and unreadable.

One witness says, "A fire company came down with their fire apparatus as if they were running to a fire, which is a very good way to collect a crowd, and headed to the front of the Mechanics Institute." After the alarm, armed men swarm the downtown streets. They wear different insignia, depending. A witness describes men "with a kind of blue badge or ribbon in the buttonhole of their coats"—the deputized police of Henry Hayes. Others wear a white handkerchief at the neck—rank and file in the fire companies. Men with a single rolled-up shirtsleeve are ex-rebel militia belonging to neither the police nor a firehouse. I think of them as freelancers for white rule.

In front of the Institute, a white newsboy taunts the black demonstrators and starts a fight with one of the black men. A dozen others get ready to join a brawl. A marcher fires a shot, and the fight with the newsboy spreads. At this, a number of police pull their guns and open fire on the men and women in the parade. The shooting begins, and it is general. The beating of men and women starts, and it, too, is general. Knives are brought out by whites not fortunate enough to possess a pistol.

The crowd of blacks in front of the building is attacked, charged from both ends of the street. There is no direction to retreat, and the crowd divides itself into two groups to face the twin assault. Hundreds of whites are armed, only a few blacks have guns. The marchers from the parade, caught in crossfire, fight back with sticks and stones. According to witnesses, the police and firemen act together. A survivor named James Thomas reports, "After the alarm I saw squads from all the fire companies with clubs and sticks. If the police could not kill all those at the convention, the plan was that they were to disperse them, and those they could not kill, the firemen were to kill outside."

Police and others shoot many to death at point-blank. They chase people down alleys and into nearby houses. The editor of the *New Orleans Tribune* is on the scene, but he somehow escapes. He writes, "What is the most hideous are the yells and calls of these savages whenever a defenseless man falls." Ecstatic shrieks are heard when the mob seizes a victim. One survivor quotes some of the shouts he hears during the riot. "Kill the Yankee nigger!" "Shoot the nigger son of a bitch!" "There goes another nigger!" And "Another damned Yankee!"

The white mob throws itself on the locked doors of the Mechanics Institute. Inside, several hundred now expect to die, and the scene is panic. The gangs fire into the windows. Police and firemen break down the doors, force their way upstairs and into the meeting hall. Some blacks jump from second-floor windows into the street, only to be shot on the pavement below. There are other tactics, according to the witness James Thomas. "I heard a policeman say they carried the plan out very nearly. When policemen shot and wounded people, the firemen would run up and kill them with their clubs."

Many who flee the scene and run several blocks are chased, caught, and beaten to death. Policemen stop the passing streetcars and drag black passengers off to be beaten or killed.

If he is on the scene, and I believe he is, I imagine Constant must feel twenty things. Here are some emotions I think he and others in the white mob feel: fear . . . pride . . . duty to power . . . jealousy . . . anger . . . masculine insecurity . . . anxiety . . . ambition. . . . Maybe the gangs who do the killing feel the thing we call sadism, though the word for it does not yet exist. At bottom, under all these feelings, lies a foundation on which the twenty emotions of the hour are piled, and that is the sense of a tribe in its power, acting as one.

THE RIOT IN NEW ORLEANS—MURDERING NEGROES IN THE REAR OF MECHANICS' INSTITUTE.

Constant Lecorgne is one of my people. He is one of my family. How can I respond to the discovery of what he seemingly did? In several ways. I do not feel responsible for the crimes he seems to commit—I mean, legally responsible—for the reason that the living cannot control the acts of the dead. In the frame of the law, I do not feel culpable for the Mechanics Institute massacre. However, as a matter of conscience, I feel implicated. I feel associated with this cruel and merciless festival of violence. I feel a part of it. Because he acts on behalf of his family—our family, if you like—I have a feeling of wretchedness and shame.

The family I share with Constant is remote. He is a great-great-grandfather of mine. Everyone has sixteen great-great-grandparents, and Constant, to me, is one of those sixteen. Oral tradition, customs, and stories are the drivers of family identity. I have a few stories from Constant's granddaughter, my aunt Maud. A few smooth stories are not the same as membership in a continuous family life.

But disavowal like this is a stage of grief. To disavow is to know something is true and terrible, and yet to desire that it not be true and act as though it is false. To disavow is to push away a horror. Constant is one of sixteen great-great-grandparents: the thought has a distancing effect. The reality is that Constant, my grandmother's grandfather, is a murderous actor on behalf of his family—on behalf of *us*. And it is a vile taste in the mouth. I must own it, in some way. He was a fighter for our gain, for my benefit. To say anything else is to prevaricate.

It is not a distortion to say that Constant's rampage 150 years ago helps, in some impossible-to-measure way, to clear space for the authority and comfort of whites living now—not just for me and for his fifty or sixty descendants, but for whites in general. I feel shame about it. That is not a distortion, either. I am an heir to Constant's acts of terror. I do not deny it, and the bitter truth makes me sick at the stomach.

Whites are my people, my tribe. They were Constant's people, his tribe. In that way he belongs to us, and to hundreds of millions. I know the honest way to regard race violence is this: American history is full of it. It is pandemic. The United States was founded upon racial violence. It is within the core of our national identity.

Here is a way *not* to see these events: The marauders like Constant are immoral, abject, and bad people. They are not like us, they belong to someone else.

It is truer to say this: the marauders are our people, and they fight for us.

That day at the Mechanics Institute, a man named Lucien Capla is on the scene. Lucien Capla is a Creole of color, age forty-five, a man with some African ancestry and some French. His family pronounces its surname, Capla, with the accent on the end, *Kah-PLAH.*

Lucien Capla is a shoe dealer, a businessman. He is born before the Civil War, outside slavery. The distinction means much. It means that he is French-speaking, literate, and that he has money. In fact, he has a good deal of money. At one point, the Capla family have a live-in servant named Étienne Dubas, their driver and factotum. They are among the colored elite.

The Caplas run a shoe store near the edge of the *Vieux Carré,* at 164 Barracks Street, where Lucien Capla has made and sold shoes for more than twenty-five years. The address is also the Capla family house. A court reporter who watches him testify to a committee of Congress describes the shoemaker as "colored slightly."

On July 30, Lucien Capla and his son Alfred go to Mechanics Hall to witness the events. Alfred is sixteen. Father and son cheer the parade and yell for the right to vote, then follow the convention delegates inside the hall. Louis and Alfred take seats among the other spectators who have pushed their way into the building.

Lucien Capla is active in the Republican Party, and he knows many of the men who have showed up. Some are like Capla himself—colored, free-born, and French-speaking. Capla and his son Alfred know that it is risky, but they are accustomed to taking risks. In the witness chair in front of a congressional committee, Capla explains how he has already been targeted. A year back, when the agitation for the black vote started, Capla made it known to everyone that he wanted the ballot. He showed up at rallies for the Universal Suffrage Association and yelled "Suffrage, now!" with the others. Capla describes the boycott of his business by whites, which started when he joined the voting campaign. "After I went with the Republicans, I did not sell a shoe to a white man for six months," Capla tells Congress.

On July 30, at 12:00 noon, Louis and Alfred Capla are in Mechanics Hall. The shooting starts outside, and they take cover. By about 12:15, the white gangs break into the building.

"They fired on us, and I saw the people fall like flies," Capla says in testimony. "Then I took my son, who was with me, and we ran out at the door among the policemen, who fired at us; and when we got down the stairs they fell on us, and if I was not killed, it was because God did not want me to be killed." Louis and Alfred somehow get free from the building, but they are chased down in the street and caught. Capla is beaten and ends the fight with deep cuts on his head. The police in the gang drag him to jail. Capla's son, Alfred, is also beaten badly. "My son was separated from me and left on the banquette for dead," Lucien Capla tells Congress. At some point in the attack, one of the gang—a policeman or fireman—pulls out a gun and shoots Alfred in the face. The bullet enters the boy's right eye, destroying it, and lodges in his head. The gang that has Alfred at its mercy thinks this is enough, and leaves him to die.

"The firemen took a great share in this affair," says Capla. "There were even women who had weapons to kill the negroes with. I heard women call out, 'Those dirty Yankees!' And 'Those niggers! Kill them! Do not let a single one of them get away!'"

I do not know whether Constant Lecorgne is on the scene when someone shoots Alfred Capla in the face. Chances are he is not. After the initial massacre at Mechanics Hall, the attackers scatter through the city, smashing black businesses and jumping black people at random.

While Lucien Capla bleeds in jail, someone picks up his boy Alfred and carries him to the hospital, where he joins a hundred or more who have been shot or beaten. The bullet has apparently not entered his brain, and miraculously, Alfred survives. He is blinded in one eye and disfigured, but after many weeks makes a recovery.

Alfred is in good enough shape to accompany his father a second time, on another outing. They attend the congressional hearings where Lucien Capla gives testimony. "My son is here," Louis says, pointing to a sofa in the room where Alfred sits, listening. "He has lost one eye, his right. He has four bullet wounds on his head, and three stab wounds. He is sixteen."

Capla is not optimistic about white opinion or white identity. "I know their sentiments. I have a great many enemies among those people. Some belong to a very decent class, and some to a very low class."

Many free people of color—after the war they are no longer f.p.c.'s but Creoles of color—remain in Louisiana for generations. It is likely

Lucien Capla has descendants in or near New Orleans. I expect it is possible to find the Capla family. I make a plan to look for them.

After the Caplas are savaged, some of the white guerrillas get the idea to attack the *New Orleans Tribune*, the black paper of Louis Roudanez.

"To the *Tribune!*" is a cry heard down the street. But when the marauders reach the newspaper's office, on Conti Street, they find it guarded by Union soldiers. Neither the publisher Louis Roudanez nor his minions can be gotten to. It is too much to risk crossing the army, and the gangs melt away.

Witnesses testify that as bunches of men swarm the streets, they sing rebel songs. One favorite song of the times is "I'm a Good Old Rebel Soldier." It goes like this—

> *I'm a good old Rebel soldier*
> *Now that's just what I am;*
> *For this "Fair Land of Freedom"*
> *I do not give a damn!*

> *I'm glad I fought against it*
> *I only wish we'd won,*
> *And I don't want no pardon*
> *For anything I done.*

> *I hates the Constitution*
> *This great republic, too,*
> *I hates the Freedmen's Bureau*
> *In uniforms of blue*

> *And I don't want no pardon*
> *For what I was and am*
> *I won't be reconstructed*
> *And I don't care a damn.*

The massacre lasts till about 3:00 p.m. "After that, there was no one left to kill," says one witness. About midafternoon, companies of

Union soldiers appear on the scene. They have come up from Jackson Barracks, the military base three miles downriver, where much of the army is quartered. Their commander blames the long delay on a mistake: someone waylaid the first calls for help.

The shooting continues in other parts of the city. "Colored persons at distant points, peaceably pursuing their lawful business, were attacked by the police, shot, and cruelly beaten," according to the report in Congress. And "the dead lying on the street were violated by shot, kick, and stab. The face of a man just breathing his last was gashed by a knife or razor in the hands of a woman."

It is time to pick up the bodies.

A white historian sympathetic to the marauders and not to the victims says about two hundred people are killed. The editor of the *New Orleans Tribune*, a man who is present on the downtown scene throughout, also reports that hundreds die. "The police and the mob, in mutual and bloody emulation, continued the butchery in the hall and on the street, until nearly two hundred people were killed and wounded," he writes. "The number was probably much larger than this; but of that number the names and residences are known." About the distribution of death, it is all black: "All of the dead belong to the unarmed crowd. Not one single person died on the other side."

Delegates to the convention number some forty whites, and three of them die. The marauders seem to spare most of the race traitors, letting them escape. Out of empathy, I imagine. Whereas none of the black supporters of the delegates get away. Dozens of working-class people in black New Orleans are killed. Dozens of businessmen, teachers, and educated leaders, too. People set a foot in politics at the first moment it becomes possible, and they are slaughtered for it.

Newspapers in the North respond. The day after the killing, on July 31, the *New-York Tribune* tells its readers to "judge the facts" of the riot. "This was almost a St. Bartholomew massacre, and it was intended to begin the Reign of Terror in the South." Louis Roudanez publishes accounts of the killing in the *New Orleans Tribune*. Writers for the paper interview witnesses and survivors and deliver these stories to the state government and to the Union Army. They send bulletins to other newspapers in the North, and they get the *New Orleans Tribune* into the hands of members of Congress.

A month later, President Johnson is on a speaking tour in the Midwest. It is a lobbying trip. He wants lenient handling of the South. On September 2, in St. Louis, Missouri, Johnson looks out on a crowd of five hundred and lays the blame for the New Orleans massacre on the people who died.

"If you take the riot at New Orleans, and trace it back to its source, you will find out who is responsible for the blood that was shed there," Johnson says. "The intention was to enfranchise one portion of the population, called the colored population, and at the same time disfranchise white men." It is whites who suffer. They are the ones victimized. "Let me say that there are many white people in this country that need emancipation," says the president. "Let white men stand erect and free."

During and after the massacre, the police arrest 261 people of color—riot, vagrancy, what comes to mind. All are beaten, many are shot by the police during arrest. Those victims are dragged to jail—the calaboose, so-called—with wounds bleeding.

There are four arrests of whites, for drunkenness.

The Mechanics Institute massacre is the first spasm of the panic that goes under the name of "Ku-klux."

The effects are deep. The sense in the North is that the white South will have the old order, by any means. The sense is that whites in defeat are not moved an inch.

A strong turn comes in politics. The *Report of the Select Committee on the New Orleans Riots* is printed and passed among newspapers from Massachusetts to California. In November 1866, three months after the killings, the midterm elections take place. The massacre brings out a big vote, and a Republican landslide sweeps every state north of Tennessee and Virginia. In early 1867, dozens of white men who are trying to think about the black South enter Congress.

In Louisiana, however, white opinion is exactly the reverse of that in Ohio and Pennsylvania. It is upside down, like the picture in a camera obscura.

"It is our general belief, fixed and unalterable," says *The New Orleans Crescent*, soon after the killing, "that this country was discovered by white men, peopled by white men, defended by white men, and owned by white men, and it is our settled purpose that none but the white man shall participate in its government."

The Mechanics Massacre triggers what historians call Radical Reconstruction. These are the years, 1867 to 1870, that black Southerners and whites try to create an interracial democracy. Maybe what is "radical" is that they face waves of white terror, some of which brings the Lecorgnes back onstage, and yet they keep trying.

The killings in New Orleans—where Constant lends a fist or a gun—are the cause of it. A call is out to defend the rights of the tribe. The directions are in, the pageant arranged. The *Ku-klux* carnival begins.

16

I look for the Capla family. I have reason to believe a descendant of
Alfred Capla, the sixteen-year-old shot in the eye, lives in Gentilly. I
drive to Gentilly, a northeast branch of New Orleans. A French Creole who once owned the land called it "Chantilly," after a wood and
chateau near Paris. When he sold off the pieces, Americans roughed
up the spelling, and "Gentilly" it became. The Lecorgnes of Bouligny
knew nothing about Gentilly. In Constant's day, the place was a dry
ridge that ran through *la ciprière*, cypress swamp.

The soldiers of whiteness have victims, killing has an aftermath.
What happens with families that whiteness fails to crush?

I come to a new and pretty house standing on a little mound
and perched a few feet aboveground. The height says it is a Katrina
house. Gentilly has partly recovered from Hurricane Katrina. In August 2005, a Category 5 hurricane, Katrina, came to New Orleans
and opened a crevasse, an old-fashioned levee break. Katrina chiseled
a gash in a concrete berm on a twentieth-century waterway called
the Industrial Canal, which runs through the city like an oily spine.
Gentilly went under some eight feet of water, and so did half of the
rest of the city. The pretty cottage is new, since the 2005 hurricane
and flood, with some bulldozed and empty lots nearby, where people
could not afford to rebuild.

I climb a wooden stair to the high front door, and a thirtyish man
answers. He is skeptical, a wrinkled brow and flat mouth. I ask for
Janel Santiago Marsalis.

It once was pretty hard to find living families who have links to
events of more than a hundred years ago. It is less so since the digital
curtain rose to display on public databases the naked life happenings

of people long dead. If you have a name from the eighteenth or nineteenth century, it is possible to locate living people who carry past events—History, with a capital *H*—as part of their *family* history. Although I am not yet sure when I knock, I think a woman named Janel Santiago Marsalis is a great-granddaughter of Alfred Capla, the boy shot in the face. The massacre took place five miles away, and about four generations back.

Ms. Marsalis appears at the door. Her brow wrinkles like that of the man, as if to say, "What do you want?" It turns out the man is her son. Ms. Marsalis possesses sensitive eyes. And she wants identification. I am a white stranger, and the visit is unannounced. She is a woman of color, and unknown whites seldom bring good news.

"Do you know of a family member named Capla—Lucien or Alfred?" I say.

At this question, she relaxes her brow. She nods.

"An event called the Mechanics Institute massacre?" Ms. Marsalis tilts back her head, clenches her mouth, and then nods again. Recognition. It was only 150 years ago. The event is somewhat fresh.

Three women in the family want to talk. We rendezvous at a safe place, a neutral coffee shop in Gentilly—beige decor, barista at the espresso counter, bland sounds on the speakers. Ms. Marsalis arrives. She comes with her sister, Alice Richard. In a while the family historian appears. She is Joann St. Cyr, sister-in-law of the first two women. The three women are in their seventies and early eighties, all mothers of grown children, and all retired.

Ms. Marsalis says she is an artist, a printmaker and painter. She says that she taught studio art for many years at Xavier University, a historically black school in New Orleans. Her sister, Alice Richard, says that she has done years of work as a seamstress, making clothes for designers. But she prefers to be a homemaker for her husband, children, and grandchildren. The third woman, Joann St. Cyr, has worked for the city of New Orleans, but she spends her real time researching Louisiana families, black and white. Her name has a beautiful ring. "St. Cyr" is the sound of the word "sincere."

Ms. Marsalis wants to know, "How did you get my name?"

"I have reason to think your family is connected to Lucien Capla, a black activist who was present at the Mechanics Institute massacre," I say.

"We are black," says Joann St. Cyr. "But we don't like to say 'black.' We're *Creole*. Creoles are black and white."

My mistake. Ms. St. Cyr puts the family a step away from "black," claiming the old tribe or social caste, Creoles of color. Creoles are like the third way in race matters, from the nineteenth century and into the present. The Caplas and maybe five thousand other Creole families were free and educated before the Civil War. The living want to remember the inheritance. After the Civil War, the campaign for white dominance pushed race into a binary—black vs. white—and the one-drop rule took over. A splash of African ancestry, "black blood," and you were black. Creoles of color disappeared into blackness, but the meaning lingered. To be Creole in Louisiana means to have membership in an antique club, the early black bourgeoisie. It is usually also a color distinction. To be Creole means to be beige, and to have hair you can comb.

"We have relatives named Capla who were in that massacre," says Ms. Marsalis. "The Caplas are our grandmother's family. And my father's people, the Santiagos, they were in it, too. But how do you know about us?"

I mention research steps, and Joann St. Cyr, the family historian, nods in agreement. Ms. St. Cyr knows her way around census lists and wills, sacramental records and marriage licenses, notarial acts and city directories, death certificates and obituaries.

I tell the Capla women that I do not know the names of each of the two hundred killed in New Orleans on July 30, 1866. No one does, but there are memories of survivors that seep down to the present. I do not know the names of all the perpetrators. None of the white terrorists were prosecuted, none even arrested. No one claimed the role of race warrior and wrote down what they did. The absence of criminal evidence is itself a piece of evidence. It is a sign of the chokehold that whiteness has on public memory.

But the U.S. Congress and the Louisiana legislature held hearings and took testimony, and Lucien Capla was a witness who testified.

"I have a copy of that testimony," says Joann St. Cyr. She pulls a photocopy from a pile of papers. "He testified Christmas Eve 1866."

Lucien Jean-Pierre Capla was the shoe dealer who got thick into Reconstruction politics. The Caplas did well in the trades. Another in the family ran a paint store that sold to contractors. A third had a cigar-making business. When Lucien Capla testified about his experience during the massacre, he was forty-five, married to a woman named Felicie Fleury, and had four children with his wife.

A mass killing of two hundred and mass wounding of another two hundred shreds four hundred families. Supposing that each victim had twenty-five family members in her orbit—children, parents, siblings, and cousins—the crudest measure counts ten thousand people subjected to the shared trauma. Add an explosion of fear. In 1866, the killings threw a shower of terror among the city's fifty thousand people of color. And disgust. The massacre meant fresh repugnance of whites. Revulsion toward whites spread among blacks, and soaked in.

The majority of whites, on the other hand, to judge from newspapers, seemed to feel comfort and satisfaction in the aftermath of the massacre. I mean, in the year 1866. It might be less true now.

I look for words and come up with this—

"That time was brutal for black people."

"It was," says Ms. Marsalis, laconic.

"I am interested in how families recovered from the trauma and what they are doing now. Family history has long effects that may still shadow us today. It is like opening a box and finding things we have not come to terms with."

"Can I see your book?" says Ms. Marsalis. She wants to see a book with my name on it, some kind of credential. Book in hand, she nods. She puts the book aside.

"I make art," she says. "I am the first person of color to receive an M.F.A. at Tulane University, and I paint portraits. I am finishing one commissioned by the city of New Orleans for its 300th anniversary. The painting depicts Dr. Norman Francis, the first African American president of Xavier University, here in New Orleans. My branch of the family, coming from the Caplas, the Santiagos, has been a family of musicians and businesspeople. But I am the first in our group to focus on the visual arts."

Janel Marsalis uses the words "musician" and "artist." Joann St. Cyr uses the word "Creole." A picture forms. In the nineteenth century, the Caplas were educated, creative, and professional. Which they remain today.

Ms. Marsalis turns to Ms. St. Cyr.

"Joann is the family historian. She is running over with information."

"From a little girl I was always a nosy child," says Ms. St. Cyr. "I wanted to know who, and I wanted to know why."

"Are you still nosy?" I ask. "Yes," she answers.

Some laughter.

"What are your names? I mean, your family names in New Orleans?" Ms. St. Cyr asks.

It is the family history question. The names of families are the front doors of history. Most historians, however, enter the house of memory through the garage, where papers and artifacts are stored. I mention two names—Rowley, my mother's surname, and Lecorgne, my grandmother's.

"I see," says Ms. St. Cyr. "That's the English and the French influence. I believe that before we had a present, we had to have a past. It's good to go back, no matter what you find. Everybody finds so many different things. Nobody is just one thing. That's a fiction."

She means, I think, that nobody living is only what her grandmother the pretty hostess used to be. And no one living is just what the marauder in the family used to be and do, in the old days.

Photographs of Lucien Capla have not survived, and no picture of his son Alfred. But a family member from the same era named Edward Capla sat for a portrait. The image is a photograph worked over by hand to make it look like a drawing, a technique of the day. Edward Capla's picture gives an idea of what Alfred Capla might have looked like—long-faced, self-possessed, and high-toned—had he not been shot in the face.

"It's a miracle that Alfred survived," says Alice Richard. "We wouldn't even be here if things had turned out differently."

Pencil drawing on photograph of Edward Capla

Alfred's father, Lucien Capla, stayed in politics. In December 1866, four months after the killing, he was appointed to the state's Republican executive committee. The goal of the party at the time was to get the vote for people of color.

His son Alfred lost his right eye and suffered terrible head injuries in the Mechanics Institute massacre. It took time, but he recovered. Then he learned a trade, tailoring. Despite having one-eyed vision, Alfred Capla trained to become a clothier and a good hand at needlework. He planned to open a store and make formal clothes for men. Alfred also followed his father, Lucien, into politics. In his early twenties, he represented the Sixth Ward of New Orleans at the state convention of the Republican Party. A reporter who knew Alfred Capla described his personality: "industrious and efficient."

A few years later, another act of violence coming from a white man almost ended the life of the boy who survived the massacre. In 1873, Alfred Capla, now twenty-five, single and living alone, was working as a clerk in the city's Recorder's Court, processing filings and small claims. It was a second job. He had begun in the tailoring trade and was gathering customers. On a Wednesday night in July, on Burgundy Street in the French Quarter, Capla was walking home. He happened to pass a Creole woman of color, and then a white man named Adam Navarre. It was about 10:00 p.m. Capla overheard Adam Navarre make a sexual remark to the woman. Capla knew the woman, and he told Adam Navarre to quit harassing her. It was not common at the time for a black man to chastise a white stranger about anything, let alone tell him to shut down his lust. Capla continued on his way and reached home. A half hour later, the street harasser Adam Navarre turned up at the front door holding a gun.

It turns out that Adam Navarre had served time for murder and had recently been released from prison. Alfred Capla possibly knew this, possibly did not. At the door, Navarre cursed Capla before firing a single shot at him, which missed. The industrious and efficient tailor flew into rage and fear, and a hand-to-hand fight followed. Capla found his way to a knife during the fight and stabbed Navarre three times. The man with the gun bled to death on the sidewalk in front of the house. With that, Alfred Capla walked to the Third Precinct police station and turned himself in.

The white legal establishment knew Capla, the courthouse clerk. Capla produced witnesses of the shooting and the fight. Police and prosecutor, seldom friendly to people of color, declined to bring charges. The case was ruled one of self-defense. Capla went back to his quiet life.

In 1876, Alfred's father, Lucien, died, age fifty-five. The same year, Alfred married a woman named Harriet Phillips. He opened his tailor shop and ran it for twenty years.

Janel Marsalis has among her things a big ledger from Alfred Capla's tailoring business. It is a handwritten pattern book, dating from about 1890, a kind of manual for making and altering men's formal wear. The book is organized with headlines, like these: "To measure a stout man . . ." "Comments on drafting the sleeve . . ." "The revised 19th-century pant and vest system . . ." "Directions for drafting the oversack . . ." Alfred Capla sketched dozens of tailoring problems and steps to solve each, how to cut and sew, alter and trim. The pattern book amounts to an encyclopedia of late-1800s fashion.

Alfred Capla and his wife, Harriet Philips, became pillars of Creole society, taking a place like that of Alfred's parents. The tailor continued in politics, joining the Republican Party's executive committee, like his father before him. Alfred Capla's life was short, however. He died at age forty-five, in 1892.

"Alfred died and his wife Harriet both died," says Alice Richard, Ms. Marsalis's sister, shaking her head. They left four young children. Their maternal grandmother, a widowed chambermaid named Julia Philips, stepped in to raise them. It was a rough passage. When Alfred's children lost their parents, they fell out of the comfort of the black bourgeoisie and into poverty. The children lived in a crammed single room, looked after by a struggling grandmother who could not read. Alfred's children grew up speaking "Creole," the dialect of the working and black poor. It was a language that absorbed the Gombo of the ex-slaves and kept black speech alive and separate from the French of the white elite.

Creole is a language that can no longer be found. The dialect blended West African syntax with French nouns and verbs, and bent them in the adoption. It is possible to guess at the number of Creole speakers. After 1820, approximately seven hundred thousand blacks came to Louisiana from Virginia, Maryland, and elsewhere on the East Coast, during the domestic slave trade; they spoke black English. During the same period, approximately two hundred thousand blacks native to Louisiana, enslaved by French-speaking whites, spoke Gombo, or Creole.

The sound of the language has vanished, but pieces survive in folktales and verse. In 1885, the writer Lafcadio Hearn published a book of Creole proverbs, used by blacks and whites, like this one—

> *Neg' porté maïs dan so lapoche pou volé poule;*
> *Milâte porté cordon dan so lapoche pou volé choual;*
> *N'homme blanc porté larzan dan so lapoche pou trompé fille.*

Nigger carries corn in his pocket to steal a chicken;
Mulatto carries a rope in his pocket to steal a horse;
White man carries money in his pocket to seduce a girl.

I do not know whether this is the kind of Creole that Julia Philips spoke. If so, I want more of it.

It is on to the story of Constant Lecorgne, our Klansman. I am not sure how to approach the subject, so I dribble out the pieces.

"I am interested in a difficult time in New Orleans history, Reconstruction," I say to the three women. "It is when enslaved people have freedom, when African American men get the vote, and there is a backlash. White people are angry and resentful at new freedoms African Americans have. Now, I have read about the Mechanics Institute massacre and found the names of people—"

Joann St. Cyr speaks up.

"I have other people who was in that massacre, ancestors, but they wasn't hurt, as far as I know. They was at Mechanics Hall, too."

I share some of the white side of the story. "Now, my mother's people, I mean, a branch of them, the Lecorgnes, they were simple people," I say. "The men were carpenters—in the trades, like the Caplas. I have evidence that one or more men in the family were in white militia groups during Reconstruction. One group was called the White League."

Joann St. Cyr says, "Oh, yes."

"Circumstantial evidence and court records say that a man called Constant Lecorgne, a predecessor of mine, was in white militias— they called them all 'Ku-klux'—and he was arrested for it. The Ku-klux were attacking politicians of color, they were night riding, and doing all sorts of things to abuse people of color."

I spill the story, running at the mouth, because I feel uncomfortable with it, and because it disgusts me.

"During Reconstruction, people of color began to exercise power. They faced violent reaction. I do not have fingerprints, but there is evidence the Lecorgnes were involved in mob violence. So, I want to reach out to families who were active, like the Caplas, who lifted their heads and fought. The Caplas were almost killed. It is for personal reasons, because my family might have done damage. And it is for social reasons. I think white folks have to come to terms with our inheritance of violence. It would be good for us, good for society."

Some silence around the table. The three women look at one another.

Ms. St. Cyr says, "I know about all that." She means, I think, that she knows the story in all its wretched parts.

Ms. Marsalis looks up. "I have a question. I don't want to add to your guilt."

"You can add to my guilt if you like," I say.

"Did your ancestors take part in that massacre?" Ms. Marsalis is poised and discreet, as I imagine the Caplas were in their time.

"I have not found direct evidence, but circumstantial evidence is strong they did. I have not found direct proof, because the perpetrators got off. The police helped with the massacre, and then arrested two or three dozen black people, and charged them with riot. The evidence is that this man Constant Lecorgne was probably on the scene. A terrible and terrifying thought. I cannot say that yes, he was a trigger man. And I do not say he was not."

The women look at me, then at one another. Ms. St. Cyr smiles thinly. "I wouldn't have made it in those days," she says. "They probably would have killed me. I would have been too defiant. A few years before that, and I would have been with Harriet Tubman. I would have been out there in the swamp, trying to smuggle people." More silence. Ms. St. Cyr looks up. She nods at the revelation that a massacre lies on the table between us. It is a bitter dish.

"So, if your family did that," she says, "and you are trying to do something to mend the pain, that's all right. My mother didn't raise me to hate anybody. And I have prayed. And I love everybody."

Joann St. Cyr deflects with a non sequitur. "Back then, men of color were voting. I mean, during Reconstruction. By the time of jazz, they were taking the vote away. During Reconstruction, black men were Republicans. My grandfather was a jazz musician. He used to say, 'Don't vote Republican. The Republicans are going to turn on us.' And of course they did turn on us, eventually."

Over a few months, I visit descendants of the Caplas in New Orleans several times. We meet at kitchen tables and on sofas, with scattered papers and albums. Sometimes the memorabilia are stained and warped from soaking in the flood of Katrina. On one visit, I spend more time with Janel Marsalis, the artist in the family. Janel Marsalis paints in acrylic, paints in watercolor, and makes prints from engraved plates. She asks me to see the work and to visit her studio.

Ms. Marsalis leads the way into her garage, and from it into her art studio. It is twenty feet square, with a wall of shelves covered in paint tubes and brushes, racks of canvases, and a chest of shallow drawers to hold prints. She pulls out picture after picture that had soaked in Katrina's water. Finally she lifts a big, rolled-up canvas and lays it out—an acrylic painting four feet wide and nearly six feet tall. It shows the face of an ageless woman, somewhat resigned.

"A portrait of my great-grandmother, Melanie Gardner. It was on the wall during the flood, and the bottom of it is rotted." The subject of the portrait, Melanie Gardner, was born in 1860. She was grandmother to the painter's mother, and illiterate, according to the U.S. Census.

More pictures come out.

"Much of my work was destroyed by the flood, by Katrina," says Janel Santiago Marsalis, shaking her head. For many in New Orleans, the memory of the 2005 disaster is a trauma as big as any. "My things stayed underwater for weeks. When I went to salvage, sculptures crumbled in my hand, paint dripped off the canvas."

Janel Santiago Marsalis with her portrait of Melanie Gardner,
her great-grandmother

Ms. Marsalis brings out a print cycle from that time, what she calls the "Boxed" series. The prints are two feet square, fine line drawings in black and white of people compressed into small spaces, confined.

"It is as though we are in a box that is invisible to those on the outside of it," she says. The people outside, I infer, are white. Ms. Marsalis nods yes. "We are boxed-in and can't break out."

She describes the first print as "a Malcolm X type who is going to get out of the box, no matter what" and the second as "a Martin Luther King Jr. type using his intellect and kindness to get out of the box." A third is "a person confounded, outdone, and defeated." Ms. Marsalis explains the process as "etchings on matte acetate, with graphite, and then images layered in like collage, with acrylic. The whole image is etched on a zinc plate, which is inked."

She pulls one more print that shows a mouth, wide open and talking. "It's called 'Communication.' Meaning, no matter how much we communicate, they still don't understand." She raises her eyebrows and smiles. "'They' are your people."

After graduating from Tulane, Ms. Marsalis started teaching part-time at the University of New Orleans, then moved to Dillard University. Both are historically black schools. She taught studio art at Dillard for fifteen years and moved to Xavier, another black university. She retired from Xavier in 2005.

"Recently I did images of Frederick Douglass and W.E.B. Du Bois, two of my heroes. And one of Harriet Tubman, when it was decided that she would be on the twenty-dollar bill." The Tubman picture is a fine print that depicts a woman in middle age with wire-rimmed eyeglasses.

"I sent one copy to President Obama and one to the U.S. treasurer, and I said, 'Do her when she was young and active and not old and in a shawl.'"

On a near table is a letter from the Democratic Party thanking Ms. Marsalis for a contribution. Pictures of the forty-fourth president, Barack Obama, peek out from under a pile, on newspapers and postcards. When Ms. Marsalis leads me back to her living room, I glance in the corner at a life-size cardboard cutout of President Obama.

It is one of the few pictures in the house that Ms. Marsalis did not make herself.

The descendants of Lucien Capla make a big family, maybe one hundred. And to hear the women tell it, a lot of them know the story of the Mechanics Institute. In 1918, Emily Capla, the grandmother who spoke Creole, married a musician and housepainter, Willie Santiago. One of their sons, Alton Santiago, married a woman named Ethel Oliver, who produced eleven children. Janel Marsalis and Alice Richard are two of them. Many of the eleven brothers and sisters stayed in Louisiana and raised families. Some moved away, in the American style, and put down roots elsewhere. Living family members who trace their ancestry to Alfred Capla the tailor live in Alabama, California, Missouri, New Jersey, New York, and Texas.

One line in the family, which leads to Joann St. Cyr and the two sisters, passes through the heart of black music. I visit Ms. St. Cyr, the woman who stressed the word "Creole" when we first met. And she shares the story of her grandfather, a jazz musician.

"My father was named John St. Cyr, and his father was John Alexander St. Cyr, my grandfather. That was *Johnny* St. Cyr, and he had the music. He was a banjo player and guitarist. And he played with Jelly Roll Morton." I am a little startled at this news, a gentle Creole woman linked to some of the pioneers of jazz. Jelly Roll Morton was a Creole of color, born in New Orleans in 1885. He boasted that he invented jazz, and it is fifty percent true. "Along with Jelly Roll," says Ms. St. Cyr, "my grandfather played with Louis Armstrong and the Hot Five." That does it for me. I did not expect that a race massacre would lead down a hallway to great inventors in music. Louis Armstrong was not a Creole of color. In 1901, he was born poor and black in a section known as "Back of Town," a hard half-mile west of the French Quarter.

Ms. St. Cyr's story means that a branch of the Capla family was present during the birth hours of a black American art form. The connection of the banjo-and-guitar player Johnny St. Cyr with the massacre survivor Alfred Capla is a little distant but real.

Johnny St. Cyr married into the Capla family. He knew Alfred Capla, and he played with another jazz pioneer in the Capla family, named Willie Santiago, a second banjo player, as well as the grandfather of Janel Santiago Marsalis. These two, Johnny St. Cyr and Willie Santiago, played the ballrooms and riverboats of Prohibition-era New Orleans. And what they did with music swept the table clean.

Johnny St. Cyr was a handsome Creole, soft-spoken and lean, with a beautiful baritone speaking voice. "He was a plasterer," said his granddaughter, Joann St. Cyr. "A lot of the jazz men worked construction for a steady income when they weren't doing regular gigs." In the era before Sheetrock, Johnny St. Cyr shaped the walls of old New Orleans houses with wet cement, switching between the banjo and the trowel for much of his life.

Johnny St. Cyr (banjo) with Louis Armstrong (trumpet) in Chicago, 1925

When he was sixteen, in 1906, Johnny St. Cyr heard Jelly Roll Morton play piano with a dance orchestra in New Orleans, and he was hooked. The banjo would be his ticket to the life. In 1908, St. Cyr married sixteen-year-old Marguerite Peralt. "I come from Marguerite Peralt," said Joann St. Cyr, her papers and pictures scattered on a coffee table. "She was my grandmother."

About 1910, ragtime, with its mid-speed syncopation, started to give way to "hot bands" that cranked up the tempo and melodies. A cornet player named Manny Gabriel asked St. Cyr to join his band, the National Orchestra, and he stayed for two years, playing rhythm guitar and banjo.

"We played parties, balls, picnics, banquets, parades and on advertising wagons," Johnny St. Cyr remembered in a taped interview with folklorist Alan Lomax in 1949. "We played both for white and colored, all over New Orleans. One night might be on St. Charles Avenue at a private party for wealthy white people, next night we might play in the District."

The District was Storyville. Most agree that jazz surfaced in the brothels and dance halls of Storyville, the prostitution quarter of the city. Storyville measured about a mile square and lay just northwest of the *Vieux Carré*, beyond Congo Square. It got its name from Sidney Story, a city councilman who wrote an ordinance that created the city's legal sex trade zone—the District. Commercial sex was legal in Storyville for twenty years, between 1897 and 1917, and jazz was born in its naked rooms.

In 1918, St. Cyr graduated from $2.50-per-gig work to a weekly payday with a dance orchestra on the *S.S. Capitol*, a paddlewheel riverboat that plied the Mississippi. The *Capitol* docked half the year in New Orleans and half the year in St. Louis, Missouri, and it cruised the river at night, a floating dance hall. It was whites-only all week, with Monday nights pegged for Negroes. St. Cyr was twenty-eight.

The banjo player told an interviewer that he helped Louis Armstrong—a cornet player, then age seventeen—to get a job on the *Capitol*. And that he persuaded the boat's manager to buy the teenage Louis Armstrong the first horn he actually owned. According to St. Cyr, he and Louis Armstrong went together to a music store in St. Louis in 1918, bought a $67 cornet, and sent the bill to the steamship company.

About 1910, jazz emerged out of the rattling tempos of ragtime. Jazz was a syncopated stomp that sped up the bass and rhythm, carried by piano and by Johnny St. Cyr's guitar, and put the melody instruments out in front of the band. St. Cyr was one of the two hundred or so musicians who first heard and then created the new form.

With World War I, jazz players started moving from New Orleans to Chicago, including a bandleader named Joseph "King" Oliver, a cornet player. The money was better, the dance halls full, and the race codes not set in concrete. At the same time, a still-young recording industry, getting rich on gramophone disks, decided money could be made with black music. White promoters had a name for the big sounds coming north with the black migration—blues from Mississippi, jazz from Louisiana. It was "race music." In Chicago, King Oliver recorded as well as played live. In 1923, Oliver sent a telegram to Johnny St. Cyr in New Orleans asking him to come a thousand miles north to join his act. Oliver sent the same telegram to Louis Armstrong, and both Armstrong and St. Cyr found themselves in Chicago on the bandstand with King Oliver and his Creole Jazz Band.

St. Cyr went to Illinois with his wife, Marguerite. Armstrong married a singer and pianist in Chicago, Lillian Hardin. In Chicago, New Orleans jazz went onto gramophone records and from there traveled out to stores and into living rooms throughout the country. After two years in the dance halls with King Oliver, Louis Armstrong formed his own band, the Hot Five, and recruited Johnny St. Cyr to play his banjo.

Louis Armstrong and the Hot Five went to the office of a race music company called OKeh Records and recorded some of the most important tracks in twentieth-century American music. Johnny St. Cyr played on fifty of the Hot Five's jazz and blues tunes, and today they sound like a foundation for popular music. The titles only gesture at the content, but they have funk: "Potato Head Blues," "Big Butter and Egg Man," "Heebie-Jeebies," "Gut Bucket Blues," "The King of the Zulus," "Skid-Dat-De-Dat" . . . In the scat singing alone, on "Heebie-Jeebies" and "Skid-Dat-De-Dat," you might locate the kernel of rap music.

While in Chicago, Johnny St. Cyr and his wife, Marguerite, had two children, including the father of Joann St. Cyr. Ms. St. Cyr is the woman in New Orleans who says about the long-ago massacre, "My mother didn't raise me to hate."

In 1926, Johnny St. Cyr recorded with a second New Orleans genius, Jelly Roll Morton. Born with the name Ferdinand LaMothe, the pianist renamed himself "Jelly Roll Morton" when he made a living at the keyboard in the brothels of Storyville, the jelly roll a joke that pointed to sex for sale. In Chicago, he led a band he called the Red Hot Peppers. With Jelly Roll Morton, St. Cyr again found himself recording songs in blues and jazz that throw a shadow over the next hundred years of popular music—"Black Bottom Stomp," "Cannonball Blues," "Doctor Jazz Stomp," a dozen more. St. Cyr himself sings on "Dead Man Blues."

By 1930, musicians started to come home from Chicago to New Orleans. As the money drained out of hot jazz, and the Depression arrived, Johnny St. Cyr retreated to the Crescent City. He went back to plastering. St. Cyr spent the next twenty-five years in New Orleans, playing with part-time bands, working in construction, and eventually recording an album of his own material.

In New Orleans in 1940, Joann St. Cyr was born, giving the banjoist a granddaughter.

Johnny St. Cyr moved to Los Angeles in the 1950s. He spent the last years of his life on a lucrative but strange bandstand—at Disneyland. Until his death, in 1966, St. Cyr led a seven-piece band that played on the *Mark Twain*, a miniature steamboat that cruised the theme park, the banjo player doing cheerful arrangements of early jazz. By that time, the sound of a hot band was tamed. The white crowds of Disneyland sipped Coke on the pint-sized steamboat and looked over at St. Cyr and his band. I imagine they found the Negroes to be quaint.

"My mother says we are Creoles, but I do not have that problem. I completely identify with the African American experience in this country."

Ricardo Coleman says he is forty-three, but he looks thirty. He is handsome and vigorous and deep-voiced, with leather jacket and beard. His mother is Joann St. Cyr, his great-grandfather was guitarist Johnny St. Cyr. Ricardo Coleman, one of the Capla family circle, has a tranquil manner. He is not an artist, like Janel Marsalis, but a historian in training. Coleman is in a graduate program in history and is writing a thesis about Creoles of color in politics after the Civil War.

"I do not think you can separate Creole life from African American life. The paramilitary organizations like the Ku Klux Klan did not make those distinctions."

It is Carnival season when I visit Ricardo Coleman. Mardi Gras is a week away, and every day a dozen parades ripple through the city. We meet at a coffee shop and sit out on the patio. Within sight is Veterans Boulevard, a commercial strip through the New Orleans suburb of Metairie. It is a parade route for the day. The loud cavalcade of the Little Rascals Krewe rolls past. Bands, floats, and marching clubs, costumes, plastic beads flying, thousands lining the road. A fantastic and foolish scene, and almost everyone is white. The suburb of Metairie, a ten-minute drive from uptown New Orleans, bloomed during the 1960s and '70s as two hundred thousand whites left the half-black center city and moved west.

I spent my teenage and high school years growing up in Metairie. It was a big place, the white younger brother of majority-black New Orleans—a three-bedroom sprawl over a filled-in swamp, with shopping malls, drive-through daiquiri bars, a golf course, the New Orleans airport, and some nice cemeteries.

Ricardo Coleman lives in Metairie. "Primarily we get microaggression," he says. "I walk into a coffee shop and there is tension. People watch you in the parking lot, clutch their pocketbooks. It happens every day. It is highly Republican out here, highly conservative, and it reflects what they want New Orleans to be."

A loud high school band overwhelms the conversation. When it passes, I share one interpretation with the historian in training. "I have the feeling there is white supremacy that is violent and aggressive and white supremacy that is psychological and soft. And that they are in communication."

"What started the white flight out to Metairie from New Orleans?" Mr. Coleman asks himself. "The first thing is the change in city government. A mayor called Moon Landrieu, white, was elected in 1969. He campaigned on inclusion and tried to make the city government look like the city. Before Landrieu, twenty percent of the city's workforce was African American, and after him it was fifty percent or sixty percent. He put African Americans in important positions. That began the talk, 'We gotta get outta New Orleans.' The move sped up with the election of Dutch Morial, first black mayor, in 1978—he was a working-class Creole—and then people started moving out to Metairie overnight."

I throw a question—"When did white supremacy get its legs . . ."—and he catches it—

"You mean with the White League, the Knights of the White Camellia, the KKK?" He skips from Reconstruction back to the present. "As far as the legacy of those things, it is invisible, not something you can point to. In some places, it is open, and you can smell it and feel it. But here, people go to parades. Whites talk to blacks, but they don't see one another. Here, people just want to have a good time. It is a legacy of silence."

I ask about the massacre, and Ricardo Coleman says—

"Most people, if you ask, say, 'There was a massacre downtown?' They don't know of it.

"After the fights of Reconstruction, eventually the white redemption came, and Jim Crow laws were written," Coleman says. "At that point, many members of the Creole community understood that reality was changing, and not for the better. Some felt they had no choice, and they crossed over into whiteness. A lot of people went up to Chicago, or to Detroit. People saw Reconstruction had ended, and it was a failure. They had been betrayed, and they had no choice but to pass into whiteness in order to get jobs and to survive."

Coleman is talking about families he has known personally. Within each family, people disappeared from one race and joined the other. That is, if they were Creole enough, and light enough to pass for white.

"Imagine the terror, the isolation. The idea that you can never any longer be who you are," he says. "That there is a part of you that is locked away. That you had to carry a lie. Some came back to visit their families, at night. Some did not."

No one has counted the number of Louisiana Creoles who passed out of blackness into whiteness, but there were many thousand, and perhaps hundreds of thousands.

"But by the way, back to the legacy of the militias, see that guy? The cop?" He waves at a beefy white policeman, one of a dozen manning the Little Rascals parade. "You want to know the legacy of paramilitary organizations? He is the inheritance. People used to look out their windows and see hooded guys with torches. In a similar way, we look out our windows today, and we see a cop."

"Louisiana has the most black people in prison, per capita, in the nation," I say.

"Louisiana is first in the nation, and the United States first in the world. So Louisiana is first in the world. True." Ricardo Coleman shakes his head.

"The paramilitary organizations may be coming back. Since the election of 2016, we have seen an increase in these militia groups, a normalizing of some of these people."

On Veterans Boulevard, the parade is ending, and street sweepers swoosh past. Hundreds walk to their cars. Children dressed as alligators, mothers dressed as insects, but also a lot of invisible men in dad jeans. It feels like pattern recognition when I see, climbing into a pickup truck, a familiar sight. It is a white man wearing blackface. He has a handful of plastic beads in one hand, a basketball in the other, and he wears a numbered jersey. He is doing it like the other tribe does it. He knows he has it just right.

PART V

WHITE TERROR

The stage is arranged, the Ku-klux pageant begins.

On March 4, 1867, a Monday at 10:00 a.m., two thousand firemen jostle left and right into parade columns on Canal Street, near the levee of the river. Their costume is full dress uniform. Marshals from the Firemen's Charitable Association yell the lines into order, and the procession moves: thirty-five fire companies, thirty-three marching bands, hundreds of horses, two dozen fire trucks. The firemen carry banners, horns, hoses, and ladders prettily draped with flowers.

Constant Lecorgne appears somewhere in the middle of the long snake of a march. The eighty-five men of Home Hook & Ladder are the eighth company in line, behind the sixty-two men of William Tell Hook & Ladder and in front of the seventy-two of Philadelphia Engine Company, whose draft horse—black and shiny—is named "Nig." A rustle of laughs whenever the driver yells, "Git, Nig!"

Newspapers run pages of detail, description, and praise. A reporter clocks it: fifty-five minutes for the parade to pass.

Wending from downtown to Jefferson City and back, the firemen's march is a two-mile-long victory parade. "New Orleans turned out *en masse* to greet and crown her heroes," says a reporter. One paper estimates the crowd on the *banquettes* to number one hundred thousand. If true, it is half the population of the city. Reporters say nothing about black spectators. African Americans, now a third of the population, seem conspicuous in absence.

The big crowd has something to do with fires, I think, and something with events at the Mechanics Institute. The *en masse* want to thank some of their fighters.

Home Hook & Ladder is "uniformed beautifully, in blue and

white, with Old Stonewall, the company's noble horse, walking proudly on, feeling monarch of all he surveys," says a witness. At the end of the day, some firemen move on to banquets and dancing, others to receptions and barbecues. But the heroes and their fans have no rest between drinks, because the following day, Tuesday, is Mardi Gras.

People say the culmination of Carnival season, coming March 5, is late this year. It is the fault of the stars. Mardi Gras, Fat Tuesday, always falls forty days before Easter Sunday, and the date of Easter shifts with the astral calendar in logic no one understands.

The firemen who crowd the streets on Monday are out again Tuesday. But instead of marching, they carouse, many with their families. While the firemen's parade was white, Carnival is black and white. Mardi Gras lowers the walls of difference and hostility between tribes, or at least so it is said by both species that crowd the streets.

On the big day, the Lecorgnes are probably in the mix with everyone, probably masking, costumed as one thing or another. Many people put on a character. Men and women dress as animals or plants, archangels or demons, princes or paupers, roles from a play or from folklore. If Constant and Gabrielle follow a common pattern, they drift from street to street with their children, everyone in an outfit, stopping for food and a laugh on a friend's porch, or kissing to greet before sitting to drink at some sister's silver-strewn dinner table.

It is common for a white woman or man to dress as one of them, *les nègres*. Probably several thousand whites wear blackface and dress as they think African Americans might, or should. To "black up" is a reassuring custom. To imitate the black race proves the gulf between the white and black worlds, a gap that must be shown again and again.

When whites pretend to be black, they do so on stage as well as in the street. It is the minstrel troupe that shows the Carnival crowds just how to play at color. Minstrelsy is the most popular of all forms of theater, from Louisiana to Atlanta, New York to Chicago. It is the nation's schoolhouse for "niggering." Everyone learns tricks from minstrel men—the loud dressing, the shucking and shuffling, the blackface and black talk, the singing like howling, all those things colored people do. All those things make superb material for masking at Mardi Gras. Whites pretend to be black as though pretending to be an animal or a character in myth.

I wonder whether the six Lecorgne siblings, Constant and his brothers and sisters, are blacked up. Maybe Constant wipes grease or the ash of burned cork on his face and pulls on a ragged pair of pants. It would not surprise me, and he would have much company.

On Mardi Gras, whites can black up, but black people do not dress as crackers at Carnival. To do so might be dangerous. It might cause trouble among the considerable number of crackers who do not see themselves as ridiculous, or like animals. It might bother the large number of whites who do not have a sense of humor.

Maybe Gabrielle and Constant are in light costume, with only a mask on the face. Constant might be wearing a plain "domino" mask, which covers the eyes and nose but leaves the lower half of the face exposed. The domino mask is the least disturbing of Carnival disguises. But it is possible that Constant wears a "moretta" mask, the one that is menacing to look at. Moretta masks cover the whole face, except for the nostrils and eyes. They are blank of expression and held in place by a button clenched between the teeth. With its empty coldness, and because it prevents the wearer from speaking, the moretta causes the most discomfort of any mask in a room. Most are entirely black. To wear one is to broadcast pure and monstrous blackness.

The six Lecorgne siblings—Yves of God, Ézilda, Constant, Joseph, Aurore, and Eliza—do not carouse with rich and pretentious whites. They are family people, parents in their thirties and forties, and they have drifted down from their old perch among the slaveholding elite. Their social circles are more plain, except for the starchy Yves of God, who keeps finer company. The Lecorgnes mask with hoi polloi, more common whites. They have little to do with the businessmen and moneychangers who float in the city's richer class. Those families, or some of them, are pulled toward one Carnival group, to which the Lecorgnes do not belong, the Mistick Krewe of Comus.

A few businessmen set up "Comus" before the Civil War. (In the same love of alliteration that gives birth to the word "Ku-klux," they coin the word "krewe.") The Krewe of Comus takes its name from

John Milton's play *Comus*, in which the named character is the de-bauched god of revelry, who captures a woman, brings her to his pal-ace, ties her to a chair, and tries to seduce her with flourishes of a large wand. (He fails.) The Krewe of Comus puts on a nighttime parade, a procession that moves by torchlight on Mardi Gras, with cos-tumes and music and rolling floats decorated with scenery—*tableaux roulants*. It is a parade that ends in the ballroom of the Varieties Theater, on Gravier Street, where the Krewe puts on a bal masqué, masked ball, and members perform a tableau, a silent bit of costumed theater.

The Krewe of Comus marching on St. Charles Avenue, Mardi Gras 1867

It is all so tasteful and restrained. While most of Mardi Gras, both black and white, is louche and wanton.

Comus is bigger than the heads and wallets of the Lecorgnes. I imagine that Constant and family, like many in the city, watch on Mardi Gras night as the masked men of Comus guide their mule-drawn tableaux along St. Charles Avenue toward the theater. The Lecorgnes watch, and they wave. On one float, Constant might see a familiar face. Or he might see a familiar beard, because the face itself is masked.

It is the face of Henry Hayes, sheriff of New Orleans, a man with a foot-long black beard. Hayes is the sheriff in the Mechanics Institute massacre, the man who deputizes ex-rebels to assist in the killing. He appears on a Comus wagon draped in a robe, mask, and half hood, an outfit that is becoming common Carnival gear. The hands of Henry Hayes are two of the bloodiest in the city. It is coincidence, of course, that the sheriff is president of the Mistick Krewe of Comus. Constant and Gabrielle wave as the tasteful and restrained leader of Mardi Gras revelry trundles past.

News of the outrage comes from Washington. The Radical Republican Congress pushes through the Reconstruction Act. The law removes the rebel legislatures from around the South and replaces them with military government. Voting by ex-rebels is cut, and the vote for black men is promised. President Andrew Johnson vetoes the bill in the afternoon, and the new Congress overrides the same day. The first Reconstruction Act is followed by three more. The four laws are Washington's answer to the New Orleans massacre; they are a backlash and a crackdown. Congress requires each state in the South to approve the Fourteenth Amendment, the 435-word footnote to the Constitution that makes black people citizens; and Congress compels each state to write a new, black-friendly constitution.

Everyone thinks that whiteness is back on its throne, but Congress decides to throw it out of the temple.

Louisiana is placed, with Texas, in the so-called Fifth Military District. And the U.S. Army general Philip Sheridan is named regional chief. Sheridan takes command in New Orleans, dissolves the state legislature, and ejects the mayor and the governor from office. On May 1, 1867, Sheridan orders his officers to start registering black men for the vote.

Captains in Yankee blue uniforms take files and fan out from New Orleans. Blacks sign up by the tens of thousands, placing an X on the signature line. Most African Americans are illiterate, due to the old law that barred enslaved people from school. All register as Republicans, the party of Lincoln the Emancipator. They register as Republicans, because they know the Democratic Party would prefer to see them in slave cabins.

Alcibiade DeBlanc, the Lecorgne friend who signed the secession order, is not happy. At this point, DeBlanc lives in the town of Franklin, in the rural pocket of St. Mary Parish, where he is part of a small white minority. He is in Franklin for a job as a district judge. It is the first time he has needed a job. An ex-slaveholder, and a lawyer, DeBlanc is accustomed to living from his wit in the courtroom and whip in the field. But the war took all of that away. The good judge Alcibiade DeBlanc regards "emancipation" as a personal theft.

In Franklin, Judge DeBlanc meets a newspaperman, Daniel Dennett, who runs a weekly called the *Planters' Banner*. The pages of the *Planters' Banner* are full of taunts aimed at Republicans and sarcasm about black rights. DeBlanc and Dennett become friends, each regarding the other as useful. Dennett the journalist is a gossip, Alcibiade the lawyer is an orator. They decide to form a talkers' club. They want a place where men like themselves can say what they feel. The club, made up of war veterans, starts to meet in Franklin. Dennett and DeBlanc give their little guild a name, the Caucasian Club.

Meetings are one night a week. Ten or twenty men drink and grieve for the lost cause of the Confederacy. For a month or two, it is enough to grouse about the Radicals and Reconstruction. But the Caucasians want more.

Alcibiade DeBlanc is ten years older than Constant. The two men are like cousins, but they are not close. DeBlanc is educated and commanding. In Constant's eyes, DeBlanc is another of the more successful men who crowd his life and make him small.

The Caucasian Club grows. Membership is held to whites with a strong sense of the tribe, whites who see themselves as a people with destiny. DeBlanc dominates the room full of resentful veterans. He is intelligent and cunning, a man of parts. Sometime in summer 1867,

DeBlanc renames the guild. The "Caucasian Club" is too limiting. The group needs a name that reflects an ambition.

In the Deep South, pretentious names for groups filled with angry men are not in short supply. DeBlanc knows of a particular name that has seen good use: the Knights of the Golden Circle. The Knights of the Golden Circle is a secret society that comes to life in Texas and Louisiana during the 1840s. Its members are Southern nationalists. The Golden Circle numbers ten thousand by the time of the Civil War and stretches from Virginia to Texas. Its members are rich, a chivalry of Southern elites, and secretive, like a Masonic order.

During the years before the Civil War, when slavery is coming under threat, the Knights of the Golden Circle devise an ambitious plan to defend it. The Knights will extend the scope of the South by annexing Cuba and Central America. The idea is to invade the countries of the Caribbean in order to create a slave empire, a "Golden Circle" that consists of the slave areas of the United States, plus territories around the Gulf of Mexico. With the defeat of the Confederacy, the dream of a slave empire decays to dust. Yet Judge Alcibiade DeBlanc knows all about the Knights of the Golden Circle and their failed plans. It is even possible he once took part himself, during the good old days, in the grand Golden Circle scheme.

DeBlanc changes the name of the Caucasian Club. From here forward, it is the Knights of the White Camellia. The new name of the guild is valiant and medieval, it sounds like a roundtable of men in armor. The camellia flower will be its symbol, a flower that is lavish, white, and stuns with a sweet fragrance. Because Judge DeBlanc is a Creole, like the Lecorgnes, the club must have a twin name in French—*les Chevaliers du Camélia Blanc*.

The Democratic politician John Ellis is a founding member of the Knights of the White Camellia, or KWC. About this time, Ellis writes in his diary that the purpose of the KWC is "to protect our race from amalgamation and miscegenation and other degradations." The mixing of the black and white species, Ellis says, and the decay of the white tribe, are things that the "dominant radical party," the Republicans, want to force on embattled Caucasians. The White Camellia will not allow it.

There is a saying in the black French of the day—*Faut jamais porté déil avant défunt soit dans cerkeil*, "Never wear mourning before the dead man is in his coffin." Do not expect white rule is dead until it is buried.

Constant is thirty-five, Gabrielle thirty-one. They have four young children—Numa, Louis, Estelle, and George. The last one, George, is a year old, a boy born during the month of the Mechanics Institute massacre. Gabrielle minds her four without the help of black hands. The economy is recovering. Cotton is high again in the fields upriver, and money spills into the city. If you are a carpenter, there should be work for the taking. Constant, the *charpentier de navire*, looks for jobs and picks up a few things. Add a porch to a house, mend a staircase in a boatyard. Meanwhile, Yves of God, comptroller for Jefferson City, hands out work to friends. Yves is a man with tax money to spread around. I find a bit of evidence that Constant does things for Yves, like repairing a few blocks of the *banquettes*, the wooden sidewalks in Bouligny. Gabrielle tries to make up for her husband's indifferent earnings. She is good with a needle, and I imagine she takes in piecework. There is some evidence that she earns money with music. A capable pianist, Gabrielle pads the small family income by teaching keyboard to young pupils.

Gabrielle and Constant scratch for money, but some of the Lecorgnes rake it in. With Yankees all around with their cash, Lecorgnes take advantage by flipping pieces of land.

Most of the older whites in town hate the newer whites, the ones from up North. These are people from Ohio or Pennsylvania, Connecticut or New York, especially New York. Maybe five thousand come to New Orleans alone. The older whites in town call the new ones who get into politics "carpetbaggers." Carpetbaggers are said to travel with cheap luggage, bags made from old rugs, sewn up into sacks—"carpetbags." They are operators, and they eat away at the power of decent Creoles. The Northern men and women also siphon money. They make deals, they start businesses, they lease plantations. Half look for land to buy or cotton to sell. The other half—the carpetbaggers—hunt favors in the courthouse, spread graft in the statehouse, or run for offices they don't deserve. At least, that is what the good local whites say.

For the Lecorgnes, however, the money spread around by Northerners helps them to forget. In one year, Constant's sister Eliza sells two pieces of land to a man named Swords and two more to a man named Hotard. Yves of God sells one piece of land to a man named Andre and two to a man named Kimball. New whites every one.

Constant and Gabrielle regard these deals skeptically, maybe enviously. They have no cash to buy even one building lot for themselves, much less seven lots to unload on Yankees.

Sister Eliza Lecorgne is twenty-eight. She is the Lecorgne who teaches in the public schools, until she marries. In 1866, Eliza marries a man named Charles Lagroue, and she is asked to leave her job, because schoolteachers, if they are women, are expected to be single. Charles Lagroue is a plantation overseer who makes decent money. Eliza has a one-year-old daughter, Adelaide, her first child.

In September 1867, Eliza Lecorgne makes a pile of money, earning more cash in one land deal than any of the men in the family has ever made. And she does it with the biggest carpetbagger of all, the Yankee invader, the U.S. Army. Worse, she does it by making a deal that helps *les nègres*.

Eliza owns land in Shrewsbury, a settlement just outside the city. Shrewsbury lies eight miles upstream, next to the U.S. Army garrison, Camp Parapet. Camp Parapet is two things: it is a refugee camp, with a city of tents that is a destination for perhaps ten thousand blacks, and it is headquarters of the Freedmen's Bureau, the relief operation for ex-slaves, run by the army. In Shrewsbury, Eliza Lecorgne owns five acres and two houses on Arlington Road, which forms the border of Camp Parapet. General Absalom Baird, the camp commander, wants to build new barracks and expand the army's relief operation. Baird says he needs the Lecorgne land, and the U.S. Army offers Eliza $4,000.

Eliza Lecorgne is lucky, and she is smart. It is her name on the deed, not that of her husband, Charles Lagroue. She takes the deal. To make $4,000, her brother Constant would have to build forty houses. To Constant, Eliza must look like a disgrace to the family. The money comes from the dirty hand of the U.S. Army, his former enemy in the war, and now carpetbagger-in-chief. In the end, however, Constant deflects. When Eliza asks him to cosign the sale contract, Constant goes down to the courthouse with his sister and does it. She is his blood, after all.

It is a year since the massacre, and the black tide is rising. The first election in which men of color can vote is set for October. In Bouligny, the firemen of Home Hook & Ladder believe it is time for another fight. On September 28, a Saturday, several men from Home Hook walk the streets, looking for trouble. They come to the Jefferson City Courthouse. Republican canvassers stand at a table outside, showing black voters how to use their first paper ballots. At this point, the year 1867, voting is not yet a private act; there is no such thing as a secret ballot. To vote Democrat requires a ballot printed by the Democrats. To vote Republican takes a ballot handed out by the Republicans. When you vote, everyone watches you stuff these garish pieces of paper into ballot boxes at the polling station.

Constant may be on the street when the Home Hook men walk up to the Republican table in front of the courthouse. Newspapers describe what happens. A Home Hook fireman named Harry Rolande stares down the black voters around the table. Rolande snatches a ballot from one of the canvass men, tears it up, and curses. I imagine he says something gentle, like "Fucking niggers cannot even read the thing." Standing with Rolande is another fireman, Henry Reese.

The shouting starts, a brawl follows, and guns come out. A report says forty shots are fired. Several white and black bystanders are wounded, as well as two policemen who run to the scene.

The gunfire ends, and the courthouse steps are empty, except for the victims who lie groaning on the pavement. Firemen carry Rolande and Reese to the firehouse of Home Hook & Ladder. The wounds spill a trail of blood two blocks long. At the firehouse, Harry Rolande soon dies. Henry Reese holds on for several hours, then he also dies.

Home Hook & Ladder has two martyrs, and vengeance is required. The marauding begins as roving gangs of whites pick out black men in the street and savage them with fists and clubs. A sense of dread falls, and African Americans in Bouligny lock themselves indoors. White newspapers say that a "black uprising" is imminent. It is likely there are deaths, but court records do not cite them, and the Jefferson City Police arrest no one. That is because the Bouligny police do not intervene when a black man is being beaten.

Felicity Street, near Bouligny, resembles the Lecorgne family's neighborhood.

Someone gets word to the Union Army, whose barracks are five miles downtown, beyond the *Vieux Carré* at Fort Jackson. A company of sixty soldiers marches into Bouligny and surrounds Lawrence Square. The Yankees brandish rifles in front of St. Stephen Church, where the Lecorgnes worship. The men of Home Hook put their truncheons away, and the army pitches its tents on the square. They plan to stay for a time.

Things have come to this—we have the army in the neighborhood. Their blue uniforms insult the eyes. Yankee bastards are here for no other reason than to pamper *les nègres*.

The Radical Republicans have taken half the white voters off the rolls, using a new loyalty oath. In order to vote, whites must swear they never supported the rebellion, and only half choose to lie. Meanwhile, ninety thousand black men vote in Louisiana for the first time. The referendum on making a new constitution passes, and delegates to write it are voted in. Half of the ninety-eight delegates are white, half are black or Creoles of color. They meet in Mechanics Hall, at the end of November 1867.

A joke goes around: it is the "black and tan convention." The joke is about hunting dogs, raccoons, and "coons." The black and tan coonhound is a dog—mostly black, with pale tan markings on the snout and legs—that hunters train to track raccoons. Some people, also known as "coons," used to be forced to run from coonhounds. Now some of them will make the new constitution—at the black and tan convention. It is a nasty joke, really.

In Washington, President Johnson is angry. He sees the new constitutions being cooked up around the South as poison. Johnson sends a message to Congress—

"The subjugation of the States to negro domination will be worse than military despotism," he says. "People will not degrade themselves by subjection to the negro race." President Johnson defends the principle of white rule. Power for black people is "clothing torn from white men," he tells Congress. "The great difference between the two races in physical, mental, and moral characteristics is obvious. . . . Of all the dangers which our nation has yet encountered, none are equal to the effort now to Africanize the half of our country." The president is afraid of the tide of blackness. An ugly fear, really.

Republicans in Congress do not care for the president's lectures on race. Three months after the warning about "Africanization," in March 1868, the House of Representatives votes to impeach the man in the White House.

The fight between President Johnson and Congress is about black rights, black power, and white rule. But the conflict moves to an area where it wears a mask. Congress writes Articles of Impeachment with charges about a law called the Tenure of Office Act. A year old, the Tenure of Office Act requires Senate approval for changes that the president makes in the cabinet. The law is meant to keep Johnson from firing Republicans left in office since Lincoln. When the president fires Secretary of War Edwin Stanton, a Lincoln man, it is a pretext for impeachment.

President Johnson is about to go on trial, and everyone knows that the reason is the way things are going down South.

"The place of meeting, the constitutional convention, is the place where white manhood is degraded to the level of the ignorant, brutal, untutored African," says the thoughtful *New-Orleans Times*.

Delegates write for three months before wrapping their business. The new constitution affirms that black men can vote and bans segregation in public services like transportation and schools. It tries to level the field of race in the law. The charter is published March 7, 1868, and a plebiscite is announced: the constitution is to be ratified by voters. Five days later, the guerrilla resistance surfaces. The word "Ku-klux" appears for the first time in the New Orleans press. On March 12, the *Crescent* newspaper—which backs the Democrats, like eight of ten city papers—runs a single sentence: "There appears to be a new secret political and social organization in Tennessee, known by the queer name of the 'Ku-Klux-Klan.'"

Another five days pass. Other papers pick up the thread. *The Daily Picayune* tells of a planning meeting for the Ku-klux. The paper runs this strange advertisement:

In hoc signo, X 22.
The Great Past Grand Giant commands you.
The dark and dismal hour draws nigh.
Some live today—tomorrow die.
The bullet red and the right are ours.
Today, the 17th of the mortal's month of March, you will begin to
scatter the clouds of the grave. By order of Great Grand Cyclops,
G.C.T.

It is a cute piece of code. The notice describes a meeting set for March 22 at 10:00 p.m. But where the meeting is to take place, I cannot decipher. Similarly I cannot place the initials, "G.C.T." The Kuklux, from the first, is hard to read.

It appears that at this moment, Constant steps forward to take part.

The new guerrillas have their meeting. Black voters are set to cast another ballot—in April, for a new state assembly. A week before the election, there is the eruption. According to the *Tribune*, gangs of whites wearing disguises carry out raids "in the country parishes," the rural districts outside New Orleans. Close to the city, in Jefferson and St. Bernard parishes, "the Ku Klux Klan parade the streets, masked, visiting the houses of well-known Republicans, white and black. The gangs affix to their doors threatening placards, breathing blood and murder, and bearing such emblems as pistols, bowie-knives, death's heads, and coffins." Louis Roudanez's paper predicts that New Orleans is next. "We may expect soon to see this new organization boldly parading our streets, and committing outrages."

It is the moment when the branches of whiteness produce their flower.

Alcibiade DeBlanc and the Knights of the White Camellia come to the surface. Witnesses at Congress put the date of appearance of the White Camellia and the Ku Klux Klan at the same time, in spring 1868. In early April, DeBlanc and his comrade Daniel Dennett run an editorial in white newspapers around the state.

Klansman, circa 1868

THE RELATIONS OF THE RACES

That the black man is not the equal of the white man in any respect, and was never intended by the Creator of the universe to be so, is a fact. There is not prejudice about it, because Nature has implanted the distinction. It has been the pleasure of the Creator to give every being in the universe his place, and to make the negro a servant to his white brother. This is a fact which no body denies.

It is a fact that no one denies if you believe the teachings of science, if you accept the ideal of whiteness in the work of Samuel Morton, the skull collector. It is a truth that no one refutes if you absorb the notion of polygenesis, which Louis Agassiz and Arthur Gobineau and Samuel Cartwright develop into theories of separate races. It is a flattering story that Josiah Nott and James DeBow have massaged into fact.

These ideas and these people are all present. The science of "niggerology" is in public circulation, implicit to thought and speech.

DeBlanc moves the headquarters of the White Camellia to New Orleans. He leaves rural St. Mary Parish to take up a campaign in the capital of the state. A killing announces the move. On April 17, election day, a white man named Philip Michael shoots and kills in the street a black man named David Hutchinson. The offense of Hutchinson is that he says aloud, "We are ratifying the Constitution." I am not certain, but Philip Michael may be under orders from DeBlanc.

In New Orleans, the KWC begins recruitment. DeBlanc probably makes a personal appeal to family and friends, and Constant belongs to that group. The ship carpenter is militant, and he is a joiner.

Democrats win the mayor's race in the April election, thanks to what one paper calls "perversions of the ballot," or vote fraud. The Republicans sweep the legislature and win the governor's office, thanks to black votes. Ninety percent of black voters approve the constitution; only three percent of white voters approve it. In Jefferson Parish, population seventeen thousand, the charter wins only seventy-five white votes. I do not think the Lecorgnes of Jefferson City are within the handful. The tide of black ballots lifts the constitution into law.

Ten days after the vote, white gangs promise revenge, publicly and anonymously. The Ku-klux runs newspaper ads with verses about coming attacks, signing the little doggerel "Ku-klux." On April 29, in *The Louisiana Democrat*:

> *Thrice hath the lone owl hooted,*
> *And thrice the panther cried,*
> *And swifter through the darkness,*
> *The Pale Brigade shall ride.*
> *No trumpet sounds its coming,*
> *And no drumbeat stirs the air,*
> *But noiseless in their vengeance,*
> *They wreak it everywhere.*
> *Ku-Klux*

The verses appear in many papers and end with a boast about the killing to come:

> *The misty gray is hanging*
> *On the tresses of the East,*
> *And morn will tell the story*
> *Of the revel and the feast.*
> *The ghostly troop shall vanish*
> *Like the light in constant cloud,*
> *But where they rode shall gather*
> *The coffin and the shroud.*
> *Ku-Klux*

We have fallen into a tactic, accidentally. The Ku-klux figures out the formula for menace, namely, keep threats half hidden, under a mask. It magnifies the fear.

Here we come to the uncanny part of Constant's story, and the story of the Ku-klux. Things "uncanny" are like a scene or a lurid memory that is meant to be secret and disguised, and yet has instead come into the open. The Ku-klux and the White Camellia are uncanny. They are like things known but unseen, or things seen but unknown. They are the way that we arrange race itself, into background and foreground, into scene, seen, and unseen.

Rumors of gangs called "Ku-klux" come in from the country parishes. The reports are that guerrillas ride horseback into black villages, but they are robed and masked, like at Carnival, or like minstrel men.

But the Ku-klux does not exist, says *The Daily Picayune*. The "hell-born cabal" is a fiction. "We have heard nothing of the kind," the paper tells readers. "Men who have a real purpose do not express themselves in such ridiculous rodomontade."

In fact, many whites like the excitement. There are a few months of uncanny menace, reports of night-riding by Ku-klux, and attacks on black people. Then in June in New Orleans, the Ku-klux is celebrated in a playhouse—with a musical show. The *Commercial Bulletin* announces the opening of an exciting new piece of theater at the Academy of Music, on St. Charles Avenue.

"A Fresh Bouquet of June Flowers," says the paper. "The first night of the New Sardonic, Sensational, Musical Mysticism, by J. E. Durivage, called 'Ku-Klux-Klan.'" The mysterious night riders, whoever they might be, deserve the welcome. Before six months have passed, the Ku-klux are made into characters on a stage.

After the Ku-klux musical closes, the Knights of the White Camellia hold a convention in New Orleans. It is a recruitment drive. The white newspapers know that Alcibiade DeBlanc is running the event but honor the guerrillas by publishing nothing. Hundreds of angry men—including, I believe, Constant—are drawn to the auditorium by word of mouth. The meeting probably fills Odd Fellows Hall, a lodge on Camp Street near Lafayette Square.

I am trying to imagine my way into the room. It is June, and the scene is a hot hall, with two hundred or more men. Cigars for the rich, pipes for the common. Drinks go around. Wine or liqueur for Creoles; ale or lager for Anglos and Germans. Voices are high from the drink and from the cause. Music warms the crowd. Maybe a band plays "Dixie," or the newer standard, "A Good Old Rebel Soldier." Regnant and manly, Alcibiade DeBlanc climbs the platform. He gives a speech full of menace. The nigger is taking it all from us. The White Camellia will make things good again. Constant sees the man he knows, the man he admires. The lawyer and ex-colonel is high, the carpenter low. It is sweltering in the room. DeBlanc waves a handful of papers. The White Camellia has its constitution, and the author stands in front of you, he says. Our constitution is nothing like the dirty new charter of the wounded state of Louisiana. Ours is a precept of the clean and the right. The White Camellia does things *comme il faut*, the way they should be done.

Copies of the KWC constitution are circulated. The text lays out principles and rites. It names passwords, diagrams secret handshakes. It describes special door knocks and coded greetings to be used by recruits on the street. It gives a script for the induction of members, and it contains an oath of allegiance. The constitution of the Knights of the White Camellia is a white supremacist manifesto. I believe it is the first statement of its kind in the United States, the first paper platform that announces race superiority and claims political power on the basis of it. To read through this document—which Constant would have known, and which he may have studied—I am somewhat disgusted, and also fascinated.

I want to be in the room with these conspirators at Odd Fellows Hall. Alcibiade DeBlanc takes a page and reads aloud from the text—

> Brothers: You are being initiated into one of the most important Orders which have ever been established on this continent. . . . Our main and fundamental object is the MAINTENANCE OF THE SUPREMACY OF THE WHITE RACE. History and physiology tell us that we belong to a race which nature has endowed with an evident superiority over all other races. The Maker intended to give us over inferior races a dominion from which no human laws can derogate. . . . It is a remarkable fact that as a race of men is more remote from the Caucasian and approaches nearer to the black African, the more fatally that stamp of inferiority is affixed to its sons, and irrevocably dooms them to eternal imperfectability and degradation.

A murmur in the room, and grunts of assent.

> We know, besides, that the government of our Republic was established by white men, for white men alone, and that it never was in the contemplation of its founders that it should fall into the hands of an inferior and degraded race.
>
> It then becomes our solemn duty as white men to do everything in our power in order to maintain, in this Republic, the supremacy of the Caucasian race, and restrain the black or African race to that condition of social and political inferiority for which God has destined it.

Cheers, maybe applause. DeBlanc is commanding as he sprays out what needs to be said. I have to picture the part when DeBlanc reaches out to Constant. I am sure he says something direct and touching to the carpenter.

—Think of your father. Our parents were close. I remember them, and I know they would want this. They would want you to be with us.

The manifesto contains all of the rules, all of the secrets. DeBlanc assigns his deputies to teach the little mysteries. If one member of the KWC meets another, they are to use a secret greeting—

"The sign of recognition on the street is made by drawing the index finger of the left hand across the left eye (all the other fingers of that hand closed). If the person addressed be a member of that order he will respond in like manner. If either party have any doubts he will ask the question, 'Where were you born?' The answer is, 'On Mount Caucasus.'"

For a new recruit to seal his membership, he must pass through initiation. It is possible that at this meeting, on the night of Tuesday, June 4, 1868, Constant is inducted. According to script—

> The Candidate is introduced into an anteroom, accompanied by a Guard. He is blindfolded and led to the door of the Council Chamber. The Guard shall give two raps on the door. The Commander shall open the door. The following dialogue shall take place between the Commander and the Guard.
>
> COMMANDER: Who comes there?
> GUARD: A son of your race.
> COMMANDER: What must be done?
> GUARD: The cause of our race must triumph.
> COMMANDER: What must we do?
> GUARD: We must be united as are the flowers that grow on the same stem.
> COMMANDER: Let him enter.

DeBlanc is the author of these lines. The ceremony, the greetings, and the handshakes show a familiarity with Greek orders and secret societies. They resemble fraternity rites. I do not think anymore it is necessary to imagine how Constant and the Knights of the White Camellia do their business. The script supplies the scene in every detail.

> The Guard shall take the candidate by the right hand and conduct him into the presence of the Commander, who shall offer the following questions . . .
>
> COMMANDER: Do you belong to the white race?
>
> CANDIDATE: I do.
>
> COMMANDER: Did you ever marry any woman who did not, or does not, belong to the white race?
>
> CANDIDATE: No.
>
> COMMANDER: Do you promise never to marry any woman but one who belongs to the white race?
>
> CANDIDATE: I do.
>
> COMMANDER: Do you believe in the superiority of your race?
>
> CANDIDATE: I do.
>
> COMMANDER: Will you promise never to vote for any one for any office of honor, profit, or trust, who does not belong to your race?
>
> CANDIDATE: I do.
>
> COMMANDER: Will you take a solemn oath never to abstain from casting your vote at any election in which a candidate of the negro race shall be opposed to a white man attached to your principles?
>
> CANDIDATE: I will.
>
> COMMANDER: Are you opposed to allowing the control of the political affairs of this country to go in whole or in part, into the hands of the African race, and will you do everything in your power to prevent it?
>
> CANDIDATE: Yes.
>
> COMMANDER: Will you under all circumstance defend and protect persons of the white race in their lives, rights and

property, against all encroachments or invasions from any inferior race, especially the African?

CANDIDATE: Yes.

There is no room for deviation in the script, no place where a person
questions or shows doubt. It is a road to obedience. The candidate
consents and raises his right hand in the oath:

> I swear to maintain and defend the social and political supe-
> riority of the White Race on this Continent; always and in all
> places to observe a marked distinction between the White and
> African races; . . . and to protect and defend persons of the
> White Race, in their lives, rights and property, against the en-
> croachments and aggressions of an inferior race.

When the meeting ends at Odd Fellows Hall, the gang of recruits
walks out and fans into the night.

Random killings spread. According to a report of the Freedmen's Bureau, in early June, after the White Camellia meeting, "a colored man,
name unknown, is killed on the road by a Frenchman, cause unknown."

Also in June, a white man named François Saleson "kills a colored
man, name unknown."

A man named John Sentinger shoots "through the body" a black
man named Alexander Washington.

Matthias Vandervall, white, shoots a black man named Eli Brown,
though "not fatally."

Outside New Orleans, "a number of freedpeople are whipped and
burned, and two women are ravished by four white men."

Some of the people who carry out these assaults are named in reports of the Freedmen's Bureau. They have surnames that are French
Creole, German American, and Dutch. No perpetrators, as yet, appear to be Irish American or Italian American.

———

The violence grows in Louisiana, Mississippi, Alabama, and beyond.

In Washington, the White House is paralyzed. Andrew Johnson has been on trial in the Senate since March 7, and things move slowly. He is indifferent, anyway, to the growing attacks. Johnson is a Democrat, much liked by white Southerners. He has no desire to act. He is well liked because he wishes to keep the white South in charge of the black South.

On May 16, the Senate calls the trial to a halt and schedules a vote. Conviction requires a two-thirds majority. Thirty-five senators vote to remove Johnson, nineteen to acquit; the ballot falls short by one vote. Later in May, the Senate tries to convict Johnson on different charges. The outcome is the same, one vote short of conviction.

Johnson stays in office for the last five months of his term. Congress is split. Democrats, in the minority, support the president. The Republican majority despises him.

Gangs that use the name "Ku Klux Klan," having appeared briefly in March, seem to disappear from the southern half of Louisiana and retreat to the northern part of the state. There they flourish. The Ku Klux Klan recruits thousands in the parishes of Caddo and Ouachita, Claiborne and Bienville, Tensas and Catahoula. Meanwhile, the Knights of the White Camellia carry the mission in the lower half of the state—in the Catholic parts, in the French parts. The White Camellia launches guerrilla cells in the parishes of Rapides and St. Landry, Terrebonne and Lafourche, St. Tammany and St. Bernard. Many in the White Camellia are Creole, and they are merciless.

White militias are strongest in Louisiana, Mississippi, Texas, and South Carolina. But they appear in all states that take part in the rebellion of the Civil War. In Mississippi, gangs call themselves "Ku-klux" in the northern and western parts of the state, the Red Shirts elsewhere, and the White Line in some counties. In Texas, the Ku-klux appears, and another group, the Knights of the Rising Sun. Virginia does not see as many rampant white militias, and Arkansas finds a way to dampen the night-riding gangs. Around the South, there are groups that call themselves the Red Hands (for blood?), the Black Horse Cavalry (after a rebel company people remember), and the Pale Faces, pointing with a smile at skin color. Some terror groups have no names. With closeness and understanding, whites call them "slickers."

The new governor of Louisiana, Henry Warmoth, is a young and magnetic Republican. A former Union officer, Warmoth is a lawyer raised in Illinois who appears in New Orleans with the occupation. He is a carpetbagger. Most whites in the state dislike Warmoth. Most blacks like him. It is black men who vote him in.

Reports grow of White Camellia attacks. Governor Warmoth does not believe the New Orleans police force can be trusted. They are five hundred officers, all of them white. With votes from the new state assembly, now one-third black, and mostly Republican, Warmoth creates a new unit of lawmen, the Metropolitan Police. The new "Metropolitans" are seven hundred men in New Orleans and Jefferson City. A third are blacks or Creoles of color, two-thirds are white. The Metropolitans become the police who push for Reconstruction, the cops who try, at least some of the time, to make a difference for African Americans.

Black politicians have power for the first time. Of 20 Republican state senators, 7 are black. Of 101 members of the Louisiana House, 56 are Republicans, nearly half of them black. The 45 Democrats are all white. One Republican senator has a pleasing name, Pinckney Pinchback. A thirty-year-old from the second electoral district of New Orleans, Pinchback uses one of his first speeches, to a joint session of the legislature, to denounce the White Camellia.

"The next outrage of the kind which they commit will be the signal for the dawn of retribution, of which they have not yet dreamed," Pinchback says. He denounces the reports of whippings carried out by gangs at night. Another episode of this kind, and "it will be a signal that will cause ten thousand torches to be applied to this city. Patience will then have ceased to be a virtue and this city will be reduced to ashes."

The black politician makes a threat of arson, no less. Pinchback is called to order by the president of the senate and forced to sit down. He is a Creole of color trying to be heard. He knows the torch is a weapon that frightens whites. The torch is a sign of "nigger insurrection."

Two newspapers support Reconstruction, Roudanez's *Tribune* and the *Republican*, a new daily set up by the Republican Party. The two report atrocities against blacks. Meanwhile, the half-dozen newspapers that call for white rule are silent about the violence. Often the white newspapers say such stories are invented—they are fake news. Writers in all the papers use "KWC" and "Ku-klux" interchangeably, sometimes in a single paragraph, as though they are one and the same. The KWC spreads from Louisiana into Mississippi. The Ku-klux grows from Tennessee and bleeds into Alabama, Georgia, and the Carolinas. In Louisiana, where the Ku-klux rides at night, a branch of the White Camellia cannot be found. Where the KWC has a gang, there is no Ku-klux. Sometimes the papers use "Ku-klux" as a generic term to designate all white-on-black violence, no matter who the perpetrator.

In New Orleans, the White Camellia recruits fifteen gangs, or "councils," and assigns each to a meeting hall.

KWC Council No. 14 holds meetings at Magazine and Philip streets.

Council No. 13 does business from a hall at the Fair Grounds horse track.

No. 11 plans its strikes at a theater on the corner of Poydras and Carondelet streets.

No. 10 operates out of the University of Louisiana's School of Medicine, on Common Street.

No. 9 has its own clubhouse, Eagle Hall, on Prytania and Felicity Streets.

No. 8 plans actions at the corner of Canal and Rampart streets.

No. 4 meets at a private house at the corner of Bienville Street and Exchange Alley, in the French Quarter.

And so on.

The KWC clubhouse closest to Home Hook & Ladder is Eagle Hall, on Prytania and Felicity streets. This must be the place where Constant mimes the secret greeting to gain entry and shows his face indoors.

From a photograph of three night riders wearing typical
costume of the Knights of the White Camellia

A Grand Council of three men directs all the White Camellia
gangs. Alcibiade DeBlanc acts as chief. He is the principal snakehead
on the Medusa.

The KWC keeps no membership rolls. They wish to torment
without making a list of tormentors. But some talk. A couple of years
later, during an investigation by Congress into the white rampages
in the South, a few guerrillas break the code of silence to testify about
how they do things. The men claim anonymity and do not use their
names, but they allow Congress to record their testimony. I imagine
a deal of some kind. You caught me; give me immunity and nameless-
ness, then I talk.

One witness at Congress explains the method in assassinations—

"When a member wants a man killed he will say to the Grand
Commander in council, 'I want ___ attended to,' and give the reason.
It is voted, and if a majority of votes are in favor, it is done.

"When a man is to be killed in a different district, word is sent to the council adjacent, and from there a member is sent to do the work, giving the members in the district where the victim lives due notice of the time it is to take place."

In other words, guerrillas travel to places they do not know, kill one or several people, and travel back out.

It is not the same as during the Civil War. Most men in the KWC, veterans, remember the sound of artillery in the distance, the screaming charge, the rifle shots when you see the outline of a figure. This is different. The night-riding and whippings and beatings—and sometimes, the killings—are more consuming work. They are close fights, and personal. A man has a relationship with his victim, something like a liaison. The victim is terrified, he shrieks and he pleads. His wife weeps, begging for her husband's life. The liaison lasts for thirty minutes, usually not more.

"Every man who has a white heart is a walking arsenal," one of the KWC tells Congress. "And it is the determination of whites to remain united until the last Radical and the last nigger are out of office."

By September, the White Camellia claims a membership of fifteen thousand men in New Orleans and the near parishes—Jefferson, Chalmette, St. Bernard, and Orleans. I imagine the figure is overstatement. At this time, the white male adult population in New Orleans is thirty-two thousand. To exaggerate their scale is part of the method of the Ku-klux. Still, the number of guerrillas is large, and they are busy.

It is fall 1868, and the biggest election since the war is set for November. The race for president puts General Ulysses Grant against Governor Horatio Seymour. Grant is a Republican. He is a war hero in the North, with both whites and blacks; in the South, he is a hero to blacks only. Horatio Seymour is a Democrat, the ex-governor of New

York State and an antagonist of Reconstruction. Grant is for black rights, Seymour against.

Someone among the Democrats writes a campaign song for the party's candidate, Horatio Seymour. It has a catchy title: "The White Man's Banner." The party sends out sheet music with the song's memorable chorus—

> *Let, then, all free-born patriots join,*
> *With a brave intent,*
> *To vindicate our Father's choice,*
> *A white-man's government.*

The White Camellia and the Ku-klux decide they will do anything to defeat Grant and elect Seymour.

The KWC launches its campaign. Near New Orleans, on July 7 at 10:00 p.m., according to an investigation, "a party of men in disguise" rides up to a cabin on a plantation owned by a man named Maurice Richard. These are raiders who probably mask at Carnival. Tonight they mask for a killing. On Richard's plantation, the gang makes its way to the house of the farmworker Spencer Stewart, "colored." They surround the house and shoot into its windows and doors. Inside, Stewart is hit in the arm and shoulder; his wife is hit in the chest and killed. His granddaughter, age ten, is also shot. She dies at the house. Witnesses identify the masked Camellias as fifteen men. Their names are Gardner, Louney, Meche, Moore, others. The name Lecorgne is not on the list.

Outside the city, a state report says, "Bob Owens, colored, is hung by persons unknown. A coroner's jury examines the case, but are unable to obtain any facts." Elsewhere, "Tom Ford, colored, is shot and killed by one Howell Rayburn. A warrant is issued, but no arrest made."

The White Camellia raids black villages and houses. Guerrillas torment women by humiliating them in front of their partners, sometimes whipping them, sometimes raping them.

The stories are raw. Yet they are our stories. Not only are they our family stories, and as vile as any can be. They are tribal stories.

266 | LIFE OF A KLANSMAN

In St. Landry Parish, "A colored boy is whipped to death with a double-stranded rawhide and another large whip." Alcibiade De-Blanc is in St. Landry Parish during this particular killing. He gives a speech on the steps of the courthouse, and his remarks appear in the local paper.

"I fought four years in the Confederate army and I am ready to fight in six months—or now, if you say so, boys!" DeBlanc tells his crowd. "Why do you not kill these carpetbaggers? There are only five or six in every parish. We are a hundred to one!" Later the same night, near the town, the teenage boy is whipped to death.

By midsummer, "the murder of negroes is a daily occurrence," says a report to the legislature.

People like to hear about the disguises of the Ku-klux. They like stories of the masked and robed men. I cannot put my hands on eyewitness accounts of White Camellia disguises, but there is little doubt these night riders wear masks and camouflage. They mask like Carnival revelers to protect their identity, and they mask like minstrel players, who sometimes dress as ghosts onstage.

For their night rides in the northern parishes, Ku-klux guerrillas wear red or white robes. On the head, they wear a hood, sometimes with a grimace mask affixed to it. The origin of the hood seems to me to lie in the minstrel shows. Some performers in minstrel acts wear painted meal sacks over their heads while performing skits in which they pretend to be ghosts.

Closer to New Orleans, the Knights of the White Camellia wear decorated jackets, sometimes robes. Sometimes the armed horsemen of the KWC wear no robes, and instead, they black up, painting themselves with blackface, using grease or burned cork, because the important thing is to cover the face. It is common for night riders to smut their faces. Sometimes they wear black masks. Carnival is a good source of masks and disguises. The tradition contains a deep catalog.

A man called John C. Lester is a member of the first cell of the Ku Klux Klan in Tennessee. In 1884, Lester publishes a memoir about his life with the Ku-klux. It contains a description of the costume that raiders wear in the state of Mississippi, next to Louisiana. I am sure the White Camellia uses a similar visual repertoire.

> Each member provides himself with the following outfit: a white mask for the face, with orifices for the eyes and nose; a tall, fantastic cardboard hat, so constructed as to increase the wearer's apparent height; a gown or robe, of sufficient length to cover the entire person. No particular color or material is prescribed . . . each selects what in his judgment will be the most hideous and fantastic. . . . The robes, of different colors, add vastly to the grotesque appearance of the assembled Klan.

A newspaper cartoon that promises lynching for carpetbaggers

The variety in costume has several motives. Anonymity is most important. During acts of sadism and cruelty, guerrillas do not wish to be recognized. Constant Lecorgne, on a ride into a black village, is not a man who wants to be identified by witnesses. Another reason for costume is theater. Men on rampage add the enjoyment of performance to their attack. A third purpose is to spread fear. The Ku-klux are in the business of terror. Cloaks and faceless hoods are the pretend costumes of death. Fear generated by the act of torment has high value to the tormentor. To magnify the fear in victims and in witnesses is an important aim of those who violate other people. Fear is the ingredient that permits us to call the Ku-klux the first American terrorists.

The blood chronicle continues.

"A man named John Sentinger shoots and nearly kills a black man called Solomon Wilson, without cause," testimony says. That is all I can say about Solomon Wilson. Single shootings are common enough to yield just one sentence of a report.

I do not know, and I come to the conclusion that it is impossible to learn, what specific atrocities Constant participates in—probably participates in—with the White Camellia and with family friend Alcibiade DeBlanc during the summer and fall of 1868. The evidence is not there, or it does not survive. And family tradition does not say. My aunt Maud, late carrier of the story, does not say. I doubt that she knew, when she was alive.

In cases of mob violence, absence of individual evidence is not evidence of individual absence. I do not know—there is no testimony—whether Constant wears a homemade disguise of robe and mask. Probably he has something like this in hand. I cannot say whether Gabrielle, at home with the children in the rented house, and a person who is good with a needle and thread, stitches together a robe with appliqués, like demons or snakes. I do not know whether she makes her husband a hood with the blank face of death. Many upon many women do this sort of thing for their men in the Ku-klux. They are women who know what their men want.

20

Grand Commander Alcibiade DeBlanc, using coded channels, makes an announcement. All White Camellias who want firearms may go to a particular gun store in downtown New Orleans. Its owner is one of the Knights. Fighters can take what weapons they want, and the Grand Commander himself will pay for them.

An assessment meeting is called. Sometime in October, seventy-two guerrillas rendezvous at Eagle Hall, headquarters of Council No. 9, at the corner of Prytania and Felicity streets. Constant may be in the corner of the room when DeBlanc steps to the front. A man who is present later writes about the scene.

"Brothers," DeBlanc says, "all of you that can come to drill, do so. Because the armory is here." The Grand Commander draws back a curtain to reveal one hundred rifles. He hands them out among the smiling men of Council No. 9.

People stand to speak. One of the Knights mocks the governor of Louisiana and heaps special scorn on his lieutenant, a man named Oscar Dunn. Dunn is a *sang-mêlé*, a light-skinned black man elected in the last vote.

"Here is a negro that could be bought for $1500 seven years ago, and now he is lieutenant governor of the state! How long are we to put up with it?"

Governor Henry Warmoth asks Washington for federal aid. He describes the situation in a letter to President Johnson—

"There is a secret organization throughout the State known as the Knights of the White Camellia. . . . It is founded for the purpose of placing and keeping the colored people in a condition of inferiority," Warmoth tells the White House. "There are military organizations on foot in this city, under the auspices of this secret organization. They drill openly in our streets at night or in halls. . . . I fully believe that there is meditated a bloody revolution, the certain fruit of which would be hopeless confusions, disaster and ruin to the State. . . . Men women and children have recently been murdered . . . by bands of armed men. . . . From the best information, Mr. President, I have no doubt but that 150 have died . . . just in the last month."

The number of Union soldiers in New Orleans has dwindled to 2,500, and the number of Metropolitan Police is also down. Black policemen, singled out as targets, have been furloughed from the force. Warmoth asks the president for cavalry, infantry, and artillery. It is a futile plea. Andrew Johnson is weakened by his impeachment. And he does not see white terror as something he wants to restrain.

The Ku-klux in the north and the White Camellia in the south grow large, but I do not think the majority of white men join the two secret militias. Most whites express themselves tacitly. Most belong to a silent majority. Most seem to support the aims of the guerrillas, if not the tactics. They give unspoken approval of the ends, not necessarily the means.

Many whites, less overtly militant than the White Camellia, join so-called ward clubs. Political clubs arise in the wards or voting districts of New Orleans. Their members sing "The White Man's Banner" and back their candidate, Horatio Seymour. The aim of the Democratic ward clubs harmonizes with the White Camellias: it is white control in politics. Members of ward clubs wish for blanket white command in all corners of life, but they are less aggressive by half.

Democratic ward clubs have names like the Broom Rangers, Chanticleer Club, Constitution Club, Crescent City Democrats, Fossil Guards, German Democratic Club, Jewell Cadets, Johnson Rangers, Minute Men, Rough and Ready Club, Seymour Cadets, Seymour Knights, Seymour Legion, Seymour Sentinels, Swamp Fox Rangers, Tiger Club, Walker Guards, and the Workingmen's Democratic Club. One club, the Innocents, is a group more violent than the others. It has a largely Italian American membership. The men in ward clubs prefer marches and rallies to night-riding and hoods. They parade through their neighborhood with banners. They harass and sometimes beat up black people and white Republicans. But they are somewhat less bloody, and they are not secret. They reject the ritual style of the White Camellia, with its passwords and hand gestures and oaths.

The most powerful ward club in Jefferson City is the Minute Men. It is allied with Home Hook & Ladder and holds meetings in the firehouse. In all likelihood, Constant Lecorgne joins the Minute Men. (The newspapers publish the names of ward club officers, not rank and file.) Constant's friend Seymour Rapp is an officer in the club, as is a man named Maurice Lethieque, a politician close to Yves of God. Another leader in the club is Felix Lagroue, a brother-in-law of Constant. Constant's fingerprints are in many places, even if they are not quite on the doorknob.

The ward clubs like to costume, and clubmen wear coordinated uniforms. For the Minute Men it is a black frock coat, white pants, and white canvas cap with a black band. Clubmen pin a badge and insignia to the right breast of their coat. Like the twenty-odd other ward clubs, the Minute Men hold parades and rallies. They run newspaper ads encouraging the attendance of "all colored Democrats," a call that yields three or four black outliers who hope to be rewarded for showing up. One event brings one thousand whites to Lawrence Square in Bouligny. The crowd marches through the neighborhood with torches and banners, a brass band, and floats decorated with campaign slogans. When the parade ends, the mass meeting is festive and angry. It is all shouted speeches and Andouille sausage, beer and curses.

The figure of Frederick Ogden comes back into view. The ex-rebel general, a swaggering speaker on the platform, Fred Ogden is much like Alcibiade DeBlanc, only he is Anglo-American, not French Creole. A writer who sees Ogden work a crowd describes his "violent, explosive, and convincing eloquence." Among its nicknames, New Orleans is the "Crescent City" because it sits on a crescent-shaped bend in the Mississippi. In June 1868, Fred Ogden talks his way to the head of the

Crescent City Democratic Club, a ward club. He takes leadership of the group. The Crescent City Democrats count a membership of three hundred men in a ward a half mile downriver from the Lecorgnes, in the neighborhood of Lafayette. Most clubmen are English-speaking, and the Lecorgnes stay out. But the Crescent City Democrats share values with the Creoles. The reason the ward club comes together, as Ogden puts it, is "the growing insolence of the negro population."

The colors of white and black, important to these men, appear in their uniform. Crescent City Democrats wear white capes edged with a red border, a black sack coat, white duck trousers, and a white kepi—a hat from the rebel army—with a red band around it spelling the name of the club in gilt letters. They take possession of a clubhouse at the corner of Jackson Avenue and Prytania Street, a mile from Bouligny. By August 1868, squads of armed men in white capes patrol the city between Thalia Street and Napoleon Avenue, a wedge of uptown New Orleans at the shoulder of Jefferson City. It is Frederick Ogden's debut performance, but not his denouement.

It feels to me as though this world is airless. There is little room to move, no space that is not commanded by a naked idea. The setting feels claustrophobic. But I have to remember that outside of it, you have everyday life. Life goes on for black people, in the middle of and despite the proxy war that singles out activists for attack. Republicans have their own ward clubs. They are mostly black. They are smaller than the Democratic ward clubs, and they are not dressed up. They rally and parade. They are less enraged. Sometimes they are even happy. I imagine the competition for public space that pits the clubs against one another. The Republican clubmen look over at the mob of Democratic marchers on the next street.

See what the buckra man is doing with himself now. It ain't good to see, and it gets worse.

Congo Square is a symbolic heart in the black South. It is a place where West African music enters America, where traditional religions, which the church calls "voodoo," are kept alive by lay priests and priestesses. The weekly dances that Constant would have witnessed as a child ended years ago, when the city shut them down. Yet the square remains a center of blackness. It is the entrance to the neighborhoods of Tremé and "Back of Town," black stretches northwest of the *Vieux Carré*. It is because of the blackness of Congo Square that several Democratic ward clubs decide to occupy the space and stage a rally on the old dancing ground.

It is October 17, and the election, Grant vs. Seymour, is two weeks away. About a thousand whites crowd the square. Angry speakers step to the platform. The first of them takes a moment to reassure the good whites who live near the Lecorgnes. A newspaper quotes but does not name the politician, who says, "The negroes in Jefferson City need looking after, as they are becoming extremely insolent and threatening." The next speaker clarifies the challenge. "The Republicans have placed irresponsible, dishonest and greedy negroes in office," he says. "They have armed the ignorant and degraded negro. They have goaded him with malice, hatred and revenge. . . . They have left nothing undone in their power to elevate the negro upon the ruin of the white man. . . . It is the duty of every white man to vote with us. Those who do not we condemn as unfaithful to their lineage and color, and false to the trust given to our race."

On October 23, the White Camellia attacks, and this time, Constant is probably in the middle of it. The setting for him is familiar, the truck house of Home Hook & Ladder. There is a theatrical and grotesque side to the violence. In Jefferson City, at about 10:00 p.m., fifteen white men surround the house of a black man named A. J. Kemp and beat on his door. The Camellia guerrillas do not wear disguises. Robes and hoods are preferred for rural settings, less in the city. An investigation by the legislature tells the story.

"Come down, you damned son of a bitch, you are the one we are looking for," one shouts, according to testimony. The men drag A. J. Kemp from his house. They also seize a black man named Clark, hiding inside with Kemp. Actions of this kind are like certain raids Constant joined during the Civil War. You have a posse, you have stealth, you have a surprise strike. Constant takes pleasure in these memories. He remembers his face-to-face fights in the war, and it all must feel typical.

The gang takes Clark and Kemp to the truck house of Home Hook & Ladder. Inside, the men have built a makeshift gallows. It is not so high as a regular gallows, and not so wide, but recognizable as a hanging machine. To build a gallows is a straightforward business, if you have a skilled carpenter on hand. Constant is a good builder, and he can improvise. One glance at a diagram and he would be able to put up a hangman's kit in two or three hours. Maybe the diagram is even unnecessary. Here is the rope and here is the gibbet, and here is how they fit together.

The investigation by the legislature is not clear on one point. Does Home Hook use its gallows actually to hang people? Or do they merely use it to torment victims they bring to the firehouse? I would like to know, really, but the evidence is sketchy.

The gang begins with A. J. Kemp. In the shadow of the gibbet, they ask him where the guns might be that belong to the Loyal League. The Loyal League is a small group of Republicans, most of them black, a few white, who want Reconstruction to succeed. The Loyal League has held several rallies for its candidate, Ulysses Grant. The white newspapers say the Loyal League is arming black men by the hundred, that it plans a strike against white rule. The White Camellias tell Kemp that if he does not reveal the whereabouts of the guns, they will hang him at midnight.

Theater and fantasy are important to the guerrillas. Their worst fantasy is the one about an African American uprising.

Apparently there is extra room in the truck house, because the Camellias set up a mock courtroom. A judge's bench is put out, a row of chairs for defendants, a witness box for testimony. The gang arraigns its two prisoners and pretends to cross-examine them. Kemp and Clark are interrogated three times, and each time they tell the same story: they do not know of a storehouse of guns.

While Clark and Kemp are being tormented, someone back at Kemp's house manages to get word to the U.S. Army. In an hour, a squad of soldiers is dispatched, and shortly before midnight, Union

Klansmen in Alabama, 1868

men reach the Home Hook truck house. They break open the door
and put an end to the charade. Kemp and Clark are freed, and they
leave. A report on the episode does not mention arrests. Everyone
knows that the good police and courts of Jefferson would not put
these firemen in jail. The army squad moves on to the next incident,
and the guerrillas take themselves home.

A rule in history is that you tell stories based on evidence. With violent white supremacy, the evidence of the act is intermittent. The
white terror does not keep records. It does not want to leave evidence.
It undermines, it mutilates, and it disappears. It operates at night and

in secrecy. It is evidence of the aftermath that remains—bodies, scars, damaged families.

In the third week of October, there is a lynching in Jefferson City. It is executed by a gang of "disguised men," according to a news item, and takes place in the jail a few blocks from Constant and Gabrielle's rental. The men may be wearing blackface, or Mardi Gras masks, or hoods. It cannot be said: the evidence does not describe their disguise. In the event, which takes place on a Saturday morning, a gang of men shows up at the police lockup in Bouligny.

Two men, Dennis and Samuel Milton, black and apparently brothers, have been "tried and found guilty twice on a charge of outraging a white woman," as a reporter puts it. But the U.S. Army halts the case twice for lack of evidence. Proving the rule that gangs are the first form of justice, "a band of disguised men overpowers the jailor and takes summary vengeance on the two negroes." The Bouligny gang shoots the Milton brothers to death in their cells.

The perpetrators have no names, and no arrests are made, and so it is difficult to say whether Constant helps with the lynching in his neighborhood. I would like to think that he is home with the children and Gabrielle, who is eight months pregnant in October, with her sixth child. But I have no evidence of it.

It is the first time I see the word "lynching" in the story of my city, New Orleans, a place I love. The newspaper throws it in. Reporters know what they are talking about. They have seen lynching before and will see a lot more of it in a few years' time.

I find a 350-page report, a lot of evidence, about the weeks leading up to the election. It counts casualties statewide—784 killed, 85 wounded by gunshot, and 265 "maltreated," whipped or beaten or maybe raped. Ninety percent of the killings are of black people, ten percent are killings of whites. "Much larger numbers are estimated," says the legislative committee. It seems likely that half of the killings and assaults are not recorded.

You start with the evidence, but it is not enough. Here are a few things that take place in New Orleans and in Jefferson City, according to evidence in the legislative report—

THE MASSACRE IN THE PARISH OF ORLEANS IN
SEPTEMBER AND OCTOBER 1868.

Large mobs occurred and great numbers of colored men and white Republicans were slaughtered successively in the parish of Orleans on September 22, and October 24, 1868 . . . and Jefferson, on October 23, 1868.

Republican processions were continually assaulted and fired into. The streets at night were patrolled by armed men who marauded, plundered and killed at will. Flags bearing the words 'No Quarter' were borne at the head of these bands. Of the numbers thus clandestinely murdered no account can be obtained. Policemen were ambushed and shot while on duty. Private citizens were stabbed and assassinated.

It is incontestably established that the attacks were exclusively by white Democrats upon Republicans, yet an attempt was made . . . to ring a general alarm on the bells of the city, upon the hollow pretext of a "negro riot."

On October 24, an unprovoked assault was made upon a Ulysses Grant procession [Republican parade], in which a number were killed and wounded. . . . The nightly murders and robberies increased; numbers of people were compelled to flee from their residences and remain concealed for weeks.

The secret organization of the Knights of the White Camellia met and drilled with arms nightly, and it was their boast that at the looked-for signal they could demolish the United States troops in fifteen minutes.

And . . .

THE MASSACRE IN JEFFERSON PARISH
OCTOBER 23, 1868.

Bands of armed white men traversed the parish and under pretense of searching among the colored people for arms, committed murders and innumerable other outrages upon defenseless men, women and children.

Investigators emphasize the existence of a secret political and semi-military organization in this state styled, the Knights of the White Camellia. The signs, ritual and operations of this society throughout the parish of Orleans have been made known by testimony. . . . The testimony shows that the order exposed in this report is the real organization which is known to the public as the "Ku Klux."

Mima Hughes states, on oath, that she is a resident of the State of Louisiana, and is residing in Jefferson Parish, and is twenty years old. That on the morning of October 30, 1868, between the hours of 8 and 10 o'clock, she saw a gang of fifteen or twenty white men running after a colored man named Harry Scott. These men were armed with pistols, spades and axes, and they were crying out, 'Head him off!' 'Kill him!' etc. Witness then saw Henry Carroll, a resident of Jefferson, shoot Scott in the back; she also saw a son of John Linton, a keeper of a coffee-house, and a Jew named Albert Lamben, both shoot him in the back. On the same day, a body of white men came to the house of a colored woman named Polly Gill—where witness was visiting—and after destroying most everything in the room, one of the white men raised his gun and shot a colored man named Euben Lindsey in the face, and a baby four months old, which he was holding in his arms.

These are a few things that take place under the white man's banner in New Orleans and in Jefferson City, according to evidence collected by the state.

Election day comes, November 3, and the White Camellia places gangs at the polls to linger and malinger. Half the city's registered voters are white, half are black or Creoles of color. Nearly all white voters are Democrats. Nearly all Republicans are of color. On November 3, blacks do not vote at all, because they expect they will be killed for trying. In fact, two or three thousand blacks vote for Democrats, the whiteness party. They are coerced by threats or told by white employers to vote Democrat, or expect to lose a job or a limb. Ninety-five percent of white Republicans stay home, too. In New Orleans, only 276 votes for Republicans are cast, by whites who vote under armed guard. The Democrat Seymour wins Louisiana and seven other states. The Republican Grant wins twenty-six states, and the election. "The election in Louisiana was simply a sham, and a nullity," says an investigation.

White terror plays its hand, and Constant's hand is played.

After the vote, Governor Henry Warmoth sends a statement to the legislature. The society will heal, he says, "only when the dream of a natural, inborn right to supremacy shall be abandoned." A sentence that might be written at various times, perhaps even recently.

PART VI

PETITS BLANCS / LITTLE WHITES

When I was a child, I loved the book *Little Black Sambo*. It was among the handful of children's books my parents read aloud, a fifty-pager sold and read everywhere. The author, Helen Bannerman, was long dead, and we must have had an early edition, printed in the 1930s, to judge from the pickanninies and big-lipped Negroes of the illustrations. It was my mother's book when she learned to read as a little girl, growing up in New Orleans.

Sambo is a boy in southern India, with parents named Black Jumbo and Black Mumbo. Despite the setting in a nameless Indian state, Sambo and family are coons of white American fantasy. Sambo is on a walk when he runs into four tigers, who wish to eat him. He gives up his clothes and his umbrella as a bribe to save his own life, and the tigers try the things on, preening in Sambo's bright gear. Jealous of one another, the tigers chase a path around a tree until they wear it down to a pit and melt themselves into a puddle of butter. Sambo picks up his clothes, collects the butter in a tin. He takes it home to his mother, Black Mumbo, who uses the butter in pancakes.

Sambo is a cunning child. Almost mauled, he pratfalls his way to triumph. He is black as coal, with red lips. I have to wonder about the character: the boy who saves his own life by accident, because he is ignorant and happy, because he knows he has to fool the kings of the jungle. I wonder about the innocent black boy who outsmarts a mob trying to kill him. The plot sounds familiar.

Little Black Sambo, read by millions of white children during the 1900s, is a fable of tribe and species. It is hardly enough, I think, to see Black Sambo as a piece of "indoctrination" or "teaching of stereotypes." The children's story is less like an individual lesson in racial identity, and more like part of a flow. Black Sambo joins a million other droplets of popular culture to create a stream of images. Taken together, Sambo and his ilk are like a hose that helps to fill a pool. And if you test the water that the pool contains, you might find that you are taking an inventory of the unconscious.

Sigmund Freud, who died in 1939, said he did not discover the unconscious. Poets have always known of it, and they should have credit. In Freud's time—the early 1900s, Black Sambo's time—the idea that there might be a primary mind beneath the mind of the self, like a sea on which consciousness floats, seemed unbelievable (to most everyone but poets). A hundred years later, in the 2000s, more people buy in. Yet what is hard to accept, even among believers in the unconscious, is that this murky reservoir of language and images and memory is really the principal mind, and the conscious, sentient self is not. If *Homo sapiens* is "knowing man," what the woman or man wishes to deny is that awareness drifts like a lifeboat on the waters of the unconscious, whose depths can just faintly be known. And that the unconscious, with its undersea creatures, may have the greater influence on the individual's identity and behavior than her or his choices, decisions, and attempts at navigation.

We carry around, for example, forgotten matter from the years of childhood. Many of the impressions of youth are pushed into the well of the unconscious. Some become latent and inaccessible, although these may surface in dreams. What else lies in there? Pictures and fantasies, links of associations formed in language and dropped like ropes into the pool. The thing we call identity is made from aggregates of stuff that are suspended in the liquid bath beneath the waking self. The unconscious is a place independent of the waking mind, which believes it is in possession of the whole person. The unconscious does not listen to instruction from the self. It does not obey if you instruct yourself not to dream during sleep.

A waterfall of symbols that code for whiteness and blackness flows in and collects at the bottom of the self. There, the stream of images and fantasies and associations assumes shapes. The aggregate hardens like sediment and tends to stay intact. You have substances stored for good, which do not easily wear out.

For example, blackface. If you want to name one symptom that lets you diagnose that the unconscious exists and contains race identity, blackface is the sign. It is a richly pregnant symptom. What is disturbing about blackface is that it shows the contents of an unconscious that is white. To look upon blackface—now, during the 2000s—is to dig up repressed features of the racial unconscious. People respond strongly to blackface because it is a sign, which, when read down to its referent, contains a glimpse of the contents of white identity.

"Whiteness" is a body of signs that may be found in the unconscious of those who identify themselves as white. (It may also be found swimming like a creature in the minds of people who are not white.) Whiteness is coherent, it has a recognizable outline; it possesses a structure that imposes itself on waking life. It helps to determine behavior, and it helps to shape the thing known as "choice." Sigmund Freud felt the idea of unconscious determinism, the hypothesis of psychoanalysis, insulted the common belief in human agency and choice. "Mental processes are in themselves unconscious, and of all mental life, there are only certain individual acts and portions that are conscious," he said in a lecture in 1917. The thought that the sediment of old pictures and associations can be stirred up and retaliate on the self by compelling behavior still feels like a lie. It is really just an unpleasant truth.

In the *Oxford English Dictionary*, first prepared during Black Sambo's time, "unconscious," by definition #3, is a thing "not realized or known as existing in oneself." The idea appears in a couplet, three hundred years old, from the English poet Richard Blackmore:

Unconscious causes only still impart
Their utmost skill, their utmost power exert.

Inside the unconscious, I think, is a submerged island of whiteness. It is like a landmass. It forms a platform and foundation for the self. But like an underwater reef, it is unseen and unacknowledged.

An unconscious formation, like the island of whiteness, is defined by its being unrecognizable. You do not know it when you see it. It is a thing that by its nature you wish not to see. It is a fact whose existence you disavow.

We would like to disavow that the phenomenon of whiteness exists. I would like to disavow it. And yet we spend it like currency, and we take home the social goods that it buys. The ego is enlarged by whiteness. Public spaces are defined by it, and by the lack of it. When you have eyes with which to see it, whiteness becomes conspicuous.

What would be the effect for us, whites, of dredging the underwater reef of white identity? What occurs when you try to carry some of what is unconscious up into the conscious mind? It is not easy to dislodge unconscious material. Racial identity, deeply embedded, cannot be removed and replaced, like computer memory. What is possible is to acquire some awareness of racial formations inside the self and to place that awareness with other sentience possessed by "knowing man."

To peer down into one's own mental well and make an inventory of what it contains does not transform you into a new person. To examine the entity of whiteness in the recesses of the mind does not cause you to be reborn. To dredge up some of the thick sediment and release it into consciousness is to experience a slight diminishment in what is unknown, that is all. The person remains the same, maybe a little altered.

I believe there are mountains of race identity that lie unconscious, beneath the sea of the mind, and their existence is not disproved by unracist behavior. The geology of race thought is craggy and durable. If I declare my love for blackness, or if I believe in equal rights, or if I desire to redress the racial wrongs of history, those things do not mean that blackness amounts to more than piedmont next to the high cliff of whiteness on the seafloor of my unconscious.

Here is an observation that is hard to make. If I reject white supremacy, saying it is not a part of me, that does not mean that the order of things within the unconscious does not still place white over black. I suspect the self is not responsible for the contents of the unconscious. But conscious people are accountable in the end for what comes out, for the announcements of the unconscious—for behaviors, if you like. The unconscious has the raw material, the person runs the delivery system. Try as you like to deflect and to sublimate what pours out of the well. It often works. Try as you wish to modify the contents of the unconscious. It may work, doubtfully.

Constant is an agent of racist terror, and he is one of us. What lies in the unconscious of this ordinary man who cannot keep a full work calendar and who terrorizes people? Maybe a hundred things can be found, with names. Bloodlust from war. Disgust with blackness. Subservience to authority. Attraction to blackness. Insecurity of self. Fear of blackness. Rage at scapegoats, defined by their blackness. The main items, maybe, are forms of aversion and arousal around blackness. He is one of us, one of ours. Does Constant share an attraction and repulsion around blackness with other whites? He does, both with the majority of whites then, and perhaps with the majority during the so-very-enlightened 2000s. Aversion is a subliminal state. Its presence is deniable by the one who feels it. And importantly, it is always denied. Aversion is a strong condition; it is even stronger the more that it is disavowed. Consider the "I am not a racist" school of racism.

The thing itself, aversion and attraction to blackness, grows like a crystal within the cave of the unconscious. It starts as a tiny facet on the wall, its prism sending light this way and that. It is unknown to the people who host it. The facet grows. Shine a beam and the big crystal gleams.

Many whites alive during the years of Reconstruction reject the method of the White Camellia. Yet many desire the ends the marauders achieve, namely, white domination. In our time, we scorn the White Camellia and feel morally superior to it. And we nevertheless bathe ourselves in the comfort and control that Constant and his comrades leave as their bequest.

He is a mediocre man, like a middling salary worker of today. He is bland and ordinary, not heroic. Small and empty, not majestic like Satan. He is one of ours.

I am advertising some of the venal things my predecessor did. But I am not delivering him to justice. I do not scold him: he is one of us. We may say that Constant Lecorgne and his clique are ignorant, cruel, mentally ill, debased, and more. And yet what they do is legible. We can understand it as a campaign made on our behalf.

This is a story of race violence and terror that is Janus-faced. It is both exceptional and normal. It is aberrant in its cruel extreme. And yet it is typical, because the wider community tacitly supports it.

Our own years, the 2000s, come with a feeling that some call "white guilt." The experience of guilt, with scolding applied to the self, is like a screen that obscures a less conscious process. Guilt is more like a symptom that points beyond, at something else. It does not refer to things that one values, principles or ideals that have failed—or it does not point to them alone. It points instead at what or at whom one fears. The experience of white guilt is an expression of fear about the cost of race domination, the punishment that history wishes to make us pay. Guilt is productive, and it is a necessary and natural stage in the act of reckoning. We are likely to pass through it in order to come to a reckoning with the crimes committed on our behalf. In that way, guilt is something like a stage of grief. On the other hand, many of us are just as likely to desire the fruits of those crimes and to enjoy them while we still can.

It is December 1868. Campaigns of terror like the ones in Louisiana take place all around the South, from Texas to Georgia, from Kentucky to South Carolina. The Democrats lose the national election, and Ulysses Grant wins.

But *les nègres* are still down. Let them stay down.

The Crescent City Democrats quit the stage when their leader, Frederick Ogden, dissolves the ward club. He is not finished. He will come back.

Gabrielle Duchemin prepares for her sixth baby. The child is conceived during the month of April 1868—just when the marauding starts. Is rampage the hour when Constant most wants his wife? Does he desire her more intensely after the White Camellia begins its torments?

The boy comes on December 16. His parents name him Saint Mark. You have the family leader, Yves *Jean de Dieu*—Yves John of God, and now you have Saint Mark Lecorgne. In the New Testament, the author of the second Gospel, Mark the Evangelist, is a prophet. He is a saint embodied with his own symbol, which is a lion with wings, holding a book. Mark the Evangelist is like the roar of proclamation in flight. His is a great and lasting testament.

I doubt Gabrielle thinks of it this way. No doubt her unconscious would make her disavow it. But I think that this moment is the one in the history of her place, and maybe in the history of the United States, when the *cause* of whiteness is born. Gabrielle is witness to a kind of proclamation of white identity. It is sometime during these years, down South, that white supremacy becomes an American program, a coherent idea with an independent life. It becomes a project, a shape and a plan.

White rule has been with us since the first ships from Europe came and tested the dirt to plant empire. But white domination has been atmospheric, for the reason that it faces weak opposition. Prior to the Civil War, white supremacy was a natural state, a climate often invisible to those within it. Some whites see it, of course. I think of Herman Melville in *Moby-Dick*; I think of Roger Taney, chief justice of the Supreme Court, who writes in *Dred Scott v. Sandford* that people of color "have no rights which the white man was bound to respect." But whiteness commonly could not be made visible, because white supremacy was the form of everyday life. After the war, whiteness becomes nonnatural. It turns visible and contingent because it faces competing claims. It faces the idea of tribal equality. It faces the idea that whites do not possess inevitable authority. It is only with Reconstruction, when the prospect of racial equality appears above the horizon, that whiteness becomes a program to achieve rather than to defend. During Reconstruction, white supremacy takes shape as a movement that it is necessary to argue and to impose. It is necessary to do violence in its behalf. White identity may wish to return to its initial state. It wishes to disappear from public view and be made natural once again. But this cannot be done.

And there is another thing, if I am allowed to say it. It is sometime in this season that whiteness enters the social unconscious of the country. It takes invisible root in national life. I do not believe white supremacy is a regional phenomenon, an ideology that is the possession of whites in the South. Sometime in this season, white identity seeps into the collective, national mind—and there, it seizes grip.

In December, near Christmas, Gabrielle gives birth to Saint Mark. Mothers are sometimes in awe of what they have done (and rightly). A mother can see her baby as a testament.

Constant and Gabrielle have a dilapidated rental on Annunciation Street, near the corner of Austerlitz. (Annunciation was once Jersey Street, but city fathers wished to honor the pregnancy of the Virgin Mary, and so the name was changed.) The Lecorgnes are the only whites on their block; every other household, according to census takers, is "black" or "mulatto."

A black block feels like cold comfort. Considering what this man has done to launder the world clean. Constant is fully what he did not wish to become, namely, a *petit blanc*, a little white.

Joseph Lecorgne lives with his wife, Estelle Daunoy, and their children on Jena Street, close to where the Lecorgne brothers grew up. He has fallen off the government payroll. Age thirty-four, and no longer justice of the peace, Joseph sometimes advertises as a carpenter, sometimes as a gardener. He is also a *petit blanc*. Joseph appears to be absent from the guerrilla movement, and from politics. The reason may be temperamental. Just as Yves of God is a fixer in local government, and just as Constant may be militant, Joseph is content with being detached. But it may also be that during these years, Joseph is not well.

In fact, Joseph Lecorgne is sick. Doctors diagnose his condition as "Bright's disease," a kidney disorder. He is ill and getting more so. The diagnosis is the beginning of Joseph's long decline. The disease is chronic and progressive, a kind of nephritis that causes edema as well as heart trouble. Treatments for Joseph are as bad as the disease— mercury, opium, and heavy diuretics. As his nephritis worsens, it disables him, and Joseph is only sometimes able to work.

Yves of God remains steady and flush. He has the family home-stead on Lecorgne row. His neighborhood is white, except for two black servants who work for him and live in an outbuilding behind the house. Yves runs a household of nine: he and his wife, Estelle Fazende; two young children; and Estelle's mother, Sophie. Plus four more: Yves's widowed sister, Aurore; her seventeen-year-old son, Ed-gar; and two African Americans, George Parker and Frannie Joseph, who do everyone's bidding. Yves captains this big barge of family life as the comptroller for Jefferson City. And he does busy side work as justice of the peace. He has maneuvered himself back into the job, taking it from his brother Joseph, over the objection of the Freed-men's Bureau.

If I am not distorting the facts, this appears to be a cooler time during the Ku-klux ascendancy. The election brought a blaze of anti-black violence. For the next three years, New Orleans is like a pit when the flame dies. The status quo remains, somewhat charred, punctu-ated by flares from the embers.

The prevailing mood among both blacks and whites, I imagine, is a kind of fatigue and a sort of disgust. Whites get what they wanted—the Ku-klux chokes every voice that opposes white command. But the Lecorgnes and other *petits blancs* are not happy. The loathsome Ulysses Grant is in the White House, and so-called radicals run the state. The governor of Louisiana is a white Republican, Henry War-moth, his lieutenant governor a black man named Oscar Dunn. The Louisiana Senate counts twenty-three Republicans, seven of whom are black, and thirteen Democrats, all white. In the state House of Representatives are sixty-five Republicans, thirty-five of them black, and thirty-six Democrats, all white. Adding things up, three out of ten state lawmakers are black or Creoles of color. The newspapers de-scribe this black representation of one-third as "negro domination."

With a two-to-one Republican majority, the Louisiana Assembly passes the Election Act. The bill bans the kinds of things done by night riders like Constant and the White Camellia. It becomes illegal to shoot a gun in the direction of a school, a house, or a church; be-comes illegal to use threats that force people to leave town. Because white judges friendly to the Ku-klux mysteriously lose their paperwork, the Election Act makes it illegal to mutilate or pilfer court files, such as indictments for crimes.

These are niceties, some say. Let the coon politicians enforce them.

Another law is proposed that hits close to home. It bans the wearing of costumes and masks, hoods and robes, "to prevent people from going abroad disguised." The law is aimed at the Ku-klux, but New Orleans is the Carnival city, where people like to mask. The costume ban goes to a committee, where it dies. Another law that bans concealed weapons has the same fate, it goes conference and disappears.

The legislature tries other things. Politicians turn to disease and hygiene. Weirdly, a public health law makes the race war worse. In 1869, lawmakers pass the "Act to Protect the Health of the City of New Orleans." In order to stop slaughterhouses upstream of the city from fouling the Mississippi with dead animals, the law creates a monopoly company for the slaughter of livestock, with a killing plant downstream. A butchers' group files suit, arguing that the brand-new Fourteenth Amendment, with its "equal protection" clause, meant to defend freed slaves, is really meant to protect them, businesspeople. Eventually the so-called Slaughterhouse Cases, triggered by the Louisiana health law, go to the U.S. Supreme Court. And in 1873, just a few years after the Constitution stretches its tent of protection over people of color, the Court uses the Louisiana act to cut away at the Fourteenth Amendment. The Supreme Court rules that the "privileges and immunities" named in the amendment do not protect individuals from actions of state governments that may rob them of their civil rights. The result is that the federal government loses much of its power of law to shelter blacks from domination. It is another reversal, and bitter. The Slaughterhouse Cases, born on the Mississippi wharfs, are an alarm that announces the beginning of the end of the experiment in race equity.

Gabrielle and Constant probably raise an ear when another bill comes up at the statehouse. Democrats propose a law that redeems old Confederate bonds; they want the state to buy up the scrip the rebel government used to raise a war chest. The Lecorgnes lost a lot when they invested in the fight. Now it looks as though their fall from *grands blancs* to the ranks of the *petits* might be cushioned, or even reversed. Their hopes are raised; the money could very well come back. But the bill is parked in committee, where it dies. Constant and Gabrielle are disappointed. For them, it is another reversal, and bitter.

White terror is shelved, for the time being. Around the South, the Ku-klux retreats from violence. In October 1869, in Tennessee, the so-called Grand Wizard of the Ku Klux Klan, Nathan Bedford Forrest, issues a proclamation that orders the secret society to cease attacks. Forrest adds, in his bulletin, "This is not to be understood to dissolve the Order of the Ku Klux Klan," merely to keep it quiet until "any emergency that may come." Terror goes dormant in Louisiana, as the White Camellia also stops night-riding. The headman Alcibiade DeBlanc moves from New Orleans back to his hometown, St. Martinville, and disappears from notice. There is no need for terror, he would say. Blood is not needed now, since the idea of social equality, blacks and whites sharing power and money, is going nowhere. The public schools that are open to blacks in the city are not merging with schools for whites. Calls by Creole radicals like the Roudanez brothers for the redistribution of land are having no effect. There is little sharing in white and black work life, none in worship life, and not much in cash. All seems frozen in place. In the statehouse, lawmakers pass a civil rights bill, an attempt to implement the equal accommodations clause of the 1868 constitution. The *Picayune* expresses mainstream white opinion. "This . . . social equality bill . . . is a sham and a snare. It is the convocation of . . . mongrel mulattoes who have read the mischievous books of . . . ridiculous theorists." The white governor, a Republican who came to office on the votes of black men, vetoes the law, claiming he cannot enforce it.

On the other hand, this is a time when the first blacks are seated in the U.S. Congress. In 1870, the state of Mississippi sends Hiram Revels, a black minister in the African Methodist Episcopal Church, to join the U.S. Senate. At the end of the year, South Carolina sends Joseph Rainey, a black barber born into slavery, to enter the U.S. House.

Voting rights for blacks appear to be made permanent, as the Fifteenth Amendment comes within reach. The Fifteenth Amendment is a single sentence: "The right of citizens of the United States to vote shall not be denied or abridged by the United States or by any state on account of race, color, or previous condition of servitude." In February 1869, Congress sends the amendment that gives black men the vote out to state legislatures for approval. White feminists, including Elizabeth Cady Stanton and Susan B. Anthony, and no doubt tens of millions of other people, want to lengthen the single sentence of the amendment with one word, "sex," to hand the vote to women. The campaign fails. The Louisiana legislature passes the Fifteenth Amendment as written.

It is a cold kind of war, in which disaster comes less often. In 1870, the Metropolitan Police publish a status report. "We have, during the year just past," it says, "no riots to report, nor any massacres of men on account of race or color." This is the paltry definition of a good year: no race massacres to report.

The cold war comes to an end with a new eruption in Bouligny. Police and firemen in Jefferson City have decided to seal off the municipality from the Yankee army and its comrades, the Metropolitan Police. It is a kind of town coup d'état, as the suburb cuts itself off from New Orleans. It appears that the two Lecorgne brothers, Yves of God and Constant, are involved. Yves helps to lead things. As comptroller, he holds the money levers of Jefferson City, with power second only to the mayor. Yves decides that he and the town should withhold all taxes from the state and use the money instead to run the local police and courts. Next, a paramilitary force made up of Home Hook & Ladder men puts up barricades to keep the army out of Bouligny. The Home Hook men begin patrols. Constant seems to be among the two or three hundred who police the perimeter of the sealed town.

The stunt continues for eight months, until May 1869, when the "secession" comes under siege. That month, Governor Henry Warmoth appoints a new mayor, comptroller, and board of aldermen in Jefferson City. When Yves of God and the rest of the local rebels refuse to surrender their offices, the case goes to trial, and the state supreme court rules against the coup d'état. Comptroller Yves Lecorgne still refuses to leave the courthouse.

On May 17, 1869, the Metropolitan Police sent by the governor try to seize the station house of Precinct 7 in Bouligny. The contingent of twenty Metropolitans is overwhelmed and arrested by Home Hook militia. Constant may or may not be in that group of guerrillas, but I suspect he is. Three years later, he will be back at Precinct 7, this time with different commandos, to seize the same station house, and to face arrest.

The Metropolitans return the next night, May 18, now with two hundred men. They reach Lawrence Square, at the center of Bouligny, to find two hundred guerrillas defending it. The two sides open fire. Everyone has a pistol, nobody a rifle, and the two gangs stay far apart. The shoot-out lasts for an hour and involves poor marksmanship. None of the Jefferson militia is killed, but two Metropolitans die, with twelve or thirteen wounded. They retreat. It is hard to imagine Constant is not one of the gunmen.

On the third day, May 19, the U.S. Army gathers four hundred men—two companies of soldiers, two pieces of artillery, and more Metropolitans. This time, some of the soldiers are a company of "colored infantry," the better to provoke the whites. Governor Warmoth joins the force on horseback. At about 8:30 a.m., the army marches up St. Charles Avenue, turns left on Napoleon Avenue, toward the river, and enters Lawrence Square. They find the square abandoned. When a white butcher in the food market off Lawrence Square insults the company of black soldiers, the Union men drag the butcher from his stall and beat him bloody. A white crowd gathers. The army men are black, while their comrades, the Metropolitans, are white. The crowd floats words like "nigger-lover" on the air, and the police are enraged. The white cops start to beat and club local whites.

Flanked by soldiers, Governor Warmoth places the new officials at their desks. Yves of God, plus the mayor and other white-collar rebels, are driven from the courthouse. Governor Warmoth swears in the new mayor of Jefferson City, a man named Felix Leche.

As it happens, Felix Leche is a Lecorgne in-law. Aurora Lecorgne, sister of Yves, was married to Felix's brother, Numa Leche, before

Numa died of yellow fever. Felix Leche is thus the brother-in-law of Constant, Joseph, and Yves. Mayor Felix Leche of Jefferson City is one of the few in the circle of the Lecorgnes—in fact, he is the only one—who takes the side of Reconstruction. Leche is the only person who seems to believe in the failing idea that blacks and whites might belong to the same tribe.

In spring 1870, President Ulysses Grant asks Congress for laws that ban voter intimidation. Grant knows that in the South, intimidation can mean murder. The Republican majority passes three laws. The first, the Enforcement Act of May 1870, bans the infamous robes and hoods of the Ku-klux. Gangs that "go in disguise upon the public highways, or upon the premises of another" and violate the constitutional rights of citizens break federal law. In the bill's floor debate, the Massachusetts congressman Benjamin "Beast" Butler waves a shirt stained with dried blood. He says the Ku-klux in Mississippi whipped the man who wore it, the superintendent of a school for African American children.

The second Enforcement Act defines Ku-klux terror as a conspiracy, and because the blood of the South shows that states cannot run a fair vote, the law puts national elections in the hands of the federal government. A third law, in 1871, allows the president to summon the army to protect voting and to suspend habeas corpus, the limit on detention of citizens. It permits group arrests without the requirement of one-at-a-time arraignment. It is this law that acquires the memorable name the Ku Klux Klan Act.

Before long, Constant Lecorgne will find himself charged under the Ku Klux Klan Act.

In June 1870, Congress creates the Department of Justice. The department is formed expressly in order to use the Enforcement Acts against the Ku-klux. After two years, white terror is returning. White terror spreads in Louisiana, Mississippi, Alabama, Tennessee, and the other ex-rebel states. President Grant appoints a man named Amos Akerman as the first attorney general to head the Justice Department.

Akerman hires a legal staff, and the first assignment of the new department is to bring cases against the Ku-klux. Akerman picks the state of South Carolina as the place to make an example.

In South Carolina, the army rounds up more than one thousand Ku-klux members, local sheriffs among them, and prosecution starts. The Ku Klux Klan trials run for eighteen months, beginning in summer 1871.

Louisiana is safe from federal action, and so is Constant, at least for now. Or almost. Congress appoints the "Joint Select Committee to Inquire into the Condition of Affairs in the Late Insurrectionary States" and sends investigators across the South to document the Ku-klux violence. The bloody trail they find turns into a thirteen-volume report. It is an encyclopedia of terror—beatings, rapes, whippings, executions. Witness testimony chronicles perhaps one thousand individual incidents. These can only be a fraction of the actual number. A reader can spend a week and not get through half the catalog.

The city of Memphis wants to imitate New Orleans, putting on its own festival of masked balls and parades on Mardi Gras. It is Tuesday, February 20, 1872. The streets of Memphis fill up with the first Carnival processions Tennessee has ever seen. There is music, masking, and drinking. In the crowning event, a marvelous parade rumbles down Front Street, following the levee that runs beside the Mississippi. One wagon in the Memphis parade attracts more attention than the rest. A reporter for the *Daily Appeal* describes the Ku-klux float, the parade car that draws notice—

"The Ku-klux had a wagon of their own in the procession in which were representatives of the Klan from all the states of the South," the paper says. "All the terrible scenes alleged to have been enacted for years were presented, and the Ku-klux appeared in full regalia."

A deep crowd on the sidewalk waves and laughs at the Ku-klux wagon. The men on the float, wearing hoods and robes, perform a skit in which they pretend to kill a black man. The role of the victim is played by a white Ku-kluxer slathered in blackface. "One of their number impersonated a living ace of spades, the veritable butt-end of midnight," the reporter writes, "and the poor negro was executed according to all the familiar forms . . . including the death-struggle, and the efforts to escape. . . ." Parades run long on Mardi Gras, and so the revelers must entertain by repeating their sketch over and over, mock-killing the mock–African American many, many times. It is all in good fun. The laughter dies slowly, Carnival season comes to an end, and the hoods and robes return to closets.

A few months later, still in Tennessee, the Grand Wizard of the Ku-klux, Nathan Bedford Forrest, writes a bulletin and sends it to his followers, whom he estimates to number forty thousand. "It will be impossible for us to make ourselves useful until we get the reins of government out of the hands of the nigger leaders," it begins. It is July, and the race for the White House is again under way. "The cussed niggers are the cause of all our woe," Forrest writes. He adds a second source of irritation, namely, President Grant's "pigheaded refusal to remunerate the Southern people for their Slave property, of which they were so wickedly robbed by Lincoln." The bulletin is sent far and wide. It will do well to raise morale. "The South must be avenged," Forrest concludes. "The negro slave must not be our final conqueror.—Forrest, Worshipful Chief, K.K.K."

Governorships around the South are up for grabs. In Louisiana, the Republican Party runs a candidate, William Kellogg, a white U.S. senator; he pairs with the politician Caesar Antoine, a Creole of color from upstate, who runs for lieutenant governor. The Democrats put up the longtime politician John McEnery for governor. In an early campaign parade, on August 12, McEnery leads a crowd of supporters through the streets of New Orleans. The parade line carries an enormous banner that reads "White Supremacy." The *New Orleans Republican* newspaper observes, "We regard the McEnery ticket as representing the negro hating, schoolhouse burning, fire-eating Bourbonists."

The Democrats are "Bourbons," after the name of the royal family in France. A clever and caustic analogy. It is said that the Democrats, like the French royals, were run out of power by a revolution—defeat in the Civil War—and yet they expect to be restored to their place of reverence, having learned nothing.

The 1872 campaigns are quieter than the ones in 1868. I suspect Constant and other guerrillas are following the Ku-klux trials in South Carolina, where 220 have been indicted, and those events curb their enthusiasm for marauding. The Ku-klux carries out minimal gang terror—although to their victims, the half truce is little comfort.

Voting occurs November 4, and the election is full of fraud. No one knows who wins the governor's race in Louisiana. The Returning Board—a panel meant to verify elections and diminish vote rigging—

gives a split opinion. Some on the board name McEnery winner, some name Kellogg. Ulysses Grant wins the White House (and Louisiana), at least that is known. Grant's Democratic opponent, Horace Greeley, dies as returns are being counted.

Both gubernatorial candidates claim to have won, but William Kellogg gets the prize for maneuvering. He brings a case to a federal court, where a judge rules in the Republican's favor and orders the U.S. Army to protect Kellogg's government. Governor Warmoth, accused of mishandling election returns, is impeached. He resigns office in December. And when that happens, his lieutenant governor, Pinckney Pinchback, is promoted to governor. By this Byzantine accident, Pinckney Pinchback becomes the first African American governor of any state. He serves for six weeks, until Governor Kellogg is inaugurated. Governor Pinchback remains the only black governor to hold office anywhere in the United States until the year 1988.

Democrats do not like that the election goes against them, and in January 1873, both Kellogg and McEnery hold installation ceremonies. Democrats also dislike the color of the new legislature, which counts sixty-eight blacks and seventy-seven whites.

Charles Gayarré, a distinguished historian of Louisiana who lives through the events, observes, "We are completely under the rule of ignorant and filthy negroes scarcely superior to the orang-outang."

The parallel governments continue for some weeks. One meets in an auditorium, Lyceum Hall, the other in the Mechanics Institute, site of the massacre.

On February 26, 1873, President Grant sends a message to Congress saying that he recognizes the Republican governor, William Kellogg. The message prompts the Democrat, John McEnery, to raise the ante to violence. The following day, McEnery gives a speech to a roomful of supporters and asks them to take up arms and install him in office. He calls out Fred Ogden and names him to lead a guerrilla group, the "McEnery Militia."

With that, the Ku-klux is back in business, and Constant back on board.

In October 1872, an artist arrives in New Orleans from Paris. He is Hilaire-Germain-Edgar Degas, age thirty-eight. Degas paints landscapes, for the most part, although this will soon change. He has come for a visit to his family in Louisiana. The artist moves into the second floor of a house at 372 Esplanade Avenue, near the corner of Bayou Road. The house is big, but it is full. In it, Edgar Degas finds his brother René de Gas, as well as their uncle, a man named Michel Musson. He finds the wives and children of the two men. Edgar's brother René uses a fake noble spelling of his name—de Gas—although the family is not aristocratic. The painter wants no part of the charade and sticks to "Degas." He is more a realist than a fantasist.

In later years, Edgar Degas becomes a man famous for his paintings of dancers, his paintings of horses, his paintings of women. He will be loved as one of the most vivid and most decadent of the Impressionist painters, a man who can bring prostitutes to life with his brush hand and hold a glass of green absinthe in the other. But in New Orleans, Degas is largely an unknown. He is just a visitor, with links to certain white Creoles in the Ku-klux.

The painter's mother, Célestine Musson, is born in New Orleans. During the 1830s, she marries a Frenchman visiting the city, Auguste Degas, and moves with him to Paris. Edgar is her first of five children. But Célestine dies in Paris in 1847, when the boy is thirteen. In 1870, Edgar's two brothers, Achille and René, move to New Orleans to find new lives. Both go to work for their mother's brother in Louisiana, Michel Musson, a dealer in cotton.

The Musson household in which Edgar lives for half a year—fall 1872 till Mardi Gras 1873—has familiar signs of white aspiration. There are black servants. There are frequent trips to the French Opera. And there is the sale of cotton, the crop from black hands, which keeps the silver polished and the house in high comfort. Degas's uncle, Michel Musson, is a cotton factor. He buys raw cotton from planters in the upstate, sorts and grades it, then sells it to buyers for fabric mills—some in New England, some in France, some in England. In early 1873, Edgar Degas paints a picture, *A Cotton Office in New Orleans*. It shows the cotton factorage belonging to Michel Musson. In the painting, Degas's uncle sits in the foreground, wearing eyeglasses and fingering a boll of cotton. On the picture's left, wearing a top hat and doing nothing, is Degas's brother, Achille. At center reading a newspaper is René de Gas, the second of Edgar's brothers. René happens to be married to a daughter of his uncle Michel Musson—that is to say, to his first cousin. At the table holding a bunch of cotton in both hands is a man named William Bell, who is married to another of the daughters of Michel Musson.

A Cotton Office in New Orleans by Edgar Degas, 1873

This William Bell, as it happens, is the most important person in the painting. He is a leader in the white supremacist movement. William Bell appears, in the picture, merely to be visiting the Musson office. In life, William Bell is the business partner of the Ku-klux leader, Fred Ogden. Their company, Bell & Ogden, with offices on Union Street, sells cotton baling material—iron ties, rope, and bags.

A year later, Fred Ogden and William Bell will come together to set up a new enterprise. It is not a cotton business. Instead, it is a Ku-klux militia, which they call the White League. The White League is the most important band of guerrillas in the story of the supremacist movement. It is the one that will bring an end to Reconstruction and seal the success of white supremacy. And it is the final militia that Constant Lecorgne will join.

On Mardi Gras day in 1873, the men in the painting (and I think Edgar Degas himself) find themselves at yet another Carnival. Circumstantial evidence says that they attend a key Mardi Gras event, the procession of the Mistick Krewe of Comus. Several of the cotton men are members of Comus, and they would want the painter Edgar Degas to see for himself the beauty of the annual festival. They would want to show off the Comus treatment of Mardi Gras, before they allow Degas to pack and return to Paris.

This year, Comus has a theme—"Missing Links to Darwin's Origin of Species." The theory of evolution spread by the naturalist Charles Darwin in *On the Origin of Species*, published in 1859, has trickled down to the level of popular culture and festival, and Comus wishes to make good fun of it. In the middle of an hour-long parade, Edgar Degas might conclude that Mardi Gras is not about masquerade, it is really about *les nègres*. An elaborate float in the middle of the procession carries a giant black creature in papier-mâché, "the Missing Link himself, half-human, half-gorilla," as a reporter puts it. The ape-like figure plays a banjo and looks out across the float toward a "simian Cupid," a monkey in the form of the love-nymph, holding a bow and arrow. Cupid himself peers this way and that, "looking for a noble mate" to unite with the banjo-playing ape. In the Comus parade, white supremacy discovers Darwin and tries to put the scientist to work, so to speak. The theme of "Missing Links" revives the old idea of the separate species. Humor is more persuasive than the windy talk of scientists like Samuel Cartwright and Louis Agassiz. And satire is more memorable than the thought balloons of James De Bow. A Carnival joke about the genus of the blacks is one that a hundred thousand drunks can understand.

After Mardi Gras, someone sends a newspaper clipping about the "Origin of Species" parade, plus a folio of drawings of the "missing links," to Charles Darwin himself. In 1873, the naturalist is a famous and aging gentleman who lives southeast of London. He writes back, sounding confused—"Dear Sir, The abusive article in the newspaper amused me more than Comus. I can't tell whether the writer is witty or ignorant," Darwin says.

It happens quickly, because the gang members are old hands. When John McEnery calls for armed resistance, a movement comes together fast. On Friday, February 28, Alcibiade DeBlanc, old master of the White Camellia, comes out of his yearlong quiet and speaks to a rally in front of Gallier Hall, on Lafayette Square. Leaning over the platform, according to the *Republican*, and looking at the mass of faces below him, DeBlanc says—

"I see in the future nothing but negro domination! Will you submit to it?"

The crowd shouts—No! No!

"I believe we ought to resist even though the muskets of the United States are leveled at our breasts," DeBlanc says. "Do you believe that you owe any allegiance to the government of the United States?"

The crowd—No!

"We owe no allegiance! We ought to resist it and raise the flag of the white race of Louisiana. We do not intend to shed blood, but we will raise high the flag of the white race!"

Something tells me Constant is at this rally. DeBlanc is his friend, his old comrade in arms. And Constant is out of guerrilla retirement. DeBlanc calls for a coup d'état that throws out the black-loving administration of Governor William Kellogg and installs the white-loving John McEnery. He throws his support and prestige to Fred Ogden, new captain of the McEnery Militia. It is a fight for white rights, Constant's cause.

I have described the raid on Precinct 7, in Jefferson City. It begins five days later, on March 4, 1873. That night, Constant joins a commando group of about thirty. They seize a police station in Bouligny. Three miles downtown, in New Orleans, the leader of the guerrillas, Fred Ogden, runs a separate assault on the armory in the city's old court building, the Cabildo. Alcibiade DeBlanc is absent from the scene. He is probably at home in St. Martinville, pulling in recruits.

The raid on the Cabildo armory fails, but the raid on Precinct 7 succeeds. Constant and his gang occupy the police station for twenty-four hours. I imagine this feels good to him. It is the same police outpost that fell to the Yankees when Bouligny was invaded by army troops.

According to one newspaper, at 1:00 a.m. on March 6, a company of 120 Metropolitans attacks the precinct. Some of the guerrillas melt back into the neighborhood, but Constant and twelve other Ku-klux make a last stand. They are armed with pistols and shotguns. As the Metropolitans swarm the building, some guerrillas open fire. No one is hit, and the Metropolitans return fire. Inside, Constant's twenty-seven-year-old cousin, Ernest Livaudais, is shot in the arm. He survives. Another man, Kendrick Chandler, is shot in the abdomen.

The same Kendrick Chandler, eight years earlier, found himself in a jailhouse with one of the Lecorgnes. Constant's brother Joseph was a prisoner of war with Kendrick Chandler. The two men survived winter in a crude Yankee prison in Ohio, Camp Chase, before being paroled to go home to New Orleans.

The Metropolitans take the building, and Constant surrenders. Kendrick Chandler, shot in the stomach, is carried out by soldiers and brought to Charity Hospital. He dies a few days later. Constant and twelve guerrillas are made prisoner. The men know one another. They are friends. Seven of the thirteen are officers in Jefferson City fire companies. In addition to Constant, the men from Home Hook & Ladder include Émile Chevalley (who runs a coal yard in Bouligny), Charles Piper (a grocer on Chestnut Street), and four others. They have drunk together, paraded together, and raised hell together.

The men are brought downtown to the central jail. A prosecutor in the First District Court of Orleans Parish writes the bill of indictment. ("Not a true bill," he scribbles on it, meaning there is more to come.) The first charge is violating the Ku Klux Klan Act of 1871. The second charge is treason. The paperwork shows a district attorney whose anger is seething. Constant Lecorgne, he says—

> . . . wickedly intending and devising the peace and tranquility of the state to disturb and destroy . . . then and there unlawfully maliciously and traitorously conspired to levy war against

the said state and to fulfill and bring to effect the said traitor-
ous compassings intentions and conspirings. [The guerrillas]
traitorously assembled, armed and arrayed as aforesaid most
wickedly maliciously and traitorously did ordain prepare and
levy war against the said State contrary to their duty of allegiance [to it] . . . and contrary to the form of the statute of the
State of Louisiana in such case made and provided and against
the peace and dignity of the same.

Constant and comrades sit in jail for six days. On March 12, they
have a bail hearing. Yves of God bails out his younger brother, paying a bond of $500. Constant is the only man bailed out by relatives.
Other prisoners pay their own bail or get bail from friends. It means
that he is poor, and perhaps not much liked.

The day after he leaves the jail, Constant signs an affidavit about
an event the night of the raid. The affidavit has nothing to do with
the treason charge or the Klan Act. Instead, it is about Kendrick
Chandler, the guerrilla shot and killed.

According to *The Daily Picayune*, Constant says that he lives on
Belmont Street near Tchoupitoulas Street. (He and Gabrielle have
moved again.) And he attests—

> I was at the station at the time of the arrival of the police. I was
> standing at the foot of the stairs under the market and oppo-
> site the telegraph office, when a policeman came up, running
> through the market, and hailing me to surrender, which I did.
> Then the policeman took Messrs. Sanders, Regnor, and Ballant
> prisoners, and turning around fired, at Kendrick Chandler,
> who was in the telegraph office, under the market; the shot
> cutting the muzzle of a gun which Chandler held in his hand,
> with the stock resting on the floor; the barrel of the gun was
> cut about six inches from the muzzle. There were other shots
> fired by parties I do not know. Mr. Chandler had surrendered
> before he was shot. I would know the policeman who fired the
> shot which killed him. Chandler slowly fell to the floor. I was
> about two yards from him at the time. The ammunition that

we received was from Capt. Guillotte, and was in cartridges.
I would know the man who shot Chandler if I saw him again.

These are some of the only words of Constant Lecorgne that survive in print. He is one of us, one of ours. Yet the warm rush that a family historian sometimes feels when seeing the words of someone *theirs* is missing for me. I am getting tired of him, in the way you tire of a zealot.

A few days later, Constant is called again to testify, and this time he says that a white Metropolitan named Thomas McAlpine "is the man who shot Chandler." For weeks, the white press covers the death of Chandler. The newspapers and white court are changing the subject. They turn the Ku-klux-and-treason case into the story of a police killing.

On March 25, a grand jury in the First District Court indicts thirteen men with treason, including "P.C. Lacorgne." The court misspells his name.

Constant and his co-conspirators face the court. Two lawyers, James Lingan and Frank Zacharie, speak for them. The judge is a man with the harmonious name of Arthur McArthur. Judge McArthur has been in office since September 1871. He is a Democrat. He helped Democratic candidates during the election of 1872. McArthur is sympathetic to the guerrillas. Constant is not particularly worried, I think. He knows what to expect. He has seen many people get off in circumstances like his. Within minutes, Judge McArthur dismisses the treason charge against all thirteen. He pauses for a moment, and then he drops the Ku Klux Klan charge. All charges thrown out, the men leave the court and go home.

Two weeks after Constant is freed of the Ku-klux charge, on Easter Sunday 1873, squads of white guerrillas kill some 150 black men and a number of women in the town of Colfax, Louisiana. The mass murder takes place around a courthouse, two hundred miles northwest of New Orleans. It is the so-called Colfax massacre, and it takes place in Grant Parish, a rural outback, half black and half white. As it was for the Mechanics Institute massacre in New Orleans, seven years back, the frame around the Colfax killings is the question of who gets to vote. Grant Parish smolders in a political fight after the election of 1872, in which Republicans win local offices on the votes of black men. In April 1873, about one hundred African American activists take possession of the Colfax courthouse, expecting that white Democrats will try to seize the building and swear in a new, unelected sheriff and judge. On Easter Sunday, heavily armed white militias encircle the courthouse. When the black defenders surrender and give up their handguns, the militias execute them, dozens at a time. They do not stop until stacks of bodies lie in the street, and many more are thrown into the Mississippi. It is the worst episode of race killing in all of Reconstruction. I do not think Constant is involved. Colfax is far from New Orleans, too far to travel.

24

The massacre in Colfax is the last piece of bad news for Louis Charles Roudanez. For years, Roudanez is the publisher of the first black daily in the South, the *New Orleans Tribune*. He is impressive. He fights white supremacy with scathing invective. Roudanez, as far as I know, is not physically attacked for speaking out, although the threat hangs heavy. He is not targeted, I think, for the reason that he is too impressive to the *petits blancs*, the little whites who occupy themselves by setting themselves on black people. But with repeated massacres and setbacks, Roudanez grows disillusioned. Soon after the Ku-klux kill 150 in the town of Colfax, he gets out of the newspaper business, gets away from the Republican Party, and leaves politics. Roudanez returns to the private life of a doctor who happens to be of color, his waiting room crowded with white and black patients.

About 150 years later, I decide to look for the Roudanez family. With small effort, I find one of the publisher's great-great-grandchildren, a man named Mark Roudané, living in the upper Midwest.

The Mississippi River is narrow and slow as it bends around the Twin Cities, St. Paul and Minneapolis, Minnesota. The river is unrecognizable, just 100 yards wide at this point, and during some winters it carries ice. Yet here is the same stream as the one in Louisiana. The flight from New Orleans to St. Paul is 1,500 miles, three hours due north. By riverboat from Bouligny to Minnesota, it would be a monthlong, 5,000-mile slog upstream on the Mississippi.

Mark Roudané lives with his wife, Barbara, in St. Paul. Theirs is a leafy section of St. Paul, a half mile from the river; a pretty, clapboard house on a sliver of a lot, engulfed by a pleasing 1920s subdivision. Mark Roudané was a public school teacher for decades. He and his wife raised two daughters, after which he retired from teaching. For the past few years, Roudané has been investigating the story of his people in New Orleans, the ones named Roudanez. When we meet, he tells me his father changed the spelling of Roudanez to *Roudané* during the 1940s.

Mark Roudané is a gentle man in his sixties, trim and fit, easy to smile. He speaks carefully, listens, then speaks again after thought. He has a flat Midwestern accent. The cultural stamp of Minnesota is far from Louisiana, but it doesn't deter the ex-teacher from spending much of his mental life in the South.

We sit at the kitchen table. He talks familiarly about his predecessor, Louis Charles Roudanez, the doctor and newspaperman.

"He would be my great-great-grandfather," Roudané says. "I think it is 1879 when Roudanez sends his wife and children to Paris. Later, he goes back and forth from New Orleans to France to visit them—a few times, but not a lot. Finally he dies in New Orleans in 1890. He is buried in the old cemetery there, the one called St. Louis #1. Meanwhile, his children grow up entirely French. Their descendants are all over France today."

Roudané brings out photographs of a Paris family from the early 1900s. A group photo shows a woman with her family standing in a French window. She is a daughter of Louis Roudanez and his wife, Célie Saulay, now with her own husband and children.

Mark Roudané has a lot to cover when it comes to his family. It is a story of skin color, naming, and escape.

Louis Roudanez was not the only one who sent his family away, out of disappointment. Hundreds, then thousands of Creoles of color began to migrate out of Louisiana. They moved to Florida and to Kansas, to Mexico and to the Caribbean.

Take the case of Armand Belot. A Creole of color with a lucrative cigar-making business, and busy in Republican politics, Belot was burned out of his home and business by the Ku-klux in 1868. He sued the state of Louisiana and, surprisingly, won a big settlement from a sympathetic white Republican judge. But the windows in black politics closed, the number of victims rose, and during the 1870s, Belot moved to Chicago. About the same time, Julien Monette, ex-Louisiana senator, another black leader frustrated by inflexible white rule, moved to Panama. A few years later, a black businessman named Pascal Tourney moved to Niagara Falls. None of the three came back.

Some Creoles of color in bitter disappointment did not leave, but killed themselves. For instance, Jean Baptiste Jourdain. He and Louis Roudanez were friends. Jean Baptiste Jourdain had pretty gray eyes and delicate features. He was a free man of color who joined the Union Army and fought in the Civil War. He saw the Mechanics Institute massacre and narrowly escaped it. He was elected to the state legislature in the early 1870s. But in 1888, having been run out of politics, and despairing for black life, Jourdain shot himself. He was fifty-six, and he left a wife and young children.

A number of people committed an act that some Creoles came to call "race suicide." They became white. New Orleans was full of Creoles of color, raised "black" and appearing "white." In midlife, some chose to pass across the line. Blackness dies, and whiteness is born.

There was Arnold Bertonneau. He was a wine dealer in New Orleans, twenty-eight years old when the Yankee army seized the city. An African American businessman, Arnold Bertonneau was well-known and prosperous, with a large white clientele. He joined the Union Army, became a captain in the Native Guards, and fought rebels in an important battle at Port Hudson, Louisiana. For this, to many black people, Bertonneau was a war hero. Earlier I told the story of how in 1864, Arnold Bertonneau and Jean Baptiste Roudanez, brother of the newspaper publisher, traveled to Washington, D.C., and met with Abraham Lincoln. Bertonneau gave the president a petition signed by eight hundred Creoles of color that demanded the right to vote. With this, Lincoln came close to considering the vote for free men of color. Arnold Bertonneau lived a prominent kind of blackness, but the disappointments of Reconstruction weighed on him. Sometime during the 1880s, Bertonneau moved to California, and there he passed into white society. In 1912, when he died in Pasadena, his death certificate listed him as "white."

It is not that being white, with its many fears and angers, looked like a paradise to Bertonneau. Maybe he wanted to be human, to take part in all roles of humanity, including ones left off the table by tribal whites in their ideas of blackness, its limits and its taboos.

It is difficult to estimate the numbers of people, and families, who passed from black life into white during the late 1800s and early 1900s. Probably thousands in Louisiana alone. Census figures for the "black" population grow slowly during the decades of the greatest travel from black to white. Because people seemed to disappear.

It was a mass phenomenon, enough that verbs and nouns appear in order to name it. The verb, for Creoles of color, is *passer à blanc*, to "pass for white." The noun is *passe-blanc*, a person passing for white.

Mark Roudané has a photograph.

"This is Aimée Potens, the mother of Louis Charles Roudanez," he says. "The picture is probably 1844 and may have been taken by Jules Lion, a daguerreotype artist in New Orleans."

Few people hired a photographer in 1844, when the camera technology of the daguerreotype was only five years old. And almost no people of color had photographs made. Mark Roudané's portrait of Aimée Potens, his great-great-great-grandmother, is the oldest photo of a black woman I have ever seen.

"I have an oral history, taken down in 1911, in St. James Parish," Mark goes on. "It says that Aimée Potens was born in 1791 in Saint-Domingue, on a coffee plantation at a place called Dondon. The Haitian Revolution got going the same year, and a slave army came to Dondon, killing whites and people of color close to them." Aimée Potens, an infant at the time, is whisked away on a boat with her enslaved black mother and white French father. The exiles get to Louisiana and make their way to a sugar estate called Maison Blanche, or "White Hall," sixty-five miles up the Mississippi from New Orleans. Aimée's white father knows the master of Maison Blanche, the rich sugar planter Marius Bringier. Aimée Potens was raised to serve but not to work in the sugar fields of Maison Blanche. She is freed in her youth and becomes a working woman of color.

Aimée Potens of the Roudanez family, about 1844

"Aimée became an accoucheuse, or midwife," Roudané says. "She usually dressed in black and she was erect and stately in her bearing, described in papers as 'a tall mulatress.' But she kept the tignon." Roudané means that Aimée Potens continued to wear the headscarf worn by enslaved women, although she was free.

It is rare to know so much about an Afro-Caribbean woman born in slavery more than two hundred years ago. When I follow some of Roudané's research notes, good sources corroborate what he says.

In the early 1800s, a man named Louis Roudanez lived at Maison Blanche. Like Aimée Potens, Louis Roudanez was also an exile who fled the Saint-Domingue revolt as a child. He was also mixed-race. Aimée Potens and Louis Roudanez became a couple. They had two children with the surname Roudanez—Jean Baptiste, born in 1815, and Louis Charles, born in 1823; they adopted a third child, named Louise. It is the first child who would one day present the petition to Abraham Lincoln; it is the middle child who would one day run the *Tribune* newspaper.

The children grew up as free people of color, possibly in the big house at Maison Blanche. They had white grandparents and "mulatto" uncles and aunts, but no kin among field hands. The boys were carefully educated, with money from their white grandfather, Augustin Tureaud. About 1843, Louis Charles was sent to France so that he could enroll at the Université de Paris. He remained in Paris for some ten years. According to Paul Trévigne, editor of the *Tribune*, who knew him well, in 1848, during the uprising that seized Paris that summer, young Roudanez joined the popular rebellion and spent his time in the working-class districts and on the barricades. But the revolution collapsed, with thousands killed and seizure of power by Louis Napoleon, a mediocrity who gave himself the title "prince-president" of France. Twenty-five-year-old Roudanez was said to be dejected by these events. But Paris in 1848 gave him a glimpse of what could happen when an old world is turned upside down.

Roudanez finished his medical degree and came back to the United States in the early 1850s. He stopped at Dartmouth College in Hanover, New Hampshire, and there he enrolled in another medical program, acquiring a second medical degree. At Dartmouth, Roudanez wrote his thesis, in French, in obstetrics. His mother, Aimée Potens, had been a midwife. He returned to New Orleans in 1857.

"Here is a guy who is witness to a revolution," says Mark Roudané. "He saw liberty, and he saw the French government abolish slavery in all its colonies. The colonies in the Caribbean, Martinique and Guadeloupe. Roudanez came home to New Orleans, started a medical practice, got married, and began to have children."

Mark Roudané sits at his dining room table. The corner cabinets have glass doors, and behind them are rows of pretty things—little sculptures, bowls, silver. He tells the story of Louis Roudanez, his great-great-grandfather, as though he has known it from childhood. In truth, Roudané did not know much about his father's family for most of his life. He had not even known the name "Roudanez" until he came upon it, at the age of fifty-five. He says it was "life-changing."

Mark Roudané is white. He was raised white, and he appears white. He has whiteness in his speech, whiteness in his manners. What he wants to convey is this. In middle age, he learned that according to the one-drop rule of blackness, he was not white.

Before the Civil War, Dr. Louis Roudanez, Mark Roudané's impressive ancestor, was an *homme de couleur libre*. Dr. Roudanez married a free woman of color named Célie Saulay, and the couple eventually had three daughters and two sons. The first son, also named Louis, followed in his father's footsteps, got a medical degree from Dartmouth, and set up a practice in New Orleans—an African American doctor serving black patients in a now harshly segregated city. This Dr. Louis Roudanez, Jr., has a son, named Rudolph.

"That's my grandfather," says Mark Roudané. "Rudolph Roudanez is born in 1901. I never met him. His birth certificate said 'Col.,' for colored. Which is something I did not know until I was in middle age. It was the family secret."

Mark Roudané was born in 1951 in New Orleans. His parents, Louis Charles Roudané and Orient Fox Roudané, were city natives. On his birth certificate, Mark Roudané was "white."

"When my father died, in 2005, I was going through his papers and throwing stuff away, and I found an unmarked binder," he remembers.

Roudané's parents had retired to Asheville, North Carolina. His mother survived her husband and lived in the house. Her son Mark was tasked with helping to filter his father's things. Roudané's father was in the habit of filing documents in plastic sleeves, compiling them in three-ring binders, and labeling each cover with the contents. At his death, Roudané's father had hundreds of binders, all of them labeled but one, which had no label. Roudané describes what he calls "the discovery," in January 2006, after the funeral.

"I opened the binder, and the first image I see is the oldest photograph of Dr. Louis Charles Roudanez. I don't know who he is, or was. I am looking at the image and clearly he looks black to me. Underneath the picture is a caption—'Louis Charles Roudanez, founder of the *New Orleans Tribune*.' It is the first time I see our name with a 'Z.' And after the picture comes page after page of birth certificates, photographs, notes on the Roudanez family. I thought, *whoa, Dad, you are holding out on me*. I didn't know any of this. It's a miracle I didn't throw the secret binder away, because I was just tossing stuff."

Roudané says that his father was born in New Orleans in the Seventh Ward, a part of the city with many Creoles of color. His name at birth was Louis Charles Roudanez III, after the physician and newspaperman. He grew up as an only child on a street named Hope.

"I assume my dad knew about his father's ancestry," Roudané says, "but I don't know, he never talked about his father. And if the subject ever came up, he was upset by it. I never met my dad's father, whose name was Rudolph Roudanez." The family story was that Rudolph Roudanez had abandoned his wife, Mark's grandmother, and left her in New Orleans during the Depression, where she raised her son as a single mother. "For that reason, he was said to be a bad dude," says Roudané about his grandfather. "Whether that was true, I don't know. It could be a smokescreen. Rudolph Roudanez was born in New Orleans in 1901. 'Colored,' by the record."

Rudolph Roudanez moved to Los Angeles. Many Creoles of color moved to California to *passer à blanc*. In Los Angeles, state records called him "white."

The son he left behind—Roudané's father, Louis Charles Roudanez III—grew up in New Orleans. Jim Crow meant the hardest caste distinction and strict inequality, white over black, all good things for one caste, leftovers for the other. As a young man, Roudané's father applied to Tulane University, the best school in the state, where he hoped to study mechanical engineering. Had the admissions office at Tulane possessed word of the "Negro ancestry" of Louis Charles Roudanez III, he would not have been admitted. At this point, the year 1946, the nineteen-year-old's father, Rudolph, was gone to California. So the young man and his mother, Irene Warner, went to court. They arranged to have the Z dropped from the Roudanez name and an accent placed on the last letter—"Roudané." Mother and son erased the color of blackness.

"The papers for the name change were in the secret binder I found," says Mark Roudané.

As it happens, in New Orleans during the 1940s and '50s, there was a registrar in charge of birth and naming records. Her name was Naomi Drake. Under her leadership, the registrar's office performed "race" research, verifying the authenticity of claims of whiteness. Naomi Drake was a bureaucrat notorious for outing the blackness of many Creoles who lived as *passe-blancs*. But somehow, Louis Roudanez III and his mother, Irene Warner, escaped the punishing judgment of Registrar Blake.

Roudané's father was admitted to Tulane, graduated, and went to work for a New Orleans company called Simplex. He married Roudané's mother, Orient Fox, in 1950.

Mark Roudané and his father, Louis Charles Roudané III,
Mardi Gras 1954

When the fifty-five-year-old Mark Roudané discovered his father's (and his own) African American ancestry, he was stunned.

"I called my brother in Atlanta. It was very disorienting for both of us. It was a thrill to find out about our father's side of the family. Then it was mind-boggling to see the racial breaks in the family, to see that we were descended from people of color. The thing that really stunned me, on top of all that, was that we were linked to Louis Charles Roudanez, a significant figure in nineteenth-century American history. That turned my life around."

Roudané says that his father "lived white his whole life." In 1957, Louis-now-Roudané got a job in Dayton, Ohio, and moved his family out of New Orleans. He sold construction equipment. The Roudanés next moved to Chicago.

"Dad sold machinery, then worked himself up over the years to be CEO of a small corporation with a small factory. We became upper middle class. We were very comfortable," says Roudané. "Ours was an all-white environment." The family lived in Glen Ellyn, a pale suburb west of Chicago.

"My dad was a conservative Republican. He voted for Dwight Eisenhower and Richard Nixon for president. And also he was overtly racist his whole life. It was always a thing that bugged me about my father, even as a young boy," says Roudané. "I did not understand race and racism, and he was such a nice guy. He was very present, very warm, very loving to his two sons. But when it came to talking about black people, who were not part of our world, all this venom would come out. I thought, 'Why is my dad being ugly?' I didn't understand it, the tone."

It is risky to measure the behavior of a man you never met and who lived decades ago. But the reflex of anger about blackness sounds like a symptom to me, a defensive reaction. I ask Roudané to explain his father's bitterness toward black people.

"My theory is that he was an overt racist as a way to distance himself, to make himself as white as he could, to create as many barriers as he could to that history in the family," he says.

He was a white, bourgeois, successful businessman, and blackness puts that teetering ladder at risk.

Mark Roudané tells a side story to the "whitening" of his family, one that involves his mother. In June 2006, "five months after the discovery," he says, Roudané visited his father's grave with his brother, Matthew, and their mother, Orient Fox Roudané. Their mother was frail and in a wheelchair. At graveside, Roudané's mother volunteered her version of the "family secret."

"My mother said that in 1948, after my parents had married, she would go to the public library and check out two or three novels to read every week, romance novels. She read a book by a writer named Frank Yerby, called *The Vixens*. A love triangle, set in post–Civil War New Orleans. In the story, a character unexpectedly popped up, which she remembered as 'the Negro doctor Louis Charles Roudanez.' She said she confronted my father with it: 'Look, he has your name and he is a Negro.' And my father exploded, and shouted, 'Do I look like a nigger?' She backed down. But afterwards, she secretly read books on Reconstruction and the Civil War."

Roudané's mother educated herself about the blackness in her husband's family, taking notes and filing them. She and her husband had a tacit understanding that it was never to be mentioned. Twenty years passed.

"My mother called my dad 'Charlie.' In the late 1960s," Roudané says, "according to my mother, 'Charlie wanted to tell you, but he was hesitating.' At the time, the cities were exploding with riots, race was the big national issue, along with Vietnam. And she said that she told our father, 'Don't tell the boys.' Her reasoning was that we were going off into the world, and that if we understood we had black ancestry, that might increase the odds we would have relationships with black people. And it would increase the odds that we might fall in love with a black woman. She said that even if it was a small possibility—and my father went along with it—they shouldn't tell us."

Mark Roudané attended Lawrence University, a liberal arts school in Appleton, Wisconsin. After college, Roudané moved back to Chicago, where he lived with a group of political activists and became a community organizer. For five years, he ran a small school in uptown Chicago, in a poor white neighborhood.

"A lot of people I worked with came from the coal mines of Kentucky and West Virginia, and I did organizing with the Black Lung Association. I went back and forth from Chicago to West Virginia to get documentation, so they could get the benefits paid to miners suffering from lung disease," he says. Mark Roudané married his partner, Barbara Peterson, and they had children—two daughters. When young children and labor organizing in Chicago became "less viable," as he put it, the family moved to St. Paul, Minnesota. There, in 1990, Roudané became a teacher in the public schools.

"I loved it. A difficult job," he says. "I taught high school and gradually worked my way down in age. For the final twelve years I taught first grade. Age six is far and away my favorite age group."

Mark Roudané's brother, Matthew, is a professor of English at Georgia State University, in Atlanta. Mark Roudané and Barbara Peterson have two grown daughters. One lives in the Northwest, where, like her father, she is a labor organizer, advocating on behalf of day laborers. The other lives in California, where she works for an environmental action group that uses litigation as a political tool.

"Our children have had great interest in this discovery," he says, "and they are really proud of this heritage. But for them the mind-blowing aspect of racial discovery wasn't as big a deal as it was for me. They have not grown up in all-white settings, as I did."

The phrase *passer à blanc*, "to pass for white," suggests masquerade, like Carnival, or a theatrical pose. It suggests invention and disguise. I ask Mark Roudané whether it is an archaic or ugly phrase.

"I never heard the term 'passing for white' before learning about the Roudanez story," he says. "But now it is an important part of understanding my own identity. Our family story is actually common, especially in New Orleans. The only thing uncommon is that our ancestor was illustrious."

He holds up a better phrase.

"I sometimes say, 'raised to be white.' There is an aspect of cultivation to my whiteness," he says. "I could be a poster boy for white privilege. I have had the wind at my back my whole life, whether I knew it or not. I was raised to be white. I appear to be white. I have all those accrued gains of whiteness. For me to say that I am not white is not credible, because I have taken benefit from whiteness. I don't say that I am 'mixed-race.' In fact, I have only about five percent sub-Saharan DNA in my genes, according to genetic tests. By that metric, I am 95 percent white. Especially I don't want to say, 'Oh, that's cool, isn't it? It's cool that I'm part black.' Because I don't have to deal with racism. I am not affected directly." Roudané stops, looks away, looks back. "Wait, I am definitely affected by it, but I mean, I am not harmed by it."

Mark Roudané

PART VII

REDEMPTION

THE CITY OF NEW ORLEANS,
AND THE MISSISSIPPI RIVER. LAKE PONTCHARTRAIN IN DISTANCE.

The past feels like a comfortable place to make moral judgments. It is comfortable because we underestimate the people who live in it. We regard them as less than we are—or in reverse, grander than we are—but always, not like what we are. The past is a place where we can enjoy moral judgment and feel superior to a roomful of unfortunate people, not so enlightened as us, who had the bad luck to live when and where they did.

One value in spinning out the story of a plain man is to show how complex an ordinary person can be, or was; to show the multitudes a life contains. It is dreadful what this character, my unlikeable protagonist, does with himself and with others. What would it mean to say that his judgments are not different by much from our own? One value in writing this particular life is to refuse to let the past be a refuge, to decline to feel superior to it, to reject feeling good because you are better than the uncountable idiots who are conveniently dead.

The Ku Klux Klan is what everyone regards as a "bad object." They are a repugnant social formation. People who perpetrate acts of breathtaking cruelty, which cover the national story in shame. The thing that makes violent white supremacy repugnant is not its violence alone. It is that we use the Ku-klux as a vessel for our worst ideas. The Ku-klux are the boogeymen of American history. What if this band of guerrillas is fascinating and obscene because it is a scapegoat that we force to carry all of the antiblack energies of the wide, white society? It is they who are the villains, and for that, we need them. We need to project our aggressions onto them. The villains become like a screen, a place where aggression that we can disavow seems to walk and talk and breathe.

We have caricature images of the Ku-klux. Yet people, even people who are bad objects, are thick with life and contradiction. The desires and motives of supremacist zealots are within the array of desires and interests that human beings have. Do our moral judgments depend on turning the people we judge into caricatures? If so, they do not seem like very good moral judgments.

The coup attempt with Constant Lecorgne as a gunslinger fails. Whites remain desperate to get Republicans out of office, and newspapers show their frustration. "The battle between the races for supremacy must be fought out . . . boldly and squarely. The issue cannot be satisfactorily adjusted by a repulsive commingling of antagonistic races," says *The Shreveport Times*. In the town of Monroe, *The Ouachita Telegraph* sounds philosophical: "That there is a superiority of the white race over the black . . . is a truth the wide world over. That white men will yield this birthright for any form of government . . . is utopian." Few whites can tolerate a social life that includes position, power, and respect for black people.

He has one of those thick names—P.B.S. Pinchback. He uses initials only, in the style of important people. And initials are easier than his name, Pinckney Benton Stewart Pinchback. P.B.S. Pinchback is one African American leader that white terror does not target. Maybe he is good with security. Pinchback, age thirty-six, will live long and die rich in a fine house.

His father was a white slaveholder in Mississippi, his mother the man's enslaved concubine. Those facts point to one thing that helps P.B.S. Pinchback survive. He possesses the phenotype of whiteness, as a race scientist would put it. He appears to be white, with a tincture of blackness. It is blunt to say it, yet that is how he is perceived and moves through the world.

Pinchback feels rivalry with Louis Roudanez, another successful "black" man, publisher of the *Tribune*. In 1870, Pinchback starts a weekly newspaper, the *Louisianian*. He is a politician who also runs a newsroom.

The Lecorgnes probably do not know P.B.S. Pinchback, at least not personally. They certainly know of him. It is possible Constant and his siblings dislike very much what they know about Pinchback. He is the man serving as lieutenant governor when the white governor, Henry Warmoth, is impeached and steps down. Pinchback becomes governor. He seems to have some luck.

In fall 1872, Pinchback runs for the U.S. House and wins a seat as a Republican. He becomes the first nonwhite elected to Congress from Louisiana. But Democrats challenge the election, and the House refuses to give Pinchback his seat. A man named George Sheridan, his rival, is seated instead. In early 1873, Pinchback puts his name in for the U.S. Senate. It is the era before direct election, when state legislatures appoint U.S. senators. In Louisiana, the new state legislature, dominated by Republicans, appoints Pinchback to the Senate. He returns to Washington and awaits his desk. If seated, Pinchback would become only the second African American senator, after Hiram Revels of Mississippi.

Hearings are held in the Capitol. Pinchback lingers in Washington with his wife, Nina Hawthorne, and their children. He lobbies. "It is possible," Pinchback writes in a newspaper, "that there may be Senators . . . who suppose I might desire to take advantage of my official position to force myself unasked on their social life." He seems to apologize for his blackness, the tincture.

The Senate Committee on Privileges and Elections does not buy that the Republican state government in Louisiana, elected by black votes, won its 1872 election. Vote fraud is accused, but not proved. The Louisiana legislature, some loud senators argue, lacks the legitimacy to send its black politician to Washington. That is the excuse for the delay. Month passes month, as the Senate stalls and argues and stalls.

James Rapier, a black congressman from Alabama, watches the drama from his seat in the House of Representatives. Rapier gives a speech on the floor of the House about his own experiences.

"There is a cowardly propensity in the human heart that delights in oppressing somebody else, and in the gratification of this base desire we always select a victim that can be outraged with safety," Rapier says, according to the *Congressional Record*. "Here the negro is the most available for this purpose." Rapier takes a wide view. "This whole thing grows out of a desire to establish a system of caste," he says.

Pinckney Benton Stewart Pinchback, turned away by the House, is never seated in the Senate, which eventually votes him out the door. The Senate refuses to admit a tainted and tinctured politician. After two years of waiting in Washington, Pinchback and his family go home to Louisiana. He has one consolation: he remains alive.

During the years after the Civil War, industrialization rolls through the North—steel, railroads, and manufacturing. The many textile mills in New England, having closed during the war for lack of cotton, reopen and expand. They process raw material grown by black hands in the Reconstruction South. North of Virginia, the white working class or caste triples in size, and a tiny master elite of money lords begins to form. It is a period of capital accumulation, when some of the rich become superrich. Meanwhile, Louisiana and the South remain what they have always been, rural and agricultural, the land and the staple crops of cotton, rice, and sugar more important than factories and finance.

The year 1873 brings a national economic crisis. That fall, a bank in Philadelphia called Jay Cooke & Company fails to raise money in a railroad deal. Jay Cooke declares bankruptcy. The New York Stock Exchange closes, and other banks collapse. By Christmas, American credit markets are frozen, and industrial growth creaks to a halt. Meantime, the agriculture of the South sits on several years of surpluses. When the textile mills of the North that once gulped the raw cotton of the South start to waver, cotton prices fall by half, along with the other Louisiana staples, sugar and rice. Among the casualties in New Orleans is the family firm of painter Edgar Degas—the cotton factorage run by Degas's uncle, Michel Musson—which goes out of business, leaving the artist himself with a pile of debt.

Constant and Gabrielle fall farther down the income ladder, as construction and river traffic slow. Craftsmen like carpenters cannot make a living. The Lecorgnes move again. They load their belongings onto wagons, take them down to the river. Their new address, Tchoupitoulas at Cadiz Street, facing the levee, is two blocks from Lecorgne row. The rent is $20 per month.

Gabrielle and Constant are unpacking when word comes that Joseph Lecorgne is dying. Joseph and his family live three houses up the block, on Tchoupitoulas near Valence Street. Joseph is just thirty-nine. He has been sick for some time with nephritis, what doctors call "Bright's disease." He and his wife, Estelle Daunoy, have been together for thirteen years, and they have three children, the youngest ten months old, the oldest twelve.

Joseph ends badly, because treatments for Bright's disease do nothing. He might have convulsions; he might go blind; he might have a hemorrhage that sends him into a seizure. He dies November 20, leaving another house of fatherless young kids.

The day Joseph dies, a political meeting is gaveled to order downtown. It is the Colored Men's Convention. Several hundred black politicians and preachers, businesspeople and activists come together at Mechanics Hall to talk politics, and to plan. Louis Roudanez of the *Tribune* is there; and the politician Caesar Antoine; and the senator-in-waiting P.B.S. Pinchback; and Aristide Mary, a black activist; and many black legislators and aspirants in the Republican Party. The men talk about the never-ending attacks of the Ku-klux. They vote a resolution—

Resolved. We deplore with sorrow the atrocities, indignities, insults and murders that have been committed during the past year in the various parishes of this state, on those of our race who have dared to assert their opinions.

Resolved. That the odious distinctions made and ostracisms practiced in various parts of this country on our people on account of color renders the passage by Congress of [the] Civil

Rights bill absolutely necessary for our protection [and] for the
perfect obliteration of race antagonisms.

Four miles uptown, on Tchoupitoulas Street, Constant appears at
the house of his brother. Joseph's widow, Estelle, bends over the body
of her husband. The next day, Constant and Yves of God and their
sisters, plus the children of all the siblings, numbering some twenty,
gather for the funeral at St. Stephen.

Downtown, the black convention talks about the new civil rights
bill that is making its way through Congress. The legislation promises much and it is certain to carry. The convention passes another
resolution that calls the civil rights law "the last special legislation
that we trust we shall need." But in Washington, there are signs that
the law will not be enough. A month after the Colored Men's Convention, and Joseph's funeral, President Grant sends a signal that he is
getting tired of all the troubles down South. In an interview with *The
New York Herald*, in January 1874, the president says that he is losing
patience with the bloody resistance to Reconstruction.

"I begin to think it is time for the Republican Party to unload.
There has been too much dead weight carried by it," Grant tells a reporter. "I am tired of this nonsense." By "nonsense," he means the
night-riding and gang rule, the fights over elections, the targeted beatings and killings, the bloody trails of the militias. "Let Louisiana take
care of herself, as Texas will also have to do. I do not want any quarrel
about Mississippi matters to be referred to me," he says. "The nursing
of monstrosities has nearly exhausted the life of the Republican Party.
I am done with them, and they will have to take care of themselves."

It is an apt phrase, the "nursing of monstrosities." Are the mon-
sters the fights, or the fighters themselves? Is it the Ku-klux that must
be nursed?

The Colfax massacre, in which some 150 blacks die in Grant Parish,
north of New Orleans, is a fresh memory. After the killings, U.S. troops
round up one hundred whites around Colfax. The Justice Department

wants to push the Ku-klux into a box, doing the same in Louisiana as it did in South Carolina. Almost a year after the massacre, however, only nine men go on trial. And in February 1874, the nine share a smile of relief when a judge in New Orleans declares a mistrial in the case.

White opinion is lifted. "We shall not pretend to conceal our gratification at the summary and hopeful lesson the Negroes have been taught," says *The Shreveport Times*. "The wonder is not that there was one Colfax, but that there is not one in every parish."

Constant and his comrades, I imagine, celebrate the good news. A disappointed Governor William Kellogg says the mistrial "establishes the principle that no white man could be punished for killing a negro, and virtually wipes the Ku-Klux laws off the statute books." One of the commanders at the killing field in Colfax, and one of the nine prosecuted, is a man named George Waters Stafford. Stafford is inspired. He returns to his hometown of Alexandria to start a newspaper. He calls it *The Caucasian*.

"*The Caucasian* will be a white man's paper," he writes. It is "devoted to the interests of the white people of the state, and opposed to the aggrandizement of the negro to the prejudice of the Caucasian race, which is the superior of the African race in every particular, except the endurance of physical labor."

The Caucasian calls for a new movement, another wave of guerrilla subversion. Guerrillas are needed to bring back white command once and for all. George Stafford says that his paper, *The Caucasian*, "will lend its aid and espouse the cause of that white man's party—by whatever name it may be called—which shall seem most likely to relieve our downtrodden state from . . . negro ignorance and impudence."

And so it is with a four-page broadsheet that is published only on Saturdays in a country town in Louisiana that the national experiment of Reconstruction begins to unravel.

The "white man's party" is supposed to be a new thing, not yet formed. But the vessel already exists among the ad hoc Ku-klux. Within a few weeks, after meetings of enthusiasts, the thing itself comes together. It is a political party; but also, it is yet another militia. The guerrillas choose a name, like others before, that cannot be mistaken. They call themselves the White League.

It is spring 1874. Constant and Gabrielle have a full house on Tchoupitoulas Street. The forty-two-year-old carpenter and thirty-eight-year-old seamstress are raising six children: Numa, Louis, Estelle, George, St. Mark, and Corinne. At sixteen, Numa is the oldest; the youngest, Corinne, is two. But April brings cruelty. On the fifteenth, daughter Estelle, age ten, has a birthday. Estelle is the war child. During the Civil War, when the city was occupied, Gabrielle made her way across enemy lines to join Constant, encamped on Bayou Teche, and she gave birth to Estelle. Now it is her birthday in 1874, and Estelle is quite sick. In fact, she has been sick for years: she has tuberculosis. In April, the girl goes into steep decline. Her breathing grows heavy, and blood comes up with every cough. She dies April 24, nine days after turning eleven.

Constant steps into his workshop—here is a job, finally. It is time to build another casket for another child. I wonder what it is like to build a coffin for your own daughter. This box has to be bigger than the one for daughter Mathilde, who died back in 1861, when she was only eighteen months. The casket for Estelle must look good, must be lined with nice material. The Ocean Sawmill, on Tchoupitoulas, is right across the street. They know him there, and they have good poplar. If he can afford it, Constant might add a veneer of mahogany to Estelle's box. They have that, too. He can pay and then pick up the things at the Ocean lumberyard, corner of Magazine Street and Valence. Maybe Gabrielle contributes to the design. Maybe Estelle's mother puts aside her piecework as a seamstress to make the soft interior of the box, a quilted cushion for Estelle to lay her head. I think about the scene. Is it strange that a violent militant can have a dead child, and he can weep? No, it is what a father would do. It is what we would expect, given that people then are like people now, like us.

Gabrielle and Constant have only one daughter left, Corinne. They hover over her, I imagine, as though she is the only girl in creation.

The *petits blancs*, like Constant, are in more direct competition with black craftsmen, as African Americans sell their labor. The *petits blancs*, like the Lecorgnes, are more likely to live among blacks, as people of color move to get nearer a wage. Maybe these social facts provoke something in the unconscious of many working-class whites, a visceral desire to put up boundaries and to draw a brighter race line. Are the *petits blancs* more crude, more cruel, and more volatile than the sedate and cunning elites who run the economy, and who employ them? It does appear that the working poor carry the knives and clubs of white supremacy. It does seem that white businessmen and politicians prefer not to use violence themselves; they prefer others to do that necessary work. The *grands blancs*, the landlord and the entrepreneur, look out at the black and white world and do what they can to make conditions right for the militias.

The "white man's party" promised by *The Caucasian* newspaper comes together. It rises up like the thing before it, the Knights of the White Camellia, which flourished six years earlier. It involves many of the same people.

Alcibiade DeBlanc, having left New Orleans, lives where he grew up—St. Martinville, the old town on Bayou Teche. DeBlanc's domain is St. Martin Parish, in French-speaking Louisiana. Constant and Gabrielle bury Estelle about the time DeBlanc leads a meeting to form the party of the white man in St. Martinville. DeBlanc is good with names, having coined "the White Camellia." It seems to be DeBlanc who names the new movement. He calls the new party *la ligue blanche*.

La ligue blanche, the White League, erupts in St. Martin Parish, Rapides Parish, and St. Landry Parish—each one hundred miles from the other two—like mushrooms that blurt above ground. Each gang has a headman. A politician named John Moncure takes leadership at Shreveport, in the north of the state. East of Lafayette, it is Charles Mouton, a lieutenant governor before the Civil War, "fearless champion of our Caucasian birthrights," as *The New Orleans Bulletin* describes him. At the organizing meeting in Lafayette, Mouton "addressed the assemblage in both French and English, holding the audience spellbound for two hours." *La ligue blanche* does not lack publicity. In the town of Opelousas, in St. Landry Parish, the *Courier* newspaper surrenders to it: "From this date the control of the editorial columns of the *Courier* passes into the hands of the White League," the paper says. *The New Orleans Bulletin* adds a motto to its masthead: "This government was made by white men, for the benefit of white men and their posterity forever, and should be administered by white men and by none other whatsoever."

In May, a second trial for the Colfax nine begins. The first prosecution of the mass killers had ended in mistrial. In a few days, four men are acquitted and the other five found guilty of a charge much milder than murder, "conspiracy to disrupt a peaceful assembly." The five go free during appeal. Two years later, their case will end in the U.S. Supreme Court.

The White League compresses the message of race, distilling to a few words the ocean of identity. A bulletin summarizes its program. "We are for white men in everything—in our public offices, in our stores, on our steamers, on our drays and floats, in our families and in our fields. Everywhere."

New Orleans joins the White League movement six weeks after its first flourish in St. Martinville. In June, Fred Ogden, leader of the failed coup d'état, calls a meeting of the Crescent City Democratic Club. The CCDC is one of the marching clubs that menaced black voters during the election of 1868. Ogden revives the club in a rally at Eagle Hall, corner of Prytania and Felicity streets. "I can readily picture Ogden's violent, explosive, and convincing eloquence," says one man who attends. I doubt that Constant is there. It is a small meeting, mostly English speakers, and the crowd is better educated and richer than the ship carpenter. They are more *grands blancs* than *petits*. But he certainly knows about it. The event takes place at the old headquarters of Council No. 9 of the White Camellia, and Constant's two lawyers in the Klan and treason case, James Lingan and Frank Zacharie, lead the roster.

Fred Ogden steps to the front of the room at Eagle Hall. He says that he and his old comrades must join the wave of White Leagues washing in from the parishes. They must regroup. Let the old marching club come back together, now with a stiffer spine. There is a new and monstrous enemy, Ogden says. It is a nigger menace like none we have seen. It goes by the name of the Black League.

As it happens, there is no such thing as a Black League. But in a few days, on June 30, the *Picayune* runs a story about Ogden's imaginary enemy. The paper reports that black men are arming themselves outside the city, that an invasion is planned for New Orleans. Reconnaissance has uncovered the plot, and its nature is bloodcurdling, the paper says. Black League marauders plan to swarm into the city like a night-riding militia and claim their spoils. "If resisted, they are at once to light fire to businesses and kill as many white men as possible," the *Picayune* tells readers, "and then keep for themselves all the women." Fortunately, good citizens like Colonel Fred Ogden are taking measures. The *Picayune* announces the new organization, the Crescent City White League, with Ogden as president. A manifesto from the group, just drafted, happens to be available. It is the new "platform of the white race in Louisiana." The manifesto shows beyond a doubt that blacks are on a campaign to replace whites. "Anyone who has . . . overheard their private conversations knows that they dream of the exodus of the whites, which will leave Louisiana to their exclusive control, like another Haiti."

The *Picayune* publishes the White League manifesto. The White League "has solely in view the maintenance of our hereditary civilization and Christianity menaced by a stupid Africanization," it says. *La ligue blanche* will fight until whites "resume that just and legitimate superiority in the administration of our State affairs to which we are entitled by superior responsibility, superior numbers and superior intelligence."

There is a rush on Eagle Hall as hundreds of men mass to declare their allegiance. Stevedores, tinsmiths, and teamsters sign up. Carpenters, grocers, draymen, and hostlers sign. They join the money caste of factors, accountants, lawyers, insurance dealers, businessmen, and clerks. The marching clubs from the party of "the Democracy" sign up *en masse*. One paper lists thirty groups that fall in with the League cause. A few of them: the Minute Men, the Pendleton Guards, the Constitution Club, the Fulton Street White Club, the Eighth Ward Wide Awakes, the Swan Cadets, the Seymour Southrons, and the Fossil Guards. All rebrand as White League affiliates.

Among the joiners is René de Gas, brother of the Impressionist painter Edgar Degas. Another joiner, according to family tradition, is Constant Lecorgne.

In Washington, the Civil Rights Bill moves through thick resistance in the House, pushed along by Benjamin "Beast" Butler. The old overlord of New Orleans during the Civil War is now a representative from Massachusetts. The Civil Rights Bill outlaws race differences in "places of public accommodation"—anywhere you spend money—as well as in churches, schools, transportation, and cemeteries. By this time, most of the Radical Republicans in Congress are gone, having been voted out, or having sold out. Few in the Capitol feel any longer that it is their job to try to design race equity; few want to make the attempt at reducing white domination. Thanks to the Ku-klux, thanks to years of bad news, Reconstruction looks impossible and thankless. When news comes to Washington that White Leagues are cropping up in Louisiana, and then in Mississippi, in Texas, and in Arkansas, most in Congress receive the word with resignation.

The House puts off considering the Civil Rights Bill until after the fall 1874 elections. In Louisiana, the White Leagues celebrate the setback for "Beast" Butler and schedule armed drills for a show of public morale. Frank Zacharie, lawyer for Constant in the treason case, is encouraged. He writes a friend, "The North is becoming tired of the eternal nigger, to whom the greatness, glory, and prosperity of the Country has been sacrificed."

The artist Edgar Degas has left New Orleans and gone home to Paris. His uncle, the cotton dealer Michel Musson, presides over a big White League rally in the city. Musson's son-in-law, William Bell, is at the center of command. William Bell becomes treasurer of the New Orleans *Ligue blanche*, while Bell's business partner, Fred Ogden, is leader of the whole White League operation.

As tension mounts, the Catholic Church, which dominates religious life in the lower half of the state, offers its ethical guidance. The *Catholic Messenger*, newspaper of the diocese of New Orleans, runs an editorial. "They, the colored people, are and have been carrying on a relentless war upon the whites . . . a war of ruin and extermination. . . . They grow fat, strong and insolent." The message from the church is plain: black people should be made to beg. "There is but one way now to manage the negro," a clergyman writes in the church paper. "He is as a class amenable to neither reason nor gratitude. He must be starved into the common perception of decency."

A musician named Annie Bowles writes a song, the "White League March." Bands play it at rallies. The men march up and down the block, and sometimes they march in circles. Some carry broomsticks, because they do not yet have rifles. The *Republican* newspaper makes a prediction: "We declare that the organization of the order of the White League in Louisiana is the revival of the Ku-klux under another name; that it is a step toward the assassination of negroes."

The attacks resume. In late July, five black people are lynched near the town of Lafayette. The White League kills black people. But it approaches whites who support Reconstruction somewhat differently. In the towns of Natchitoches and St. Martinville, mass meetings draw up petitions demanding the resignation of white Republican judges, police, and mayors. Gangs of night riders pay visits to the homes of white officials. Most resign or leave town.

In the northwest of the state on the Red River lies the village of Coushatta. *La ligue blanche* selects it for mob action. Coushatta, population some two hundred, with two out of three people black, sees three days of skirmishes among a dozen combatants. When local whites send out the familiar tribal call that an insurrection is afoot, White League recruits stream into the parish from around the state to form a strike force of several hundred. The public mobilization shows a difference between the White League and earlier Ku-klux gangs. The White Camellias were secret; they acted at night, and they liked a good disguise. Whereas the White League hides nothing; its guerrillas swarm in large numbers during the day.

On August 29 in Coushatta, a gang takes prisoner a dozen blacks and six whites, all Republicans. A tribunal extracts confessions and promises from the prisoners that they will leave the parish. When the Republicans march off the next day, guerrillas intercept them. Six are shot to death and two are hanged.

The Coushatta massacre dominates newspapers in the North for the next several weeks. I imagine that Fred Ogden—in New Orleans, hearing the news—has a thought: It looks like the beginning of the end.

Fred Ogden and his officers recruit twenty-six infantry companies, 1,500 men ready to fight without hoods and robes. It is late summer 1874. The traditional enemies, black women and men who can be tormented one at a time, are no longer enough. The White League wants a bigger prize, state power. The government is to be brought down.

Constant is a veteran of the March 1873 coup d'état, when Ogden led a failed putsch. It was Ogden who ordered the assault on police precinct 7. When Constant and his gang succeeded, Ogden came to the station at midnight to visit. The carpenter shook the leader's hand and bathed in his charisma. Constant, I think, feels about Ogden the way he feels about his Creole commander, Alcibiade DeBlanc. If the White League says it will take the statehouse, Constant will be with them.

On September 1, a rally for the White League brings several thousand into the Varieties Theater, on Canal Street. The auditorium is lit with torches. Flagmen wave banners, and bands rattle through tunes. Speakers remind the crowd of the good news from Texas. In Austin, White League crowds have laid siege to the state capitol and driven out the Republican governor, ignoring a Texas court ruling that the Reconstruction politician won reelection to office. What's more, President Grant has refused to intervene, sending in no troops, for a change. The great state of Texas has been *redeemed*. A cheer at the word—*redeem*. The League will do the same here and in all of the South. It is the time of redemption for the superior race.

The end of the war came in spring 1865. Since then, Reconstruction has cut the first road through the rainforest of white supremacy. African Americans have gotten to vote, or some of the men have, mainly for white politicians, a few of whom try to share power. Ex-slaves have begun to earn money, or some have, those who can get free of sharecropping on the land of their ex-masters. New schools have enrolled many thousands, clearing a way for blacks to sit in class-rooms built with money from the North; it is literacy at low cost, at least until the Ku-klux burns a third of the schools down. The col-ored elite has grown during the years of Republican rule. New Or-leans has the oldest and largest class of propertied blacks in the South, free people of color, moneyed since before the Civil War. Their num-bers have gone up, but there are few things that irritate *petits blancs* as much as a prosperous Negro. The economy of New Orleans is still built on two words—cotton and sugar—moving them, selling them, a job helped by a new, third word, railroads. The city remains the rich-est in the South, with little palaces rising along a fresh, golden boule-vard, St. Charles Avenue, and along the streets between Bouligny and the French Quarter.

Constant and Gabrielle do not see the money in their hands, not the countable kind. Just maybe, they might see their whiteness as a kind of money, natural and bankable and deserved. They really do not want to see that disappear, the way the other kind of capital they once had went away, the kind you can count.

Companies of militia drill in the streets, like a field army, as though for war. The White League drills in Bouligny, in Carroll-ton, in the Marigny, and in Lafayette—all the *faubourgs*. The League identifies its main foes: the state militia, the Metropolitan Police, and the U.S. Army. By good fortune, most troops in the Union Army are gone from town. Federal commanders are afraid soldiers might catch Yellow Jack in the steam of August, the wettest month of a New Orleans summer. The Yankees have sent most of their regiments to camp in the pinelands of Mississippi, where it is hot but dry.

The Metropolitan Police are the state cops, under the leadership of a man named Sidney Badger. An integrated force, the Metropoli-tans have both black and white companies. The Louisiana State Mili-tia, the third foe, is chiefly black. Its ranks are under the command of General James Longstreet, an ex-Confederate who flipped after the Civil War and joined the Reconstruction cause.

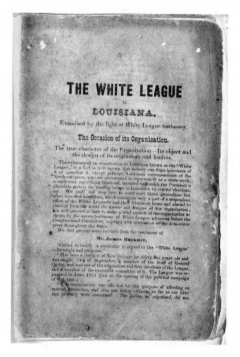

Pamphlet about the White League

The White League has staff officers, rank-and-file men like Constant, and a goal—redemption—but the guerrillas do not have the guns they want. Many have pistols or shotguns, and some have single-load muskets. They want long guns, especially Springfield rifles. In the western territories, the U.S. Army is using breech-loading Springfields to kill and drive away Native people and secure land for white settlement. It is the gun that wins when people of color are in the way.

Another election is scheduled in November. Observers in the North worry the vote in Louisiana will go to the Democrats. "Every midnight marauder and assassin from the Tennessee to the Gulf, the Ku-Klux and the White League, the fiends who strip and scourge and banish and massacre, the murderers of Coushatta, the women-whippers and the minions of the terror, all pray fervently for a Democratic success," says *Harper's Weekly*, in New York. In New Orleans, the Democrats expect to drive out the Republicans by manipulating the vote. Fred Ogden and the League plan to stage a coup just before the election in order to guarantee the outcome. *Harper's Weekly* takes them seriously, calling the new wave of Ku-klux "a band of assassins who, under the name of a White Man's League now rule by terror . . . in midnight raids and orgies in the negro cabin."

Ogden and his commanders have arranged shipments of guns from a source in New York. Hearing of the plan, General Longstreet sends a team from the state militia to look for weapons at the railroad terminal. Nothing. He sends another team to search ships docked at the wharfs. Nothing again. On September 8, a wagonful of rifles turns up at the corner of Canal and Camp streets. When this happens, the White League decides to move up the coup by six weeks, from November to September. On September 11, a team from Longstreet's militia finds six crates of Springfield rifles in a ship named *City of Dallas*. The next day, a steamer called the *Mississippi* docks near Jackson Square, within sight of St. Louis Cathedral. When officers in the state militia board, they find the ship's hold stuffed with guns.

The coup d'état is kicked into motion. On the night of September 13, rifles stored at a factory, Leeds Foundry, are handed out to White League fighters. This first force numbers 224, according to one fighter who writes a memoir. With his long battle credentials, Constant would be a good choice for the first ranks.

Ogden and his gang plan a mass meeting downtown for Monday the fourteenth. The idea is to stage a rally, then send a mob to the *Mississippi* to take the guns. From there, guerrillas can storm the statehouse. The statehouse has lately moved. It now occupies the former St. Louis Hotel, in the French Quarter. And the St. Louis Hotel, as everyone knows, was once called the City Exchange. Which means that the statehouse inhabits the old auction center of the slave trade.

On the morning of September 14, a big crowd masses downtown around a landmark, a statue of the politician Henry Clay. The life-size bronze of Clay stands at the corner of Canal and Royal streets. It is a place where the white elite gathers when it is time to take the law into vigilant hands. From the statue, five or six angry whites take turns giving speeches to one thousand angry whites. Meanwhile, Fred Ogden heads a second rally uptown, at the intersection of Prytania and Felicity streets, around the well-used Eagle Hall, a half mile from Bouligny. I believe Constant is in that crowd, as close as it is to Lecorgne row.

Ogden's gang starts to move downtown along Prytania Street toward the Canal Street mob, two miles away. By this time, late morning, the Louisiana State Militia has formed a defensive line within the French Quarter. It runs from the arsenal at the Cabildo, around the statehouse, and west along the streets next to the river. As they march downtown, Ogden's gang comes to the headquarters of city government, Gallier Hall on Lafayette Square. A contingent manages to cut the telegraph lines, so that word of the revolt spreads more slowly.

The guerrillas with Ogden stop on Poydras Street, off Lafayette Square, a quarter mile short of the rally at the Clay statue. The men build barricades at the intersections along Poydras. They knock streetcars off their tracks, drag furniture and mattresses to the middle of the road, and pile up iron fencing pulled up from buildings. At the rally around the bronze of Henry Clay, a lawyer named Robert Marr yells for the crowd to go the hell home and to come the hell back with what guns they have. Most of the mob leaves, as ordered. Three hours pass, during which Ogden's rebels fortify their barricades. By 2:00 p.m., thousands return from home with guns from closets, guns long secreted from the Union.

The White League has Poydras Street, to the west; the state militia and Metropolitans have Canal Street, to the east. The white uprising now numbers about 3,500; the defenders, some 3,000, a third of them black. I cannot place Constant in one or another company, or on one or another street, but I have no doubt he is there.

The fighting starts about 3:45 p.m. White League guerrillas move east along the levee, attempting to flank and go around the state militia. Their target is the statehouse at the St. Louis Hotel, a quarter mile away, in the French Quarter. The Metropolitans place a Gatling gun—the first machine gun, run with a hand crank—in the middle of Canal Street. They open fire on the levee. From the river, hidden behind bales of cotton, White League companies shoot back. Sharpshooters manage to kill the Metropolitans who man the machine gun—first one, and then his replacement, and then another. The Metropolitans' commander, Sidney Badger, is shot off his horse and his leg crushed under the animal. When this happens, most of Badger's men break and flee. Some ten White League guerrillas and ten defenders are killed in the first wave of the fight.

General James Longstreet, the ex-rebel who flipped, commands the black militiamen. Something happens, and he is thrown from his horse and disabled. The state defenders are leaderless. White League fighters stream off the levee and charge north on Canal Street. The state militiamen retreat into the French Quarter. Fred Ogden leaves his redoubt on Poydras Street and rides to Canal Street. Then he, too, falls from his horse. He hobbles around, shouting murderous orders.

At this point, Constant himself may be injured and carried off the street by comrades. I am reminded of something. The keeper of the Lecorgne story, my aunt Maud Lecorgne, says that her grandfather Constant "has his head split open" in this wheeling street fight, which is the biggest Ku-klux action of any during Reconstruction. With flak in the air and hand-to-hand combat, the White League coup is a good place for Constant to be smashed in the skull. Admission records for Charity Hospital, where some of the injured are taken, do not show his name. Although I do not know exactly how he fares in the climactic fight, I do know that he shares in its glory for the rest of his life.

Constant is personal friends with at least two of the dead. A Bouligny man named Albert Gautier is one. Gautier is twenty-six. His family runs the Ocean Sawmill on Tchoupitoulas Street, where Constant gets building material. Another of the dead is a man named Jean Gourdain. Long ago, before the Civil War, it is Gourdain's family that buys the last man Gabrielle and Constant enslave, Ovid. When you buy a man from someone, it is the kind of thing that seals a friendship.

What are black people in New Orleans doing during the crisis and bedlam? Most African Americans have no weapons. Most of the black city is possessed of a desire to remain alive. In the battle that will bring down the curtain, whites are mostly fighting whites. I imagine that most black people are working hard to stay out of the way, except for the handful of thousand black men who staff the state militia. They are on the front line. But about most in the city of color,

Engraving in *Harper's Weekly* depicting the Battle of Canal Street

someone might say that it is a good day when the main targets of the Ku-klux are other crackers.

The shooting goes on, and another twenty are killed. The state militia retreats toward the Cabildo and the statehouse. Many barricade themselves inside the Cabildo armory, others barricade at the statehouse. A spur of White League fighters reaches the steamship *Mississippi* and unloads its weapons. While the fighting unfolds, hundreds more men appear to join the uprising and claim some of its glory. Around New Orleans, several of these factions seize police stations. By 6:00 p.m., the uprising is armed and patrolling through the city, and the state defenders have just two buildings in hand.

At night on the fourteenth, guerrillas form cordons around the Cabildo armory and the statehouse. They demand surrender, and the soldiers give in. One at a time, and then in groups, they strip off their uniforms and disappear into the night. The White League gangs let them go.

By sunrise, the Ku-klux are telling one another that they have ended Reconstruction and restored righteousness to the world.

It is a military battle in the middle of a big city. But the harvest of dead is not so large, compared with the massacres. The White League has sixteen dead and nineteen wounded. The Metropolitans and state militia have sixty wounded and thirteen dead, seven of them black. A couple of thousand spectators watch the battle as though it is a piece of theater. Six of them are killed.

The White League coup succeeds, and for three days, the rebels put on a show of running the state. Railroad workers stall the trains so that U.S. Army regiments, away at camp in Mississippi, cannot return to the city. A Democratic politician, Davidson Penn, is sworn in as governor during a rally at the statehouse, and there is talk of seating a new legislature. Fred Ogden's officers run citywide patrols, acting the role of police.

Late on September 17, the army reaches New Orleans. White League guerrillas decide not to fight another day, and on September 18, they give up their posts. As quickly as it had appeared, the uprising surrenders. Governor William Kellogg takes back his office, and the Republican legislature meets again.

Yet most whites are exhilarated. Everyone knows that the superior race has regained its throne. The September coup wins back the narrative. It is the glorious overthrow of Reconstruction. The "Redemption" is come.

President Ulysses Grant sends three more regiments and batteries of artillery to New Orleans, showing the Washington fist, and navy gunboats appear on the Mississippi. General Philip Sheridan, army commander in New Orleans, writes the secretary of war in Washington—"I think that the terrorism now existing . . . could be entirely removed and confidence and fair-dealing established by the arrest and trial of the ringleaders of the armed White Leagues." But no one is arrested, and none prosecuted. The Enforcement Acts cannot be enforced. The Ku Klux Klan Act is a dead letter.

Harper's Weekly describes New Orleans as the author that has just written the end of the story—

> Never did so small a community as Louisiana in so few years
> exhibit such a succession of horrors. In 1868 we have the raids
> on the negro voters . . . when the White Camellias dominated

in the streets of New Orleans. . . . In 1872 they re-appear. In 1873 they burned and shot down . . . negroes at Grant Parish, and attempted an insurrection in New Orleans. In 1874 they have murdered the United States officials at Coushatta and a large number of negroes; they have risen in rebellion in New Orleans and shot thirty or forty Unionists in a deadly contest. . . . Louisiana is the most unlucky of all the States, because it has been tormented by a horde of traitors.

Extending their victory, White League fighters next attack the city's integrated schools. Vigilantes go from schoolhouse to schoolhouse, pulling black students out of the classrooms. The sons of Pinckney Pinchback, the black politician, are roughed up. Segregation is made the basis of education policy once again. Eliza Lecorgne no longer teaches in the schools, but if she shares the same opinion as her brothers, she must watch these events with satisfaction.

Six weeks after the Battle of Canal Street, the 1874 election takes place. White morale is high, black morale low. Democrats deploy familiar violence, and the "white man's party" wins parity in the state legislature, which splits 53–53, Democrat/Republican. In Washington, the Republican Party loses control of the U.S. House of Representatives for the first time in fifteen years. "Beast" Butler of Massachusetts loses his seat. He decides to finish his career by pushing through the Civil Rights Bill in his final weeks before leaving office.

White League guerrillas take up patrols, because the state militia and the Metropolitans no longer command the streets. Companies of White League guerrillas drill openly, marching like an unmasked Ku-klux, and armed.

In the North, whites are fatigued with the Reconstruction drama. Most have lost interest in its plot.

In February 1875, the U.S. Congress passes the Civil Rights Bill. But the law has no enforcement teeth and gives no one authority to prosecute. The law requires individual black litigants to sue for their rights as citizens, an infrequent event.

White Leagues do similar work in the state of Mississippi, next door to Louisiana. During an election in 1875, Mississippi falls into

White League terror, and Governor Adelbert Ames asks Washington to send soldiers. Ames gets only a skeptical telegram from Edwards Pierrepont, the new attorney general under President Grant. "Governor Ames," the attorney general writes on September 14, anniversary of the White League coup in New Orleans, "The whole public are tired out with these annual autumnal outbreaks in the South, and the great majority are ready now to condemn any interference on the part of the Government. . . . I suggest that you preserve the peace by the forces in your own State."

In Mississippi, and throughout the South, most whites either condone attacks on blacks, or they are indifferent to them. If they feel a touch of regret, as some do, they choose to ignore it.

I have to admit that some of the indifference and regret are familiar. They might even be recurring. You can feel regret about the acid hand of racism. No, it is not quite as busy in the 2000s as it was during Constant's time. But it is nevertheless front and center in life. And then you can ignore it.

White opinion acknowledges the rampage, and then washes the bloody sheets. "White men may have burned and killed in Louisiana," *The Shreveport Times* says on Christmas Eve 1875. But whites are not to blame, because "the responsibility belongs to the Radical government of the state."

The Colfax massacre, when the Ku-klux kills 150 blacks, comes to its end in a case known as *U.S. v. Cruikshank*, which reaches the Supreme Court. The case does not involve murder, but conspiracy. *U.S. v. Cruikshank* turns on the question of whether the Colfax killers conspired to deny the constitutional rights of their victims. In March 1876, the Supreme Court overturns three convictions in the case; and for good measure, undermines the Fourteenth Amendment. The Fourteenth Amendment grants rights to due process and equal protection, but the Court rules that the amendment does not apply to violations perpetrated by individuals, such as acts of discrimination or even gang violence; it applies only to state action. The decision means that both race bias and the menace of the mob are constitutional. *U.S. v. Cruikshank* vindicates the White Camellia massacre and paralyzes the federal prosecution of gang rule.

An 1874 cartoon on the common cause of the masked Ku-klux and
the unmasked White League: "Worse than slavery"

In 1876, the United States is one hundred years old, with a presidential election set for the fall. This is the year that nails down white
supremacy for good. The Redemption in Louisiana spreads to the
rest of the country in a vote that turns into a referendum on race.

Constant is forty-four, and his wife forty. Gabrielle Duchemin has
carried eight pregnancies to birth. Two of her children are dead. She
has four sons and two daughters still living—the oldest nineteen, the
youngest three. And in fall 1876, she is pregnant again.

In July, *Harper's Weekly* runs an essay, "The Ku-Klux Democracy," which asks, "Shall the Ku-Klux select the next President of the
United States?" and then answers, yes, probably. "Louisiana is the
State in which these merciless have committed their worst deeds,"
the magazine says. "The Ku-Klux [is] steeped in the blood of their
fellow-citizens, and would bring war and desolation, had they the
power, to the whole nation."

In the race for president, the Democrat Samuel Tilden wins
a majority of the popular vote, but his opponent, the Republican

Rutherford Hayes, claims a one-vote victory in the Electoral College. Democrats charge fraud. In Washington, they decide to contest the vote count in Louisiana, South Carolina, and Florida. Representatives start a filibuster in Congress, blocking the certification of Hayes's win. November ends, and Christmas season begins, with the election outcome suspended.

Gabrielle's ninth child is born December 16. Her parents call the girl Marie Constance. By custom, they set the baptism for a month later.

In mid-December, President Grant also makes a delivery. He sends to Congress a dossier that summarizes the Louisiana atrocities. The portfolio, made from reports by Freedmen's Bureau agents and Yankee officers, runs ninety-eight pages. It describes the whippings and murders, rapes and maimings perpetrated in the state by the Kuklux, the Knights of the White Camellia, and the White League. Some four thousand African Americans are disabled or dead in Louisiana, Grant reports.

Infants, according to Catholic doctrine, are born with a fallen human nature. Every person is polluted by original sin. Such is the teaching of the church, for Constant and Gabrielle. A child may be cleaned of the filth of sin by a new birth in the rite of baptism. Baptism frees the faithful from the weight of the fall and brings the possibility of redemption, cleaning the believer's eyes to see the white light of godliness, and dispelling the cloud of sin that threatens to damn the sinner.

On January 10, 1877, Constant and Gabrielle walk to St. Stephen and christen their last child, washing away the pollution and evil into which she is born.

Two days before, on January 8, White League regiments surround the statehouse, take possession of the courthouses, and occupy the police stations. Federal troops do nothing, and the state militiamen put up no fight. A slogan of "the Democracy" appears in the newspapers—"One party, one race." It is like a caption written on the times.

In Washington, the filibuster in Congress about the presidential vote rambles on.

Both parties say they won in the three states that still have Republican rule—Florida, South Carolina, and Louisiana. (Two of the three have more black residents than white.) But no one really knows who won, since both Republicans and Democrats have used vote suppression, on the one hand, and fake ballots, on the other. The arguments go up, the payoffs go down. The Democrats relent and affirm the Republican win in Florida and South Carolina. That leaves Louisiana. The choice of president falls to the White League state. What the Creole parties do with their eight electoral votes will determine the White House.

On February 13, Mardi Gras, the Mistick Krewe of Comus marches in its customary and majestic parade. Most whites are happy, but not many blacks are heard to applaud when the Krewe reveals the theme for this year's celebration. It is "The Aryan Race." In twenty-three decorated floats, Comus tells the story of the rise to command of whites. The tale begins with float #2, "Greek Tragedy, 400 B.C.," and ends with float #24, "Our Future Destiny, the year 1976." A program printed for the masked ball explains: "The Aryans have been the devotees of luxury, and from the earliest period of their existence as a distinct race, they have been the dictators."

Sixteen weeks after the election, on February 26, Democrat and Republican dealmakers come together at Wormley House, a hotel near the Capitol. The parties reach an arrangement. Democrats will lift the filibuster against the vote, Louisiana will throw its electors to the Republican side, and Rutherford Hayes will get the White House—in exchange for the national acknowledgment of white rule. For twelve years, the U.S. Army, white politicians, and black activists have tried to plant the seeds of equity between blacks and whites; they have only managed to share a little power and turn a little soil. In the election deal, Hayes is to become president, provided that he removes Washington's hand from the South. The army is to be withdrawn from the Southern states where it remains—South Carolina, Florida, and Louisiana. America is to end its quarrel with white supremacy.

W.E.B. Du Bois describes the events in his 1935 book, *Black Reconstruction*: "The Louisiana Democratic State Convention frankly called itself 'we, the white people of Louisiana'. . . . The crucial election of 1876 came and . . . the whole nation waited on the outcome in

Louisiana which would settle the presidential contest. . . . The white folk of Louisiana with threat of civil war entered into negotiations with the President and President-elect. . . . Finally the filibuster was dropped . . . and Louisiana was free for a new period of unhampered exploitation."

Rutherford Hayes is inaugurated March 4. Very soon, he orders the withdrawal of federal soldiers from South Carolina and tells U.S. Army troops stationed in Louisiana to return to their barracks. And that is all. White power wins.

In Congress, Democrats win passage of an amendment that bars the executive from using federal troops to enforce any law—the so-called posse comitatus rule. The mandate is intended to make sure Washington does not try again to engineer a different balance of tribal power.

Black people throughout the South are disarmed. In Louisiana, the Metropolitan Police and the state militia are dissolved and their guns collected. The rule of separate and unequal education is affirmed, and the schools legally segregated. Alcibiade DeBlanc, friend of the Lecorgnes and leader of the Knights of the White Camellia, is appointed to the Louisiana Supreme Court. When that happens, Yves of God, the politician in the family, acquires an ear in the state's high councils. Race segregation is made stiff as concrete in "places of public accommodation"—transport, entertainment, food service, public spaces and parks, shopkeeping, and hotels. A divided society turns permanent, and so does the hand of white command.

There are things I cannot know about what one *petit blanc* in New Orleans thinks and feels during this aftermath. There is no evidence. But I do know that Constant is a person who lives through these events and leaves a chiseled mark on them. I do know that he experiences a pair of bad omens. Gabrielle and Constant's new baby girl, Marie Constance, dies at eleven months, in November. The death record gives the cause as enteritis, an intestinal infection, probably started in contaminated food. Babies just die, even redeemed ones. With a second omen, a plague comes to the city. In summer 1878, Yellow Jack returns. The deaths mount—one thousand . . . two thousand . . . —and whites who can do so flee for the parishes. When the epidemic recedes, six months later, 3,800 are dead—mostly whites, as usual.

Constant and comrades are recruited into official power, as the White League turns into a government agency. In 1879, the League is transformed into the Louisiana National Guard, a state military force. The same happens in other Southern states, as ex-Ku-klux gangs are remade into regional military units. Companies of National Guard, paid soldiers in a local army, become strike forces run by Southern governors. And in state after state, new guard units are summoned to put down black resistance, especially efforts by African Americans to unionize and strike.

To prove it is worthy of a payroll, the Louisiana National Guard applies special violence when it is called out to crush a sugarcane workers' strike. In November 1887, ten thousand black farmworkers are on strike around the town of Thibodaux, seat of Lafourche Parish. Organized by a union, the Knights of Labor, it is the largest collective action in agriculture anywhere in the United States. At Thibodaux, the Louisiana Guard begins its work by massacring some twenty African Americans, then transporting into the parish eight hundred contract workers from convict labor camps in Mississippi. A week later, a second massacre follows at the hands of local guerrillas, who no longer find it necessary to call themselves "White League" or "Ku-klux." Another fifty black workers killed.

"Who is to rule?" one newspaper asks about the Thibodaux strike. "Either the nigger or the white man."

27

If you hear a certain kind of sermon in church, or if you have a Bible that falls open to Exodus or Deuteronomy, you might encounter a promise about the way history spirals down to reckoning. It is a familiar forecast that goes like this—

> I the Lord your God am a jealous God, visiting the iniquity of
> the fathers upon the sons to the third and fourth generation.
> Exodus 20:5–6, Deuteronomy 5:9

Do the marauders of the Ku-klux bring down calamity on their children, their children's children? Do we, does anyone, have hell to pay?

You have large numbers of people in white society who, with race identity as a motive, author violent acts of domination. We kill, we maim, and we rape. I refer to the gallant cohort of the White League and to their fellow travelers. Well short of the model they establish, we commonly use psychological torment against nonwhites, without admitting or knowing it. I refer to the plurality of Americans in possession of unconscious machines of entitlement. In the generations since the White League flourished, it is possible to name many perpetrators like them—and more continue to be made. White supremacy rises and falls, and rises again.

But back to the biblical question: Do the third and fourth generations take ownership of their fathers' crimes? I page the Bible and find another verse, one with an answer of sorts. It is in Isaiah, the book of prophecies, and it is another nasty forecast.

Prepare a place to slaughter the sons for the sins of their fore-
fathers; they are not to rise to inherit the land and cover the
earth with their cities.

Isaiah 14:21

It is an anachronistic question, really. The cult of the individual
that dominates modern minds, the ideology of the "I," prevents most
of us from seeing ourselves as products of the chronicle and choices of
our predecessors. People may make their own lives, but we do under
conditions we do not choose, with terms dictated from the past. We
can never make out our personal links to the felonies of history. "The
tradition of all dead generations weighs like a nightmare on the brains
of the living," said a German philosopher.

In 1883, the U.S. Supreme Court throws out what is left of black
rights. The court rules the Civil Rights Act of 1875 unconstitutional,
making discrimination in public places legal and opening the lock
to a cascade of laws that complete the quarantine of the black tribe
from the Aryan tribe. These so-called Jim Crow laws, named for a
blackface character in minstrel theater, harden the iron vessels of race
caste. Today, five or six generations later, what historians call segregation is ended as a matter of law. But a glance around churches and
workplaces and barrooms, hotels and restaurants and parks and suburbs, living rooms and bedrooms, is enough to conclude that Jim Crow
worked, that the vessels remain, invisible and only a little damaged.

Constant's work is done, and he knows it. He tries to return to his
measuring tapes and pencils, his saws and plane, his nails and notch
drills. Yet he cannot. The census in 1880 says the carpenter spends
half of his working year without any work at all. He is unemployed.
Meanwhile, his brother Yves of God does well. Yves calls himself a
plantation man. He buys land on the outskirts of New Orleans, near
the old Seven Oaks place. It is only thirty acres, but that is more land
than anyone else among the Lecorgnes owns. He hires eight black

workers to dig the fields and tells these farmhands to plant him some rice. In past years, Yves has called himself a judge, an architect, and a builder. Now, when he puts a notice in the city directory, he is a "planter." Yves is an absentee landlord with a single rice field, but he carries on like this in order to touch the old family glory.

Alcibiade DeBlanc, something of a father figure to Constant, dies in St. Martin Parish in November 1883, age sixty-two. A newspaper drapes the marauder-in-chief with velvet praise, calling him "a man of heroic courage, whose magnanimity divested him of all selfishness and made him champion of the rights of others."

I am trying to open a small window into U.S. history. I am trying to bring whiteness up from its unconscious storage place into nascence, which is that feeling just short of consciousness.

The years pass, the rains come. The planting season arrives, the cotton and rice and sugar harvests land on the docks.

Gabrielle and her husband watch their children marry. Numa, the oldest, is a tinsmith, cutting and stamping sheets of tin to roll onto ceilings. In 1881, at twenty-four, he moves out to marry a woman named Odile Livaudais. Gabrielle and Constant see their son Louis grow up. He graduates from the Jesuit Academy, and in September 1885, when he turns twenty-four, he marries a twenty-one-year-old named Annie Miller, who works as a hatmaker.

The Lecorgne boys marry white women. To do otherwise is illegal. More, if you peer into the mind, it is unthinkable.

Louis and Annie set up housekeeping on Berlin Street, in Bouligny, a few blocks from Lecorgne row. Louis works as a carpenter, like his father. The couple has a daughter, named Edna Lecorgne, and another, named Maud, and they have a son, Albert, the siblings I knew as a boy.

There are various templates of race talk. One of them is the sentimental, which sounds like this. How nice it is that we can see each other as humans, and that we can like each other. Another template is the past tense, in which racial processes are placed in the bad old days. It sounds like this. We are different from our grandparents and great-grandparents. They lived with the old prejudices, the old consciousness. Race is the way it used to be, and is not now.

Gabrielle and Constant make do. The rewards of the race war

are hard to detect when you are poor and feel wounded. A few months after son Louis marries, Fred Ogden, leader of the White League, dies from liver cancer, age forty-nine. I imagine Constant and friends from the guerrilla days are in the pews when an Episcopal bishop performs services at the Church of the Annunciation, on Camp Street.

The year 1886 brings an unforgettable season for the Lecorgnes. It begins with Ézilda, Constant's older sister. She is fifty-five and married to a man named François Fazende, who runs a horse stable for a streetcar company. They have four grown children and live on Felicity Street. In April, Ézilda dies of cancer.

The next one taken is a son. Gabrielle and Constant have as their youngest a boy named Stephen, who is thirteen. When Stephen Lecorgne develops a temperature, in September 1886, his parents treat it with the customary fear of an autumn fever. But he worsens quickly, and he dies. The death record names spinal meningitis, a bacterial infection of the membranes that envelop the brain and spinal cord. Stephen is the fifth child his parents bury of the nine who are born to them. Gabrielle and Constant are familiar with children who die, but I do not think they are used to it.

Constant Lecorgne in late life

Two weeks after Stephen's funeral, Constant decides to go on a hunting trip. He wants distraction, or maybe he still has no work, I do not know. Gabrielle lets him go. Maybe she wants to be alone with her grief and with the rest of the children. According to the family story, Constant goes into the state of Mississippi—not that far, two days round-trip—and brings his gun. He goes with friends, other veterans of the old gangs. It is mid-October 1886. He hunts, he returns home, and he is sick. He crawls into bed.

Family tradition, as told by my aunt Maud Lecorgne, is that Constant is ill from "bad water." He drinks contaminated water while on his hunt in the woods. Within a week, Constant is dead. He dies October 24, 1886, age fifty-four.

A doctor cites "malarial fever." It is not contaminated water, in fact, but fever that comes for him. Fevers have seized him before. Fevers of rage, fevers of white power. This time it is a fever that cannot be avoided, unlike those other kinds. The end for a man taken by malaria is quiet. His death is conveyed by the anopheles mosquito, which carries the parasite *Plasmodium falciparum*. Malaria comes with trembling and a bath of sweat. As he wilts in bed, part of Gabrielle might be thankful for a husband who shrinks toward death, rather than rages to it. After decades with guns and fighting, Constant is gone in a few groans.

He dies in Bouligny in yet another rental, one-half of a shotgun house on Napoleon Avenue. The physician who comes to the house to examine the body says Constant is "white," "married," and "a carpenter by occupation." The three features of an American identity, in order of importance: race, sex life, and job. The next day, Gabrielle walks with her children to the funeral at St. Stephen Church, across the street. It is the second time in a month that she buries one of her own.

Do his comrades from the white militias come? I suspect some do. But "our Klansman," as my aunt Maud teaches me to call him, is not given the celebration that rises around leaders of the fight for supremacy, saviors of the race, like Ogden and DeBlanc. He receives no notice in the newspapers, no obituary. The priest delivers a perfunctory eulogy, but that is all.

———

During the 1900s, the Lecorgnes stay put in New Orleans. The divide in the family between Yves Lecorgne, the man of property and the law, and his plainer siblings, including Constant, seems to carry on and harden. Some rise into the white bourgeoisie—the descendants of Yves of God. Some remain in the working class—the progeny of Constant.

Take three of the grandchildren of Constant, Maud and Edna and Albert, whom I remember. Maud becomes a teacher in the white public schools, Edna a homemaker and then a bookkeeper, Albert another carpenter. It is Maud who becomes the carrier of the story of the White League, the story I first heard when I was a boy, in New Orleans. It is not that long ago, really.

Constant was a man with little skill for money, and when he dies, he leaves a poor widow. Gabrielle has next to nothing, and she cannot afford a marker for her husband's grave. There is no sign of his interment. He lies in an unmarked grave for more than seventy years. In the 1950s, a stone is placed to mark this insignificant and yet calamitous, strange but common life. It appears during the lifetime of Maud Lecorgne, the dead man's granddaughter, and thanks in part to her. My aunt Maud wishes to memorialize her grandfather, the *petit blanc* warrior for the Redemption.

Gabrielle, "Widow Lecorgne," carries on as a single mother. She has two children to finish, fifteen-year-old Corinne and twenty-year-old George. George becomes a breadwinner, going to work as a junior carpenter. Gabrielle takes in work as a seamstress. But it is not much, and she and the children live on thin means. Maybe Yves of God shares a few dollars. In a couple of years, son George marries and moves out. Daughter Corinne marries at age nineteen to a man named Emile Jacob, and she moves out. Gabrielle is alone.

The year after Corinne marries, the victory monument goes up. It has been seventeen years since the triumph in the Battle of Canal Street, in 1874. The aging men of the White League want to celebrate themselves with a memorial. A thirty-foot granite obelisk goes up at Canal and Royal streets, the intersection where the guerrillas turned back "negro domination." It is November 1891. When she sees it, Gabrielle must wish that her husband were with her.

The stone monument is popular among whites, widely detested among blacks. An inscription is eventually added to the plinth beneath the obelisk. It reads: "The national election in November 1876 recognized white supremacy and gave us our state." One hundred forty-three years after the Battle of Canal Street, in the summer of 2017, the city of New Orleans decides to remove the monument to the White League. It is dismantled and stored.

Monument to the White League in New Orleans,
and the author

After Reconstruction collapses, after Constant dies, lynching becomes a preferred form of white mob violence. In New Orleans, the lynching years begin differently from other places, with a gang killing of Italian Americans, in 1891. Eleven "Dagoes," as the papers put it, accused of killing a sheriff—they are men who are chiefly guilty of being born in southern Europe, a place less than fully white—are themselves murdered by guerrillas who break into the city jail. After this massacre, almost all lynch mobs target African Americans. Louisiana, Mississippi, and Georgia are the states with the highest number of black lynching victims in the period 1880–1940, when the killings are most popular among whites. Lafourche Parish, southwest of New Orleans, has the greatest number, with fifty-two African Americans put to death by the noose.

As Gabrielle grows older, the straitjacket of whiteness tightens. Meantime, Creoles of color make futile efforts to untie it. In 1890, eighteen men in New Orleans form the *Comité des Citoyens*, the Citizens' Committee, to try to loosen the legal knot that binds black identity. They come together to fight the "exaggerated fanaticism about caste and segregation," as one of its members puts it. The Citizens' Committee takes aim at Act 111, the most severe segregation law, approved by the Louisiana State Assembly in 1890.

In 1892, the *Comité des Citoyens* sends a shoemaker named Homer Plessy to board a segregated railcar belonging to the East Louisiana Railroad. Plessy climbs into a white car at the Press Street Depot, east of the French Quarter. The battlefield involves no guns and no terrain, just a single wooden seat on a train, five miles from Bouligny and Lecorgne row.

Plessy is arrested and tried. When *Plessy v. Ferguson* is argued in New Orleans, Judge John Ferguson of the criminal district court for Orleans Parish hears the case. The prosecution argues that quarantine of black people is necessary on the basis of *contact-répugnant*, or "repellent intimacy." White passengers, the state says, are deeply inconvenienced by the odor of people of color. Judge Ferguson agrees, and the law is affirmed. The Citizens' Committee appeals, and for four years, the case rises through layers of the judiciary, emerging in the U.S. Supreme Court. In May 1896, the thoughtful justices of the high court, men who help to clarify national standards for everyone, determine that "repellent intimacy" is a persuasive argument. The law of quarantine is affirmed.

"We think the enforced separation of the races . . . neither abridges the privileges or immunities of the colored man, deprives him of his property without due process of law, nor denies him the equal protection of the laws," writes associate justice Henry B. Brown in a 7–1 ruling. The main point, says Justice Brown, is that "legislation is powerless to eradicate racial instincts."

The encirclement is complete. Race quarantine becomes the custom in all the land. White supremacy is acclaimed in habit, in thought, and in law.

Yves of God dies January 1, 1896, at seventy. He leaves life contented and well served. With her rich brother-in-law dead, Gabrielle's money worries appear to grow. When Gabrielle's son-in-law Emile dies young, in 1898, her widowed daughter Corinne moves back in with her three children. The household is somewhat desperate. To alleviate the strain, Gabrielle applies for her husband's Confederate pension. The state of Louisiana runs a program that pays Civil War veterans, or their widows, a monthly stipend. It is a thank-you for good service during the rebellion. Gabrielle is given a pension, $5 a month for Constant's service in the long-ago war, the war that went badly, but which the South seems eventually to have won.

Gabrielle, age sixty-five, and daughter Corinne, twenty-seven, raise the grandchildren together. They take in two boarders, a German-born laborer and a Louisiana-born streetcar driver. The boarding arrangement works for a little while, until it does not. To supplement, Gabrielle teaches piano, but this, too, is not enough. She looks for a job, because she can no longer pay the rent.

In a public school, Gabrielle finds work as a "portress." A portress is a doorkeeper; also, some of the time, a female porter. Gabrielle is hired by a primary school at 926 Berlin Street, on the corner of

Camp Street. The job is full-time, and the pay is slender, but the work comes with an important benefit, housing. Gabrielle, Corinne, and the three children move into an apartment in the back of the school. It is cramped, and the building is loud from the swarm of students during the day.

Gabrielle the portress greets the schoolchildren, keeps attendance, and makes sure the students stay in class all day. And, like a porter, she picks up a mop and broom.

The school building stands just behind the church, St. Stephen, where the Lecorgnes have baptized and buried one another for fifty years. To Gabrielle's consternation, perhaps, it is a black public school. Everyone agrees the tribes are to be kept apart. But the black tribe needs portresses, just like the white. Gabrielle works at a black school, lives with black children all around her, every day. She is glad to have the work, to take care of her own. Or maybe she is disgusted to have work, when it is work of this kind.

Gabrielle must be glad that her husband is dead. She must be relieved that Constant cannot see his wife is a portress in a black school, looking over the burr-headed pickaninnies. It is 1905. She is seventy years old, then older. She works and works, and does not stop. She reaches for her mop to swab the floor, cleaning up after the black children.

A NOTE ON SOURCES

To write a life story from scattered and thin sources is like making a mosaic. A piece of tile here, a chip with color there, and something from the scrap bin—until you have a picture. Archaeologists work a similar process. Give me a shard and I will make a village, says the digger for old pots.

I began with bits of oral tradition and the casual research of a family historian, my aunt Maud. Why would a person go beyond them to fill out a portrait of a Klansman? Behavior is overdetermined.

Some of the sources are routine for historians: wills and probate records, census data, institutional ledgers and receipt books, sacramental records, tax filings, military archives, maps, city directories, memoirs, travel accounts from the period. What is missing is the voice of the Klansman.

No, that is not true. Archives about unfamous and unrich people are not "missing": they are never made. One person in a thousand leaves a trail in personal paper (rather than in public records) that the living can follow. Almost no one keeps evidence of what they think, do, say, and dream. If they do, their children do not place it in a library. In the future, archives will differ. The accidental records of common people, traces of lives left in the digital mass brain, will be vast.

The voice of the Klansman is absent. In its place, you have a condition more promising for pleasurable prose, and that is the intermittent record. When the archive says little or nothing, it is a matter of developing trace evidence, using inference and implication. Documentation of a life that appears in bits—a legal contract, an arrest record, a single letter, marriage or divorce papers, a hospitalization record, a lawsuit, a newspaper article, or an obituary. From these threads are garments made.

I first took an interest in telling a story about "our Klansman" years ago. I began to write his life as a novel, and after twelve months, had one hundred pages. But the manuscript read as mediocre, an adventure plot here, a melodrama there. I realized that making things up robbed the story of too much truth. I put the fiction away and opened a nonfiction folder.

NOTES

ABBREVIATIONS USED IN THE NOTES

Freedmen's Bureau: Records of the Bureau of Refugees, Freedmen and Abandoned Lands

LARC: Louisiana Research Collection, Tulane University, New Orleans

Louisiana Division, NOPL: Louisiana Division/City Archives and Special Collections, New Orleans Public Library

Louisiana State Archives: Louisiana Secretary of State, Division of Archives, Records Management and History

LSU: Louisiana State University

NARA: National Archives and Records Administration, Washington, D.C.

Sacramental Records: Sacramental Records of the Roman Catholic Church of the Archdiocese of New Orleans

PROLOGUE

11   *Fred C. Trump, Klansman*: arrest—"Warren Criticizes 'Class' Parades," *The New York Times*, 1 Jun 1927, 16; reprise—Philip Bump, "In 1927 Donald Trump's Father Was Arrested after a Klan Riot in Queens," *The Washington Post*, 29 Feb 2016.

CHAPTER 1

26   *Ku-klux raid, indictment*: *The Morning Star and Catholic Messenger* (New Orleans), 9 Mar 1873; *The Daily Picayune* (New Orleans), 6, 7, 8, 13, 20, and 25 Mar 1873; *New Orleans Republican*, 6, 7, and 9 Mar 1873; *The New-Orleans Times*, 6 and 8 Mar 1873; "A Riot in New-Orleans," *The New York Times*, 6 Mar 1873; "The New-Orleans Rioting" and "The New-Orleans Mob," *The New York Times*, 7 Mar 1873; State of Louisiana v. Peter Duffy, et al., Indictment no. 5187, for Treason, and Violating the Enforcement Act of 1871 (Ku Klux Klan Act), 24 Mar 1873, First District Court, Orleans Parish, and Witness' Bond, Recorder's Office, Sixth District, City of New Orleans, 12 Mar 1873, Louisiana Division, NOPL.

CHAPTER 2

30 *St. Louis Cathedral*: Karl Postel, *The Americans as They are; Described in a Tour Through the Valley of the Mississippi* (London: Hurst, Chance, 1828), 154–56.

35 *French prisoners of war, and deserters*: Francis Abell, *Prisoners of War in Britain 1756 to 1815; A Record of Their Lives, Their Romance and Their Sufferings* (London: Oxford University Press, 1914), 208–13, 416, 445, 450; Patricia K. Crimmin, "Prisoners of War and British Port Communities, 1793–1815," *The Northern Mariner/Le Marin du nord* 6, no. 4 (Oct 1996), 17–27; Paul Chamberlain, "The Release of Prisoners of War from Britain in 1813 and 1814," *Napoléonica. La Revue* 21, no. 3 (2014), 118–29.

37 "Histoire naturelle *('Natural History')*": François Bernier, "Nouvelle division de la terre, par les différentes espèces ou races d'homme qui l'habitent" ("A New Division of the Earth, According to the Different Species or Races of Men Who Inhabit It"), *Journal des Sçavans* 12 (1684), 148–55; Ibram X. Kendi, *Stamped from the Beginning: The Definitive History of Racist Ideas in America* (New York: Nation Books, 2016), 55, 85, 137.

37 *Deserters in New Orleans*: François Furstenberg, *When the United States Spoke French: Five Refugees Who Shaped a Nation* (New York: Penguin Press, 2014), 349–402; retrocession of Louisiana, 1800—Alexander De Conde, "Napoleon and the Louisiana Purchase," in *Napoleon and America*, ed. Robert B. Holtman (Pensacola, FL: Perdido Bay Press for the Louisiana State Museum, 1988), 110–30.

CHAPTER 3

42 *Slaves speak a language, Gombo*: Edward Larocque Tinker, *Gombo, the Creole Dialect of Louisiana* (Worcester, MA: American Antiquarian Society, 1936); *"The same stick"*: Lafcadio Hearn, *"Gombo zhèbes": Little Dictionary of Creole Proverbs* (New York: W. H. Coleman, 1885), 25; *Enslaved revolt, 1811*: Daniel Rasmussen, *American Uprising: The Untold Story of America's Largest Slave Revolt* (New York: Harper, 2011), 97ff., 147ff.

44 *43 Dauphine Street, New Orleans*: Sale of Property, John Longpre to A. Lassize, 16 Dec 1815, Michel De Armas, notary; "Vente de Propriété, John Longpré à Marie Hinard," 4 Mar 1817, Marc Lafitte, notary; "Sale of Property, Marie Hinard to Jean Barbey," 20 Apr 1847, Theodore Guyol, notary; "Testament de Delle Mariane Hinard," 18 Mar 1842, Felix Grima, notary—all, New Orleans Notarial Archives Research Center; *Yves César Le Corgne household*: New Orleans, United States Census, 1830 (Washington, D.C.: National Archives and Records Administration);

"Y.C. Lecorgne, teacher, 43 Dauphin," *Michel's New Orleans Annual and Commercial Register* (New Orleans: Gaux & Sollée, 1833).

45   *Yves Le Corgne*: work as teacher—Simone de la Souchère Deléry, *Napoleon's Soldiers in America* (Gretna, LA: Pelican Publishing, 1972), 41–42; family in France—*Le Courrier* (New Orleans) for 16 Dec 1831 cites letters to "C. Lecorgne" (César Le Corgne) at post office.

46   *Free people of color / gens de couleur libres chronicled*: Charles Barthelemy Rousséve, *The Negro in Louisiana; Aspects of His History and His Literature* (New Orleans: Xavier University Press, 1937), 20–55; Alice Moore Dunbar-Nelson, "People of Color in Louisiana," in *Creole: The History and Legacy of Louisiana's Free People of Color*, ed. Sybil Kein (Baton Rouge: LSU Press, 2001), 3–41.

47   *Mixed-race terms*: Frederick Law Olmsted, *A Journey in the Seaboard Slave States in the Years 1853–1854, with Remarks on Their Economy* (New York, London: Dix & Edwards, Sampson Low, 1856), 583.

49   *Children of Yves and Marguerite Le Corgne*: Anne (b. 10 Apr 1819)—Sacramental Records; Yves Hypolite (b. 19 Jan 1820)—*New Orleans, Louisiana, Birth Records Index, 1790–1915*, Louisiana State Archives; Marguerite (b. 8 Feb 1824)—Sacramental Records; Yves Jean (b. 23 Jan 1826)—Sacramental Records; yellow fever—Karl Postel, *The Americans as They Are*, 192–94.

50   *David Walker*: *David Walker's Appeal, in Four Articles, Together with a Preamble to the Coloured Citizens of the World, but in Particular, and Very Expressly, to Those of the United States of America*, rev. ed. (New York: Hill and Wang, 1995), vii, xix–xx, 2, 7, 9–12, 16–21, 61, 62n, 71.

50   *People enslaved by Yves and Marguerite Le Corgne and by Jean-Louis and Anne Constant Zeringue*: Valentin—Jean-Louis Zeringue to Yves C. Le Corgne, sale of a slave, Valentin, age 40, 11 Feb 1830, Jefferson Parish Conveyances, Louisiana Division, NOPL; Zeringue slaves—Constance Anne Constant Zeringue, Succession no. 346, filed 15 Jul 1826, Jefferson Parish Succession and Probate Records, Louisiana Division, NOPL; further Zeringue slaves—Will of Jean-Louis Zeringue *père* (grandfather of Marguerite Zeringue Le Corgne), Jun 1813 (drafted), Jan 1824 (filed), Louisiana Division, NOPL.

51   *Constant Le Corgne*: "Constant Polycarpe Hypolite Le Corgne," b. 28 Apr 1832, baptized 1 May 1833, Sacramental Records, St. Louis Cathedral, Baptisms, vol. 14, no. 385.

CHAPTER 4

54   *P.C. grows up around enslaved blacks*: By 1830, Yves and Marguerite have three children and three slaves, a man and two women—U.S. Census,

1830; baptisms of enslaved in Zeringue household—Sacramental Records, St. Louis Cathedral, Baptisms of Slaves and Free People of Color, no. 314 (27 Apr 1839); *voodou,* exorcism—Gwendolyn Midlo Hall, "The Formation of Afro-Creole Culture," in *Creole New Orleans: Race and Americanization,* ed. Arnold R. Hirsch and Joseph Logsdon (Baton Rouge: LSU Press, 1992).

57 *Congo Square:* seen by—Benjamin Henry Latrobe, *The Papers of Benjamin Henry Latrobe: Journals 1799–1820,* vol. 3, ed. Edward C. Carter (New Haven: Yale University Press, 1980), 202–203; seen by—Christian Schultz, *Travels on an Inland Voyage Through the States of New York, Pennsylvania, Virginia, Ohio, Kentucky, and Tennessee, and Through the Territories of Indiana, Louisiana, Mississippi, and New-Orleans, Performed in the Years 1807 and 1808* (Ridgewood, NJ: Gregg Press, 1968), 187–93; seen by—James R. Creecy, *Scenes in the South, and Other Miscellaneous Pieces* (Washington, D.C.: T. McGill, 1860), 20–23; imagined by—Herbert Asbury, *The French Quarter; An Informal History of the New Orleans Underworld* (New York and London: Alfred A. Knopf, 1936), 239–43; imagined by—Joseph R. Roach, *Cities of the Dead: Circum-Atlantic Performance* (New York: Columbia University Press, 1996), 63–68; described—Ned Sublette, *The World That Made New Orleans from Spanish Silver to Congo Square* (Chicago: Lawrence Hill Books, 2008), 271–83.

60 *Jean-Louis Zeringue estate:* sixteen workers—Jean-Louis Zeringue, succession no. 6070 (filed 30 Oct 1839), Jefferson Parish Succession and Probate Records, Louisiana Division, NOPL; Camille Zeringue property—Conveyance, Jean-Louis Zeringue to Camille Zeringue, sale of habitation, 14 Jan 1830, Book BIS1, Act/page 5, Jefferson Parish Conveyances, Louisiana Division, NOPL; Camille Zeringue as slaveholder—advertisement for runaways Frank, Handison, and Jarret, *New-Orleans Argus,* 30 Jul 1828.

CHAPTER 5

62 *Carnival / Mardi Gras:* James Creecy, *Scenes in the South,* 43–46; Carol Clark, "Carnival," in *The Rabelais Encyclopedia,* ed. Elizabeth A. Chesney (Westport, CT: Greenwood Press, 2004), 28–29; Mikhail Bakhtin, *Rabelais and His World,* trans. Hélène Iswolsky (Cambridge: MIT Press, 1968), 7–11; Samuel Kinser, *Rabelais's Carnival: Text, Context, Metatext* (Berkeley: University of California Press, 1990), 41–48.

64 *Caucasians:* Samuel George Morton, *Crania Americana; or, a Comparative View of the Skulls of Various Aboriginal Nations of North and South America, to Which Is Prefixed an Essay on the Varieties of the Human Species* (London: J. Dobson Simpkin, Marshall, 1839), 3–7, 8–9, 40.

66   *Le Corgne family moves*: land purchase—Joseph Vincent à Yves C. Le
     Corgne, 20 Apr 1840, Jefferson Parish conveyances, vol. 10, Louisiana
     Division, NOPL; City of Lafayette—Lyle Saxon, Edward Dreyer, and
     Robert Tallant, *Gumbo Ya-Ya* (Boston: Houghton Mifflin, 1945), 50–75;
     Bouligny development—Fred Daspit, *Louisiana Architecture, 1820–1840*
     (Lafayette: Center for Louisiana Studies, University of Louisiana at
     Lafayette, 2005), 22–23; Terpsichore Street—*New-Orleans Annual and
     Commercial Directory, for 1846* (New Orleans: E. A. Michel, 1846).
71   De Bow's Review: idea of blackness—Josiah Nott, "The Negro," *De
     Bow's Review* (New Orleans) 3, no. 5 (May 1847), 419–22; "a distinct
     species"—Solon Robinson, "Negro Slavery at the South," *De Bow's Re-
     view* 7, no. 3 (Sep 1849), 206–25; on Solon Robinson—*American Phreno-
     logical Journal* 19 (1854), 99–101.
72   Les Cenelles *anthology*: *Les Cenelles: Choix de poésies indigènes* (New
     Orleans: H. Lauve, 1845); Armand Lanusse, *Creole Voices: Poems in French
     by Free Men of Color*, ed. Edward Maceo Coleman (Washington, D.C.:
     Associated Publishers, 1945); about *Les Cenelles*—Rodolphe Lucien
     Desdunes, *Nos hommes et notre histoire* (Montréal: Arbour et Dupont,
     1911), 13–94; Rodolphe Lucien Desdunes, *Our People and Our History*,
     trans. and ed. Sister Dorothea Olga McCants (Baton Rouge: LSU
     Press, 1973), 10–25.

CHAPTER 6
74   *Gabrielle Duchemin*: arrives New Orleans—"Louisiana, New Or-
     leans Passenger Lists, 1820–1945," database with images, *Family-
     Search*, https://familysearch.org/ark:/61903/1:1:QKNP-9BQS, 13 Mar
     2018, Eléonore Labarrière, 60, and Marie Labarrière, 11 (1847), citing
     ship *Orléans*, affiliate film no. 026, NARA microfilm M259 and T905
     (Washington, D.C.: National Archives and Records Administration,
     n.d.), FHL microfilm 200, 156; Gabrielle Duchemin lives with Laizer
     family—"G. Duchemin, age 14, F," U.S. Census, 1850 (Jefferson Par-
     ish); Laizer household—François Laizer and family live at Cadiz and
     Jersey streets in 1858, where they possess four slaves and eight building
     lots, making theirs the richest household in Bouligny—Jefferson City,
     Assessors' Office Tax Rolls, vols. 1–5 (1850–61), Louisiana Division,
     NOPL.
75   *Gabrielle Duchemin*: birth—"Marie Léonide Gabrielle, fille de Joséphine
     Perdreaux . . . et Alphonse Duchemin," b. 4 May 1836, Pointe-à-Pitre,
     Guadeloupe, État Civil 1836, Archives d'Outre-Mer, Archives Nation-
     ales de France, http://anom.archivesnationales.culture.gouv.fr; Alphonse
     Duchemin in Guadeloupe—"Alphonse Duchemin, 44, propriétaire" is

witness to a marriage in 1850: marriage no. 87 (Clément Moko and An-gèle Abiakona), 20 Dec 1850, Sainte-Anne, Guadeloupe, État Civil 1850, Archives d'Outre-Mer, Archives Nationales de France, http://anom .archivesnationales.culture.gouv.fr.

76 *Joséphine Perdreau*: In Cuba, Perdreau is named in the purchase of Julia, enslaved, by her grandmother—Sale of a slave, Julia, Victoria Moreau à Eléonore Labarrière, n.d. Apr 1844, Archivos Coloniales, Santiago, Cuba; Jean Labarrière in New Orleans—"J. Labarriere," New Orleans, Ward 1, Orleans Parish, U.S. Census, 1840; Caribbean migration to New Orleans, 1800–1850—Paul F. Lachance, "The Foreign French," in *Creole New Orleans: Race and Americanization*, ed. Arnold R. Hirsch and Joseph Logsdon (Baton Rouge: LSU Press, 1992), 101–30.

77 *Gabrielle Duchemin*: imagined youth—Eliza Ripley, *Social Life in New Orleans, Being Recollections of My Girlhood* (New York: D. Appleton, 1912), 11–12.

79 *Minstrelsy in Louisiana*: John Smith Kendall, "New Orleans' Negro Minstrels," *Louisiana Historical Quarterly* 30, no. 1 (Jan 1947), 128–48; "Dandy Broadway Swell," in Rudi Blesh and Harriet Grossman Janis, *They All Played Ragtime: The True Story of an American Music* (New York: Grove Press, 1959), 85–86.

80 *Louisiana governor Joseph Walker*: on slavery—Sidney J. Romero, *"My Fellow Citizens—": The Inaugural Addresses of Louisiana's Governors* (La-fayette: Center for Louisiana Studies, University of Southwestern Loui-siana, 1980), 102.

81 *Sale of Caroline, enslaved*: Joseph Michel to François Laizer, 10 Apr 1849 (five lots of land and a twelve-year-old girl, Caroline), Jefferson Par-ish Conveyances, Louisiana Division, NOPL; real estate—François J. Laizer and various sellers/buyers, nine transactions, 1843–55, Jefferson Parish Conveyance Books, 1827–1900, vols. 12–15, Louisiana Division, NOPL.

84 *Lecorgnes close together*: marriage of Aurore Lecorgne—Sacramental Rec-ords, Diocese of Louisiana, L. A. Numa Leche and Marie Aurore Le Corgne, 9 Oct 1852; Constant Lecorgne, work—*Gardner & Wharton's New Orleans Directory for 1858* (New Orleans: Edward Wharton, 1858).

85 *Yellow fever epidemic*: New Orleans Sanitary Commission, E. H. Barton, and New Orleans City Council, *Report of the Sanitary Commission of New Orleans on the Epidemic Yellow Fever of 1853* (New Orleans, 1854), 3–10, 104, 246, 460 (insert), 480; Edgar Leche, infant—Sacramental Records, Parish of St. Stephen, Baptisms and Marriages, vol. 1, no. 46 (18 Aug 1853); Numa Leche, death—Sacramental Records, Parish of St. Stephen, Funerals, 1851–60, vol. 1, no. 8 (20 Jun 1854).

86 *François Laizer*: mayor and treasurer, Jefferson City—"Jefferson City, Minutes of the Board of Aldermen (Journal), 1 Sep 1857–20 May 1861," AB 300, Louisiana Division, NOPL; Jefferson City described—Richard Campanella, *Cityscapes of New Orleans* (Baton Rouge: LSU Press, 2017), 16–18; "dance hall pays $50 a year"—taxes for types of business, in "Jefferson City, Minutes of the Board of Aldermen (Journal), 1 Sep 1857–20 May 1861."

87 *Lavinia, aka "Fanny," enslaved*: Succession of Eleanor Vautrin, dec., widow of J. B. Labarriere, 29 Mar 1855, Third Judicial District Court, Jefferson Parish, Louisiana Division, NOPL.

89 *Marriage of Constant Lecorgne and Gabrielle Duchemin*: "Le Corne Constantin Policarpe con Gabriela Du Chemin," Matrimonios Blancos, 1850–62, Folio 63, N°6 (3 Abril 1856), registros sacramentales, parroquia de Santo Tomás, diócesis de Santiago de Cuba, Cuba; return to New Orleans— "Louisiana, New Orleans Passenger Lists, 1820–1945," database with images, *FamilySearch*, https://familysearch.org/ark:/61903/1:1:QKNP-FY4P, 13 Mar 2018, citing ship *Elizabeth Segar*, affiliate film no. 042, NARA microfilm M259 and T905 (Washington, D.C.: National Archives and Records Administration, n.d.); FHL microfilm 200,182.

CHAPTER 7

95 *Frederick Douglass*: "What to the Slave is the Fourth of July?" *Frederick Douglass: Selected Speeches and Writings*, ed. Philip S. Foner (Chicago: Lawrence Hill, 1999), 188–206.

97 *Laizer and Lecorgne households*: François Laizer and Marguerite Lecorgne, holdings—Tax records, West Bouligny, Jefferson City, 1858, Louisiana Division, NOPL; "a scrap of land"—"Mme. V.S. Dufossat to P.C. Lecorgne," Conveyance and mortgage, 13 Jan 1857, Jefferson Parish Conveyances, Book F, p. 374, Louisiana Division, NOPL; birth of Numa Lecorgne—"Joseph Gabriel Numa, legitimate son of Polycarpe Constant Lecorgne and of Gabrielle Duchemin, born 2 September," Sacramental Records, Parish of St. Stephen, Baptisms and Marriages, 1851–60, vol. 1, no. 63 (4 Oct 1857).

99 *Josiah Nott*: "Negro slavery is consistent"—"Two Lectures on the Connection Between the Biblical and Physical History of Man, Delivered by Invitation from the Chair of Political Economy, etc., of the Louisiana University in December 1848 (New York, 1849)," 19; Josiah Nott's "polygenesis"—Josiah Clark Nott et al., *Indigenous Races of the Earth; or, New Chapters of Ethnological Inquiry; Including Monographs on Special Departments . . . Presenting Fresh Investigations, Documents, and Materials*, chap. 5, "The Monogenists and the Polygenists" (Philadelphia: J. B.

Lippincott & Co., 1857); and Josiah Nott, George R. Gliddon, Samuel George Morton, Louis Agassiz, William Usher, and Henry S. Patterson, eds., *Types of Mankind; or, Ethnological Researches Based Upon the Ancient Monuments, Paintings, Sculptures, and Crania of Races, and Upon Their Natural, Geographical, Philological, and Biblical History* (1868; Miami: Mnemosyne Publishing Co., 1969).

101 *Louis Agassiz and Arthur Gobineau*: Agassiz—Joseph T. Zealy / Louis Agassiz, daguerreotypes (15), ca. 1850, Peabody Museum of Archaeology and Ethnology, Harvard University; Gobineau, "Aryan"—Arthur de Gobineau, *Essai sur l'inégalité des races humaines* (1853–55), or *The Inequality of Human Races*, trans. Adrian Collins (London: Heinemann, 1915), 205–12.

106 *Lecorgne family*: land held—Tax Rolls, Jefferson City (West Bouligny), 1850–61, vols. 2–3 (1858 and 1859), Louisiana Division, NOPL; house sale—"P.C. Lecorgne to Mrs. Mary S. Lacoste," 14 Jan 1859, Jefferson City Register of Conveyances, book 4, p. 506, Land Records Division, Office of the Clerk of Civil District Court for the Parish of Orleans, Louisiana Division, NOPL; house purchase—"E. S. Dufossat to P.C. Lecorgne," 11 Feb 1859, Jefferson Parish Conveyances, vol. 4 (1856–58), p. 527, Louisiana Division, NOPL; birth of Françoise Mathilde—Sacramental Records, St. Stephen [aka St. Vincent de Paul, Bouligny], Baptisms and Marriages, vol. 1 (23 Jun 1859); Constant and Gabrielle Lecorgne on Bellecastle Street—*Gardner's New Orleans Directory for 1861* (New Orleans: Charles Gardner, 1861); Yves J. Lecorgne, justice of the peace—"Notice to Taxpayers," *New Orleans Daily Crescent*, 21 Nov 1859, 6; Joseph and Constant Lecorgne appointments—*The Carrollton Sun* (New Orleans), 30 Jun 1860; Constant Lecorgne sheriff's sale—*The Carrollton Sun*, 1 Aug 1860; Constant Lecorgne, collector—Valmont Soniat Dufossat v. Claudine Claude, f.w.c., 7 Nov 1861, Third District Court case no. 16372, Louisiana Division, NOPL.

CHAPTER 8

108 *Samuel Cartwright*: in New Orleans—"Dr. Samuel Cartwright, 175 Canal Street," *Gardner's New Orleans Directory for 1861* (New Orleans: Charles Gardner, 1861); *Dysesthaesia Aethiopica* ("Ethiopian dysesthesia")—Samuel Cartwright, "Diseases and Peculiarities of the Negro Race," *De Bow's Review* 11 (Sep 1851), 331–34; lecture—"Ethnology of the Negro or Prognathous Race," *New Orleans Medical and Surgical Journal* 15 (Mar 1858), 149–63; more scientific racism—"Report on the Diseases and Physical Peculiarities of the Negro Race," *New Orleans Medical and Surgical Journal* VII (Nov 1851), 369–73; "Dr. Cartwright on the Caucasians

and the Africans," *De Bow's Review* 25 (Jul 1858), 45–56; "Unity of the Human Race Disproved by the Hebrew Bible," *De Bow's Review* 29 (Aug 1860), 129–36; "Negro Freedom an Impossibility Under Nature's Laws," *De Bow's Review* 30 (Jun 1861), 648–59.

110 *Enslaved in Lecorgne households*: Marguerite Lecorgne, death—Sacramental Records, Parish of St. Stephen, Funerals, vol. 1 (2 Nov 1859); estate— Succession of M. C. Zeringue, Widow of Y. C. Lecorgne, Third Judicial District Court, Jefferson Parish, LA, case no. 1654 (19 Jan 1860); enslaved—Partition between Heirs of Mistress Marguerite Lecorgne, deceased, 18 Feb 1860, Conveyance books, 1827–1900, Jefferson Parish, Louisiana Division, NOPL; "Yves takes nine people"—the 1860 census records Yves J. Lecorgne as slaveholder of nine people, whose description matches his mother's inventory, viz., two women, ages 70 and 50, two 23-year-old men, a 3-year-old girl, and four boys, ages 15, 14, 4, and 4, Slave Schedules, U.S. Census, 1860; estate inventories of other Lecorgne siblings show movement between households of domestic slaves.

112 *Sermon*: Benjamin M. Palmer, *The South: Her Peril, and Her Duty; A Discourse, Delivered in the First Presbyterian Church, New Orleans, on Thursday, November 29, 1860, by B. M. Palmer* (New Orleans: 1860).

113 *Lecorgnes are Democrats*: Yves Lecorgne, election commissioner—*The Carrollton Sun*, 9 Mar 1861; electorate at 7%—White men voted in all states regardless of wealth by 1860, when total U.S. population is 31,443,321, of which white males comprise 13,811,381, of which 5.8 million are vote eligible (above age 21); from the national electorate, 80% vote in 1860 (4.6 million, or 15% of the population); whereas in Louisiana, 1860 population 708,000, with white males numbering 178,000, 47% of whom (84,000) are vote eligible, 58.6% of voters cast a ballot in 1860 (49,200), placing the election in the hands of 7% of the state's population.

115 *Sale of Ovid*: Polycarpe Constant Lecorgne to Jean Valsin Gourdain, Sale of a slave, Ovid, 10 Oct 1860, New Orleans Notarial Archives, Conveyances, vol. 83, p. 505.

117 *Sen. Judah Benjamin*: "servile race" speech in Senate, 31 Dec 1860—Marion Mills Miller, *Great Debates in American History*, vol. 5 (New York: Current Literature Publishing, 1913), 380–87.

CHAPTER 9

121 *New Orleans, early 1861*: Mathilde Lecorgne, death—Sacramental Records, Parish of St. Stephen, Funerals (Whites), vol. 2, p. 1, no. 2 (23 Jan 1861); Secession convention, the Marseillaise—Gerald Mortimer Capers, *Occupied City: New Orleans Under the Federals, 1862–1865* (Lexington: University of Kentucky Press, 1965), 1; Estelle is pregnant—Marie

Alice, b. 6 Sep 1861 to Joseph and Estelle Lecorgne, Sacramental Records, Parish of St. Stephen, Baptisms, vol. 2, p. 12, no. 77; Captain Constant Lecorgne—"Regimental Order," *The Carrollton Sun*, 22 May 1861.

123 *New Orleans, mid-1861*: Numbers of volunteers—Willie Malvin Caskey, *Secession and Restoration of Louisiana* (Baton Rouge: LSU Press, 1938), 41; Émile Chevalley—*The Carrollton Sun*, May 4, 15, 25, 1861; Constant Lecorgne, family, and friends in Confederate militias—Janet B. Hewett, Noah Andre Trudeau, and Bryce A. Suderow, eds., *Supplement to the Official Records of the Union and Confederate Armies, Part II—Record of Events*, vol. 24 (Wilmington, NC: Broadfoot Publishing Co., 1996), 726–27, 750–51; *The Daily Picayune*, 3 Apr 1861; *The Carrolton Sun*, 4 May 1861; "Cornerstone" speech—Henry Cleveland, *Alexander H. Stephens, in Public and Private: With Letters and Speeches, Before, During, and Since the War* (Philadelphia, 1886), 717–29; Native Guards—Mary F. Berry, "Negro Troops in Blue and Gray: The Louisiana Native Guards, 1861–63," *Louisiana History* 8, no. 2 (spring 1967), 165–90.

124 *Constant Lecorgne's Confederate service, 1861*: Fourteenth Company B, Jefferson Cadets, Louisiana Regiment muster rolls, Louisiana Historical Association Collection, Series 55-BB, folder 153, LARC; Andrew B. Booth, *Records of Louisiana Confederate Soldiers and Louisiana Confederate Commands, in Three Volumes*, vol. 3, book 1 (New Orleans, 1920), 701.

127 *Fourteenth Louisiana Regiment mutiny*: Christopher Blackburn, "The Grand Junction Riot of 1861," *West Tennessee Historical Society Papers* 47 (1993); Hewett et al., *Supplement to the Official Records*, 309–16; *The Memphis Daily Appeal*, 7 Aug 1861; *The Daily Picayune*, 5 Aug 1861; Col. Valery Sulakowski's regiment—Lawrence Lee Hewitt, "'Wildcats' in the Army of Northern Virginia," in *Louisianians in the Civil War*, ed. Lawrence L. Hewitt and Arthur W. Bergeron (Columbia: University of Missouri Press, 2002), 122–25; Valery Sulakowski to Leroy Pope Walker, 11 Aug 1861, Letters Received by the Confederate Secretary of War, 1861–65, RG 109, NARA publication m437, no. 3249–1861, reel 7.

128 *Louis Constant Lecorgne*: born 1 Sep 1861—Sacramental Records, St. Stephen Church, Baptisms, vol. 2, p. 12, no. 76.

CHAPTER 10

140 *New Orleans, 1862–64*: Joe Gray Taylor, *Louisiana Reconstructed, 1863–1877* (Baton Rouge: LSU Press, 1974), 2–50; Union gunboats— *The Daily Picayune*, 5 Apr 1862; Yankee capture and Gen. Benjamin Butler—Capers, *Occupied City*, chaps. 1–2; Prime Minister Viscount Palmerston—quoted in Capers, *Occupied City*, 69; Julia Le Grand,

imagined as Gabrielle Duchemin: Julia Ellen (Le Grand) Waitz, *The Journal of Julia Le Grand, New Orleans, 1862–63*, ed. Kate Mason Rowland and Agnes E. Browne Croxall (Richmond, VA: Everett Waddey, 1911), 58–60, 74; loyalty oath—Amnesty Oaths, 1864–66, Record Group 59, General Records of the Department of State, NARA, Washington, D.C.; Agassiz letter—Louis Agassiz to Samuel G. Howe (member of the American Freedmen's Inquiry Commission, established by President Lincoln), letters of 9 and 10 Aug 1863, quoted in Stephen Jay Gould, *The Mismeasure of Man* (New York: W. W. Norton, 1996), 79–82.

146 *Constant Lecorgne in Eighteenth Louisiana Regiment*: Marie Gabrielle Lecorgne, Widow's Application for Pension, #2506, Orleans Parish, 19 Nov 1903, Confederate Pension Application Index Database, reel CP1.83, microdex 3, sequence 30, Louisiana State Archives; actions of Eighteenth Louisiana—Michael Dan Jones, *General Mouton's Regiment: The 18th Louisiana Infantry* (CreateSpace, 2016), 72, 82–93; Christopher G. Peña, *Scarred by War: Civil War in Southeast Louisiana* (AuthorHouse, 2004), 147–212; John William De Forest, *A Volunteer's Adventures: A Union Captain's Record of the Civil War* (New Haven: Yale University Press, 1946), 50ff.; Arthur Bergeron, Jr., "Dennis Haynes and His 'Thrilling Narrative of the Sufferings of . . . Western Louisiana,'" in *Louisianians in the Civil War*, ed. Lawrence L. Hewitt and Arthur W. Bergeron (Columbia: University of Missouri Press, 2002), 37–49; Arthur Bergeron, Jr., "Yellow Jackets Battalion," in *Louisianians in the Civil War*, ed. Lawrence L. Hewitt and Arthur W. Bergeron (Columbia: University of Missouri Press, 2002), 50–71; Arthur W. Bergeron, Jr., ed., *The Civil War Reminiscences of Major Silas T. Grisamore, C.S.A.* (Baton Rouge: LSU Press, 1993); Barnes F. Lathrop, "The Lafourche District in 1862: Confederate Revival," *Louisiana History* 1, no. 4 (1960), 300–319.

CHAPTER 11

149 *New Orleans, 1863*: star cars—Capers, *Occupied City*, 93–96; "negroes . . . not fit for freedom"—Waitz, *Journal of Julia Le Grand*, 100–102.

152 *Marie Estelle Lecorgne*: b. 15 Apr 1863—"Louisiana Births and Christenings, 1811–30; 1854–1934," database, *FamilySearch*, https://familysearch.org/ark:/61903/1:1:FWGF-HLK, 10 Feb 2018, citing St. Martinville, LA, FHL microfilm 6,010,604.

156 *Sergeant "Terrance Lecorgne" and Yellowjackets*: Winter camp—Jones, *General Mouton's Regiment*, 96–97; Battle of Fort Bisland—Bergeron, *The Civil War Reminiscences of Major Silas T. Grisamore*, 109–17; Peña, *Scarred by War*, 219–22; "Incomprehensible wandering"—Bergeron, *The Civil*

War Reminiscences of Major Silas T. Grisamore, 118–36; Jones, *General Mouton's Regiment*, 98–148; Battle of Mansfield—Hewett et al., *Supplement to the Official Records*, 118–19.

CHAPTER 12

161   *Camille Zeringue and Seven Oaks plantation revolt*: "*les nègres* are grown children"—Camille Zeringue (to Nathaniel P. Banks), 10 Feb 1863, box 4, Letters Received by the Provost Marshal General, 1862–65, Department of the Gulf and Louisiana, 1861–66, Record Group 393, NARA; Workers at Seven Oaks—Statistics of Plantations for Orleans and Jefferson Parish Right Bank, 20 Mar 1863, box 2, Letters Received, 1863–66, Record Group 393; Seven Oaks revolt—Provost Marshal, Jefferson Parish to Captain ———, 24 Feb 1863, Letters Received, 1863–65, Record Group 393; John W. Ela to (unnamed), 23 Feb 1863, Letters Received, 1863–65, Jefferson Parish (LA), Record Group 393; wide resistance of enslaved—W.E.B. Du Bois, *Black Reconstruction: An Essay Toward a History of the Part Which Black Folk Played in the Attempt to Reconstruct Democracy in America, 1860–1880* (Philadelphia: A. Saifer, 1935), chap. 4, "The General Strike."

165   *Abraham Lincoln, Jean Baptiste Roudanez, and Arnold Bertonneau*: Joseph Logsdon and Caryn Cossé Bell, "The Americanization of Black New Orleans, 1850–1900," in *Creole New Orleans: Race and Americanization*, ed. Arnold R. Hirsch and Joseph Logsdon (Baton Rouge: LSU Press, 1992), 220–30; Paul Trévigne editorial—*L'Union* (New Orleans), 14 Apr 1864.

166   *Louis Charles Roudanez and the* New Orleans Tribune: Mark Charles Roudané and Matthew Charles Roudané, "The Color of Freedom: Louis Charles Roudanez, New Orleans, and the Transnational Origins of the African American Freedom Movement," *South Atlantic Review* 73, no. 2 (spring 2008), 1–6; issue #1—*New Orleans Tribune* 1, no. 1, 21 Jul 1864.

173   *Joseph Lecorgne, Confederate service*: enlistment—Joseph E. Lecorgne, "United States, Civil War Unfiled Papers of Confederate Soldiers, 1861–1865," Papers of and Relating to Military and Civilian Personnel, 1861–65, NARA microfilm M347; actions of regiment—Arthur W. Bergeron, Jr., *Guide to Louisiana Confederate Military Units*, 1861–65 (Baton Rouge: LSU Press, 1989), 142, 169–70, 181; Battle of Nashville—Joseph T. Wilson, *The Black Phalanx: A History of the Negro Soldiers of the United States in the Wars of 1775–1812, 1861–65* (Hartford, CT: American Publishing Company, 1888), chap. 8; capture—John H. King, *Three Hundred Days in a Yankee Prison: Reminiscences of War Life, Captivity, Imprisonment at Camp Chase, Ohio* (Atlanta: J. P. Daves, 1904),

chaps. 1–3; prisoner of war—Registers of Prisoners, Compiled by the Office of the Commissioner General of Prisoners, Dec 1863–Jun 1865, *Selected Records of the War Department Relating to Confederate Prisoners of War, 1861–65*, Camp Chase, Ohio, Military Prison, NARA microfilm M598: roll 94 ("Jos Lecorgne"), roll 92 ("Joseph Lecorgne," 2 Jan 1865), roll 23 ("Joseph Lecorgne," 13 May 1865), roll 36 ("J. E. Lecorgne," 6 May 1865), Register of Receipt of Articles Delivered to Prisoners (Mar 1864–May 1865), and roll 26 ("Jos E Lecorgne," 13 May 1865), List of prisoners released, March 1863–May 1865; Camp Chase, Ohio prison— William Hiram Duff, *Terrors and Horrors of Prison Life; or, Six Months a Prisoner at Camp Chase, Ohio* (Lake Charles, LA: Orphan Helper, 1907), 11–26; Lonnie Spear, *Portals to Hell: Military Prisons of the Civil War* (Mechanicsburg, PA: Stackpole Books, 1997), 79–82; Confederate soldiers returning—*The Daily Picayune*, 18 May 1865.

CHAPTER 13

184   *New Orleans, 1865–66*: "insult and oppression"—*The Daily Picayune*, n.d., quoted in Whitelaw Reid, *After the War: A Southern Tour, May 1, 1865 to May 1, 1866* (Cincinnati: Moore, Wilstach & Baldwin, 1866), 422; "Bellecastle Street is turned black"—U.S. Census, 1870, New Orleans, "Constant and Marie G. Lecorne," with four children, and neighboring households; "naked, hungry and destitute"—Frederick Douglass, *Life and Times of Frederick Douglass, Written by Himself* (Boston: De Wolfe & Fiske, 1892), 458–59; thousands seeking amnesty: Reid, *After the War*, 239; New Orleans described—James Keith Hogue, *Uncivil War: Five New Orleans Street Battles and the Rise and Fall of Radical Reconstruction* (Baton Rouge: LSU Press, 2006), 17–26; "no rights which the white man was bound to respect"—Dred Scott v. Sandford, 60 U.S. 393 (1856).

185   *"degradation of our race"*: Alcibiade DeBlanc, "Loyalty in the Parishes," *The Courier of the Teche* (St. Martinville, LA), 15 Jul 1865, reprinted in *New Orleans Tribune* (21 Jul 1865).

186   *Republican Party activists*: Thomas J. Durant—Joseph G. Tregle, "Thomas J. Durant, Utopian Socialism, and the Failure of Presidential Reconstruction in Louisiana," *Journal of Southern History* 45 (Nov 1979), 485–512; Durant described—Reid, *After the War*, 232–33; Friends of Universal Suffrage—Joe Gray Taylor, *Louisiana Reconstructed, 1863–1877* (Baton Rouge: LSU Press, 1974), 73–76; "there are buzzards"—Lafcadio Hearn, *"Gombo zhèbes,"* 24.

187   *Paul Fazende shooting*: Fazende plantation—Inspection Reports of Plantations, Jan–May 1866, Assistant Commissioner for the State of Louisiana, Bureau of Refugees, Freedmen, and Abandoned Lands, 1865–69, NARA

microfilm M1027, reel 28; Records Relating to Murders and Outrages, Report of 21 Jul 1865, NARA M1027, roll 34; Letters—W. M. Vaudain to W. E. Dougherty, 21 Jul 1865, and W. E. Dougherty to Thomas W. Conway, 24 Jul 1865, Letters and Telegrams, Freedmen's Bureau, NARA M1027, roll 7; Thomas Conway to W. M. Vaudain, 24 Jul 1865, Thomas Conway to ___ Hoffman, 25 Jul 1865, Thomas Conway to ___ Hoffman, 7 Aug 1865, all in Letters and Telegrams Sent, vol. 1, M1027, roll 1.

187 *Yves J. Lecorgne*: white witnesses—A. Morse (to Joseph Fullerton), 13 Oct 1865, Letters and Telegrams, Freedmen's Bureau, NARA microfilm M1027, roll 5.

188 *Democratic Party activists*: Frederick Ogden—Justin A. Nystrom, *New Orleans After the Civil War: Race, Politics, and a New Birth of Freedom* (Baltimore: Johns Hopkins University Press, 2010), 60–61; "government of white people"—Platform of the Democratic Party of Louisiana, 1865, reprinted in Walter L. Fleming, *Documentary History of Reconstruction*, vol. 1 (Cleveland: A. H. Clark, 1906), 229–30.

189 *François Laizer*: slaveholder—Slave Schedules, U.S. Census, 1850, NARA microfilm M432; indenture of Randall—F. J. Laizer, 3 Apr 1866, Indenture and Apprenticeship Records, 1865–72, Labor Contracts, New Orleans, Freedmen's Bureau, NARA microfilm M1905, roll 8.

191 *Origins and early years of Ku-klux*: Letter, James Crowe to Walter Fleming, 22 May 1905, Walter L. Fleming papers, 1685–1932, MSS 1029, New York Public Library; Albion Winegar Tourgée, *The Invisible Empire (Two Parts Complete in One Volume)* (New York: Fords, Howard, & Hulbert, 1880), 385–500; L. M. Rose, *The Ku Klux Klan; or, Invisible Empire* (New Orleans: L. Graham, 1914), 18–24; Elaine Frantz Parsons, *Ku-Klux: The Birth of the Klan During Reconstruction* (Chapel Hill: University of North Carolina Press, 2015), chaps. 1–2.

CHAPTER 14

194 *Fire companies*: in Jefferson City—"Fire Department," *The Daily Picayune*, 2 Mar 1865, and *The New-Orleans Times*, 26 Feb 1865; Home Hook & Ladder—Thomas O'Connor, *History of the Fire Department of New Orleans, from the Earliest Days to the Present Time* (New Orleans, 1895), 144; *A History of the Proceedings in the City of New Orleans, On the Occasion of the Funeral Ceremonies in Honor of James Abram Garfield, Late President of the United States* (New Orleans: A.W. Hyatt, 1881), 240–41; and *The New-Orleans Times* 1 Apr 1875; Home Hook & Ladder parades—*The Daily Picayune*, 2 Mar 1865, and *The New-Orleans Times*, 26 Mar 1867; Mardi Gras ball—*The New-Orleans Times*, 7 Feb 1865; banquets—"Fireman's Ball," *The New-Orleans Times*, 8 Feb 1866; truck house—"Obituary," *The*

New-Orleans Times, 2 Sep 1866; eighty-five volunteers—*New Orleans Daily Crescent*, 5 Mar 1866; Émile Chevalley on Lecorgne row—1851 and 1859 Tax Records, West Bouligny, Jefferson City, Louisiana Division, NOPL; firemen group photo—"The City," *The Daily Picayune*, 19 Nov 1866; Theodore Lilienthal, photographer—Gary Van Zante, *New Orleans 1867: Photographs by Theodore Lilienthal* (New York: Merrell, 2008).

195   *Yves Lecorgne, fiscal officer:* "Y. J. Lecorgne to Council of the City of Jefferson," City of Jefferson, Louisiana, Board of Aldermen, Minutes, vols. 3 & 4 (1861–68), and City of Jefferson, Louisiana, Treasurer, Journals of Accounts (1868–70), Louisiana Division, NOPL; Yves Lecorgne accused of malfeasance—"Grand Jury Report of the Parish of Jefferson," New Orleans *Daily Picayune*, 11 Feb 1870.

195   *Lecorgne households: Gardner's New Orleans Directory for 1861*, 272, and *Gardner's New Orleans Directory for 1866*, 268.

198   *Politics, 1865–66:* Andrew Johnson veto—James D. Richardson, ed., *A Compilation of the Messages and Papers of the Presidents*, vol. 4 (Washington, D.C.: Government Printing Office, 1907), 405–13; concealed carry law—M. P. Hunnicutt to A. M. Jackson, 1 May 1866, box 11, Letters Received by the Provost Marshal General 1862, State of Louisiana, 1862–63, Military Installations, Record Group 393, NARA; Seymour Rapp, police officer—*New Orleans Republican*, 26 Mar 1874; assaults and killings—Michael G. Wade, "'I Would Rather Be Among the Comanches': The Military Occupation of Southwest Louisiana, 1865," *Louisiana History* 39, no. 1 (winter 1998), 49, 60.

CHAPTER 15

212   *Mechanics Institute massacre:* New Orleans, First District Court, Grand Jury, *Grand Jury Report, and the Evidence Taken by Them in Reference to the Great Riot in New Orleans, Louisiana, July 30th, 1866* (New Orleans, 1866); "Report of the Select Committee on the New Orleans Riots" and "Testimony," U.S. Congress, House of Representatives, 39th Cong., 2nd sess., report no. 16 (Washington: Government Printing Office, 1867); "New Orleans Riots, Message from the President of the United States, in Answer to a Resolution of the House of the 12th Ultimo, Transmitting All Papers Relative to the New Orleans Riots," U.S. Congress, House of Representatives, 39th Cong., 2nd sess., executive doc. no. 68, 1867; incidents and quotations—from "Report of the Select Committee," 5, 17, 110; from "Message from the President," 64, 70, 71; from "Testimony," 3, 4, 13, 33, 38, 50, 78, 80, 87, 110, 180, 181, 446; testimony of Lucien Capla, 119–23; rebel song—"O I'm a good old rebel"

(1861), Notated Music, Civil War Sheet Music Collection, Library of Congress.

213   *Massacre aftermath*: two hundred people killed—Ella Lonn, *Reconstruction in Louisiana After 1868* (New York: G. P. Putnam's Sons, 1918), 4; several hundred—Jean-Charles Houzeau, *My Passage at the New Orleans Tribune: A Memoir of the Civil War Era*, ed. David C. Rankin, trans. Gerard F. Denault (Baton Rouge: LSU Press, 1984), 128–33, 155–60; Andrew Johnson speeches—Walter L. Fleming, *Documentary History of Reconstruction*, vol. 1, 226, 466–67; further on July 30, 1866, massacre— John Rose Ficklen, *History of Reconstruction in Louisiana*, ed. Pierce Butler (Baltimore: Johns Hopkins University Press, 1910), 146–79; Frank J. Wetta, *The Louisiana Scalawags: Politics, Race and Terrorism During the Civil War and Reconstruction* (Baton Rouge: LSU Press, 2012), chap. 5; "none but the white man"—*The New Orleans Crescent*, 11 Jan 1867, 5.

CHAPTER 16

215   *Capla family*: descendants of Lucien Capla, New Orleans, interviews (Jul and Oct 2017, Mar 2018).

216   *"I mention research steps"*: Genealogists make family trees using birth and death records, marriage papers, census records, Social Security applications, wills, and other public notes about private lives; members of the Capla family confirm this research when they examine it.

219   *Lucien Capla*: whereabouts—*Edwards' Annual Directory to the Inhabitants . . . in the City of New Orleans and Suburbs, for 1870* (New Orleans: Southern Publishing, 1869), 117; United States Census, 1870, New Orleans, Ward 6; in politics—"Comité Central Executif," *New Orleans Tribune*, 14 Dec 1866.

220   *Alfred Capla*: tailor—U.S. Census, 1880, New Orleans; in politics— "Delegates to the Convention," *The Daily Picayune*, 26 May 1872; "Republican Executive Committee," *New Orleans Republican*, 13 May 1876; killing—"Adam Navarre Killed," *New Orleans Republican*, 10 Jul 1873; "Another Tragedy," *The Daily Picayune*, 10 Jul 1873; tailor's pattern book, ca. 1890, private collection; death—*Vital Records Indices*, State of Louisiana, Division of Archives, Records, and History; children—U.S. Census, 1900, New Orleans, Ward 5, and U.S. Census, 1910, New Orleans, Ward 6.

221   *Gombo or Creole dialect*: "White man carries money"—Lafcadio Hearn, *"Gombo zhèbes,"* 25n.

230   *Johnny St. Cyr*: life—Johnny St. Cyr, recorded interview with Alan Lomax (New Orleans, Apr 1949), Alan Lomax Archive, Association for Cultural Equity, New York, culturalequity.org, accessed 12 Feb 2019;

"Johnny St. Cyr," in *The New Grove Dictionary of Jazz*, 2nd ed., ed. Barry Dean Kernfeld (New York: Grove, 2002); "Johnny St. Cyr," in Leonard Feather and Ira Gitler, eds., *The Biographical Encyclopedia of Jazz* (New York: Oxford University Press, 1999).

CHAPTER 17

239   *Carnival, 1867*: firemen's parade—*The New-Orleans Times*, 5 Mar 1867; masking and Ku-klux display—Elaine Frantz Parsons, "Midnight Rangers: Costume and Performance in the Reconstruction-Era Ku Klux Klan," *Journal of American History* 92, no. 3 (Dec 2005), 811–36.

241   *Radical Reconstruction*: overview—Eric Foner, *Reconstruction: America's Unfinished Revolution, 1863–1877* (New York: Harper & Row, 1988), 228–71; First and Second Reconstruction Acts—*Acts and Resolutions*, 39th Cong., 2nd sess., 60, and Supplementary Reconstruction Act—*Acts and Resolutions*, 40th Cong., 1st sess., 260 (both Mar 1867); Third and Fourth Reconstruction Acts (Jul 1867, Mar 1868)—Fleming, *Documentary History of Reconstruction* (Arthur Clark, 1906), vol. 1, 415–19.

243   *Alcibiade DeBlanc and Knights of the White Camellia*: Alcibiade DeBlanc obituaries—*The Times-Democrat* (New Orleans), 10 Nov 1883; *L'Observateur* (St. Martinville, LA), 10 Nov 1883; Caucasian Club—U.S. House of Representatives, *House Miscellaneous Documents*, 41st Cong., 1st sess., serial 1402, no. 12 (Washington, D.C., 1870), 517; genesis of KWC—James G. Dauphine, "The Knights of the White Camellia and the Election of 1868: Louisiana's White Terrorists; A Benighting Legacy," *Louisiana History* 30, no. 2 (spring 1989), 173–90; and similar militias—Taylor, *Louisiana Reconstructed*, 162–77; "miscegenation and other degradations"—E. John Ellis Diary, E. P. Ellis and Family Papers, 1812–1914, Louisiana State University Libraries, Special Collections, quoted in Nystrom, *New Orleans After the Civil War*, 74.

CHAPTER 18

246   *Lecorgnes and carpetbaggers*: sales to carpetbaggers—Eliza Lecorgne Lagroue to Matthew Swords, 8 Sep 1866, Yves J. Lecorgne to William Kimball, 12 Sep 1866, Yves J. Lecorgne to Louis Andre, 26 Jul 1866, Louisiana Division, NOPL; Shrewsbury land sale—Eliza Lecorgne Lagroue to Adolphe Hotard, 27 Sep 1867, in Jefferson Parish conveyances, books I–J, record no. 958, Louisiana Division, NOPL.

249   *New Orleans, 1867–68*: courthouse shoot-out—*The New-Orleans Times*, 29 Sep, 1 and 2 Oct 1867; 1868 constitutional convention—Richard L. Hume and Jerry B. Gough, *Blacks, Carpetbaggers, and Scalawags: The Constitutional Conventions of Radical Reconstruction* (Baton Rouge: LSU

Press, 2008), chap. 6; constitution vote—Donald W. Davis, "Ratification of the Constitution of 1868: Record of Votes," *Louisiana History* 6, no. 3 (1965), 301–305; "Africanize . . . the country"—Andrew Johnson, Message to Congress, 3 Dec 1867, quoted in William E. Gienapp, *The Civil War and Reconstruction: A Documentary Collection* (New York: W. W. Norton, 2001), 352–54; Andrew Johnson indictment—Articles of Impeachment, in Fleming, ed., *Documentary History of Reconstruction*, vol. 1, 458–70; "Untutored African," *The New-Orleans Times*, 4 Mar 1868.

254 *Militias emerge*: "queer name of the 'Ku Klux Klan'"—*The New Orleans Crescent*, 12 Mar 1868; Ku-klux advertisement—*The Daily Picayune*, 17 Mar 1868; "Ku Klux and the Why of It," *The Daily Picayune*, 18 Apr 1868; "Ku Klux is a mysterious association," *The Daily Advocate* (Baton Rouge), 27 Mar 1868; Knights of the White Camellia—Louisiana General Assembly, *Supplemental Report of Joint Committee of the General Assembly of Louisiana on the Conduct of the Late Elections, and the Condition of Peace and Good Order in the State* (New Orleans: A. L. Lee, 1869), 211–21, 262–66; Dauphine, "The Knights of the White Camellia and the Election of 1868," 182–85; Ku-klux verses—*The Louisiana Democrat* (Alexandria), 29 Apr 1868; *The South-Western* (Shreveport, LA), 6 May 1868; *Tri-Weekly Advocate* (Baton Rouge), 13 Nov 1868; Ku-klux musical—*New-Orleans Commercial Bulletin*, 2 Jun 1868, advertisement.

CHAPTER 19

256 *Knights of the White Camellia (KWC)*: constitution and rites published—*New Orleans Republican*, 2 Dec 1868; "Constitution and Ritual of the Knights of the White Camellia, Adopted at a General Convention Held in New Orleans, June 4, 1868," pamphlet (1904), in Papers of Walter L. Fleming, New York Public Library; "Constitution and Ritual of the Knights of the White Camellia," in Walter L. Fleming, ed., *Documents Relating to Reconstruction* (Morgantown: West Virginia University Press, 1905).

261 *White militias*: around the South—Foner, *Reconstruction*, 412–44; "Ku-kluxery"—Philip Dray, *Capitol Men: The Epic Story of Reconstruction Through the Lives of the First Black Congressmen* (Boston: Houghton Mifflin, 2008), 77–102; spread of Klan—Parsons, *Ku-Klux*, introduction.

262 *State response*: Metropolitan Police—Report of the Metropolitan Police, 1869–70 (New Orleans, 1871), John Minor Wisdom Collection, LARC, 5–14; "ten thousand torches"—*The New York Times*, 6 Sep 1868; "nigger insurrection"—Lonn, *Reconstruction in Louisiana*, 22.

264   *KWC*: councils in New Orleans—Louisiana General Assembly, *Supplemental Report*, 211–13; "When a man is to be killed"—*Supplemental Report*, 217–18.

264   *Constant Lecorgne and the Knights of the White Camellia*: The claim that Constant Lecorgne falls in with the Knights of the White Camellia and marauds with the sometimes-costumed gangs of family friend Alcibiade DeBlanc grows from circumstantial evidence, which is extensive, and from oral tradition. A secretive cult with many semiliterate actors, the KWC (probably) did not keep paper files. Or, if they did, records do not survive. I use these methods to tell the story of Constant and the White Camellia: deduction from clues, inference from symptoms, and reasonable projection from trace evidence.

266   *"murder of negroes is a daily occurrence"*: Louisiana atrocities—"Desperate Attack on a Freedman's House," *New Orleans Republican*, 15 Jul 1868; "List of Murders and Outrages," in Louisiana General Assembly, *Supplemental Report*, 258–75; U.S. Congress, *Report on the Alleged Outrages in the Southern States by the Select Committee of the Senate* (1871).

268   *Ku-klux costume*: J. C. Lester and D. L. Wilson, *Ku Klux Klan: Its Origin, Growth, and Disbandment*, published 1884 (reprint ed., New York: Neale Publishing, 1905), 58; photographs—a handful of photos survive of Ku-klux and KWC marauders in Alabama, Mississippi, and Tennessee (pages 251, 263, and 275).

CHAPTER 20

270   *Henry Warmoth letter*: Warmoth to Andrew Johnson, 1 Aug 1868, printed in *The Bossier Banner* (Bellevue, LA), 15 Aug 1868.

271   *Ward clubs*: *The New-Orleans Times*, 6 and 8 Aug 1868; *New Orleans Republican*, 22 Aug 1868; *New Orleans Daily Crescent*, 12 Aug and 4 Oct 1868.

273   *Election of 1868*: context—Taylor, *Louisiana Reconstructed*, 161–73; incitement—"Radical Negro Mob in Jefferson," *The Daily Picayune*, 13 Aug 1868; Frederick Ogden observed—"Origin and Activities of the White League in New Orleans (Reminiscences of a Participant in the Movement)," *Louisiana Historical Quarterly* 23, no. 1 (1940), 523–38; mobbing—"Mass Meeting at Congo Square," *The New Orleans Crescent*, 18 Oct 18.

278   *Election violence*: lynching—*The Weekly Advocate* (Baton Rouge), 31 Oct 1868; beatings and killings—Register of Murders and Outrages, May–Dec 1868, and Miscellaneous Reports and Lists, Mar 1867–Nov 1868, State of Louisiana, Freedmen's Bureau, NARA microfilm M1027, reel

34; U.S. Congress, *Testimony Taken by the Sub-committee of Elections in Louisiana*, serial 1435, H. misc. doc. 154 (1870), 200+ references to KWC, several hundred to assaults and murders, in 1,500 pp.; Coroner's Office, Record of Inquests and Views, 1868–70, Louisiana Division, NOPL.

279   *Election aftermath*: *The Daily Picayune*, 4 Nov 1868; "Address of the State Campaign Committee of the Republican Party of Louisiana, New Orleans, 10 Nov 1868," pamphlet (New Orleans: J. E. Stephens, 1868); *Report of the Senate Committee on Elections in the Case of W.B. Gray v. A.B. Bacon* (1869), pamphlet, John Minor Wisdom Collection, box 13, folder 22, LARC.

CHAPTER 21

285   *"Unconscious causes"*: couplet—Richard Blackmore, *Creation: A Philosophical Poem, in Seven Books* (1712), III.

289   *Saint Mark, the baby*: Honorius St. Mark Lecorgne, b. 16 Dec 1868, Sacramental records, Parish of St. Stephen, Baptisms, vol. 2, no. 162.

CHAPTER 22

292   *Lecorgne households*: *Gardner's New Orleans Directory for 1869* (New Orleans, 1868); *Edwards' Annual Directory to the Inhabitants, Institutions . . . etc. in the City of New Orleans, for 1872* (New Orleans: Southern Publishing, 1871); United States Census, 1870.

293   *Slaughterhouse Cases*: Lonn, *Reconstruction in Louisiana*, 42–44; Charles Lane, *The Day Freedom Died: The Colfax Massacre, the Supreme Court, and the Betrayal of Reconstruction* (New York: Henry Holt, 2008), 110–26; case law—*Slaughter-House Cases*, 83 U.S. 36 (1872).

295   *Terror goes dormant*: Nathan Bedford Forrest—"How Grant Broke Old Ku Klux," *The New York Times*, 17 Aug 1924; cold politics—Taylor, *Louisiana Reconstructed*, 173–83; "mongrel mulattoes"—*The Daily Picayune*, 22 Sep 1868; no massacres—Report of the Metropolitan Police, 1869–70 (New Orleans, 1871), John Minor Wisdom Collection, LARC, 5–14.

296   *Jefferson City, 1869*: municipal coup—City of Jefferson, Board of Aldermen, Minutes, vol. 4 (1868–70), Louisiana Division, NOPL; militia—*Testimony Taken by the Sub-committee of Elections in Louisiana*, 246, 469–71; May 1869 battle—*The Daily Picayune*, 19, 20, and 21 May 1869, 1 Aug 1869; *The New York Times*, 23 May 1869, 1 Aug 1869; *New Orleans Republican*, 23 May 1869; *The Opelousas Courier*, 29 May 1869.

297   *1870–72 Enforcement Acts*: summarized—Dray, *Capitol Men*, 88–98; narrated—Xi Wang, "The Making of Federal Enforcement Laws, 1870–72," *Chicago-Kent Law Review* 70, no. 3 (Apr 1995), 1013–58; statutes—

Act of 31 May 1870, ch. 114, 16 Stat. 140 (enforcing voting rights); Act of 14 Jul 1870, ch. 254, 16 Stat. 254 (on naturalization); Act of 28 Feb 1871, ch. 99, 16 Stat. 433 (expanding law of May 1870); Act of 20 Apr 1871, ch. 22, 17 Stat. 13 (enforcing Fourteenth Amendment); and Act of 10 Jun 1872, ch. 415, 17 Stat. 347 (appropriation to pay for legislation).

298 *Encyclopedia of terror*—U.S. Congress, *Joint Select Committee on the Condition of Affairs in the Late Insurrectionary States*, 13 vols. (Washington, D.C.: Government Printing Office, 1872).

CHAPTER 23

301 *1872–73*: Ku-klux parade float—"First Celebration of Mardi Gras in Memphis," *The Memphis Daily Appeal*, 14 Feb 1872, 4; "Worshipful Chief, K.K.K."—Nathan Bedford Forrest, "A Letter of Advice: To the Grand Order–the K.K. Klan–throughout the U. States and Territories of America" (1872), Library Broadside Collection, Tennessee State Library and Archives, Nashville; 1872 campaign and election—*New Orleans Republican*, 26 Jul and 13 Aug 1872; Taylor, *Louisiana Reconstructed*, 230–52; Nystrom, *New Orleans After the Civil War*, 120–38; Lonn, *Reconstruction in Louisiana*, 167–204; Grant's message to Congress—*New Orleans Republican*, 26 Feb 1873.

304 *Edgar Degas, Krewe of Comus*: Christopher E. G. Benfey, *Degas in New Orleans: Encounters in the Creole World of Kate Chopin and George Washington Cable* (New York: Knopf, 1997), 164, 184–85; "Missing Links" Carnival theme—Perry Young, *The Mystick Krewe: Chronicles of Comus and His Kin* (New Orleans: Carnival Press, 1931), 118; Reid Mitchell, *All on a Mardi Gras Day: Episodes in the History of New Orleans Carnival* (Cambridge, MA: Harvard University Press, 1995), 65–66.

305 *Alcibiade DeBlanc rally*: *New Orleans Republican*, 1 Mar 1873.

307 *Raid on Precinct 7*: *The New-Orleans Times*, 6 Mar 1873; "Capture of the Jefferson City Police Station by the Metropolitan Police," *The Daily Picayune*, 6 Mar 1873; "The New Orleans Mob," *The New York Times*, 7 Mar 1873.

308 *Case chronicle*: court papers—State of Louisiana v. Peter Duffy, et al., Indictment no. 5187 . . . 24 Mar 1873, and Witness' Bond, Recorder's Office . . . 12 Mar 1873, op. cit.; "The Citizens Captured" and "Dead," *The Daily Picayune*, 7 Mar 1873; affidavit of Constant Lecorgne—"The Chandler Murder," *The Daily Picayune*, 13 Mar 1873; "The City," *The Daily Picayune*, 15 Mar 1873; "The Chandler Murder Case," *The Daily Picayune*, 20 Mar 1873; "The Chandler Murder Case—Verdict of the Jury," *The Daily Picayune*, 21 Mar 1873; "The Courts," *The Daily Picayune*, 25 Mar 1873; *New Orleans Republican*, 21 and 25 Mar 1873.

CHAPTER 24

311 *Roudanez family*: Mark Roudané, St. Paul, MN, interviews (Apr 2018).

312 *Suicides by Creoles*: David C. Rankin, "The Impact of the Civil War on the Free Colored Community of New Orleans," *Perspectives in American History* 9 (1977–78), 394–95, 400–407.

315 *Louis Charles Roudanez in 1848*: obituary, Paul Trévigne, "Dr. Louis Charles Roudanez," *The Crusader* (New Orleans), 22 Mar 1890.

CHAPTER 25

328 *Summer–fall, 1873*: "superiority of the white race"—*The Ouachita Telegraph* (Monroe, LA), 21 Jun 1873; P.B.S. Pinchback in Washington—Dray, *Capitol Men*, 102–34; "desire to establish . . . caste"—Rep. James Rapier, speech, in Gienapp, *The Civil War and Reconstruction*, 362–63; Colored Men's Convention—*New Orleans Republican*, 20 Nov 1873.

329 *Lecorgnes on Tchoupitoulas*: lease—Theodore Soniat Dufossat to P.C. Lecorgne, 9 Sep 1873, New Orleans Notarial Archives; Joseph Lecorgne, death—20 Nov 1873, Death Records, 1804–76, vol. 59, p. 865, Louisiana State Archives.

332 *Winter–summer 1874*: Ulysses Grant to *The New York Herald*, 20 Jan 1874, quoted in Gienapp, *The Civil War and Reconstruction*, 393–94; "not pretend to conceal our gratification"—*The Shreveport Times*, 10 Jul 1874; *The Caucasian* newspaper—prospectus, *The Louisiana Democrat*, 25 Mar 1874; Estelle Lecorgne, death—24 Apr 1874, Sacramental Records, Parish of St. Stephen, Funerals (whites), vol. 2.

336 *The White League*: formation—Taylor, *Louisiana Reconstructed*, 279–84; Hogue, *Uncivil War*, 124–31; Nystrom, *New Orleans After the Civil War*, 163–65; H. Oscar Lestage, "The White League in Louisiana and Its Participation in Reconstruction Riots," *Louisiana Historical Quarterly* 18 (Jul 1935), 617–95; C. H. Mouton, spellbound—*The New Orleans Bulletin*, 20 Jun 1874; "*Courier* passes into the hands of the White League"—*The Opelousas Courier*, 25 May 1874; *La ligue blanche*—"Political Chambords of Louisiana," *New Orleans Republican*, 17 Jun 1874, masthead; "benefit of white men"—*The New Orleans Bulletin*, 20 Jun 1874; "white men in everything"—*New Orleans Republican*, 19 Jun 1874; Eagle Hall meeting—"Origin and Activities of the White League," 533–35; White League manifesto, and ward clubs join White League—*The Daily Picayune*, 2 Jul 1874.

338 *White League observed*: "He must be starved"—*Catholic Messenger*, 14 Jun 1874; "assassination of negroes"—*New Orleans Republican*, 5 Aug 1874.

338 *Coushatta massacre*: Taylor, *Louisiana Reconstructed*, 287–91; Nicholas Lemann, *Redemption: The Last Battle of the Civil War* (New York: Farrar, Straus and Giroux, 2006), 76–77.

CHAPTER 26

345 *September 1874*: street battle—"War; The Uprising of the Citizens," *The Daily Picayune*, 22 Sep 1874; September 14 narrated—Hogue, *Uncivil War*, 128–43; white supremacy restored—James Joseph Alcée Fortier, *Carpet-Bag Misrule in Louisiana: The Tragedy of the Reconstruction Era Following the War Between the States . . . Louisiana's Part in Maintaining White Supremacy in the South* (New Orleans: T. J. Moran, 1938); coup d'état—misc. in White League Papers, LARC; "Redemption"—Stuart Omer Landry, *The Battle of Liberty Place; The Overthrow of Carpet-Bag Rule in New Orleans, September 14, 1874*, pamphlet (New Orleans: Pelican, 1955); and Nystrom, *New Orleans After the Civil War*, chap. 7, "The Redeemer's Carnival."

346 *Constant Lecorgne joins the White League*: Family tradition says he is in the middle of the fight. The September 1874 White League coup makes the 2,500-man guerrilla army into heroes among the white population. Sometime later, several units of the League assemble muster rolls, but the lists are unreliable, because many men outside the militias want to claim glory. Constant probably fights with a White League unit known as the First Louisiana Regiment. Prior to 1874, a piece of this group calls itself the McEnery Militia, and Constant, when he is arrested and charged with treason in March 1873, is tagged as a marauder with that particular gang. The McEnery Militia enters the White League and falls in with the First Louisiana Regiment, an infantry led by an ex-Confederate colonel named John G. Angell.

349 *Aftermath of September 14*: "Official Report of General Ogden," *The Daily Picayune*, 2 Oct 1874; "minions of the terror," "band of assassins," "horde of traitors"—*Harper's Weekly*, 17, 24, and 31 Oct 1874; "Vox Populi—The Procession in Honor of Louisiana's Deliverance," *The Daily Picayune*, 8 Nov 1874; Edwards Pierrepont to Gov. Adelbert Ames—quoted in Gienapp, *The Civil War and Reconstruction*, 406–407; "White men may have burned and killed"—*The Shreveport Times*, 24 Dec 1875, quoted in Taylor, *Louisiana Reconstructed*, 313; "steeped in the blood"—*Harper's Weekly*, 15 Jul 1876; Hogue, *Uncivil War*, 144–49.

350 *Grant dossier*: *Congressional Record*, 44th Cong., 2nd sess., vol. 5 (6 Dec 1876), 68ff.; *Executive Documents*, 44th Cong., 2nd sess., no. 30.

350 *Their last child*: Marie Constance Lecorgne—b. 16 Dec 1876, Sacramental records, Parish of St. Stephen, Baptisms, vol. 3, no. 327; dies, eleven months—d. 20 Nov 1877, *Orleans Death Indices 1877–1895*, vol. 70, 147, Louisiana State Archives.

351 *1877 Carnival*: the Aryan Race—Young, *The Mystick Krewe*, 141–44, 150, 222.

353 *Tilden-Hayes compromise*: W.E.B. Du Bois, *Black Reconstruction*, 483–84; Foner, *Reconstruction*, 572–82; aftermath of Redemption—Hogue, *Uncivil War*, 177–94.

CHAPTER 27

355 *1875 Civil Rights Act abrogated*: Civil Rights Cases, 109 U.S. 3 (1883).

356 *Alcibiade DeBlanc*: life—*Dictionary of Louisiana Biography* (Louisiana Historical Association, 1988); death—*The Louisiana Democrat*, 14 Nov 1883; *The Opelousas Courier*, 17 Nov 1883.

357 *Frederick Ogden*: death—*The Daily States* (New Orleans), 27 May 1886; *L'Abeille* (New Orleans), 26 May 1886.

358 *Polycarp Constant Lecorgne*: death—New Orleans Health Department, Recorder of Births, Marriages, and Deaths, vol. 89; burial—Oct 1886, Lafayette Interment Records, vol. 8, 1873–96, Louisiana Division, NOPL.

361 *Lynching*: Lafourche Parish—Equal Justice Initiative, "Lynching in America: Confronting the Legacy of Racial Terror," 3rd ed. (Montgomery, AL, 2017), https://lynchinginamerica.eji.org/report/, accessed 24 Sep 2019; Ida B. Wells, *Southern Horrors: Lynch Law in All Its Phases* (New York, 1892).

362 *Homer Plessy*: Desdunes, *Our People and Our History*, 143–45; case—*Plessy v. Ferguson*, 163 U.S. 537 (1896).

362 *Gabrielle Lecorgne, pension*: Gabrielle Marie Duchemin Lecorgne / Polycarpe Constant Lecorgne, 19 Nov 1903, Confederate Pension Applications, Louisiana State Archives.

ACKNOWLEDGMENTS

The Cullman Center for Scholars and Writers gave me a fellowship and a year in-house at the New York Public Library in 2015–16. Many thanks to the Cullman's former director, Jean Strouse, and her colleagues. The Radcliffe Institute for Advanced Study at Harvard University offered a yearlong fellowship in 2016–17. I am grateful to Radcliffe's former director, the late Judith Vichniac, the ex-dean Lizabeth Cohen, and Harvard comrades. The National Endowment for the Humanities awarded me a much-appreciated Public Scholar Grant in 2015–16.

In New Orleans, Tulane University's Center for the Gulf South gave timely support, while Tulane's retreat for artists, A Studio in the Woods, offered many weeks of housing. Thank you to Rebecca Snedeker and Ama Rogan of those university branches.

I appreciate the support of family in Louisiana, especially those named Rowley (Ann, Cissy, Edward, George, Judy, Renée). Thanks to the Lecorgne cousins Jennifer Fagan, Laura Lecorgne, and Parker Lecorgne. Greg Osborne of the New Orleans Public Library and the genealogists Jay Schexnaydre and Katy Shannon brought facts to the surface from court cases, property and tax filings, sacramental records, and other submerged reefs of family history. Appreciation to the researcher Agnès Renault for similar work in the city of Santiago, Cuba. In Connecticut, Lily Walton drew the Lecorgne family tree. Pembroke Kyle of Picture Research Consultants, in Massachusetts, retrieved many images and permission to publish them.

Others in Louisiana helped this book: Theodore Ball, Augusta Elmwood, Roberta Gratz, Erin Greenwald, Jari Honora, Andy Horowitz, Norman and Sand Marmillion, Peter Patout, Sally Reeves, and

S. Fred Starr. John Bardes, graduate student in history at Tulane University, has the most gratitude. Without the research of John Bardes, who contributed much of the factual texture of the story, the book would have lacked a thousand pieces and might not have come together. I am grateful to Janel Santiago Marsalis, Joann St. Cyr, Alice Richard, Ricardo Coleman, and others in the latter-day family of Alfred Capla, in New Orleans, who shared their family story like a gift. The same thanks to members of the Roudanez family, formerly of Louisiana, especially Mark Roudané, in St. Paul, Minnesota.

Gratitude to Saidiya Hartman, who read chapters of the manuscript in draft form. Friends and historians Claire Potter, Beverly Gage, and Paul Sabin read early parts of the text and removed some of its unattractive clothing. Much appreciation to the Louisiana historian Larry Powell, who read the book when it was done and gave advice.

Thank you to my agent, Andrew Wylie, who put the book in front of many eyes. I appreciate the generosity of Penguin Press: the Penguin editor Scott Moyers initially acquired the book, and the company was gracious enough to hand it to another publisher when I made the request. Gratitude to Jonathan Galassi at Farrar, Straus and Giroux, who more than twenty years ago published my first book, *Slaves in the Family*, and who acquired this one, number six. And many thanks to Alex Star, editor at FSG, the most sensitive of prose readers, whose pencil raised the educational attainment of every page.

I acknowledge that my partner, Candace Skorupa, is part author of this story: when the Klansman made me go away, mentally or physically, she asked me to return, and held the door. Thank you, and love, to her.

275 *Carte de visite*, Huntsville, Alabama, 1868, Pictorial Press, Ltd., Alamy Photo

282 Gorilla costume design from Mistick Krewe of Comus 1873 parade (theme: "Missing Links to Darwin's *Origin of Species* . . . by Comus"), New Orleans, 1873, Tulane University, Louisiana Research Collection

303 Edgar Degas, *A Cotton Office in New Orleans*, oil on canvas, 1873, Musée des Beaux-Arts de Pau, France

314 Aimée Potens, grandmother of Louis Charles Roudanez, daguerreotype, Louisiana, ca. 1844, private collection

318 Mark Roudané and his father, New Orleans, photograph, 1954, private collection

322 Mark Roudané with protest sign, 2016, private collection

324 City of New Orleans and the Mississippi, Currier and Ives, 1885, Library of Congress, Prints and Photographs Division

331 *The Caucasian* newspaper (Alexandria, Louisiana), 4 Apr 1874, Library of Congress

341 Pamphlet about the White League, 1875, White League Papers, Tulane University, Louisiana Research Collection

345 "The Louisiana Outrages—Attack upon the Police in the Streets of New Orleans," *Harper's Weekly*, 3 Oct 1874, Library of Congress

349 Thomas Nast, "The Union as It Was," *Harper's Weekly*, 24 Oct 1874, Library of Congress, Prints and Photographs Division

357 Polycarp Constant Lecorgne, private collection

360 White League monument, and the author, New Orleans, 2016, photograph by Claire Bangser

Edward Ball is the author of six books, including *The Inventor and the Tycoon*, about the birth of moving pictures in California, and *Slaves in the Family*, an account of his family's history as slaveholders in South Carolina, which received the National Book Award for Nonfiction. He has taught at Yale University and has been awarded fellowships by the Radcliffe Institute at Harvard and the New York Public Library's Cullman Center. He is also the recipient of a Public Scholar Award from the National Endowment for the Humanities.